D0915546

The Collected Essays of
CHRISTOPHER
Hill

By the same author:

The Century of Revolution, 1603–1714
Society and Puritanism in Pre-Revolutionary England
Intellectual Origins of the English Revolution
The World Turned Upside Down
Milton and the English Revolution
The Experience of Defeat: Milton and Some Contemporaries

Christopher Hill

The Collected Essays of
CHRISTOPHER
Hill

Volume One
Writing and Revolution in
17th Century England

THE UNIVERSITY OF MASSACHUSETTS PRESS
Amherst

© Christopher Hill 1985

First published in the United States of America
in 1985 by the University of Massachusetts Press
Box 429 Amherst Ma 01004

Printed in Great Britain

Library of Congress Cataloging in Publication Data

Hill, Christopher, 1912–
  The collected essays of Christopher Hill.

  Includes bibliographical references.
  Contents: v. 1. Writing and revolution in 17th-century
England.
  1. English literature—17th century—History and
criticism—Addresses, essays, lectures. 2. Literature
and society—Great Britain—Addresses, essays, lectures.
3. Great Britain—History—Stuarts, 1603-1714—Addresses,
essays, lectures. 4. Great Britain—Intellectual life—
17th century—Addresses, essays, lectures. I. Title.
PR433.H54 1985   082   84-16446
ISBN 0-87023-467-6 (v. 1)

Contents

Preface

The pieces contained in this volume are based on lectures, articles and reviews written over the past thirty years or so. I have rewritten some of them. I hope readers will make allowances for the very diverse origins of these pieces. In most cases I did not select the subjects: I was asked to review a book or deliver a lecture. I suppose I accepted the assignments because they interested me. So such unity as this book possesses derives from what I hope is a fairly consistent, though developing, attitude towards the history of England in the seventeenth century. Now that they are collected together, certain patterns seem to emerge. From the time I published my first book, over forty years ago, I have been fascinated by the connections between social change and literature in the seventeenth century. In particular, I have felt that the effects of the censorship before 1640 and after 1660 have been underestimated, as also have the long-term consequences of the intellectual turmoil of the revolutionary decades. These themes recur in the present collection.

I have made acknowledgments in the notes where I am conscious of specific debts. But there are many more. I am very grateful to Dena Goldberg, Nicholas Jose, John Laydon, Hugh Ormsby-Lennon, Ian McCalman, Wilfrid Prest, André Rannou, Michael Roberts, Paul Salzman, P.L. Thirlby, and Michael Wilding for letting me read their work in advance of publication. I received help and encouragement of various kinds from Penelope Corfield, Andrew Foster, Charles Hobday, and Dev Moodley. I owe much more to the stimulus of Harriett Hawkins's witty writings than I have been able to acknowledge. My greatest debt is to Margot Heinemann, who has contributed so much to our understanding of the relation between literature and politics in this period. In addition she very generously read three of these chapters in re-draft, and saved me from many howlers. I have benefited enormously from discussing many aspects of this book with her. I am especially grateful to the patience and skill of the long-suffering staff of the Harvester Press. Bridget helped, stimulated and encouraged at every stage, and undertook the tedious task of reading the proofs. None of the above however are responsible for the errors which remain.

Spelling and punctuation have been modernized, except in titles of books and in chapters 7 and 11. All dates are in the New Style, but I take the year as beginning on 1 January.

December 1983.

Acknowledgments

Earlier versions of many of the pieces collected in this volume were originally published elsewhere. I am grateful for permission to include them in this collection.

"From Marprelate to the Levellers" appeared in *Essays in Criticism*, (Vol. XXXII, 1982). Also published in *Essays in Criticism* were "Sir John Berkenhead (1617–79)" (Vol. XX, 1970), parts of "Francis Quarles (1592–1644) and Edward Benlowes (1602–76)" (Vol. III, 1955) and "Samuel Butler (1613–80)" (Vol. XIX, 1969). "Daniel Defoe (1660–1731)" was published in *History Workshop Journal*, 10, Autumn 1980; part of "Francis Quarles (1592–1644) and Edward Belowes (1602–76)" in *The Times Literary Supplement* of 23 May 1980; "Thomas Traherne (1637–74)" in the Swiss periodical *Feuillets*, No. 8 (Fribourg, Switzerland, 1985); "John Evelyn (1620–1706)" in *History*, (Vol. XLII, 1957); parts of "Samuel Pepys (1633–1703)" in the *New Statesman* of 27 September 1974 and in *The New Republic* of 9 July 1983. "John Wilmot, Earl of Rochester (1647–80)" appeared in *The London Review of Books* of 20 November–4 December 1980.

"George Wither (1588–1667) and John Milton (1608–74)" originally appeared in a *Festschrift* published by the Oxford University Press for Dame Helen Gardner (*English Renaissance Studies*, ed. John Carey, 1980); "John Milton (1608–74) and Andrew Marvell (1621–78)" in *Approaches to Marvell: York Tercentenary Lectures*, (ed. C.A. Partrides, Routledge and Kegan Paul, 1978).

Abbreviations

The following abbreviations have been used.

C.S.P.D.	*Calendar of State Papers, Domestic.*
D.N.B.	*Dictionary of National Biography.*
E.H.R.	*English Historical Review.*
Heinemann	Margot Heinemann, *Puritanism and Theatre: Thomas Middleton and Opposition Drama under the Early Stuarts* (Cambridge U.P., 1980).
H.M.C.	Historical Manuscripts Commission.
M.C.P.W.	Ed. D.M. Wolfe, *Complete Prose Works of John Milton* (Yale U.P., 8 vols., 1953–82).
M.E.R.	C. Hill, *Milton and the English Revolution* (1977).
M.P.L.	Ed. H.M. Margoliouth, *Poems and Letters of Andrew Marvell* (Oxford U.P., 2 vols., 1927).
P. and P.	*Past and Present.*
U.P.	University Press.
W.T.U.D.	C. Hill, *The World Turned Upside Down* (Penguin edn., 1975). First published 1972.

I *Introductory*

1. *The Pre-Revolutionary Decades*

"Sometimes a passage from an imaginative genius provides us with an intensity of insight quite unattainable any other way".

It does not seem to me possible to understand the history of seventeenth-century England without understanding its literature, any more than it is possible fully to appreciate the literature without understanding the history. Increasingly this has come to be recognized by literary critics and historians of seventeenth-century literature: the liveliest and best workers in the field are fully aware of the importance of the connections; some, like Margot Heinemann, Michael McKeon and Susan Staves, write better history than many historians.[1]

Not all historians, unfortunately, read literary criticism (and I fear some do not even read English literature). If they did, they would realise that there was a revolution in English literature as well as in science, even if they cannot persuade themselves that there were revolutions in politics, economics and society. Those historians who concentrate on Parliamentary debates, state papers and the correspondence of the gentry, fail to notice what is going on elsewhere. It is one of the disastrous consequences of specialization. If you look only at Parliament, counting M.Ps. and tellers, it is easy to convince yourself that the civil war was an accident, caused by the cost of foreign war, the factiousness of the nobility, or the folly of the King. If you look only at religion and the church, it is easy to convince yourself that Laud was responsible for the breakdown of confidence between King and country. If you look only at political science, one can accept that the sudden emergence of great political thinkers in England—Hobbes, Harrington, the Levellers, Winstanley—was another accident; similarly with the revolution in English law, symbolized by the transformation of Sir Edward Coke, dismissèd

*J.H. Hexter, "Property, Monopoly and Shakespeare's *Richard II*", in *Culture and Politics: From Puritanism to the Enlightenment* (ed. P. Zagorin, California U.P., 1980), p. 18.

from the bench by James I, highly suspected by Charles I, into the father of English law, behind whom it is not necessary to go. If you look at literature in isolation from society, it is easy to blame Shakespeare's early retirement, the separation of coterie from popular theatre, and the censorship, for the decline of English drama, for the replacement of tragedy by heroic drama.

In my view, England's mid-century crisis embraced literature and the arts as well as economics, politics, law and society. That is what so sharply differentiated it from the contemporaneous revolts on the continent, whose causes have been subsumed with those of the English civil war under the formula "court versus country", but whose outcome was so startlingly different. Historians disagree about speaking of an English Revolution, but no one has ever suggested applying the word "revolution" to any of the continental upheavals. The English Revolution is as unique as Elizabethan and Jacobean drama. Could the uniqueness of the one relate to the uniqueness of the other?

After the cultural florescence from the fifteen-nineties to about 1620, years of a considerable degree of national unity, there followed a period of growing disunity which was reflected in the deterioration of drama and a literature crippled by censorship.[2] We can see the great literary triumph of the Authorized Version as a monument to this unity; by 1624 a similar unity in London, when Puritans flocked to see Middleton's *A Game at Chess*, was nipped in the bud by government repression.[3]

Literary critics and historians have posed other questions, even if they have not answered them. If literary taste relates to social structure (as L.B. Wright argued many years ago),[4] how are we to explain the rise and decline of drama, the rise and disappearance of the metaphysical mode and its supersession by the rhymed couplet, in drama and in lyric poetry? Milton in 1674 spoke of the "bondage" of rhyme; and he was not one to use so political a term lightly. What happened to satire under James and Charles I?[5] How did the quatrain, with its deep roots in popular ballad poetry, used so effectively from Spenser to Rochester, then get lost? (The question was asked by George Saintsbury).[6]

Drama is especially important for our purposes, since it necessarily involves discussion, including discussion of ideas. The dramatist could not agree with everything said by all his characters. And given the stress laid on debate in the English educational system, especially at the universities, the habit of making out the best case for a particular argument was almost universal.

From the start the theatre was a socially ambiguous institution. Its origins have been traced in popular folk drama and gild pageants. But the London theatre evolved under the protection of great lords like the Earl of Leicester; the players started as dependent feudal servants. An act of 1572 treated "common players" as vagabonds, except for those "belonging to any baron or honourable person of greater degree". The City authorities could easily suppress players, Gosson told them in 1578, "if their letters of commendation were once stayed." Yet when permanent theatres, charging for admission, were established in London, actors came to depend on their audiences no less than on their aristocratic patrons.[7] As Robert Weimann has brilliantly shown, the fact that the theatre straddled the growing social divide contributed enormously to the power of drama in Elizabeth's reign and the first half of James's.[8]

After Essex's rebellion of 1601 (in which Shakespeare's *Richard II* had played a part) drama dealing with all but the remotest periods of English history, like satire, came to an end. Shakespeare switched to tragedy. English history plays had flourished in Elizabeth's reign: they assumed a united nation. They declined as English society divided, and as government control increased.[9] James took the best organized theatre companies into the service of himself and his family, and licensed only theatres in which these companies' capital was invested.

Wickham sums up: "By 1642 acting in England was permitted by the royal prerogative or not at all". As royal servants, actors and dramatists were drawn and driven into dependence on the court. This "could not but serve to divorce the theatre from the popular audience on which it had previously been based and from which it had drawn its vigour". The process was hastened by tighter censorship and increasing court emphasis on spectacle rather than drama. Inigo Jones defeated Ben Jonson.[10] Cultural consequences followed. The florescence of City comedy towards the end of Elizabeth's reign had petered out by the middle of James's.[11] The tone of the drama favoured by the court and by the coterie theatres became increasingly "Cavalier".

The theatre thus came to share, and to add to, the growing unpopularity of the court. As early as 1598 Donne had used "courtier" in a pejorative sense.[12] The more independent dramatists

—Webster, Tourneur, Middleton, Massinger, Ford—denounced
court corruption, though always of course by reference to courts in
Italy or other foreign parts. Hamlet is clear about the corruption of
the court of Denmark. Beaumont and Fletcher became the favourite
playwrights of the court and the coterie theatre. The growing
divisions in society enabled them to speak more convincingly to one
section, the future Cavaliers: they increased the isolation of this
group from the rest of the community.[13]

There has been something of a reaction recently against Harbage's
sharp distinction between the audiences of popular (plebeian) and
coterie (court) audiences; and against the view that the sixteen-
thirties were an epoch of complete decadence in drama. Plays by
Marlowe and Heywood continued to be acted at the popular
theatres. There was more mixing than Harbage allowed.[14] But
Carew referred contemptuously to

> the men in crowded heaps that throng
> To that adulterous stage[15]

Contemporaries clearly thought there were social distinctions to be
drawn.

The royal takeover of the theatre had direct political consequences.
In 1625 an anonymous pamphlet appealed to Parliament against the
theatre. Sixteen years later a pamphleteer pointed out that Parliament
had abolished monopolies, High Commission, Star Chamber, and
bishops were on the way out; it might well be the theatre's turn
next.[16] The theatre had become an appendage of unpopular royal
power.[17]

A special form of court/country polarization was that between
court and City. Unlike Elizabeth, James disliked crowds; Charles
refused even to make a civic entry into his capital until—typically—
1641, when it was too late. The Lord Mayor's show usurped the place
formerly occupied by royal pageantry. It became a political occasion.
The pageant of 1614, *The Triumphs of the old Draperies: or the rich
Cloathing of England*, written by Antony Munday, defied the crown
by opposing James's Cokayne Project, which was soon to collapse
with disastrous consequences for the clothing industry. In 1624 the
City used the occasion for criticism of the government's pro-Spanish
foreign policy.[18]

Massinger is a dramatist who differentiates himself from both
court and City. A spokesman for an anti-Spanish foreign policy, he

seems also to express the viewpoint of gentry who are not "in" at court. His *A New Way to Pay Old Debts* (c. 1625), as everybody knew, was an attack on Sir Giles Mompesson and his patron the Duke of Buckingham. Mompesson was a country squire who had attached himself to the court, but Sir Giles Overreach in the play is depicted as a low-born City usurer. "Massinger blandly assumed that the prodigal gentry, as they lapsed increasingly into debt, retained a basic decency entitling them to their position as the rightful inheritors of England".[19] There had, Overreach says,

> "ever been
> More than a feud, a strange antipathy
> Between us and true gentry". (II. i. 87–9; cf. IV. i. 220–6)

So the honour of the gentry was safeguarded, just as Parliament covered up for Buckingham in impeaching Mompesson rather than his more powerful patron. The transformation of Mompesson into Overreach, Miss Bradbrook suggests, points to an audience increasingly alienated from the City.[20] The Master of the Revels would not allow "persons of great quality" to be impersonated on the stage.[21]

Dramatists more sympathetic to City values could retort only indirectly. Thus Webster clearly approves of the Duchess of Malfi's marriage beneath her, though it horrified her court; similarly Middleton's *Women Beware Women* opposed City morals to those of the court—though both under cover of Italian settings. Webster, son of a wealthy City merchant, was himself a member of the Merchant Taylors' Company by patrimony and wrote a provocatively political Lord Mayor's pageant in 1624. Middleton wrote seven Lord Mayor's pageants and a number of other City entertainments. He became City chronologer in 1620.[22]

The rise of the Lord Mayor's show paralleled that of the masque. Court masques have received more than their due share of attention recently: twentieth-century critics probably understand many of them better than seventeenth-century courtiers, over whose heads the words often passed.[23] What must be stressed is the close association of the masque with the court and with the government. Chapman in 1613 thought opposition to masques comparable with opposition to lawful government.[24] The main point of the masque had always been its conspicuous expenditure; this was recorded with greater care sometimes than the words. It was the court, not the poets, who favoured the masque. Jonson stood it as long as he could, and then revolted.

The theme of court masques was always basically the same: social harmony, idealization of a united nation under a strong monarch. All problems were solved at the end by the King descending from the clouds like a God. Such heavy insistence on harmony betrays fear of discord, anarchy lurking to seize the moment when the central power loses control. Exposing anxieties that had haunted Elizabethan and Jacobean tragedy from Shakespeare onwards, the masque trivialized but did not solve them. It was a dead end in literature: not even in 1660 could it be revived. But it was significant in the sixteen-thirties as a symbol of the conflict of cultures.[25] Milton was unique in trying to bend the masque to carry wider and more serious themes.[26] "When court poets invoke the halcyon, revolution is round the corner", Miss Wedgwood wrote.[27] She was referring to 1685, but in the early sixteen-thirties Carew thought that

> Tourneys, masques, theatres, better become
>   Our halcyon days

than concern for the struggle for protestant survival then going on in Germany.[28]

Before 1640, and to an almost equal extent after 1660, the hope of a budding author without means was to obtain the patronage of some great man, to be taken into his household as tutor or chaplain, to be presented to a living, or at least to enjoy financial largesse in exchange for adulatory dedications. Only a precarious livelihood could be made by the pen before 1640. Patronage was traditionally the responsibility of the King and the aristocracy. Under James I and Charles I it was increasingly monopolized by the court. Only a few great aristocrats could now play the role that the Earl of Leicester had done under Elizabeth. As the gentry became more and more dependent on the court for the pickings which kept some of them solvent, so authors were forced to rely on sales, on appealing to the expanding market for literature. Robert Greene had sixteen different patrons for seventeen books.[29] Marston and Wither showed their contempt for the system by dedicating books to themselves.[30] Patronage continued to be a necessity for those out of favour with the authorities: Margot Heinemann has shown how Middleton looked to the patronage of the Earl of Pembroke as well as having friends in the City.

After 1642 a large number of the great men found themselves in exile or in financial difficulties: the Cavendish family could no longer maintain Hobbes. "Dedications begin nowadays to go out of fashion", Fuller noted in 1647.[31] State office was one alternative that offered itself (Milton, Marvell, Dryden). Another was to earn one's living as a literary free-lance writing for the vastly expanded market. Journalists as able as Marchamont Nedham and James Howell may have managed this. The profession of letters was only just beginning; but it opened up new possibilities of freedom for the author who could hit the taste of the public—though men continued to seek aristocratic patronage for a long time to come.

"The crisis of confidence in those holding power is addressed in play after play", writes Mr Dollimore. "The corrupt court is . . . a recurrent setting for the drama; far from being (as is sometimes suggested) a trans-historical symbol of human depravity, this setting is an historically specific focus for a contemporary critique of power relations".[32] I think Mr Dollimore is right. The most cursory reading of Elizabethan and Jacobean plays would tell us that the powers and duties of monarchs are being questioned. The problem of a disputed succession and the possibility of civil war naturally concerned Elizabethans. *1 Henry VI*. IV. i gives expression to fears of an aristocratic faction fight for the crown: the interests of "simple men" are opposed to the "jarring discord of nobility". Against noble faction the saintly King is powerless, king on sufferance only.[33] In *1 Henry VI* citizens quell potential revolt by bishops and nobles whose patriotism cannot be relied on. In *King John* true patriotism is found in the speeches of the Bastard Falconbridge—though he is a King's bastard. Popular anti-papal patriotism wins through in spite of the King. Even in *Henry V* the authority of monarchy is maintained by the treacherous slaughter of rebel prisoners. (Lack of a standing army is one obvious weakness in the position of fifteenth-century English kings: Richard III had to curry favour with the Lord Mayor even to control London.)

Shakespeare focuses continually on the role and function of monarchy. Richard II is compared and contrasted with Henry IV, Richard III with Henry VII, Henry V with Prince Hal. No longer could monarchs be simply idealized as symbols of the independent English commonwealth; the actual occupants of the throne diverged too markedly from the ideal; and the aspirations of members of the politically important classes began to diverge from one another too.

From Marlowe's *Tamburlaine the Great* and *Edward II* the divinity that doth hedge a king is contrasted with the all too human attributes of some monarchs.[34] "The dramatists anticipated in imagination what the later generation would experience, and by this anticipation helped to set patterns of thought and emotion which determined how that generation would react to its experience".[35] The last point is impossible to prove or disprove, but it is worth bearing in mind. It has been calculated that during the civil war Puritan pamphleteers quoted Shakespeare and Ben Jonson twice as often as royalist.[36]

Historians argue about whether or not men felt themselves to be on a high road to civil war in the first decades of the century: it may be we should not look only at Parliamentary debates to answer this question. Cecil in 1601 was appalled that "Parliament-matters are ordinarily talked of in the streets"; he had heard men say "God prosper those that further the overthrow of these monopolies! God send the prerogative touch not our liberty!"[37] Nine years later the letter-writer John Chamberlain said that "our monarchical power and regal prerogative [are] strained so high and made so transcendent every way that if the practice should follow the positions we are not like to leave to our successors that freedom we received from our forefathers".[38] Such views were more likely to be expressed in private conversation or correspondence than in public debates, where conventional respect for the King was always shown. But many even of the formal documents of Parliament were treasured in men's memories and were rushed into print in the early sixteen-forties, as soon as the censorship could no longer prevent it.[39]

Shakespeare's *Richard II* could be read as an eerily accurate anticipation of Charles I.[40] Richard, passionate and headstrong, held divine right views urged on him by the clergy. He was ruled by flattering favourites who played up to his tastes and fashions: he was deaf to other advice, and became isolated from his people, not least through his financial exactions, in disregard for property rights and the law of the land. Richard frequently compared himself to Jesus Christ. Charles in his turn consciously prepared for martyrdom. He was above all the actor King, as Milton and Marvell both noted. He had been a God in many a masquing scene in the sixteen-thirties: in 1649 he had a real role to play as a tragedy king and his triumphant performance did as much to save monarchy in England as the rest of his life had done to ruin it. Finally Richard, like Charles, was unstable and irresolute, liable to bouts of uncertainty and despair. His most eloquent and high-flown speeches are invariably followed by disastrously bad news.

> Not all the water in the rough rude sea
> Can wash the balm off from an anointed king (III. ii. 54)

leads on to

> With mine own tears I wash away my balm (IV. i. 206)

It is the usurper Richard III who describes himself as "the Lord's anointed" (IV.iv.149). The oft-quoted words in *Hamlet*, "such divinity doth hedge a king", are given to the usurping regicide Claudius.[41] In Sir Francis Hubert's *Edward II* it is the despicable favourite Piers Gaveston who asserts the divine right of kings; in a stanza added before publication in 1629 Edward himself proclaims the doctrine at the moment of his deposition.[42]

Harriett Hawkins noted how Shakespeare held the balance in *Richard II*. The case against the King is stressed in the first half, the arguments against Bolingbroke in the second. In each phase the underdog has our sympathy. But Richard's place in contemporary protestant mythology was rather different. In 1578 Sir Francis Knollys used the phrase "King Richard the Second's men" to describe the court flatterers and parasites who opposed a protestant foreign policy.[43] Twenty-three years later Essex's followers thought it worth while to arrange for Shakespeare's *Richard II* to be acted on the eve of his rebellion, and Elizabeth regarded it as a seditious play. ("I am Richard II, know you not that?"). She was particularly angry that it was "played forty times in open streets and houses".[44] Henry Parker in 1642 drew a parallel between the evil advisers of Charles and Richard,[45] and Colonel Rainborough in the Putney Debates spoke of Richard being deposed because "he did not concur with and agree upon those wholesome laws [which] were offered him by the Council for the safety of the people".[46] As late as 1680—a dangerous year—a play on Richard II, even though favourable to the monarch, was banned; and the theatre was closed for putting on an amended version.[47]

If Richard is Charles, Henry IV has some of the characteristics of Oliver Cromwell, or of a personification of the Parliamentarian Cause. Henry was a self-made hero, a meritocrat owing little to his birth, a bourgeois individualist overthrowing an anointed king. He appealed for popular support when he opposed forced loans. Henry, Daniel said, was "raised by his worth, and by their own consent", just as Cromwell was to be.[48] Hexter has plausibly argued that "the inheritance of real property is the heart" of *Richard II*, a theme which appealed not merely to the aristocracy but to London artisans among the groundlings, from whom court-favoured monopolists had taken "their property in the form of their craft". "Men had a property in their liberty".[49]

In *Richard II*, III. iii, lines 42-4, Henry uncannily anticipates Marvell's *Horatian Ode*. Richard's murder was a necessary part of a natural process: Henry required the blood of the defeated King as a plant requires rain.[50] But it was Henry V rather than his father who claimed the support of God's special Providence.[51] In *King Lear* the monarch who expects total and absolute obedience is petulantly impotent when it is refused: Charles I again.[52] When in *Women Beware Women* the Duke tells Bianca "I can command" he is reminding her of her duty of passive obedience to authority. Obedience will be richly rewarded: the alternative is rape. The theme of Middleton's play is very subversive. It shows a fairly ordinary middle-class household wrecked by the court. Leantio had "normal" aspirations to social mobility; for him the court is not the centre of social harmony, it is at best irrelevant, at worst its power is devastatingly malignant.

In Sidney's *Arcadia* it was accepted that the commonwealth was greater than the king. "The King is but a man as I am", Henry V recognized. In Fletcher and Massinger's *Sir John van Olden Barnveldt* (1619), although the censor insisted on considerable rewriting, the suggestion that the Prince of Orange was "but . . . a servant to . . . the state" was allowed to remain.[53]

>   There must a people be
>   When we shall not be kings,

Henry VI told his rival, the future Edward IV, in Samuel Daniel's *The Civil Wars*.

>   What chair soever monarch sate
>   Upon on earth, the people was the state.

Daniel had been called before the Privy Council in 1605 because the theme of his play *Philotas* was thought to recall the Earl of Essex. Daniel made significant revisions before republishing *The Civil Wars* (1595) in 1607. He covered himself by some snide remarks about Parliamentary agitators: "Those fair baits these trouble-states will use".[54]

"What is the city but the people?" one of the tribunes asked in *Coriolanus* (III. i.) In this play Shakespeare got below questions of monarchy to discuss government as such. The play is about how to deal with the people. Coriolanus's technique for ruling was "to carry it . . . by the suit of the gentry . . . and the desire of the nobles": the people were to be disfranchised (II. i–ii). "In soothing . . . the rank-scented many . . . we nourish 'gainst our Senate/The cockle of rebellion . . . by mingling them with us, the honoured number" (III.i). Menenius has no disagreement with Coriolanus's objectives, but he thinks they can be better secured by guile and flattery, by deceiving the people for their own good. He and the other patricians are embarrassed by Coriolanus's outspokenness: wooing the people's voices with ostensible humility is necessary in order to preserve the social order peaceably (III. ii).

Coriolanus puts his personal feelings of honour and aristocratic virtue above his loyalty to his country: "Let the Volsces plough Rome and harrow Italy" (V. iii). But Shakespeare shows that the "patriotism" of Volumnia and the patricians is self- and class-interested too. "In *Coriolanus*", Miss Bradbrook wrote, "Shakespeare, by sensitive response to pressures from his theatre and audience, had produced a work of strict political relevance"—an "explanation of conflicting systems in terms of personal relationships" which "goes far beyond what could at that time have been formulated politically".[55] It was a pre-view of how City democracy was to be dealt with in the forties and fifties: *Coriolanus* is a wholly urban play—though it was first acted in 1608, a year after Midlands enclosure riots.

In *The Gentleman Usher* (1606) Chapman produced what looks like a direct protest against the principle of monarchy:

> What's a prince? Had all been virtuous men,
> There never had been prince upon the earth,
> And so no subject; all men had been princes.
> A virtuous man is subject to no prince,
> But to his soul and honour.[56]

It has been argued that around 1610 a series of plays (Fletcher's *The Maid's Tragedy* and *A King and no King*, Webster's *Duchess of Malfi*, Chapman's *The Revenge of Bussy D'Ambois*, Dekker's *Match Me in London*) all discuss divine right and the limitations which the law lays on monarchs—not without reference to events in Parliament in 1610.[57] Fletcher's *Valentinian* (1614) shows the impasse into which believers in the divine right of kings found themselves when faced with an intolerable monarch. Murder or suicide seem the only possible alternative courses of action, since popular revolt will lead to mere anarchy (see esp. II. vi, III, i, V. iii–iv, viii).[58] It was this sense that there was no way out that led Fulke Greville to give his plays a Turkish setting. Philip Edwards has argued that Ford's *Perkin Warbeck* (probably early sixteen-thirties) and Massinger's *Believe as You List* (1631), both produced under an even tighter censorship, depict "good" pretenders, but not in any anti-monarchical spirit. "The force behind the pretender figure is the feeling that Charles was betraying the monarchy". "It is the merchants who are most obviously suffering".[59] In Shirley's *The Cardinal* (1641) "the King's response [to violence] each time is prompt, authoritative, confident and entirely ineffectual"—a mirror of Charles's position.[60]

The censorship made it difficult for lower-class viewpoints to come across. The nearest we can get to these is through literature. Contemporaries recognized that there were at least three social groups—landed aristocracy and gentry, citizens, and peasantry and unprivileged artisans. Sidney in *Arcadia* had given pungent expression to their divergent interests: "The peasants would have all the gentlemen destroyed; . . . the citizens would have them reformed".[61] Consciousness of a three-handed class struggle was widespread. Marston in *Histriomastix* (1610) depicted the third class as "the rude commons", "russetings and mechanicals" as well as peasants.[62] Spenser had captured some authentic lower-class voices.[63] Something of the citizens' viewpoint was partially expressed in City comedy by Dekker and Middleton. With the shifting economic balance a new respect for the yeomanry began to develop. "The notion of every man in his place", Conrad Russell observed, "was hard to combine with the effect of inflation on the social structure".[64] In *1 Henry VI* (II. iv) "yeoman" had been used as a term of abuse. But Peacham's character of a plain country fellow in 1638 showed him resisting payment of Ship Money.[65] One reason for Fulke Greville's opposition to unparliamentary taxation had been that it fell heavily on the yeomanry.[66] As the century progressed, Derek Hirst has shown, the Parliamentary gentry had to pay more attention to the feelings of their electorate.[67]

Henry V's conversations with common soldiers show that they too have ideas about how the state should be run. In *Richard II* it is suggested that gardeners do a better job that rulers (III. iv). "The King's Council are no good workmen", say Cade and his followers;

"the nobility think scorn to go in leather aprons. . . . Let the magistrates be labouring men". (*2 Henry VI* IV. ii). Mr Hobday insists on the symbolic nature of gardening. "And Adam was a gardener", Cade replies to a sneer at his humble origins (*ibid*., IV. ii). He alludes no doubt to the old rhyme

> When Adam delved and Eve span,
> Who was then the gentleman?

"There is no ancient gentlemen but gardeners, ditchers and grave-makers", says the grave-maker in *Hamlet*. (V. ii. 33–42).[68]

Paralleling Cade's demand for all in common, the crowd in Marston's *Histriomastix* cries "all shall be common, . . . wives and all". "We came all of our father Adam!"[69] In Middleton's *Hengist King of Kent* (c. 1620) it was Vortigern, tyrant and murderer, who denounced "that wide-throated beast, the multitude" and the inconstancy of the people. The irony in this case can hardly be accidental.[70]

The contempt for the lower orders shown by Coriolanus, who "stuck not to call" Roman citizens "the many-headed multitude", need not necessarily represent the dramatist's point of view, any more than need Sir Humphrey Stafford, who described Cade's followers as "rebellious hinds, the filth and scum of Kent"; "a ragged multitude of hinds and peasants". Shakespeare depicts Cade's rebels with a certain detachment. They are indeed "rude and merciless", as Stafford says; but the arguments which Shakespeare puts into their mouths are not implausible. Prices are too high, lawyers and clerks fleece the poor. J.Ps. "call poor men before them about matters they were not able to answer". Cade looked upon education as a class privilege, as indeed it often was: "Because they could not read, thou hast hanged them". (Ability to read the "neck verse" saved a first offender from the gallows). Cade proposed to burn all legal records. He and his supporters are much more patriotic than the aristocracy who have relations with the national enemy—just like Coriolanus.[71]

"It was never merry world since gentlemen came up": similar remarks had been made in Kett's rebellion in 1549, in Gloucestershire in 1586 and in the Oxfordshire rising of 1596. Dr Hunt has produced much evidence of calls for revolt in Essex during Elizabeth's reign. "What can rich men do against poor men if poor men rise and hold together?" These even took the form of looking for Spanish support.[72]

When Fulke Greville, unusually, raised the subject in the House of Commons, he said—anticipating Menenius's already hackneyed analogy—"if the feet knew their strength, as we know their oppression, they would not bear as they do".[73] That was one of the secrets of government that had to be kept from the governed. In *King Lear* servants are appalled by the tyranny of Regan and Cornwall, even to the extent of resisting it forcibly (III. vii). The Fool, and sometimes Lear himself, gave forcible expression to the lower-class point of view, in a manner very different from the uncommitted reportage of *2 Henry VI*. "Which is the justice, which is the thief? . . . The great image of authority: a dog's obeyed in office" (IV. vi).

> Thou rascal beadle, hold thy bloody hand!
> Why dost thou lash that whore? Strip thine own back;
> Thou hotly lusts to use her in that kind
> For which thou whippst her. The usurer hangs the cozener,
> Through tattered rags small vices do appear,
> Robes and furred gowns hide all. . . . (IV. vi)

The passion behind those words anticipates Abiezer Coppe's *A Fiery Flying Roll* of 1649.

> Poor naked wretches, whereso'er you are
> That bide the pelting of the pitiless storm. . . .
>   O I have ta'en
> Too little care of this! Take physic, pomp;
> Expose thyself to feel what wretches feel.

I do not think anyone else in the seventeenth century so vividly entered into the feelings of that large minority of the population who were condemned to a life of outcast vagabondage. C.S. Lewis suggested that the literature of roguery, treating vagabonds as interesting anthropological specimens, may tell us less about them than about the guilty consciences of the rich, in face of a problem which would not go away.[74]

Raymond Williams sees Shakespearean drama as contemplating "the interaction of social order and social disintegration". "The crisis of *Hamlet* or *King Lear* is a simultaneous crisis of public and private breakdown".[75] "*Macbeth* might almost be described as dramatic prelude to the historical drama of the sixteen-forties and fifties", wrote Christine Berg and Philippa Berry.[76] A familiar theme in Elizabethan and Jacobean literature is the depiction of powerfully Machiavellian individualistic "heroes", whose desires are unlimited, aiming at power beyond power, a quest which ends only in death. The road leads direct from Marlowe's *Tamburlaine* and *Faustus* through Shakespeare and Jonson to Hobbes. Normally such characters are viewed with ultimate disapproval: "Richard loves Richard". "There is no creature loves me, and if I die, no soul will pity me" (*Richard III*, V. iii). "I am myself alone" (*3 Henry VI*, V. vi). "I love myself" (*Richard III*, V. iii). Coriolanus intended to behave

> "As if a man were author of himself
> And knew no other kin". (V. iii)

The aims of such characters are completely anti-social: Ulysses in *Troilus and Cressida* sees them as wolves. And yet the dramatists must have enjoyed depicting Tamburlaine and Faustus, Macbeth and Iago, Edmund, Goneril and Regan in *King Lear*, Antonio in *The Tempest*, Volpone; and audiences enjoyed seeing them. Webster's Flamineo, an alienated intellectual as well as an unprosperous gentleman,[77] is another of the tribe:

> I do not look
> Who went before, nor who shall follow me;
> No, at myself I will begin and end. (*The White Devil*, V. vi. 256–8)

It is the self-made man owing nothing to birth. When Dekker's Barterville (a merchant who has become a court office-holder) says

> Nature sent man into the world alone
> Without all company, but to care for one
> And that I'll do,

the devil Lurchall comments "True City doctrine, Sir".[78]

"My golden time was when I had no gold", said Mosbie in *Arden of Feversham* (III. v). This factually accurate play shows violence employed in the quest for property. Elsewhere there is much denunciation of the corrosive power of gold, from Shakespeare, Jonson, Nicholas Breton and many, many others.[79] Yet Shakespeare makes it clear that Timon's indebtedness was due to reprehensible ostentatious expenditure; it is associated with the feudal violence of Alcibiades, opposed by the money-lenders of "the usurious city", which is clearly London as well as Athens.[80]

The trouble with Timon was that there is no circuit of giving in capitalist society. In feudal society, and in peasant societies today, you may expect returns for gifts and services rendered: they rather than love make the world go round, as is demonstrated for Henry VIII's court by *The Lisle Correspondence*. But Timon discovered that his giving was one-way: in a commercial society men would give nothing for nothing.[81] Money and unscrupulous skill are upsetting traditional stabilities and expectations.

In *The Changeling* De Flores counterposes deeds to mere social rank:

> Fly not to your birth, but settle you
> In what the act has made you;
> You're no more now.

Beatrice-Joanna's actions have brought her down to De Flores's level, made him her equal. Commercial values were the only values of the society which Marlowe imagined in *The Jew of Malta*. As early as 1607 men were arguing that "the good individual is the good general"; "under colour of private enriching himself he [the citizen] laboureth for the common good" (1616). "The poor man's inheritance is in his hands".[82] Such views were to triumph after the Revolution.

"The cause of plagues is sin", declared Thomas White in a sermon at Paul's Cross in 1577; "and the cause of sin are plays. Therefore the cause of plague are plays".[83] The point was echoed after the plague of 1625 by the famous Puritan preacher at Gray's Inn, Richard Sibbes.[84] National sin would inevitably bring punishment on the people, no doubt through the frightening power of continental Catholicism. Simonds D'Ewes, as early as 1623, was preparing himself for "worser times", which "without God's admirable and infinite mercy we could not but shortly expect".[85] We should not underestimate such contemporary expressions of alarm, which perhaps had more to do with emigration to New England than historians have recognized. In 1629 John Winthrop expected "heavy affliction upon this land, and that speedily". Thomas Hooker, Mrs Anne Hutchinson and many others agreed with him.[86] In 1628–9 letters received by Lady Barrington are full of such anxieties. ("God's heavy judgment—most like to befall us"; "the foundations of the earth out of order"; "these dead and declining times").[87] Donne had a sense of impending doom. Nor was the feeling restricted to clergy and godly laity. As early as *Tamburlaine* Marlowe was depicting an irresistible destructive force which swept aside traditional societies, traditional states and traditional religions. Caesar in *Antony and Cleopatra* thought we should

Let determined things to destiny
Hold unbewailed their way (III. vi).

'Tis madness to resist or blame
The force of angry heaven's flame

wrote Marvell after the kingdom old had been cast in another mould.
Did the expectation help to bring about the catastrophe?

But religion did not lead only to a sense of imminent catastrophe: it
also gave men and women courage and self-reliance. Bible-reading
contributed to the rise of individualism no less than did economic
developments: the inner light anticipates the hidden hand. Puritanism
helped to create a sense of solidarity as well as confidence among the
unprivileged: if God was with them who could be against them?
"Seeing we cannot compass these things by suit nor dispute", said the
Presbyterian leader John Field, probably in 1587, after defeat in
Parliament, "it is the multitude and people must bring the discipline
to pass which we desire".[88] If the Presbyterian discipline "come in by
that means which will make all your hearts to ache, blame
yourselves", warned John Udall in 1588.[89] Many after the event said
that George Wither's *Brittans Remembrancer* had foretold the civil
war: certainly he predicted in 1628 that clerics—the ideologists of the
society—would "blow the flame" on both sides as polarization took
place.[90]

Margot Heinemann has pointed out the difficulty of representing
bad parsons on the Elizabethan, Jacobean and Caroline stage.[91]
Disreputable clergymen had to be Catholics or Puritans. Nevertheless, the dramatists were able to exercise some finesse. The only
wholly admirable bishop in Shakespeare, Margot Heinemann tells
me, is Cranmer: he had to be. The good kings Henry V and Henry
VIII stand up to their priests, as the less good John and Richard II do
not. But Henry V failed to carry out his father's intended
expropriation of church lands, even to pay for his French wars: unlike
Henry VIII in that. There were frequent proposals for a further
confiscation of church lands under the monarchy down to 1626: they
were expropriated in the forties. Webster in both *The White Devil*
and *The Duchess of Malfi* shows how the secular power of the
Catholic church is associated with the ruler's tyranny. The protests
of the Cardinal are ineffective in *Women Beware Women*.

It is an heretic that makes the fire
Not she which burns in it

said Paulina in *The Winter's Tale* (II. iii); something of a contrast with Shakespeare's treatment of Joan of Arc as a witch and a whore in *I Henry VI*. There is a connection, which has not yet been properly studied, between popular heretical religion and theories of revolt, between what contemporaries called atheism and rejection of the values of traditional society. Marlowe appears to have embraced the very radical heresy of mortalism: the soul dies with the body, a heresy against which Sir John Davies directed *Nosce Teipsum*. It was proclaimed in 1643 by Richard Overton, the future Leveller leader; it was shared by Milton and many other radicals.[92]

Nashe denounced those, Familists presumably, who thought the devil was only an allegory.[93] This idea too surfaced after 1640, just as Milton's Satan repeated Mephistophilis's "Where I am is hell". It was argued that religious liberty would lead through complete freedom of speculation on to atheism. "Atheism" was commonly thought of as rejection of a Creator God: all comes by nature only. This view was attributed to Marlowe and the Ralegh circle; it too reappeared among the Ranters of the sixteen-forties and fifties.

Another way of envisaging social and political change was by way of millenarianism. For John Foxe England was the chosen nation. Judith Doolin Spike has suggested that this conception of a historical destiny for the English people permeates the history plays of the early seventeenth century.[94] Many saw England's destiny in the New World, where God's glory could be served by converting the Indians after liberating them from the cruel and antichristian tyranny of the Spaniards. This combined with more mundane motives—"to seek new worlds for gold, for praise, for glory", Ralegh sang.[95] He was presumably thinking of gain and glory for younger sons of the aristocracy and gentry, many of whom were suffering economic difficulties in that inflationary age. As well as gold, there were raw materials and markets to be won, and above all there was the slave trade. Colonies in America could also be used as a dumping ground for the surplus population of vagabonds which frightened propertied Englishmen.[96] On a more realistically pessimistic assessment Winthrop and others envisaged the New World as a refuge for God's people against the rising power of Antichrist in Europe, and of his henchmen in England. Even George Herbert, far from being a committed Puritan, saw religion "ready to pass to the American strand".[97]

This vision of empire was there from Elizabeth's reign. John Dee,

Richard Hakluyt, Sidney, Ralegh and Bacon were its outstanding exponents. Fulke Greville, in his poetical treatises as well as in his *Life of Sidney*, set out a long-term political programme for representative government and Parliamentary control of taxation to pay for a forward foreign policy in the interests of God and England. This meant war against Spain in alliance with the Netherlands, and following the Dutch model at home.[98] The point was made by Robert Burton, who, like Greville and Thomas Scott, approved of industry and was critical of aristocratic idleness.[99] George Chapman, a former member of Ralegh's circle, put forward empire as the solution to all social problems.[100] Bartoldo in Massinger's *The Maid of Honour* (I. i) advocated development of Sicilian (sic!) sea power and aggressive use of it to solve the island's problems of over-population and under-endowed younger sons. Sidney and Ralegh had been admirers of the Dutch republic, whose commercial success depended on using sea power to expand trade. The Dutch government was controlled by merchants; state power was directed to the maximization of national profit—initially to finance the war of liberation against Spain. Early Stuart governments could never have carried out such a commercial policy. Nor would they have wished to, though merchants and M.Ps. repeatedly demanded it. Only in the sixteen-fifties did the Commonwealth carry it out. Parliamentary control of taxation after 1660 ensured that the policy survived the restoration.

Bacon's ideas too contributed to millenarian optimism by giving men a sense of the possibility of historical change, akin to the sense of co-operating with God's purposes which Calvinists enjoyed. If the Moderns can out-do the Ancients, progress is possible, change for the better: perhaps it can be planned? Bacon showed that science might be used for the relief of man's estate, to abolish poverty. Disregarded by the court in his lifetime, many of his works were first published, or published in English, only after 1640.

It was then a fragmented world in which late Elizabethan and Jacobean intellectuals lived. All coherence had gone because quite new possibilities were opening for individuals and for society—new potentialities frustrated by old institutions and old ideas. It is easier to see this in retrospect; but the more sensitive contemporary writers had grasped something of it. Faustus was already in a divided world. He rejected traditional philosophy and divinity for magic, by which he meant useful knowledge, science. Bacon's separation of religion from science was intended to achieve the same effect by more

acceptable means. Marston and Donne as well as Marlowe were
critical of traditional Christian humanism; Shakespeare's last plays
have been taken in the same sense. Ritual obeisance was still made to
the great chain of being so eloquently laid out in the Book of
Homilies; but men clearly knew that it was under attack.[101]
Protestantism had taught men and women to look inwards to
ascertain God's will, not outwards to the hierarchy of the church.
"'Fool', said my Muse to me, 'look in thy heart and write'".[102]

> Arks now we look for none, nor signs to part
> Egypt from Israel; all rests in the heart.[103]

But hearts gave different answers. Greville's lines are almost as
well-known as Donne's:

> O wearisome condition of humanity!
> Born under one law, to another bound:
> Vainly begot, and yet forbidden vanity,
> Created sick, commanded to be sound.

They lead on to the conclusion:

> Yet when each of us in his own heart looks
> He finds the God there far unlike his books.[104]

Everywhere we find phrases like "the double heart". From Greville
himself,[105] Robert Heywood,[106] and Joseph Beaumont,[107] through
preachers like Henry Smith,[108] Richard Sibbes,[109] Joseph Hall,[110] and
John Owen,[111] it extended to Robert Burton,[112] Marvell,[113] Gerrard
Winstanley,[114] Cowley,[115] and *The Cabal*, an anonymous poem of
1679.[116] Hamlet personifies the double heart, the divided will.

> The time is out of joint. O cursed spite
> That ever I was born to set it right!

Like Hamlet, Marston's Malcontent "in his own soul is at variance
with himself.[117] For Donne, says Mr Wilders, "to be human was, by
definition, to be in a state of civil war".[118]

We may compare the revealingly entitled *Automachia, or Self civil
war*, translated by John Sylvester from the Latin of George
Goodwin:

> Unto myself I do myself betray. . . .
> Myself agrees not with myself a jot. . . .
> I trust myself, and I myself distrust. . . .
> I cannot live, with nor without myself.[119]

It is interesting that these lines attracted the Grindletonian Roger Brearley, who died in 1637.[120] "Why should I war without the walls of Troy", Troilus asked, "That find such cruel battle here within?" (I. i. Cf. V. ii). The battle raged both among the Trojans and in Troilus's own heart. "The histories", said F.P. Wilson, "are tragedies of a divided state; the tragedies are tragedies of a divided mind".[121] Analogous expressions can be found everywhere in the poems of William Arblaster,[122] Giles and Phineas Fletcher,[123] George Wither,[124] Henry More,[125] Thomas Traherne.[126]

> My thoughts are all a case of knives
> Wounding my heart,

wrote George Herbert.

> O that thou shouldst give dust a tongue
> To cry to thee,
> And then not hear it crying!
>
> God chains the dog till night; wilt loose the chain,
> And wake thy sorrow?[127]

"Mansoul it was the very seat of war", sang Bunyan in *The Holy War* (1682).[128] Consciousness of agonizing internal division is characteristic of no one religious or political tendency: it is universal. In Donne, for instance, paradoxes and contradictions abound:

> Those are my best days when I shake with fear.
> No cross is so extreme as to have none[129]

Or in Crashawe's vision of Christ coming

> Lightly as a lambent flame,
> Leaping upon the hills to be
> The humble King of you and me.[130]

We may compare Vaughan's

> Here in dust and dirt, oh here
> The lilies of his love appear[131]

with Tourneur's "to have her train borne up and her soul trail in the dirt,"[132] and with Joseph Beaumont:

> Lilies are cleanly, white and sweet
> And yet they have but dirty feet.[133]

Or Marvell:

> Therefore the love which doth us bind,
> But fate so enviously debars

> Is the conjunction of the mind
> And opposition of the stars

That is why we have to

> Tear our pleasures with rough strife
> Thorough the iron gates of life.[134]

Sir Thomas Browne spoke of "passion against reason, reason against faith, faith against the devil, and my conscience against all".[135]

Analogous is the metaphor of rape, from Donne

> For I,
> Except you enthrall me, never shall be free,
> Nor ever chaste, except you ravish me[136]

to Edward Taylor in New England.[137] Taylor was a belated metaphysical poet. In old England the metaphor of the double heart is rarely found after the restoration, until it reappears in C. Day Lewis in the nineteen-thirties, concurrently with the revival of interest in metaphysical poetry. But in the early seventeenth century men of very differing outlooks were far more acutely aware of inner tensions than in the preceding or succeeding centuries.

I hope I need not disclaim any intention of suggesting that Shakespeare foresaw the execution of a King of England, still less that he would have welcomed it; or that the poets I have cited anticipated the civil war. What I am suggesting is that the great tragedians and the metaphysical poets—whatever they may have thought themselves —are not dealing with "the human condition", with "man", but with specific problems which confronted rulers and their subjects in a specific historical situation—problems which were bloodily resolved in the sixteen-forties. Faced with the apparent collapse of traditional values, some clung desperately to "the Elizabethan world picture" and "the great chain of being". But few serious students now suppose that such ideas were generally accepted. The great dramatists— Shakespeare, Webster, Middleton—can no longer be adequately categorized as "Christian humanists".[138] "Statements of a subversive and startling kind" have been found in Massinger.[139]

Few have had the courage of Mr Dollimore in putting forward an alternative theory which stresses the radical implications of Jacobean drama—a drama in which the established institutions of state and church "and their ideological legitimation were subjected to sceptical, interrogative and subversive representation",[140] or of Margot Heinemann who shows two worlds in conflict in the drama of

Middleton. Whether these dramatists—or any of the metaphysical poets—had conscious alternative value systems is undemonstrable and, in Winstanley's phrase about the historical truth of the Gospel, "it matters not much". They provide us with "an intensity of insight quite unattainable any other way." We should take fuller advantage of this richness in our attempts to explain what happened in seventeenth-century England.[141]

NOTES

1. Margot Heinemann, *Puritanism and Theatre: Thomas Middleton and Opposition Drama under the Early Stuarts* (Cambridge U.P., 1980); M. McKeon, *Politics and Poetry in Restoration England: The Case of Dryden's* Annus Mirabilis (Harvard U.P., 1975); Susan Staves *Players' Scepters: Fictions of Authority in the Restoration* (Nebraska U.P., 1979). See also the writings of Robert Weimann and M.C. Bradbrook, *passim*; and a special issue on restoration drama of *The Eighteenth Century: Theory and Interpretation*, 24 (1983).
2. My *Intellectual Origins of the English Revolution*, esp. pp. 10–13. Cf. pp. 34–49 below.
3. Heinemann, *passim*.
4. L.B. Wright, *Middle-Class Culture in Elizabethan England* (North Carolina U.P., 1935), p. 95. This remarkable book raised most of the questions historians have been trying to answer during the last half century.
5. See pp. 34–5, 98–9 below.
6. Ed. G. Saintsbury, *Minor Poets of the Caroline Period* (Oxford U.P., 1905–21), I, p. 488. See p. 326 below.
7. Bradbrook, *The Rise of the Common Player* (1962), pp. 39–42, 53, 65, 71, 75.
8. Weimann, *Shakespeare and the Popular Tradition in the Theatre: Studies in the Social Dimension of Dramatic Form and Function* (Johns Hopkins U.P., 1978), pp. 169–85 and *passim*.
9. Cf. J.D. Spike, "The Jacobean History Play and the Myth of the Elect Nation", *Renaissance Drama*, New Series, VIII (1977), pp. 10–49.
10. G. Wickham, *Early English Stages, 1300 to 1600*, II, Part i (1963), pp. 17, 90–5, 104–5, 136. But see note 141 below.
11. Brian Gibbons, *Jacobean City Comedy* (1968), pp. 25, 202–3 and *passim*; cf. Malcolm Smuts, "State Culture and Patronage", in *Patronage in the Renaissance* (ed. C.F. Lytle and S. Orgel, Princeton U.P., 1981), p. 187.
12. A.F. Marotti, "John Donne and Patronage", *ibid.*, p. 215.
13. J. Danby, *Elizabethan and Jacobean Poets* (1965), pp. 19, 165, 182, 204; cf. P.W. Thomas, "Two Cultures? Court and Country under Charles I," in *The Origins of the English Civil War* (ed. C. Russell, 1973), p. 75.

14. Alfred Harbage, *Shakespeare and the Rival Traditions* (New York, 1952); cf. K. McLuskie, "The Plays and Playwrights, 1613-1642", in *The Revels History of Drama in English*, IV, *1613-1660* (1981), p. 168.

15. "To my worthy friend, Master D'Avenant", in *Minor Poets of the 17th Century* (Everyman edn.) pp. 142-3. Carew was consoling Davenant for the flop of "his excellent play, *The Just Italian*".

16. [Anon.], *The Stage-Players Complaint* (1641), quoted in *The Cambridge History of English Literature*, VI (Cambridge U.P., 1950), pp. 407, 403.

17. D.M. Bergeron, *English Civic Pageantry, 1558-1642* (1971), pp. 108-9; Wickham, *op. cit.*, II, pp. 237-9.

18. M.C. Bradbrook, "The Politics of Pageantry: social implications in Jacobean London", in *Poetry and Drama, 1570-1700: Essays in Honour of Harold F. Brooks* (ed. A. Coleman and A. Hammond, 1981), pp. 70, 72-4.

19. Julia Briggs, *This Stage-Play World: English Literature and its Background, 1580-1625* (Oxford U.P., 1983), p. 35.

20. Bradbrook, *The Living Monument: Shakespeare and the Theatre of his Time* (Cambridge U.P., 1979), p. 200. Massinger's *The City Madam* (1632) attacks usury.

21. G.E. Bentley, *The Profession of Dramatist in Shakespeare's Time, 1590-1642* (Princeton U.P., 1979), pp. 192-3.

22. Bradbrook, *John Webster, Citizen and Dramatist* (1980), Chapters 1 and 8; Heinemann, *passim*.

23. G. Parry, *The Golden Age Restored: The Culture of the Stuart Court, 1603-1642* (Manchester U.P., 1981), pp. 63, 152 and *passim*.

24. Chapman, *Dramatic Works* (1873), III, p. 105; McLuskie, *op. cit.*, p. 141.

25. See P.W. Thomas, "Two Cultures?", *passim*; S. Orgel, *The Illusion of Power: Political Theatre in the English Renaissance* (California U.P., 1975), *passim*.

26. Jonathan Dollimore interestingly suggests that the anti-masque could carry a subversive message (*Radical Tragedy: Religion, Ideology and Power in the Drama of Shakespeare and his Contemporaries*, Brighton, 1984, pp. 27-8, 275).

27. C.V. Wedgwood, *Poetry and Politics under the Stuarts* (Cambridge U.P., 1960), p. 173.

28. "In Answer of an Elegiacal Letter upon the Death of the King of Sweden", *Minor Poets of the 17th Century*, p. 127.

29. P. Sheavyn, *The Literary Profession in the Elizabethan Age* (Manchester U.P., 1967), p. 24; cf. E. Rosenberg, *Leicester, Patron of Letters* (New York, 1955), *passim*.

30. Briggs, *op. cit.*, pp. 137-8. Smollett dedicated *Ferdinand Count Fathom* to himself in 1753. Dr G.S. Rousseau takes this as evidence of mental collapse on Smollett's part (*Tobias Smollett: Essays of Two Decades*, Edinburgh, 1983). I should see it rather as evidence that aristocratic patronage still mattered.

31. T. Fuller, *Good Thoughts in Worse Times* (1647), To the Christian Reader.

32. *Radical Tragedy*, p. 4. Unfortunately this brave and powerful book appeared too late for me to make full use of its insights. Cf. also Nicholas Brooke, *Horrid Laughter in Jacobean Tragedy* (New York, 1979), *passim*.

33. Glynne Wickham suggests that Cymbeline is intended to be an image of James I ("Riddle and Emblem: A Study in the Dramatic Structure of *Cymbeline*" in *English Renaissance Studies Presented to Dame Helen Gardner*, ed. J. Carey, Oxford U.P., 1980, p. 100.)

34. My *Intellectual Origins of the English Revolution* (Oxford U.P., 1965), pp. 174-5, where I acknowledge a debt to W.M. Merchant.

35. P. Cruttwell, *The Shakespearean Moment and its Place in the Poetry of the 17th Century* (1954), p. 189.

36. E. Sirluck, "Shakespeare and Jonson among the pamphleteers of the first civil war", *Modern Philology*, 53 (1955-6), p. 90.

37. Ed. R.H. Tawney and E. Power, *Tudor Economic Documents* (1924), II, p. 292.

38. Ed. N.E. McClure, *The Letters of John Chamberlain* (Philadephia, 1939), I, p. 301. Chamberlain cites disparaging use of the term "royalist" as early as 1624 (*ibid.*, II, p. 540).

39. See pp. 44-5 below.

40. Cf. Heinemann, p. 68.

41. The point is made by Charles Hobday, "Clouted Shoon and Leather Aprons: Shakespeare and the Egalitarian Tradition", *Renaissance and Modern Studies, xxiii (1979)*.

42. *The Poems of Sir Francis Hubert* (ed. B. Mellor, Hong Kong U.P., 1961), pp. 17-18, 323.

43. H. Hawkins, *Poetic Freedom and Poetic Truth* (Oxford U.P., 1976), p. 71; P. Collinson, *Godly People: Essays on English Protestantism and Puritanism* (1983), p. 381.

44. C. Hobday, "Clouted Shoon and Leather Aprons", p. 77.

45. Parker, *Observations upon some of His Majesties Late Answers and Expresses* (1642), in *Tracts on Liberty in the Puritan Revolution, 1638-47* (ed. W. Haller, Columbia U.P., 1933), II, pp. 195-6.

46. Ed. A.S.P. Woodhouse, *Puritanism and Liberty* (1938), p. 121.

47. R.D. Hume, *The Development of English Drama in the late Seventeenth Century* (Oxford U.P., 1976), p. 345. The play was by Nahum Tate.

48. Daniel, *The Civil Wars* (ed. L. Michel, Yale U.P., 1958), p. 172.

49. Hexter, *op. cit.*, esp. pp. 14-16.

50. Cf. D.A. Tapton, "Shakespeare's Henry IV: A New Prince in a New Principality", in *Shakespeare as Political Thinker* (ed. J. Alvis and T.G. West, Carolina Academic Press, 1981), p. 88.

51. Cf. an interesting article on Shakespeare's ambivalence towards Henry V in John Arden's *To Present the Pretence* (1977), pp. 196-208.

52. M.C. Bradbrook, *The Living Monument*, p. 147.

53. S. McLuskie, *op. cit.*, p. 132.

54. Bentley, *op. cit.*, pp. 168-9; Daniel, *op. cit.*, pp. 34, 189, 256, 293; cf. pp. 172, 272, 274, 159, and Heinemann, p. 41.

55. Bradbrook, *The Living Monument*, p. 176.

56. Chapman, *Dramatic Works* (1873), I, p. 331.
57. S. Shepherd, *Amazons and Warrior Women: Varieties of Feminism in Seventeenth-Century Drama* (Brighton, 1981), p. 120; cf. McLuskie, *op. cit.*, p. 138.
58. This play was revived in 1684, partly rewritten by Rochester (see p. 308 below).
59. Edwards, "The Royal Pretenders in Massinger and Ford", *Essays and Studies* (1974), pp. 34–5.
60. Catherine Belsey, "Tragedy, Justice and the Subject", in *1642: Literature and Power in the Seventeenth Century* (ed. F. Barker *et. al.*, Essex University, 1981), pp. 167–85.
61. Sidney, *Arcadia* (ed. H. Friswell, 1867), p. 226. First published 1590.
62. *The Plays of John Marston* (ed. H.H. Wood, Edinburgh, 1934–9), II, pp. 278–91.
63. See esp. Spenser, *Mother Hubberds Tale*, ll. 132–66; *The Faerie Queene*, Book V, canto ii, stanzas 32–8.
64. Russell, *The Crisis of Parliaments* (Oxford U.P., 1971), 196, quoted very effectively by Dollimore, *op. cit.*, p. 284.
65. D. Bush, *English Literature in the Earlier Seventeenth Century, 1600–1660* (Oxford U.P., 2nd. edn., 1962), p. 201.
66. Greville, *Life of Sidney* (1907), pp. 52–4. First published 1652.
67. D. Hirst, *The Representative of the People? Voters and Voting in England under the Early Stuarts* (Cambridge U.P., 1975), *passim*.
68. Hobday, "Clouted Shoon", gives many more examples of Shakespeare's awareness of class-consciousness. "Clouted shoon", like "leather aprons", were a social symbol, dating back at least to Kett's rebellion in 1549. Hobday quotes Lilburne in 1653 claiming the support of "the hobnails, clouted shoes, the private soldiers, the leathern and woollen aprons and the laborious and industrious people in England". Cf. the First Citizen's speeches in *Coriolanus*, I. i.
69. Marston, *Plays* (ed. Wood), III, p. 289.
70. Middleton, *The Mayor of Queenborough, or Hengist, King of Kent*, I. i, II. ii.
71. Hobday, "Clouted Shoon", p. 68.
72. W. Hunt, *The Puritan Moment: The Coming of Revolution in an English County* (Harvard U.P., 1983), pp. 58–62, 147–9; cf. p. 167.
73. S. D'Ewes, *A Compleat Journal of the . . . House of Commons* (1693), p. 490.
74. C.S. Lewis, *English Literature in the Later Sixteenth Century* (Oxford U.P., 1954), p. 59.
75. Raymond Williams, *Culture* (1981), pp. 156–9.
76. "Spiritual Whoredom: An Essay on Female Prophets in the 17th century", in *1642* (ed. P. Barker *et al.*), p. 42.
77. Brooke, *Horrid Laughter*, pp. 28–9, 130.
78. Dekker, *If it be not good the Divel is in it* (1612), in *Dramatic Works* (ed. F. Bowers, Cambridge U.P., 1953–61), III, p. 179.
79. Jonson, "Epistle to Elizabeth, Countess of Rutland", in *Poems* (ed. Ian Donaldson, Oxford U.P., 1975), pp. 107–8; Breton, "Old Mad-cappes,

new Gally-mawfrey", in *Poems* (ed. J. Robertson, Liverpool U.P., 1967), pp. 120–33.

80. *Timon of Athens*, III. v; cf. *Cymbeline*, II iii.
81. *The Lisle Letters* (ed. M. St Clare Byrne, Chicago U.P., 6 vols, 1981), *passim*. Cf. The Bastard on "commodity" in *King John* (II. i).
82. Quoted by L.B. Salingar, "The Social Setting", in *The Age of Shakespeare* (ed. B. Ford, Penguin, 1955), p. 40.
83. Quoted by E.K. Chambers, *The Elizabethan Stage* (Oxford U.P., 1923), IV, p. 197.
84. Sibbes, *Complete Works* (Edinburgh, 1862–4), VI, pp. 153–4.
85. *The Diary of Sir Simonds D'Ewes, 1622–1624* (ed. E. Bourcier, Paris, n.d., ?1975), p. 130; cf. p. 145.
86. P. Collinson, *The Religion of Protestants: The Church in English Society, 1559–1625* (Oxford U.P., 1982), p. 283; cf. Joseph Hall in 1624: "there is a storm coming towards our church" (*ibid.*, p. 90).
87. *Barrington Family Letters, 1628–1632* (ed. A. Searle, Camden 4th Series, 28, 1983), pp. 29, 37, 77; cf. pp. 36, 58, 60, 94, 96.
88. A.F. Scott Pearson, *Thomas Cartwright and Elizabethan Puritanism* (1925), pp. 252–3; cf. P. Collinson, *The Elizabethan Puritan Movement* (1967), p. 297. Zeal-of-the-Land Busy appears to echo this phrase in *Bartholomew Fair* (V. iii).
89. Udall, *A Demonstration of Discipline* (1588) (ed. E. Arber, 1880), p. 7.
90. See pp. 136–7 below.
91. Heinemann, pp. 73–5.
92. For mortalism see M.E.R., Chapter 25.
93. T. Nashe, *Pierce Penniless his Supplication to the Devil* (first published 1592), in *The Unfortunate Traveller and Other Works* (Penguin, 1972), p. 127.
94. J.D. Spike, "The Jacobean History Play and the Myth of the Elect Nation", pp. 117–49.
95. *The Poems of Sir Walter Ralegh* (ed. Agnes M.C. Latham, 1951), p. 27.
96. For examples cf. Thomas Cooper, *The Blessing of Japheth*, a sermon dedicated to the Lord Mayor, Aldermen and Sheriffs of London and the Commissioners for Plantations in Ireland and Virginia, quoted in my "Till the Conversion of the Jews", in *Millenarianism in English Thought and Literature* (ed. R. Popkin, California U.P., forthcoming) and T. Scott, *Vox Populi* (1620), Sig. B4–4v.
97. See pp. 216–17 below.
98. Greville, *Life of Sidney*, Chapters 15–17 and *passim; Poems and Dramas* (ed. G. Bullough, Edinburgh, n.d.,?1939), I, pp. 99, 128–30, 146; II, pp. 74, 81, 129; *Remains* (ed. G.A. Wilkes, Oxford U.P., 1965), pp. 107–12, 135–9, 144–7.
99. Burton, *Anatomy of Melancholy* (Everyman edn.), I, pp. 86–93, 136. First edition published 1621.
100. Chapman, *Poems and Minor Translations* (1875), pp. 51–5. The poem is about Guiana, Ralegh's colony. Chapman addressed another poem to Hariot, Ralegh's mathematician.
101. P.N. Siegel, *Shakespearean Tragedy and the Elizabethan Compromise*

New York U.P., 1957), p. 78; J. Danby, *op. cit.,* p. 97. For the great chain of being see pp. 57-8 below.

102. Sidney, *Poems* (ed. W.A. Ringler, Oxford U.P., 1962), p. 165. Cf. Gerrard Winstanley, "read in your own book, your heart" (*The Works of Gerrard Winstanley*, ed. G.H. Sabine, Cornell U.P., 1941, p. 213).

103. Greville, *Remains*, p. 226.

104. Greville, *Poems and Dramas*, II, pp. 136-7.

105. *Ibid.*, I, p. 116; cf. pp. 11-14, 117, 168, 194-5; cf. II, p. 116.

106. R. Heywood, *Observations and Instructions in Verse, Divine and Morall* (ed. J. Crossley, Chetham Soc. publications, 1869), p. 33: "my womb two nations doth embrace". Heywood died in 1645.

107. Joseph Beaumont, *Civil War*, in *Minor Poems* (ed. E. Robinson, 1914), p. 13.

108. H. Smith, *Sermons* (1631), p. 119.

109. Sibbes, *Complete Works*, VII, p. 411: "a double eye as well as a double heart".

110. Hall, *Works*, VIII, p. 147: "set me at war with myself, that I may be at peace with thee".

111. Owen, *Works* (1850-3), VI, p. 173.

112. Burton, *An Anatomy of Melancholy*, I, pp. 11-13: "The Author's Abstract of Melancholy".

113. Marvell, *A Dialogue between the Soul and Body*, in *M.P.L.* I, p. 20.

114. Winstanley, *The Law of Freedom and Other Writings* (Cambridge U.P., 1983), p. 58.

115. A. Cowley, *Poems* (ed. A.R. Waller, Cambridge U.P., 1905), p. 113.

116. Quoted by K.H.D. Haley, *The First Earl of Shaftesbury* (Oxford U.P., 1968), p. 529.

117. *The Malcontent*, I. ii, in *Plays*, I, p. 146.

118. Wilders, "Rochester and the Metaphysicals", in *Spirit of Wit: Reconsiderations of Rochester* (ed. J. Treglown, Oxford, 1982), p. 44.

119. J. Sylvester, *The Complete Works* (ed. A.B. Grosart, 1880), II, pp. 260-3. Goodwin seems to have had Puritan sympathies; an attack on Catholicism by him, dedicated to Sir Francis Naunton, was translated by John Vicars in 1620.

120. The lines were printed among Roger Brearley's poems in *A Bundle of Soul Convincing. . . and Comforting Truths* (1677), p. 94. I mistakenly cited them in *W.T.U.D.* as though Brearley had written them.

121. F.P. Wilson, *Elizabethan and Jacobean* (Oxford U.P., 1945), p. 112. A similar double heart arose simultaneously in historical writing, Dr Merchant suggests ("Lord Herbert of Cherbury and 17th-century Historical Writing", *Trans. of the Hon. Soc. of Cymmrodorion* 1956-7, pp. 53-63).

122. Alabaster, Sonnet 73, in *The Sonnets of William Alabaster* (ed. G.M. Story and H. Gardner, Oxford U.P., 1959), p. 40.

123. G. and P. Fletcher, *Poetical Works* (ed. F.S. Boas, Cambridge U.P., 1908-9), I, pp. 18-19, 182; II, pp. 19, 257.

124. Wither, *Emblemes* (1635), IV. i, quoted on p. 150 below.

125. H. More, *Poems* (ed. Grosart, 1878), pp. 17, 181.

126. Traherne, *Poems, Centuries and Three Meditations* (ed. A. Ridler, Oxford U.P., 1966), pp. 43, 46, 68, 104, 110; cf. pp. 226–7 below, and Peter Sterry, quoted on pp. 232–3 below.
127. G. Herbert, *Works* (ed. R.A. Willmott, n.d.), pp. 89, 78, 153.
128. Bunyan, *Works* (ed. G. Offor, 1860), III, pp. 253–4.
129. Donne, "Holy Sonnet XIX;" "The Crosse", in *Complete Poetry and Selected Prose* (ed. J. Hayward, Nonesuch edn., 1929), p. 288.
130. Crawshawe, *Poems* (ed. J.R. Tutin, Muses Lib., n.d.), p. 266.
131. *The Works of Henry Vaughan* (ed. L.C. Martin, Oxford U.P., 1914), p. 643; cf. pp. 414–15, 476. Cf. M. Drayton, *Poetical Works* (ed. R. Hooker, 1876), III, p. 275.
132. Tourneur, *The Revengers Tragedy* (IV. iv).
133. J. Beaumont, *Minor Poems* (ed. E. Robinson, 1914), p. 21; cf. Benlowes, "Theophila's Spiritual Warfare"—see p. 201 below.
134. *M.P.L.*, I, pp. 27, 37.
135. Cf. J. Briggs, *op. cit.*, p. 8. Cf. Bush, "Browne is a completely harmonious microcosm of an age of contradictions" (*op. cit.*, p. 353).
136. Donne, *op. cit.*, p. 285.
137. Karl Keller, *The Example of Edward Taylor* (Massachusetts U.P., 1975), p. 214.
138. Dollimore, *op. cit.*, pp. 6–8, 19, 50, 60–1, 139.
139. McLuskie, *op. cit.*, p. 200.
140. Dollimore, *op. cit.*, p. 4.
141. If Martin Butler's important book, *Theatre and Crisis, 1632–1642* (Cambridge U.P., 1984) had been available before I wrote this chapter I should have taken advantage of his demonstration that significant drama could be written and produced even in the sixteen-thirties. The argument of Robert Weimann's suggestive "Shakespeare und Luther", in *Shakespeare Jahrbuch*, 20 (1984), is relevant to the problem of authority.

2. *Censorship and English Literature*[1]

The most effective way of enforcing censorship, Terry Eagleton observed, is to keep the mass of the population illiterate.[2] Although only a minority of the English people in the sixteenth and seventeenth centuries could read, protestant emphasis on Bible-reading as well as the needs of a developing business society acted as stimuli to literacy. In any case, as we have learnt from the Third World in the present century, illiteracy does not necessarily debar men and women from participating in politics. There is evidence in England during our period of pamphlets being read aloud in taverns, ale-houses and market-places—and later in the New Model Army. But in normal times illiteracy plus the censorship effectively excluded the majority of the population from being able to take part in politics, probably even from contemplating the possibility of participation.

Censorship in England started soon after printing. The reformation owed a great deal to print, and especially to the import from the continent of prohibited books. Henry VIII tried to abolish diversity of opinions by statute, and his daughter Mary by proclamation. Neither was successful. Historians of literature and of ideas, and some straight historians, seem to me seriously to underestimate the significance of censorship. Those who believe we should study only the words on the page, only texts, do not ask themselves whether there were certain words, or certain ideas, which could not be printed; and others which of conventional necessity had to be. The constraints shaping "the text" might be social and economic (patronage, the market) or political (the censorship in all its forms. I use the word "censorship" loosely to cover all restraints on the freedom of the press).

What was the object of censorship in sixteenth- and seventeenth-century England? It was less moral than political and religious, or ideological, corresponding more to censorship in eastern Europe today than to that in England.[3] Its object was to prevent the circulation of dangerous ideas among the masses of the population. Manuscripts, even if unorthodox, could pass from hand to hand among the ruling élite, as they had done before the invention of printing, without serious danger. But when a printed book was put on sale to the general public authority lost control of it; anyone who had the money could buy it and convey its contents to others. Printing was "a sort of appeal to the people", it was said after the restoration: that was why it had to be controlled.[4] It may be that the reluctance of aristocrats and gentlemen to publish, their preference for private manuscript circulation, was in part a reluctance to undergo the indignity of having their thoughts vetted by some bishop's chaplain. Much better to have their manuscript pirated. Then the pirate had to attend to these sordid details, and the author could disavow his book if it was not well received.

The censorship, then, was required because there were ideas about in society which the authorities thought dangerous: the reformation had shown the power of the press to advance new ideas. Here however caution is needed. It is easy, in reading sixteenth- and seventeenth-century literature, to note the recurrence of certain ideas, and to assume that they recur because everyone accepted them. It is equally possible that they were repeated (often eloquently and emphatically) because they were under attack. Robert Burton wrote with heavy irony "We . . . hold them most part wise men that are in authority, princes, magistrates, rich men, they are wise men born, all politicians and statesmen must needs be so, for who dare speak against them?"[6] It is worth remembering that Ralph Holinshed's *Chronicle*, the primary source for most Elizabethan history plays, was carefully edited by the royal censors. So was John Hooker's *Continuation*.[7]

There was a dual system of control. Books were supposed to be licensed by the ecclesiastical authorities; and the Stationers' Company (which had a monopoly of printing) exercised a reasonably effective control over works issued by its members. Between 1586 and 1640 there was no legal printing outside London, Oxford and Cambridge. Illegal presses could be set up; they were small, inexpensive and light-weight bits of equipment. The Marprelate Tracts were printed on the run in 1589.[8] But if the government attached importance to it such printers could be rounded up—or made ineffective—without too much difficulty: use of the rack helped. Works smuggled in from the continent presented greater problems; but as long as government remained effective there was little chance of such books obtaining wide distribution.

From at least 1576 onwards the Stationers' Company's monopoly came under frequent attack.[9] The Company incurred additional unpopularity since its searchers, in the process of enforcing their monopoly, also acted as a detective agency which assisted in uprooting heresy and disaffection. Just as ecclesiastical licensing ended with the abolition of High Commission in 1641, so the Stationers' monopoly broke down when Star Chamber was abolished. The attempt to get censorship restored provoked Milton's *Areopagitica*, among many principled defences of freedom of the press from pre-publication censorship. The Leveller leader, John Lilburne, attacked the Stationers' monopoly in 1645,[10] a year in which there was a campaign for greater democracy within the Company. Hobbes said that "the privilege of stationers is (in my opinion) a very great hindrance to the advancement of human learning".[11]

The end of monopolies in 1641 helped in other ways to make printing technically possible for the hitherto unprivileged. Many of the raw materials required by the trade had been monopolized. The best paper was made from linen and cotton rags: the right to collect either of them had been a monopoly. The cheapest binding material was parchment—sheepskin dressed with alum; and alum was a monopoly.

The censorship had been tightened up after the Marprelate scandal; in the fifteen-nineties economic crisis combined with two outbreaks of plague in London (1593, 1597) and the possibility of a disputed succession to make rulers feel especially insecure. There was a drive against Sir Walter Ralegh's alleged "school of atheism", whose most notorious member was the great mathematician Thomas Hariot. In 1598 George Chapman suggested that Hariot's writings could not be published "now error's night chokes earth with mists".[12] In 1599 satires by Joseph Hall, Ben Jonson, Chapman, Marston, Nicholas Breton, Drayton and Middleton were called in and burnt, together with John Davies's epigrams and Marlowe's translation of Ovid's *Amores*. The sudden rise of satire in the nineties has been explained as a reaction to the expanding market for literature, so that what is produced reflects public opinion, not necessarily the views of aristocratic patrons. The clamp-down of June 1599 saw the end of published satire in England for many a decade.

George Wither, who did publish, was in and out of prison despite the patronage of the Earls of Southampton and Pembroke. But his *Abuses Stript and Whipt* (1613) ran to seven editions in four years. Wither advised John Taylor to get himself arrested: "then shall you thrive".[13]

Under James I censorship over the theatre was tightened still further. From 1607 the Master of the Revels, a court official, had the duty of licensing plays for publication, over and above the licence required from him for presentation on the stage. Fees were charged whether or not a play was licensed. Even when the Master of the Revels disliked a play so much that he burnt it, he charged £2.[14]

Nicholas Breton, one of those whose writings were suppressed in 1599, was particularly sensitive to the dangers of writing satire:

> For the Star Chamber is a dangerous court. . . .
>   It much more credit bears
> To be held simply plain, without disgrace,
> Than to be counted witty without ease,
> With shoulders lashed, or stigmatized face,
> Or head in hole, in public market-place.[15]

Wentworth Smith similarly wrote:

> What pen dares be so bold in this strict age
> To bring him while he lives upon the stage?
> And though he would, authority's stern brow
> Such a presumptuous deed will not allow.[16]

Many plays which attracted packed houses in the sixteen-twenties were not published; and the "lost" plays of the thirties are also numerous.[17]

Middleton's *A Game at Chess* (1624) is an exceptional example of a play thoroughly critical of royal policy which nevertheless managed to hold the stage for nine days, to the delight of packed audiences. Middleton is perhaps unique among Jacobean dramatists in that Puritans "seemed much to adore him".[18] But even plays on apparently remote subjects like Jonson's *Sejanus* (1603), Day's *Isle of Gulls* (1605–6) and Middleton's *Hengist, King of Kent* (c. 1620) got their authors into trouble.

There is much evidence of contemporary unhappiness about the effects of the censorship, from Shakespeare's "Art made tongue-tied by authority" onwards. Dekker in *The Noble Spanish Soldier* (before 1631, printed 1634) has a daring passage in which a poet refuses Onaclia's request to write against the (Spanish) King:

The King! Should I be bitter 'gainst the King
I shall have scurvy ballads made of me
Sung to the hanging tune.

Onaclia replies (with a reminiscence of *Lear*?):

This baseness follows your profession:
You are like common beadles, apt to lash
Almost to death poor wretches not worth striking,
But fawn with slavish flattery on damned vices,
So great men act them; you clap hands at those
Where the true poet indeed doth scorn to gild
A gawdy tomb with glory of his verse
Which coffins stinking carrion; no, his lines
Are free as his invention; no base fear
Can shake his pen to temporize even with kings,
The blacker are their crimes, he louder sings.
Go, go, thou canst not write: 'tis but my calling
The Muses' help, that I may be inspired:
Cannot a woman be a poet, Sir?[19]

In 1605 Hariot wrote to Kepler, "Things with us are in such a condition that I still cannot philosophize freely. We are still stuck in the mud. I hope Almighty God will soon put an end to it".[20] Two generations later the Royal Society went to great trouble in an attempt to recover the writings which Hariot had been unable to publish. William Gilbert left much of his scientific work unpublished; some of it appeared during the interregnum.

Even private correspondence was unsafe. "These times are dangerous for men to write", declared a Kentish gentleman in the nineties, "much more to write opinions". Another gentleman's steward corresponded in cypher.[21] John Young's Diary in 1617 reveals a critical attitude towards the workings of the censorship.[22] Religious radicals felt themselves especially unable to get their views across in print: this added to their zeal for preaching. John Everard in 1618 complained that "the liberty of the pulpit is too little, but that of the press, in our affairs, is much less".[23] "The times are dangerous, and the world grows tender and jealous of free speech", wrote John Chamberlain to the ambassador Sir Dudley Carleton in February 1622.[24]

Parliaments seem to have been less than enthusiastic about the way in which the censorship was exercised by the ecclesiastical hierarchy. William Prynne's "dear friend", Michael Sparke, who was imprisoned ten times in eleven years for "seditious" printing, "would print anything in Parliament-time"—or so Attorney-General Noy reported him as saying.[25] Suppression indeed seems to have been especially effective in the years without Parliament, 1626–8 and 1629–40.[26] In 1629 Sparke told the High Commission that the Star Chamber decree entrenched on "the hereditary liberty of the subject's person and goods, . . . contrary to Magna Carta, the Petition of Right and other statutes".[27]

Further restrictions were imposed in the sixteen-thirties under Laud. In 1633 the Master of the Revels insisted that old plays being revived must be resubmitted to censorship, "since they may be full of offensive things against church and state, the rather that in former times the poets took a greater liberty than is allowed them by me".[28] John Vicars was refused permission to reprint a play of 1617 dealing with Gunpowder Plot, because we "are not so angry with the papists now as we were 20 years ago".[29]

By a new Star Chamber decree of 1637 the number of authorized printers in London was cut to twenty. Unlicensed printers were to be pilloried and whipped. All imported books were to be vetted by bishops before being put on the market; printing English books abroad was declared illegal. Books previously licensed had to be re-licensed before reprinting. Henceforth licences were required even for ballads. Almanacs were censored more severely in the thirties. In 1631 William Beale's almanac was burnt. John Booker tells us casually that his almanac was censored in 1639 in consequence of a reference to an eclipse—"as they usually did in my almanacs".[30] Corporal penalties were imposed on those who offended against these decrees, regardless of rank. The Rev. Alexander Leighton in 1630 was whipped and branded, had his ears cropped and his nose slit, and was imprisoned for life. When released in 1640 he was seventy-two years old. The lawyer William Prynne had his ears cropped twice, in 1634 and 1637, and was also imprisoned. Dr Henry Burton and the Rev. William Bastwick lost their ears in 1637, and received swingeing fines and life imprisonment. Lilburne, a gentleman's son, was flogged through the streets of London for handling illegal pamphlets.

During this period Laud was alleged to have refused licences for Luther's *Table Talk*, Foxe's *Book of Martyrs*, Bishop Jewell's *Apology for the Church of England*, Bishop Bayley's *The Practice of Piety*, the Geneva Bible and the last three books of Richard Hooker's *Laws of Ecclesiastical Polity*. Laud blue-pencilled even the writings of his own adherents, William Chillingworth and Bishop

Joseph Hall. Aubrey tells us that Laud frustrated the printing of the second part of Sir Henry Spelman's glossary of legal terms because it contained naughty words like Magna Carta and Magnum Concilium Regis.[31] A translation of an Italian devotional work "well approved by George Herbert" was refused a licence for publication. On the other hand Cowell's *Interpreter*, banned in 1610 because too favourable to absolutism, was reprinted in 1637.

Plays were strictly censored. Cuts were made in Middleton's *Hengist King of Kent* to remove references to the poverty of the common people and to the vulnerability of even an usurping king to revolt by the commons.[32] Thomas Drue's (if it was his) *The Duchess of Suffolk* (1624, not printed till 1631) was "full of dangerous matter" and had to be "much reformed" by the censor before being allowed on the stage. It remained provocatively nationalist and anti-Catholic in its sentiments.[33] Massinger was repeatedly in trouble for expressing critical views on government policy. So were the popular theatres in the thirties.[34]

As in the fifteen-nineties, men feared that private letters were liable to be intercepted and read: this is clear from the Barrington correspondence in 1628-9.[35] Joseph Mede concluded a private letter of July 1635 "I dare go no further; it may be I have said too much already".[36] John Selden employed anagrams in his correspondence.[37] As early as 1622 D'Ewes kept his diary in cypher, like Samuel Pepys later, "that I might write more freely as of the public occurrences so of mine own private occasions". Certainly his remarks about James I's homosexual tendencies would have done him no good had they become known.[38] In 1636 John Vicars remarked that, since printing was not open to them, manuscripts were the best help God's people had to vindicate the truth.[39] A text-book on shorthand of 1641 recommended its use as a defence against "bloody inquisitors". The explicit reference was to foreign countries: but some might find the disguise useful nearer home.[40] Shorthand—for taking notes of sermons—seems to have been especially popular in England, particularly among mechanics—the class to which Puritanism was held to have the greatest appeal.[41]

"I might have said more of this subject", wrote Robert Burton, "but forasmuch as it is a forbidden question" by "the Preface or Declaration to the Articles of the Church, printed 1633, . . . I will surcease, and conclude with Erasmus, . . . 'it is neither safe nor pious to harbour and spread suspicions of the public authority. It is better to endure tyranny, so long as it does not drive us to impiety, than seditiously to resist'".[42]

Before 1640 there were no printed newspapers, and publication of home news of any sort was a legal offence. Newsletters for the rich circulated privately at £5 *per annum*: they were suppressed in 1632. But there was great hunger for news, brought out by Ben Jonson's *The Staple of News* (1625), itself suppressed. In 1638 Bastwick's brother-in-law was reading intelligencers' news in Colchester streets on market-days. "Zealots", we are told, flocked about him "as people use when ballads are sung".[43] In 1639 Richard Overton, writing from Scotland but not printed until 1640, reported "I had once good store of news in my pocket-book", but he burnt it "else the hangman had done it for me, and perhaps burned me with it".[44] As soon as the censorship collapsed pamphlets like Overton's could be printed, and there was an explosion of newspapers—four in 1641, 167 in 1642, 722 by 1645.[45] The press proved strongly Parliamentarian in sympathy: in 1644 John Berkenhead—best of the royalist journalists—looked nostalgically for a royalist victory and a society in which there would be no newspapers.[46]

Most significant writers suffered in one way or another from the Elizabethan or early Stuart censorship. The following lists are certainly not complete; I have included only well-known names, and I am sure I have missed many. But they will give some idea.[47]

Playwrights: George Chapman, Samuel Daniel, Robert Davenport, John Day, Thomas Dekker, John Fletcher, Ben Jonson, Thomas Kyd, Thomas Lodge, Christopher Marlowe, Philip Massinger, Thomas Middleton, Anthony Munday, Thomas Nashe, William Shakespeare, James Shirley. *Sir Thomas More*, in which Shakespeare is believed to have had a hand, remained unpublished until 1922. A large number of plays has been lost, no doubt because they could not obtain the licence necessary for publication: though it is also true that theatre companies did not like plays to be printed so long as they were in their acting repertoire. Some authors may have been under contract not to publish without permission.[48] The above list may help us to appreciate Glynne Wickham's remark that what he regards as the decadence of Jacobean and Caroline drama was due in far greater measure to censorship than to the inadequacy of dramatists.[49]

The following other poets at one time or another had difficulties with the censor: Spenser, John Davies of Hereford, John Donne, Michael Drayton, Fulke Greville,[50] Edward Guilpin, Joseph Hall,

George Herbert,[51] John Marston, Samuel Rowlands, John Taylor, George Wither.

Among prose writers I omit extreme Puritans and sectaries, the latter of whom could not expect to publish in England, and published abroad if at all. There remain: Nicholas Bownde,[52] Robert Burton,[53] William Camden, Sir Edward Coke,[54] Nicholas Ferrar, John Hales,[55] Joseph Hall,[56] Gabriel Harvey, Sir John Hayward,[57] Lord Herbert of Cherbury,[58] Ralph Holinshed and his continuator John Hooker, Lord Henry Howard, Edward Misselden,[59] Thomas Nashe, Sir Walter Ralegh, Sir Edwin Sandys,[60] John Selden,[61] Sir Henry Spelman,[62] John Stowe and Archbishop Ussher.[63] On the other hand tracts against the Laudians Peter Heylyn and Richard Montagu were suppressed.

"Were the press open to us", said Bastwick in the pillory in 1637, "we would scatter his [Antichrist's] kingdom".[64] They did. As the Long Parliament met in November 1640 the censorship collapsed. "There is no law to prevent the printing of any books in England", Selden had told the House of Commons in 1628; "only a decree in Star Chamber".[65] But Star Chamber was abolished in July 1641. This "opened many mouths", as Bastwick's fellow-victim Henry Burton more modestly put it.[66] The effects were indeed sensational. In 1639 the Archbishop of York had proposed reviving the practice of burning heretics, which had done "a great deal of good in the church".[67] The ending of ecclesiastical control seems to me the most significant event in the history of seventeenth-century English literature: it is too easily taken for granted. Milton's friend the bookseller George Thomason tried to buy a copy of every book and pamphlet published during these exciting times. In 1640 he purchased twenty-two titles; in 1642, 1966. This rate of publication was maintained for the next decade. There was an equivalent increase in the number of almanacs and ballads. Almanac writers, severely censored in the thirties, gave pretty solid support to Parliament during the civil war, even before it was clear who was winning.[68] They were said to have contributed more than anything else to the King's defeat. In the sixteen-thirties a monopolist kept the price of Bibles too high for the poor to be able to buy them, though cheaper copies were illegally imported from the Netherlands. But in the sixteen-forties Bibles circulated in cheap editions, as Josselin noted with pleasure.[69]

Pamphlets and newspapers were of crucial importance in the struggle for men's minds during the forties. An early sign of the new age was that the petition of twelve peers in August 1640 asking Charles to summon a Parliament was at once published—not by the King. The Scots, with Charles's grudging consent, published the Treaty of London which the King was forced to sign in August 1641.[70] "The Parliament is far too nimble for the King in printing", wrote Sir Marmaduke Langdale to Sir William Saville in November 1642. Unfortunately, he added, "the common people believe them".[71] "The main end of printing the votes of 41", observed Sir Roger L'Estrange long after the event, "was to solicit the concurrence of the common people to the subject matter of them". He echoed Samuel Butler in alleging that these votes came back to the houses in the form of petitions, addresses and declarations.[72] In all the King's negotiations with Parliament in 1641–2 he insisted on a restoration of censorship to suppress seditious pamphlets and sermons. Charles was especially outraged by the fact that the lower orders could not be prevented from reading such pamphlets. When the Grand Remonstrance was published—an appeal to the people, whose printing had been fiercely opposed in the Commons—Charles commented: "we are many times amazed to consider by what eyes these things are seen, and by what ears they are heard". It was criminal folly to extend political discussion beyond the charmed circle of the ruling class.[73] Parliament for its part ordered the Lord Mayor of London not to allow the King's Answer to the Nineteen Propositions of 1 June 1642 to be printed. They had previously attacked printers for publishing royal proclamations.[74]

Another way of considering the effects of the censorship is to look at books which could not be published before 1640 (and in some cases were for that reason not written); and books which, previously unpublishable, appeared after 1640. I have already mentioned the failure to publish of scientists like Hariot and Gilbert, of Biblical scholars like Joseph Mede. Fulke Greville's *Life of Sidney*, believed to have been written 1610–12, was not published until 1652. Its contrast between the achievements of Queen Elizabeth and her successor was too outspoken. Greville wanted to write a history of Elizabeth's reign, but Cecil would not allow him access to the national archives.[75] Greville himself destroyed his play *Antonie and Cleopatra* ("apt enough to be construed or strained to a personating of vices in the present governors and government") at the time of the downfall of the Earl of Essex. Greville intended none of his poems to be published in his lifetime.[76]

Court memoirs and contemporary histories published after 1640 include Sir Robert Naunton's *Fragmenta Regalia* (1641), *The Five Years of King James* (1643), attributed to Fulke Greville but more probably by Arthur Wilson, Sir Anthony Weldon's *The Court and Character of King James I* (1650), Michael Sparke's *The Narrative History of King James For the first 14 years* (1651), Sir Edward Peyton's *The Divine Catastrophe of the . . . Stuarts* (1652), Arthur Wilson's *History of Great Britain* (1653),[77] Francis Osborne's *Traditional Memoirs of the Reigns of Queen Elizabeth and King James I* (1658). Sir John Harington's *Brief View of the State of the Church*, though written for Prince Henry, did not appear until 1653. Bishop Godfrey Goodman's *The Court of King James the First* remained in manuscript until 1839. Goodman would have liked to reply to Bacon's *Advancement of Learning* in 1603, "if I durst have printed it". A treatise by Bishop John Williams, *Vindex Principis et Patriae* which could not be printed, nevertheless in 1638 "passeth through many noblemen's and gentlemen's hands".[78]

Other works on affairs of state could appear after 1640. Sir Thomas Fanshawe's *The Practice of the Exchequer Court*, written in 1572, was printed in 1658. Sir John Burrough's *The Soveraigntie of the Seas of England*, written in 1633 and widely circulated in manuscript, was first published in 1651, the year of the Navigation Act. *The Compleat Ambassador* by Sir Dudley Digges (d. 1639) was printed in 1655. Various tracts by Lord Chancellor Ellesmere, who died in 1617, were published in 1641-2 and 1650.[79] Bacon's *Advertisement Touching the Controversies of the Church of England* (written for private circulation in 1589) was published in 1640, when it proved as topical as other echoes of the Marprelate controversy. Foxe's *Book of Martyrs* could be printed again, including now a memoir of the martyrologist by his son Simeon, written as long ago as 1611 but not published until 1641.[80] Books VI and VIII of Hooker's *Laws of Ecclesiastical Polity* were at last printed in 1648; Book VII appeared in 1662. The *Commentaries* of Sir Francis Vere (died 1609) were published in 1657.

All these had some public implications, like Coke's *Reports* and *Institutes*. But private men too decided not to publish—Sir Henry Spelman, for instance.[81] Another antiquarian, Sir Simonds D'Ewes, in May 1628 "began an elaborate work which I called 'Great Britain's Strength and Weakness'". His object was "to show . . . how both church and state might yet be upheld" (the "yet" is significant). But after the dissolution of Parliament in 1629, "I thought my labour would be too full of truth and plainness to endure the public view of the world, and so laid aside my further searches in that kind till a fitter opportunity and better times might encourage me to the finishing of them".[82] He turned to earlier (and safer) history, and composed his *Primitive Practice for Preserving Truth* in 1637; even this was not published until 1645.

History proved an especially dangerous subject. Sir John Hayward was imprisoned and threatened with torture because *The First Part of the Life and Reigne of Henry IV* happened to come out in 1599. Two-thirds of the book dealt with the dangerous subject of the deposition of Richard II; it was moreover dedicated to the Earl of Essex. Among the interrogatories administered to Hayward was "might he think that his history would not be very dangerous to come amongst the common people?"[83] That was what censorship was mainly concerned with. From that date onwards English histories were to be printed only by allowance of some of the Privy Council. But D'Ewes was reading Hayward in 1623.[84] James I prevented the publication of Camden's *History*: it appeared posthumously, at Leiden, in 1625. Samuel Daniel described writing "a true history" as "a liberty proper only to commonwealths, and never permitted in kingdoms but under good princes". He promised James that he would "tread as tenderly on the graves of his magnificent predecessors as he possibly could".[85] The many revisions and modifications which he made to his verse *The Civil Wars* between 1595 and 1607 show how hard he was trying.[86] Ralegh too intended not to follow truth too near the heels, and his *History of the World* ended before the Christian era. Yet James called it in.[87]

Histories of English kings were risky undertakings. William Martin's *Historie, and Lives, of The Kings of England* (1615) led to him being hauled before the Privy Council to make "humble submission and hearty repentance and acknowledgment of his fault", though we do not know exactly what the fault was.[88] Cotton's *Short View of the Long Reign of Henry III* (1627) was reprinted twice in 1641–2, and again in 1651. The edition of 1642 was bound up with a reprint of Hayward's *Henry IV*.[89] Sir Francis Hubert's long poem on Edward II was forbidden publication in 1597, and appeared (in modified form) only in 1629.[90] Lord Falkland's *Edward II* was not published until 1680, forty-five years after his death. William Habington's *Edward IV* appeared in 1640. Sir George Buc's *Richard*

III, written before 1619, was published in 1646. Sir Henry
Bourchier's Latin work on Henry VIII, circulating in manuscript in
1632, remained unpublished because the government's closure of
Cotton's library prevented him checking his references.[91] Lord
Herbert of Cherbury's life of the same King was printed,
posthumously, in 1649. Drayton amended his *Englands Heroical
Epistles* before publication in 1599–1600. "Histories are lately come
abroad", Drummond of Hawthornden observed in the sixteen-
forties, "allowed and approved by the present rulers of the state,
which to read in the days of Queen Elizabeth and King James was
treason and capital".[92] He was quite right. When the censorship
closed down again after 1660, the great histories of the civil war
written by participants had to wait until after 1688 for publication—
Ludlow in 1698, Clarendon in 1702–4.

The case is similar with printing or reprinting historical documents.
As we shall see, radicals were busy reprinting and echoing the
Marprelate Tracts in 1641–3; the many allusions to Martin Marprelate
show that he was still a vivid memory.[93] Other documents from that
period were reprinted or printed for the first time. In 1641 a letter of
John Reynolds to Sir Francis Knollys against Bancroft's Paul's Cross
sermon attacking Marprelate was printed, with some other tracts of
his.[94] Walter Travers's *Directory of Church Government*, written
1586–9, was published for the first time in 1644–5. An account of
John Udall's trial in 1590 was printed in 1643, fifty years after his
death.[95] *Leicester's Commonwealth*, called in by Elizabeth in 1584,
was reprinted in 1641.

Other publications in 1641–2 show how very conscious men were
of the part played by earlier Parliaments in opposing the monarchy.
Though most of these documents had never been printed, they must
have circulated in manuscript, and came into print on the first
possible occasion. Many dated from the Parliament of 1604–10—the
Parliament which Professor Elton selected for his idiosyncratic
argument that there was no continuity in opposition between earlier
Parliaments and the Long Parliament.[96] Most of the following were
printed by the latter Parliament's authorization or with its tacit
approval: Nicholas Fuller's tract of 1607 against impositions;
William Hakewill's House of Commons speech on Bate's Case; a
speech of Whitelocke's in the same Parliament. An alleged answer to
the King's speech dissolving Parliament in 1610 was also published in
1641.[97] The report of a conference between Lords and Commons in

April 1628 was printed for the first time in 1642.[98] Richard Callis's *Case and Argument against Sir Ignoramus of Cambridge*, a defence of common lawyers dating from 1618, was published in 1648.[99] Contemporaries may have been more aware of continuities across these thirty years (fifty years in the case of Marprelate) than Elton and his followers have wished to admit.

Also published by order of the Commons were the *Modus Tenendi Parliamentum*, William Ames's *Marrow of Sacred Divinity* (1643), a translation of his *Medulla* (1623), and a translation of Joseph Mede's *Clavis Apocalyptica (The Key of the Revelation)* (1643). *The Mirror of Justices* appeared in 1646; in 1651 "A Narrative of the Burning of Bartholomew Legatt" in 1612, published no doubt by those who shared his anti-Trinitarian heresies and were briefly free to express them.[100] Leonard Bussher's *Religious Peace* (1614—probably published abroad) was reprinted in 1646. John Hales's *Tract concerning Schism and Schismaticks*, held up by Laud, was published (anonymously) in 1642. *His Golden Remains* appeared in 1659.

Of lesser interest except to those concerned is that John Traske, condemned in 1618 for his seventh-day sabbatarianism, was able in 1648 to publish his *Meditations*. Theophilus Brabourne, involved with Traske, also published in the sixteen-fifties.[101] John Etherington's *Defence against Stephen Denison*, written from prison in 1627 to counter a sermon preached at St Pauls against his Familist views, could at last be published in 1641. The works of the antinomian theologians John Everard, John Eaton and Tobias Crisp were published posthumously after 1640.[102]

Very important for the development of radical ideas was the publication of foreign works which could not have been printed in England before 1640. John Henry Alsted's *The Beloved City, Or, The Saints Reign on Earth A Thousand Years* (1627) was not published in English until 1643. Translations of the works of Jacob Boehme began to appear in the same year. James I had caused David Pareus's works to be publicly burnt in Oxford in 1622,[103] but in 1644 *A Commentary upon the Divine Revelation of . . . John* appeared in English translation, followed by his *Theologicall Miscellanies* the next year. John Everard's translation of what a Laudian administrator called "that cursed book" *Theologia Germanica*, circulating in manuscript since at least 1628, was at last published in 1648.[104] Everard also translated Hermes Trismegistus, Nicholas of Cusa, Sebastian Franck, Hendrik Niclaes, and various alchemical works, all of which

had to wait for publication until after his death in 1641. Everard's
hope was to appeal to "tinkers, cobblers, weavers, poor slight
fellows", who were "mean, poor and despised by the world".[105] Giles
Randall also made translations of heretical books which circulated in
manuscript before 1640 and were published thereafter.

In 1575 an English version of Hendrik Niclaes's *Terra Pacis* had
been smuggled over from the Netherlands; it was reprinted in 1649.
Two others of his works were published in the same year, and more in
1652, with two reprints in 1656. Also in 1649 appeared the Koran,
translated from the French by Alexander Ross. Like the translation
of the Socinian *Racovian Catechism* (condemned to be burnt in 1614,
approved for publication by Milton in 1650, condemned by
Parliament in 1652), the Koran stimulated anti-Trinitarian ideas.[106]
Cornelius Agrippa's *Three Books of Occult Philosophy* appeared in
English translation in 1651. Campanella's *The City of the Sun* came
out in English in 1654. Henry Pinnell and others translated
Paracelsus. Robert Fludd's *Mosaicall Philosophy* appeared in 1659,
twenty-one years after the Latin text had been published abroad.
Last but perhaps not least significant, Puritan England saw the first
translation of Aretine's *Dialogues* in 1658. A great many very
unpuritanical works were published between 1657 and 1660, including
the Laudian Peter Heylyn's *Ecclesia Vindicata* (1657) and *Examen
Historicum* (1659).

When Nicolas Fiske printed Sir Christopher Heydon's *An
Astrological Discourse* in 1650, he said it was "the malice of the
clergy" which had prevented such important astrological writings
from seeing the light of day, as well as his own "servile fear."[107]
The works of the Puritan Thomas Taylor, published in 1653, twenty
years after his death, had been held up "because of the iniquity of the
times", we are told on the title-page. *A True and Faithful Relation of
What passed . . . between Dr. John Dee . . . and Some Spirits*, written
mainly in the fifteen-eighties, was not published until 1659. Thomas
Mun had died in 1641 without publishing his seminal *Englands
Treasure by Foreign Trade*, written in the sixteen-twenties but
dangerously critical of royal policy: it came out in the more congenial
atmosphere of 1664. Keith Thomas has drawn attention to "the
unprecedented number of traditional prophecies" published after
1641, which previously could circulate only orally or in manuscript.[108]

We do not often reflect how many important works of English
literature were first printed in the sixteen-forties and fifties, although

in most cases their authors had died earlier. Carew's and Francis Beaumont's Poems (1640), Corbett's Poems in 1647 and 1648; Beaumont and Fletcher's *Comedies and Tragedies* (1647),[109] Ben Jonson's *Underwoods* and *Timber* (1640); plays by Massinger, Middleton, Dekker, Ford, Shirley, Suckling; Donne's *LXXX Sermons* (1640), *Biathanatos* (1647), *Fifty Sermons* (1649), *Essays in Divinity* (1651), *Paradoxes* (1652); Herbert of Cherbury's *De Causis Errorum* and *Religio Laici* (1645); Suckling's *An Account of Religion by Reason* (1646), *Reliquiae Wottonianae* (1651). George Herbert's *Remains* (including *The Country Parson*) was published in 1652.

Authors who before 1640 could not, or did not wish to, publish in England went to the Netherlands or protestant Germany. William Harvey's *De Motu Cordis* appeared at Frankfurt in 1628. It was not translated into English until 1653. His *De Generatione* (1651) suffered no such delay: the English version came out two years later. Camden's *History* was published at Leiden, as we saw. [110] Marlowe's translation of Ovid's *Amores* appeared, incongruously, at the Brownist sanctuary of Middelburgh in 1597. John Penry's *Historie of Corah, Dathan and Abiram* came out in Amsterdam in 1609, sixteen years after his execution.[111] So did Lady Eleanor Davies's eccentric but dangerous prophecies, in 1633.[112] Samuel Hieron published either in the Netherlands or in Scotland.[113] All Thomas Brightman's influential treatises interpreting the Biblical prophecies were published abroad, until in the sixteen-forties it was possible for translations and popular summaries to appear in England. Hugh Broughton's similar studies appeared in Middelburgh. George Wither published *The Psalmes of David* in the Netherlands in 1632, no English publisher being willing to risk taking them on.

There was in consequence a smuggling trade in illicit literature from the Netherlands. The traffic increased in the thirties, despite Laud's efforts to control it. It is difficult to document, since good smugglers leave no traces; but Mr Foster has done his best. One of Thomas Scott's lively pamphlets, *Vox Populi*, ran to five editions between 1621 and 1623, so there can have been no lack of purchasers. There seems to have been a network for distribution in England, in which itinerant south-western cloth merchants played a part.[114] Laud's failure to control this trade helps to account for the savagery of the sentences on Prynne, Burton, Bastwick and Lilburne. Sibbes and Preston had to be read in smuggled Dutch editions.[115]

In the light of the foregoing we can understand Milton's

denunciation in 1641 of "this impertinent yoke of prelaty, under whose inquisitorious duncery no free and splendid wit can flourish".[116] Wither, who had even greater first-hand acquaintance with the censorship, thought it was the bookseller who brought "authors, yea the whole commonwealth and all the liberal sciences, into bondage".[117] Some authors were protected by high-placed patrons. That was one advantage of having a patron, and it became more important as social tensions increased. Judicious pressure from a patron might help an author to get a licence; or a patron might protect the author of an unlicensed book.[118] Margot Heinemann has shown the significance in this respect of the third Earl of Pembroke, who succeeded to the role played by the Earl of Leicester in Elizabeth's reign.[119]

Even under Charles's personal government in the sixteen-thirties the court was not monolithic. Henrietta Maria led a party of "Puritan lords", including the Earls of Holland and Northumberland, who were staunchly anti-Spanish.[120] Great magnates still retained a good deal of independence. William and Philip Herbert, third and fourth Earls of Pembroke, successively held the office of Lord Chamberlain, "the most important government official in the lives of players."[121] The Master of the Revels was their kinsman, Sir Henry Herbert. Their interest in the drama was of long standing. Shakespeare's First Folio was dedicated to them; the 1647 volume of Beaumont and Fletcher's plays was dedicated to the fourth Earl, now a supporter of Parliament. The Earl of Pembroke was one of the most powerful figures in the land. When a Parliament was called, he controlled the election of fifteen to twenty M.Ps.—far more than any other peer after the death of the Duke of Buckingham.[122] The third Earl almost certainly protected Middleton and the actors from the consequences of their daring production of *A Game at Chess* in 1624,[123] and the fourth Earl appears to have continued patronizing Massinger, whose father had been steward to the Herbert family.

Massinger was repeatedly in hot water for reflecting the Herberts' views on foreign policy.[124] In 1638 Charles intervened personally to insist on cuts in *The King and the Subject* to remove references to arbitrary taxation which he found "too insolent"—and no doubt too relevant to Ship Money.[125] But no other action was taken against Massinger. There is room for further study of Massinger and his patrons, on the lines of Margot Heinemann's pioneering book on Middleton. It would throw light on the connection between court rivalries and the increasing ideological rift in City and country.

Despite the censorship, then, opposition views did get expressed on the stage, however mutedly, even in the sixteen-thirties, especially at the popular theatres. We know as yet far too little about new plays produced at the Red Bull and the Fortune, since they mostly remained unprinted. But there is evidence that they were at times critical of government policy. In 1639 the Fortune suffered fines and shut-downs for putting on plays dealing with affairs of state;[126] it seems to have been responding to the political atmosphere of that year.

Another mitigating factor was the inefficiency of the workings of the censorship. Fuller tells us that Bownde's treatise on the Sabbath doubled in price after suppression, "as commonly books are then most called for when called in". And he gives us an insight into a process which we cannot otherwise document when he adds "it ran the faster from friend to friend in transcribed copies".[127] Printing after all was barely a century old; books had circulated in manuscript for hundreds of years. Gazeto, in Dekker's *Match Me in London* (1625), confirms that suppressed books enjoyed enhanced sales.[128] The printer of Prynne's *Histriomastix*, Michael Sparke, was reported to have anticipated that "it would be called in, and then sell well".[129] Sales of Francis Osborne's *Advice to his Son* are said to have leapt after its suppression by Oxford University in 1658.[130] On 3 September 1668 Pepys recorded that Hobbes's *Leviathan* "is now mightily called for, . . . it being a book the bishops will not let be printed again". Its second-hand price quadrupled.

Moreover, even in the sixteen-thirties the licensing system seems frequently to have been ignored. Apparently 65% of books published in 1640 were unlicensed.[131] It is not clear whether this was typical, or whether it gives advance warning of the impending breakdown of the whole system.

The facts we have been considering throw light on an optical illusion from which historians have suffered. "Between 1625 and 1640", wrote J.W. Allen, "there seems to have been considerable change in men's political outlook. It is unfortunate that contemporary literature throws so little light on the nature and extent of that change".[132] Unless we consider the evidence very carefully we may be led to suppose that Machiavelli, Bacon, Hakewill, Harvey, Gilbert, were almost without readers or influence before 1640; and that they then leapt suddenly into the public consciousness. It is at least equally probable that these authors could be freely discussed in print only after the breakdown of the censorship; but this by no means entails that their writings had been ignored earlier.[133]

Thomas Hobbes waited until he was fifty-four years old before publishing his first original work. This extraordinary fact has aroused insufficient comment: Shakespeare after all died at the age of fifty-two. It was another nine years before Hobbes published in English. It is only when we consider the content of his writings in relation to the pre-1640 censorship that this behaviour becomes comprehensible. We may compare traditional views on Milton's orthodoxy, which survived because his most unorthodox writings could not be published.[134] Historians looking only at the words on the page risk entering into an unwritten conspiracy with seventeenth-century censors.

For this reason we should take very seriously evidence from what Rushworth afterwards called "the late printing age".[135] Not only is the ferment of speculation let loose by the breakdown of controls of great intrinsic interest, but it also suggests that ideas may have been bubbling beneath the surface for some time before they were free to break through. In this book I have tried to use evidence drawn from the sixteen-forties and fifties to throw light on what came before and after. If I appear obsessive in this emphasis, it is because I feel that inadequate use has hitherto been made of such evidence. My exaggerations, if any, can easily be discounted.

As we have seen, Parliament was by no means libertarian in its attitude towards printing. In November 1641 the Commons established a committee to advise on restraint of the press; they were particularly concerned about the publicity given to proceedings in Parliament.[136] Royalist and radical pamphlets were suppressed. In February 1642 the Commons ordered the Stationers' Company to seize copies of Sir Edward Dering's speeches, though he was a member of the House.[137] Books were still supposed to be licensed, but in 1642 only seventy-six were registered, though Thomason collected over 700 titles. In the first six months of 1643 the discrepancy was even greater.[138] In June 1643 Parliament passed an ordinance regulating printing and appointed new press licensers. Milton's *Areopagitica* was one of many tracts on the other side, glorifying the freedom of the press which had established itself in defiance of authority, and suggesting that new Parliamentarian censors were no better than old bishops'.

In September 1647 Parliament issued an ordinance forbidding publication of unlicensed books, ballads, etc.; but its authority was insufficient to get this enforced. As soon as the Army effectively controlled power in 1649 it took steps to restore censorship. Newsbooks were drastically reduced by an Act of 8 April 1649; in 1655 they were cut to two. Censorship broke down again in 1659–60, when there was an outburst of pamphlets defending the republic and dealing with seditious subjects like law reform, decentralized courts, stable copyhold, etc. The desirability of re-establishing control over the press was one of the many reasons leading to the restoration of 1660.

From 1660 to 1678 the censorship was back in nearly all its old severity, handicapped only by the lack of prerogative courts to implement it. Ecclesiastical control was restored. Henceforth all books on history or affairs of state had to be licensed by a Secretary of State; books on divinity, philosophy and science by the Archbishop of Canterbury, the Bishop of London or the Vice-Chancellor of Oxford or Cambridge (acting of course through their agents). In 1662 the Royal Society was added to those entitled to license books on science—a privilege of which the Society did not make full use.[139] Lilly's almanacs were strictly censored.[140] Charles II on occasion intervened personally to have a play suppressed—for instance Edward Howard's *The Change of Crowns* in 1667 and Sir Robert Howard's *The Country Gentleman* in 1669.[141] Printers were reduced to twenty again. The only newspaper published between 1660 and 1679 was an official government sheet.

"A public mercury should never have my vote", said the editor of this, Roger L'Estrange: "It makes the multitude too familiar with the actions and counsels of their superiors".[142] "It is with the unruly populace", he explained, "as it is with raging tides; they press where the bank is weakest, and in an instant overrun all". Another revealing remark of his was "You shall sometimes find a seditious libel to have passed through so many hands that it is at last scarcely legible for dust and sweat; whilst the loyal answer stands in a gentleman's study as clean and neat as it came from the press".[143] When in 1663 L'Estrange issued proposals for licensing the press, his main target was "the great masters of the popular style" of the interregnum, who "speak plain and strike home to the capacity and humours of the multitude" because they wrote "in times of freedom".[144] Secretary Jenkins called printing "a sort of appeal to the people"—as indeed it had been in the sixteen-forties. Controversy in the press is like a civil war, said one royalist.[145] In 1664 a printer was hanged, drawn and quartered for refusing to reveal the name of the author of a book deemed seditious.[146]

Censorship was exercised not only against religious and political radicals. Thomas Hobbes was afraid the bishops might try to burn him. Resumption of burning was discussed in the House of Commons in 1666. Hobbes published none of the serious works on religion and politics which he wrote after the restoration, though he had been a prolific publisher in the fifties. The bishops would not let *Leviathan* be reprinted.[147] *Behemoth*, written in 1668, was not published until a pirated edition appeared in 1679, a year of brief liberty. Edmund Waller refused to praise Hobbes in print because he was afraid of the churchmen. Aubrey was worried in 1683 lest his *Brief Lives* should fall into the wrong hands and he should be charged with *scandalum magnatum*.[148] In the same year Oxford University solemnly burnt the political writings of Knox, Goodman, Rutherford, Hunton, Parker, Hobbes, Milton, Baxter, Owen and other distinguished thinkers. Coffee houses were suppressed in 1675 as discussion centres, "the great resort of idle and disaffected persons, . . . tradesmen and others". Richard Baxter, who suffered severely from the censorship, was told that it was directed against an author's reputation as well as against any particular book. He was very wary of publication in the sixties.[149] Nathaniel Bacon's *An Historical Discourse of the Uniformity of the Laws and Government of England*, published in two parts in 1647 and 1651, was suppressed when reprinted in 1665; there were other editions in 1672, 1676 and 1682, one of which led to the prosecution of the printer, who had to go into exile. It was finally reprinted in 1689.

The consequences of this sudden reversal of press freedom were drastic and have never been properly analysed. A great deal of self-censorship must have been exercised. Locke kept many of his ideas to himself even after 1689: so did Newton. Samuel Butler and Thomas Traherne left much unpublished. The great dissenting educationalist Charles Morton wrote a republican utopia called *Eutaxia*. It circulated only privately, in manuscript, and has not survived.[150] Henry Stubbe's *Account of the Rise and Progress of Mahometanism, with the Life of Mahomet* was too strong meat to be printed: it had to wait till 1911.[151] What a difference it would have made to historical scholarship in England if this work of Gibbonian irony and scepticism about the origins of the Christian church had appeared in the seventeenth century! George Fox wielded a *de facto* censorship over Quaker publications, which became semi-official from 1672.[152] We get a glimpse of what might happen in one of Oliver Heywood's *Reflections* for 1683. His printer returned a manuscript because "he found some smart reflections", and thought "it was not safe to print them, being then a very hazardous time". On second thoughts Heywood agreed, and made amendments: even so his book was denounced as "a seditious piece", "full of faction"; "some of my friends censured me". But no action was taken against him.[153]

As in the sixteen-thirties, men feared that their private correspondence would be tapped. Marvell frequently expresses uneasiness about this in his letters to Hull corporation, and clearly says only part of what he thinks.[154] "All prudent persons have ever been wary of writing . . . court news," Henry Saville reminded Rochester on 4 June 1678, "especially since Mr. Lane [Groom of the Bedchamber] was once turned out about it".[155] Pepys wrote his Diary in cypher, like D'Ewes in the twenties; nevertheless he kept its existence secret.[156]

There was a temporary relaxation of political censorship in 1670–3 when the Cabal was in office and Charles was planning a policy of indulgence for protestant and catholic dissenters. Baxter was amazed that Fulke Greville's *Treatise of Monarchy* could be printed in 1670, "a poem . . . for the subject's liberty, which I greatly wonder this age would bear". No book had been published since the restoration "that I more wonder at".[157] But Marvell's *The Rehearsal Transpros'd* (1672), though approved by Charles II, suffered some cuts, and Milton's *Of True Religion, Heresy, Schism, Toleration* in 1673 was markedly more moderate than his pamphlets on behalf of religious liberty in 1659. Marvell's *Mr. Smirke* (1676) and *The Growth of Popery and Arbitrary Government* (1677) were published anonymously.

The crisis of the Popish Plot and Exclusion (1679–81) led to the suppression of many plays suspected of alluding to contemporary affairs.[158] But the expiry of the Licensing Act in 1679 released a flood of pamphlets. A royal proclamation of 1680 against unlicensed publications had only a temporary effect. Chief Justice Scroggs reasserted the pre-1640 principle that to print or publish any newsbooks or pamphlets of news whatsoever without authority is illegal. "No private man can take upon him to write about government at all", added Justice Allybone in 1688.[159] But before the defeat of the Whigs in 1682 the courts could not enforce this doctrine

against the opposition of juries and sheriffs' officers.[160] Some
interesting publications got through during this brief interlude—
Hobbes's *Behemoth* in 1679 and a cluster of Parliamentarian histories
around 1680, including a resumption of Rushworth's *Historical
Collections*, publication of which had been suspended since 1659.[161]
The *Memorials* of Bulstrode Whitelocke (died 1673) appeared in
1682. In 1681 Marvell's *Poems* had been published (though not the
most political of them even then). It is surely no accident that
Bunyan's major literary works—*The Pilgrim's Progress, The Holy
War, Mr. Badman*—came out between 1678 and 1682. Selden's
irreverent *Table Talk*, Petty's *Political Arithmetic*, written 1676–7,
and Rushworth's later volumes all had to wait till after 1688.

In 1695 the Licensing Act was not renewed; pre-publication
licences were no longer required. The effective arguments against
renewing the Act were less libertarian than economic; licensing was
an interference with freedom of production. But the consequence was
no explosion of seditious tracts. Toland reprinted Milton and
Harrington, and published a carefully edited version of Ludlow's
Memoirs; but not the writings of Levellers, Diggers or Fifth
Monarchy Men. The deist tracts which shocked the orthodox were
not plebeian rabble-rousers; they were more likely to appeal to upper-
class libertines or rationalizing Presbyterians. By now radical
dissenters had either been driven out of active politics, or had
voluntarily withdrawn. Publishing had become a profitable business,
and publishers censored themselves rather than risk offending against
the accepted standards of a society to which there was no apparent
alternative except Jacobitism.[162]

So long as the censorship existed, authors had to take evasive
action, and this has its bearing on literary forms and styles. Allegory
is often discussed as a self-sufficient literary form, whose pedigree can
be traced from the Middle Ages. But late sixteenth and early
seventeenth-century practitioners of allegory and pastoral were clear
about their political usefulness. Sidney said that "sometimes under
the pretty tales of wolves and sheep [pastoral poetry] can include the
whole considerations of wrong-doings and patience".[163] "Representing of virtues, vices, humours, counsels and actions of men in
feigned and unscandalous images is an enabling of free-born spirits to
the greatest affairs of state". Puttenham had employed very similar
words in his *Arte of English Poesie* (1589).[164] Spenser used *The
Shepheards Calendar* and *Colin Clouts come home again* to make

veiled political comment; and he admitted that in writing *The Faerie Queene* "I chose the history of King Arthur as . . . furthest from the danger of envy and suspicion of present times".[165]

A whole school of Spenserian poets continued to use pastoral as (among other things) a simple means of eluding censorship. Browne's *Britannia's Pastorals* is full of political comment.[166] The Fletchers, Wither, Milton in *Lycidas*, all employed the technique, just as in 1654 John Ogilby's translation of Virgil used the "occult" passages of the *Aeneid* to foretell "the restoration of the golden age under the happy government of Augustus", and the "future greatness" of princes. Lest his readers should mistake his intention (kingship for Oliver Cromwell was in the air in 1654), illustrations showed a lion under an oak and a lion being crowned.[167]

Allegory and pastoral decline after the Revolution: their use is over. So did utopianism as a way of presenting political ideas. When Gabriel Plattes published *Macaria* in 1641 he could be more open than some of his utopian predecessors. Under Laud he had had to express himself very guardedly.[168] Harrington's *Oceana*, putting forward republican ideas under Cromwell, is almost the last of its kind. Harrington could safely abandon the utopian form in his hectic pamphleteering in 1659.[169] Dialogue is another way of avoiding full responsibility for dangerous opinions, from More and Starkey under Henry VIII through Sir Thomas Smith, Sir Thomas Wilson, Spenser and Ralegh to Harrington and Neville.

There were other evasive techniques. Dramatists who wished to write about monarchy or court corruption under James or Charles I—and again after the restoration[170]—were well-advised to choose a classical or Italian theme; though very early English history might do. The cautious Fulke Greville took the Turkish empire as the scene of his studies in tyranny. In 1631 the censor insisted that the plot of Massinger's *Believe as You List* should be switched from Sebastian, King of Portugal (*floruit* 1580) to a story from ancient Rome.[171] Heywood's *Troia Britanica* (1609) is about London, just as Shakespeare's Timon lived near a "usurious City". In *The Exemplary Lives and Memorable Acts of Nine of the Most Worthy Women of the World* (1640), Heywood's Boadicea stands out against a corrupt court: Levellers were citing her a few years later.[172] Miss Bradbrook pointed out that the political conflicts in seventeenth-century England resembled those in a classical *polis* more than those of fifteenth-century England. This, she suggested, reflects changes that were coming about in England: the citizen was becoming less of a subject, the community less hierarchical.[173] So it is difficult to distinguish between cause and effect. Hobbes thought that the study of classical republicanism had brought about the civil war.[174] Sprat and the Royal Society were determined to get rid of classical mythology, no doubt for other reasons.[175]

There were other types of language which could be used to deceive. The author of *Persecutio Undecima* in 1648 said that Puritans "took up a canting language, . . . abusing phrase of Scripture, thereby to understand one another, to colour their seditious practices".[176] An example of this technique occurred in Thomas Hooker's assize sermon of 1626, cited by William Hunt. Hooker prayed that God would "set on the heart of the King" Malachi II. 11-12. He did not quote the text: "an abomination is committed; Judah hath married the daughter of a strange God. The Lord will cut off the man that doth this". Hooker could hardly have more openly urged Charles I to repudiate his new French bride, Henrietta Maria.[177] Fifth Monarchists used similar techniques to denounce Cromwell in December 1653 and early 1654. Christopher Feake preached on the Little Horn in Daniel VII ("'I will name nobody', said he, but he gave many desperate hints").[178] In January Captain John Williams in Radnorshire used 3 and 8 Amos to similar effect.[179] The godly took their Bibles with them to church, so that they could check the preacher's references. Milton at the end of the first edition of *The Ready and Easy Way to establish a free Commonwealth* applied to Charles II "what God hath determined of Coniah and his seed for ever" in Jeremiah 22, without specifying that this fate was an ignominious death in exile.[180]

The possibilities were endless here. Gerrard Winstanley declared "I do walk in the daily practice of such ordinances of God as Reason and Scripture do warrant", without reminding us that for him Reason and Scripture do not authorize prayer, preaching, holy communion, baptism or Sabbath observance.[181] Selden and Hobbes were masters of the art of using Biblical texts to make a wholly unorthodox point. "Of the maintenance of our Saviour and his Apostles we read only that they had a common purse (which was kept by Judas Iscariot)".[182] In the context the implication could only be that tithes are unlawful. Similarly Robert Burton covered himself by making his riskiest points—and there were many—by means of quotations from classical authorities.[183] Henry Vaughan conveyed political messages likely to be unpopular in the fifties by inserting passages of his own in translations of devotional works.[184] There is room for much more serious study of such techniques for conveying a message without actually committing oneself to it—and there are no doubt more. Twentieth-century experience of writers under censorship could give us a number of leads.[185]

A favourite method of political denigration within acceptable limits was to praise Queen Elizabeth—often excessively—in order by implication to criticize her successors. The *locus classicus* is Fulke Greville's *Life of Sidney*, though he realised that it could not be published. Among others who used the same ploy we may list Shakespeare, Chapman, Dekker, Webster, Nicholas Breton, Daniel, Heywood, Middleton, Massinger, Ford, Sylvester, Wither, Ralegh, Browne, Quarles, Marvell, Milton, Burton, D'Ewes, Thomas Scott, Robert Bolton, Sir Edward Coke, Sir Robert Cotton and a number of speakers in the Parliament of 1628, John Preston, Prynne, Sir Robert Naunton, Tom May, and many, many others. In the unglorious sixteen-twenties Sir Francis Drake was a useful reminder of what an aggressive foreign policy could do.[186] Prince Henry, especially after he was dead, played something of the same role as Elizabeth I, as did Elizabeth of Bohemia after Henry's death.[187]

We might also be a little readier to spot irony in seventeenth-century writers, especially when dealing with hallowed commonplaces. I suggest below some instances of this in Shakespeare. Take for example the great chain of being. Tillyard did a very good job all those years ago when he reminded us that this mediaeval idea still survived in Tudor England. It is in the Book of Homilies and in Shakespeare. Undoubtedly a lot of people still found it a useful framework for their thought, as well as a useful defence of their own privileged position. But it needs very little reflection to suggest the possibility that this traditional idea was expressed with such frequency and vigour not because everybody accepted it but because it was being challenged. It is of the nature of theories justifying a hierarchical society that they appeal much more to those at the top than to those at the bottom. The Homily against Disobedience and wilful Rebellion supplied ready-made sermons for those who were incapable of preaching themselves, or who could not be trusted to say the right things. There would be no point in having a homily on degree if everybody accepted it, just as there would be no point in having a censorship controlled by the state church if nobody disagreed with its doctrines.

So as Anne Barton has forcefully argued, we need not suppose that Ulysses's speech in *Troilus and Cressida* is to be read without regard to the character who makes the speech. It is eloquent; but Ulysses is not a neutral character: he is no doubt intended to be regarded as a sententious old bore.[188] Similarly Lear in his madness is not to be taken as conclusive evidence of what Shakespeare himself thought. Marlowe certainly did not accept the great chain of being. Nor did Robert Greene, Webster, Middleton and many others. We admire De Floris in *The Changeling* for his determination even in evil; he compares with Iago and even, in an odd way, with Milton's Samson. Whatever these three characters have in common, it is not that other tired cliché, Christian Humanism.

Some historians are rather naive about this. Peter Laslett once said that "all of our ancestors were literal Christian believers, all of the time" in the seventeenth century.[189] Unless he has a very unusual definition of Christianity, this is a surprising statement. The trooper in the sixteen-forties who asked "Why should that mug on the table not be God?" may have been drunk at the time, but the many others who said the sun was God or that God was in all things were not. Laslett asserts that (apart from imaginative literature) "it would seem impossible to cite statements which contemplated permissiveness of any sort in [sexual] matters", and that "witnesses in ecclesiastical courts . . . left no doubt that sexual intercourse outside marriage was universally condemned".[190] Only a lunatic would go out of his way to bring serious trouble on himself by attacking monogamy in front of ecclesiastical judges, but plenty of people, including Milton as well as Ranters, rejected it in theory as well as in practice as soon as church courts had ceased to function.

There were in short so many new ideas about, even if few of them could be developed in print, that it would be absurd to suppose that everybody still accepted traditional ideas uncritically. One of the great virtues of Elizabethan and Jacobean drama is that it shows people influenced by untraditional ideas; they were "in the air".

We do not need to read very deeply in Elizabethan and Jacobean literature to find expositions of individualism, for instance, the idea that a man may do what he will with his own. Such ideas were not necessarily presented approvingly; but in a world of new industries, of investment in trade, exploration and commercialized agriculture, positive approval was not necessary. Similarly with stage Machiavellian utilitarians: they tell us how men acted, not how they ought to act; and that is the significant fact about them. Scientific experiment and exploration (new animals, new plants, new medicines) were calling in question the authority of Aristotle, Galen and the Ancients generally. The new astronomy and the telescope, the possibility of life on other planets, made men ask whether the Christian scheme of salvation was unique. Acquaintance with the old civilizations of India and China stimulated ideas of comparative religion. Simultaneously Bible-reading was suggesting or confirming subversive heresies: that God might be a better Lord than the Earl of Derby or even than the King; that there was no ecclesiastical hierarchy in the New Testament, and perhaps no Trinity; that the Second Coming was at hand, and with it (in Milton's phrase) "an end to all earthly tyrannies"; that perhaps all men might be saved. Few indeed of these new ideas could be systematically expounded before 1640, but no one can read the literature without being aware of their existence. The novelty after 1640 was only in freedom to publish and discuss. Similarly, were it not for the freedom of the press in the Netherlands we should know very little of the views which drove sectaries to put up with the hardships of exile in order to escape from a state church which they regarded as antichristian.

An example of what the censorship could do comes with the question of enclosure. The rights and wrongs of it were hotly disputed in the forties, with a good deal of strong moral disapproval expressed. But the discussion died out in the mid-fifties: historians are apt to say that by then public opinion had come to accept the desirability of enclosure. What is at least equally likely is that the censorship stopped opposition to enclosure being expressed in print (except in the years of liberty, 1659–60); that henceforth only the public opinion of the propertied classes was heard.

In 1646 Walwyn published a mock recantation for Thomas Edwards, the great defender of censorship. He had acted, Walwyn makes Edwards say, "out of the pride and vanity of my own mind, out of disdain that plain unlearned men should seek for knowledge any other way than as they are directed by us that are learned; out of base fear, if they should fall to teach one another, that we should lose our honour, and be no longer esteemed as God's clergy, or ministers *jure divino*, or that we should lose our domination in being sole judges of doctrine and discipline. . . . All this I saw coming in with that liberty

which plain men took to try and examine all things".[191] It is a slanted
statement; but it helps us to understand how things must have
seemed to some "plain men" before they got the chance to express
themselves freely. "The art of printing", the author of *Macaria*
hoped in 1641, "will so spread knowledge that the common people,
knowing their own rights and liberties, will not be governed by way of
oppression".[192] The fullest aspirations of the Hartlib circle which
produced *Macaria* were not realised; but the brief period of freedom
between 1640 and 1660 had immeasurable consequences for English
society and its literature.

More than England was affected. Professor Eisenstein pointed out
how crucially important for the development of world science was
the existence of a free press in the Netherlands and England.[193] Isaac
Newton rightly congratulated himself on being born an Englishman,
not subject to the Inquisition, like Galileo, not compelled to publish
abroad and to accommodate himself to papal dogma like Descartes.[194]
Would there have been a European Enlightenment so soon without
the free press in the Netherlands and England?

When in books published before 1640 or after 1660 we meet with
even a flicker of unorthodoxy we should never exclude the possibility
that there is more heresy underneath, or that opinions are being
mitigated for political or other purposes. These are only possibilities;
but we neglect them at our peril. J.R. Jacob in his pioneering book on
Henry Stubbe, and the editors of the Yale edition of Milton's prose,
have shown how close and careful reading can reveal nuances which
escape those who restrict themselves to the words on the page. So
have recent studies of Marvell, and Michael McKeon's book on
Dryden.[195] To date this has been done most effectually for the post-
restoration period, which followed an age of relative freedom from
censorship; an oblique approach to unorthodox ideas could be more
easily taken. Before 1640 the problem is more difficult, since there is
no base-line, so to speak. The émigré literature which circulated
illegally in England, the writings of Thomas Scott, John Robinson,
William Ames, may provide some suggestions. So might careful
consideration of the contrast between public and private utterances,
such as those of Sir Simonds D'Ewes or Joseph Mede. But it will need
much detailed research.

In the post-restoration period we can use Marvell's unbuttoned,
irreverent correspondence with his nephew William Popple as a
check on his formally correct letters to his Hull constituents; and his

satires to check *The Rehearsal Transpros'd*. Stubbe, Butler, Traherne, Milton, Locke and Newton all left unorthodox material with which we can compare work published in the author's lifetime.[196] Lilly's drafts for his almanacs can be compared with what the censor passed.[197] But for the period before 1640 the job has still to be begun.

In *Milton and the English Revolution* I compared Chekhov's wrestle with the Russian censor—here making a compromise, there deciding not to publish rather than say less than he wanted to say—with Milton's position before 1640 and after 1660.[198] Georgia Christopher has argued that *Comus* is a masque *à clef*, and that words like "chastity" may mean more than they say.[199] Certainly the very class-conscious lines which the poet added (or restored) in 1645,

> If every just man that now pines with want
> Had but a moderate and beseeming share
> Of that which lewdly-pampered luxury
> Now heaps upon some few with vast excess . . .
> The giver would be better thanked (lines 768–75)

suggest a wider social context than that in which the masque is sometimes read. The headnote which Milton was free to add to *Lycidas* in 1645 gives us a clue without which some critics would no doubt have wished to resist the idea that the poem was anti-episcopal. (Milton first owned *Lycidas* in 1645; it was originally published over the initials J.M.).

After 1660 Milton was a marked man, fortunate to have escaped with his life: censors would certainly be alert to anything written by him. It is not very sensible to argue that because there is no overt mention of anti-Trinitarianism in *Paradise Lost*, therefore we can reject the plain evidence which we find in Milton's "best and dearest possession", the *De Doctrina Christiana*, on which he was working whilst composing *Paradise Lost* but which he recognized he could not publish.[200] *The History of Britain* (published 1670) was cut by the censor because it was thought to attack bishops by attacking popery; and Milton fairly clearly censored himself in his references to Presbyterians—now potential allies—in *The Character of the Long Parliament*. He could not put his heresies or his political opinions into *Paradise Lost*, *Paradise Regained* or *Samson Agonistes*. His name was not on the title-page of the first edition of *Paradise Lost*, only his initials. But the invocation to Book VII,

> I sing . . . unchanged
> . . . though fallen on evil days,
>   On evil days though fallen, and evil tongues,

would alert readers who recognized the initials and remembered Milton as spokesman for the republic, defender of regicide and of "divorce at pleasure", author of *Areopagitica*. This was the public Milton whom we too often forget: few thought of him as a poet before 1667.[201] The sonnets to Cromwell, Vane and Fairfax could not be published, nor his prose works be collected, until after 1688.

Milton had to work by indirection: the founder of monarchy was Nimrod (though Milton did not even name him) whom his readers would recognize as a wicked man. The heresies of the *De Doctrina Christiana* could only be hinted at. Defoe—a trained theologian—noted unsoundness on the Trinity; polygamy was covertly approved;[202] Milton's belief that baptism should be performed in running water was slipped into *Paradise Regained*—in words given to Satan. Milton's alterations to the Biblical story of Samson—Samson destroying the Philistine *aristocracy* and *priests*, whilst "the vulgar only 'scaped who stood without"—closely related to post-restoration politics in England.[203] Dalila reminds us that history is written by victors; but alternative points of view still exist and can be preserved:

> Fame, if not double-faced, is double-mouthed
> And with contrary blasts proclaims most deeds.[204]

At the end of the play the Chorus speaks of God's Cause as an undying phoenix, which "lay erewhile a holocaust", but

> Revives, reflourishes, then vigorous most
> When most unactive deemed,
> And though her body die, her fame survives,
> A secular bird, ages of lives.[205]

We must get the habit of reading between lines like these.

Milton, that political animal, was no doubt more conscious of the censorship than most of his contemporaries. But its limiting presence was there for other writers too: those least conscious of it may not have been the least frustrated. And it stopped some from writing at all. If we are to read seventeenth-century English literature with proper appreciation, we should be sensitive to the implications of these facts.

NOTES

1. An earlier version of this paper was delivered at a post-graduate seminar held at Le Louverain, Switzerland, by the Universities of Geneva, Lausanne, Fribourg and Neuchatel. I am very grateful to the participants in this seminar for a lively and helpful discussion.
2. Eagleton, *Criticism and Ideology* (1976), p. 58.
3. But after a statute of 1606 oaths in plays were censored (G.E. Bentley, *The Profession of Dramatist in Shakespeare's Time*, Princeton U.P., 1971, pp. 146, 155–6). William Whateley's *Bride-Bush* (1611) put forward ideas on divorce so shocking to orthodox churchmen that the High Commission ordered him to retract them (L.B. Wright, *op. cit.* p. 22). Marriage was a social as well as a religious institution, as the uproar over Milton's divorce pamphlets in the sixteen-forties illustates.
4. See p. 51 above.
5. See p. 33 above.
6. Burton, *Anatomy of Melancholy*, I, p. 41; cf. p. 118.
7. Conyers Read, "Good Queen Bess", *American Historical Review*, XXXI (1926), pp. 658–9; ed. F. Chiappelli, *First Images of Man in America* (California U.P., 1976), p. 524. See pp. 43–4 above.
8. See pp. 76–7 below.
9. F.S. Siebert, *Freedom of the Press in England, 1476–1776* (Illinois U.P., 1952), *passim*; C. Blagden, *The Stationers' Company: A History, 1407–1959* (1960), p. 67; cf. Haller, *Tracts on Liberty*, I, p. 9; III, pp. 268–9.
10. Lilburne, *Englands Birthright Justified*, in *Tracts on Liberty*, III, p. 257; Siebert, *op. cit.*, pp. 169–70.
11. J. Aubrey, *Brief Lives* (ed. A. Clark, Oxford U.P., 1898), I, p. 381.
12. G. Chapman, *Poems and Minor Translations* (1875), pp. 53–5. See p. 36 above for Hariot.
13. Quoted by Wallace Notestein, *Four Worthies* (1956), p. 177.
14. Bentley, *op. cit.*, pp. 152–8; Heinemann, pp. 36–47.
15. N. Breton, *The Mothers Blessing* (1621).
16. Wentworth Smith, *The Hector of Germany* (c. 1615), quoted by L.B. Wright, *op. cit.*, p. 625. Cf. Voltimar in Dekker's *The Welsh Ambassador*: "To th' gallows, upon a ladder a man may talk freely and never be sent to prison" (*Dramatic Works*, IV, p. 331); cf. Wallace Notestein, *The House of Commons, 1604–1610* (Yale U.P., 1971), p. 16.
17. Heinemann, pp. 204–5, 231–2.
18. For the circumstances which made presentation of this play possible, see *ibid.*, pp. 39, 44, 61–2, 141–4; McLuskie, *op. cit.*, p. 138.
19. Dollimore has an unusual appreciation of the effects of censorship (*op. cit.*, pp. 22–5, 119, 128, 136); cf. Massinger, *The Roman Actor*, I, iii.
20. J. Jacquot, "Thomas Hariot's Reputation for Impiety", *Notes and Records of the Royal Society*, IX (1952), p. 167.
21. P. Clark, *English Provincial Society from the Reformation to the*

Revolution: Religion, Politics and Society in Kent, 1500–1640 (Hassocks, Sussex, 1977), p. 266.

22. Ed. F.R. Goodman, *The Diary of John Young* (1928), pp. 58–9.
23. Quoted by Margaret Judson, *The Crisis of the Constitution: An Essay in constitutional and political thought in England, 1603–1645* (Rutgers U.P., 1949), p. 311.
24. *Letters of John Chamberlain*, II, p. 423.
25. J. Rushworth, *Historical Collections* (1659–1701), II, p. 224.
26. I owe this point to the unpublished Ph.D. thesis of Dr P.L. Thirlby, *The Rise to Power of William Laud, 1624–1629* (Cambridge, 1958), esp. pp. 187–8, 195–6, 256. Cf. p. 10 above.
27. For Sparke see *C.S.P.D., 1628–9*, pp. 525, 528; *1631–3*, pp. 3, 231; *1633–4*, pp. 135–6; Rushworth, *op. cit.*, II, p. 234. Had Sparke been talking to Selden? See p. 40 above. Justice is done to this early hero of the struggle for economic freedom and freedom of the press by Leona Rostenberg, *Literary, Political, Scientific and Legal Publishing, Printing and Bookselling in England, 1551–1700: Twelve Studies* (New York, 1965), pp. 11–12, 161–202; Blagden, *op. cit.*, pp. 131–4.
28. Ed. J.Q. Adams, *The Dramatic Records of Sir Henry Herbert* (Yale U.P., 1917), p. 21; Bentley, *op. cit.*, pp. 155–65, 172–3, 177, 179–81, 192–5.
29. The play was printed in 1641 as *The Quintessence of Cruelty*.
30. B.S. Capp, *Astrology and the Popular Press: English Almanacs, 1500–1800* (1979), pp. 29, 47–50; C.R. Gillett, *Burned Books: Neglected Chapters in British History and Literature* (Columbia U.P., 1932), p. 149; [John Booker], *Mercurius Coelicus* (1644), pp. 1–2.
31. Aubrey, *Brief Lives*, I, p. 230.
32. Heinemann, pp. 142, 272.
33. *Ibid.*, pp. 205–9; McLuskie, *op. cit.*, p. 134.
34. See pp. 48–9 above.
35. *Barrington Family Letters*, pp. 53, 100.
36. J. Mede, *Works* (3rd. edn., 1672), p. 829.
37. G.P. Gooch, *The History of English Democratic Ideas in the Seventeenth Century* (Cambridge U.P., 1898), p. 72.
38. Ed. Bourcier, *The Diary of Sir Simonds D'Ewes, 1622–1624*, p. 55; cf. pp. 92–3 and J.T. Cliffe, *The Puritan Gentry* (1984), p. 196.
39. Ed. F.S. Boas, *The Diary of Thomas Crosfield* (1935), p. 89.
40. F.E. Manuel, *A Portrait of Isaac Newton* (Harvard U.P., 1968), p. 409.
41. V. Salmon, *The Study of Language in 17th-century England* (Amsterdam, 1979), pp. 157–9.
42. Burton, *Anatomy of Melancholy*, III, p. 424.
43. Hunt, *The Puritan Moment*, p. 262.
44. Overton, *Vox Borealis* (1640), quoted by Marie Gimelfarb-Brack, *Liberté, Egalité, Fraternité, Justice! La vie et l'oeuvre de Richard Overton, Niveleur* (Berne, 1979), p. 509.
45. Siebert, *op. cit.*, p. 203; cf. pp. 143–4, 157, 191.
46. J. Frank, *The Beginnings of the English Newspaper, 1620–1660* (Harvard U.P., 1961), p. 58. See p. 98 below.

47. I normally give no reference when the relevant facts are to be found in *D.N.B.* or standard modern editions.
48. Bentley, *op. cit.*, pp. 143, 265, 273–9, 285–97.
49. G. Wickham, *op. cit.*, pp. 94, 17.
50. The 1633 edition of Greville's *Works* starts at p. 23, the preceding *Treatise of Religion* having been removed whilst printing was proceeding. Greville's plays were never intended for the stage, but lines in his *Mustapha* ("Kings' life kept but in flesh and easily pierced;/Kings' crowns no higher than private arms may reach") were deleted before publication in 1609, perhaps by Greville himself (see *Poems and Dramas of Fulke Greville*, I, p. 14, II, p. 26).
51. See p. 217 below.
52. For his *The Doctrine of the Sabbath* (1595).
53. Not perhaps censored, but his remarks in *Anatomy of Melancholy*, I, pp. 41–2, 63, 96, 118; III, pp. 424, show that he was being very wary.
54. Coke's *Reports* were criticized by James's Privy Council; the last three parts of his *Institutes* were suppressed by Charles. The latter were published by order of the House of Commons in 1644.
55. See p. 45 above.
56. James I forbade Hall to publish his *Via Media*.
57. See p. 43 above.
58. See p. 44 above.
59. M. Beer, *Early British Economics* (1938), pp. 182–3.
60. On account of his *Europae Speculum* (1605), printed in 1632 by Michael Sparke (Rostenberg, *op. cit.*, p. 188).
61. Selden had to make formal expression of regret to the High Commission for publishing his *History of Tythes* (1618), and was threatened with imprisonment if he or any of his friends replied to attacks on it. Selden remained of the same opinion still (see his *Opera*, 1726, II, pp. 1422–3).
62. See p. 38 above. Spelman's *History of Sacrilege* was judged unfit for publication in 1663 lest it should offend the nobility and gentry (Philip Styles, "Politics and Historical Research", in *English Historical Scholarship in the Sixteenth and Seventeenth Centuries*, ed. Levi Fox, 1956, p. 68). It appeared ultimately in 1698.
63. Ussher's proposal to publish the letters of Polycarp and Ignatius was turned down by Oxford for fear of offending Laud (R. Parr, *The Life of . . . James Ussher*, 1686, II, p. 399). They appeared in 1644.
64. T. Fuller, *The Church History of Britain* (1842), III, p. 387.
65. Rushworth, *Historical Collections*, I, p. 665.
66. Burton, *Englands Bondage and Hope of Deliverance* (1641), p. 14, quoted by M. Walzer, *The Revolution of the Saints: A Study in the Origins of Radical Politics* (Harvard U.P., 1965), p. 266.
67. *C.S.P.D.*, *1639*, pp. 455–6. I owe this reference to Mr Andrew Foster.
68. Capp, *Astrology and the Popular Press*, pp. 72–9.
69. Ed. J. Gutch, *Desiderata Curiosa* (1732), I, pp. 275–6; ed. A. Macfarlane, *The Diary of Ralph Josselin, 1616–1683* (Oxford U.P., 1976), p. 173; Rostenberg, *op. cit.*, pp. 185–6.

70. C. Carlton, *Charles I: The Personal Monarch* (1983), p. 228.

71. *H.M.C., Portland*, I, p. 70.

72. Quoted by P. Fraser, *The Intelligence of Secretaries of State and their monopoly of licensed news, 1660-1688* (1956), p. 127; S. Butler, *Hudibras*, Part I, canto ii, ll. 609-14.

73. J. Nalson, *An Impartial Collection of the Great Affairs of State* (1682), II, pp. 747-8.

74. Ed. W.C. Abbott, *Writings and Speeches of Oliver Cromwell* (Harvard U.P., 1937-47), I, p. 179.

75. Greville, *Life of Sidney*, pp. 216-19.

76. *Ibid.*, pp. 156, 219-20; *Remains* (ed. G.A. Wilkes), p. 5.

77. In the same year the anonymous *A Cat May look upon a King* attacked James.

78. Goodman, *The Court of King James* (1839), I, p. 283; Lambeth MS. 1030, f. 94.

79. L.A. Knafla, *Law and Politics in Jacobean England: The Tracts of Lord Chancellor Ellesmere* (Cambridge U.P., 1977), Chapter 8.

80. Collinson, *Godly People*, p. 506.

81. See p. 65 note 62 above.

82. *Autobiography of Sir Simonds D'Ewes* (ed. J.O. Halliwell, 1845), I, p. 374; cf. Cliffe, *op. cit.*, p. 207—Robert Parker.

83. *C.S.P.D., 1598-1601*, p. 404; cf. pp. 449, 452-3, 539-40.

84. Bourcier, *op. cit.*, p. 138.

85. Daniel, Epistle Dedicatory to Sir Robert Carr, Viscount Rochester, in his *Collection of the History of England* (1612) (*Complete Works in Verse and Prose*, 1896, IV, p. 78); cf. p. 12 above.

86. Daniel, *The Civil Wars*, pp. 28-48.

87. Ralegh, *History of the World* (Edinburgh, 1820), I, p. lviii. *The Prince*, wrongly attributed to Ralegh, appeared in 1642; *The Cabinet Council* in 1658.

88. W.R. Prest, "Common Lawyers and Culture in Early Modern England", *Law in Context*, I (1983), p. 99.

89. A collection of Cotton's tracts appeared as *Cottoni Posthuma* in 1657.

90. Ed. B. Mellon, *The Poems of Sir Francis Hubert*, pp. xvi, xxiv, 175.

91. *Original Letters illustrative of English History* (ed. H. Ellis, 1825-7), 2nd series, III, p. 270. A manuscript of Bourchier's on the state of Ireland in James I's reign was published in 1923.

92. David Masson, *Drummond of Hawthornden: the Story of his Life and Writings* (1873), p. 393.

93. See pp. 75 and 79 below.

94. J. Strype, *Annals of the Reformation during Queen Elizabeth's happy reign* (Oxford U.P., 1824), III, Part ii, p. 101.

95. L.M. Carlson, *Martin Marprelate, Gentleman: Master Job Throkmorton Laid Open in his Colors* (San Marino, 1981), pp. 352, 359. See Chapter 3 below.

96. G.R. Elton, "A High Road to Civil War?" in *From the Renaissance to the Counter-Reformation: Essays in Honor of Garrett Mattingly* (ed. C.H. Carter, New York, 1965), pp. 325-47.

97. F. Thompson, *Magna Carta: Its role in the making of the English Constitution, 1350–1629* (Massachusetts U.P., 1948), pp. 252, 369; Notestein, *The House of Commons, 1604–1610*, pp. 368, 432–3, 559–61.

98. Ed. R.C. Johnson and M.J. Cole, *Commons Debates, 1628* (Yale U.P., 1977), II, p. 332.

99. I owe this information to Professor Wilfrid Prest.

100. In *Truth brought to light and discovered by time, or a Discourse and Historical Narrative of the first XIII yeares of King James's Reigne* (1651).

101. D.S. Katz, *Philo-Semitism and the Readmission of the Jews to England, 1603–1655* (Oxford U.P., 1982), pp. 28–36.

102. Everard, *The Gospel-Treasury Opened* (1657); Eaton, *The Discovery of the most dangerous dead Faith* (1641); *The Honey-Comb of Free Justification by Christ alone* (1642); Crisp, *Christ Alone Exalted in seventeene Sermons* (1643). Another volume was published in 1648. *A Comfort for Believers* by the millenarian John Archer (died c. 1642) was printed in 1645 (when it was condemned to be burnt). The sermons of the antinomian Roger Bearley were not published until 1670.

103. *Letters of John Chamberlain*, II, p. 439.

104. W. Haller, *The Rise of Puritanism* (Columbia U.P., 1938), p. 207; cf. Acontius's *Satans Stratagems* (1648). First published 1565.

105. Everard, *The Gospel-Treasury Opened* (2nd. edn., 1659), I, Sig. a, p. 86.

106. *W.T.U.D.*, p. 266; *M.E.R.*, pp. 73, 184, 292.

107. Capp, *Astrology and the Popular Press*, p. 181; ed. C.H. Josten, *Elias Ashmole (1617–1692)* (Oxford U.P., 1966), II, pp. 21–2. See p. 81 below.

108. K.V. Thomas, *Religion and the Decline of Magic* (1971), pp. 410–13.

109. Plays are perhaps in a different category, since the theatre companies did not want them to be published whilst they were still in the repertoire. See p. 39 above.

110. See p. 43 above.

111. Carlson, *op. cit.*, p. 397.

112. Theodore Spencer, "The History of an Unfortunate Lady", *Harvard Studies and Notes in Philology and Literature*, XX (1938), pp. 49–50.

113. Heinemann, pp. 157, 290–1.

114. S. Foster, *Notes from the Caroline Underground* (Hamden, Conn., 1978), Chapters 5 and 6 and p. 90; cf. C. Bridenbaugh, *Vexed and Troubled Englishmen, 1590–1642* (Oxford U.P., 1968), p. 343; W. Hunt, *The Puritan Moment*, p. 13; B.R. White, *The English Separatist Tradition* (Oxford U.P., 1971), pp. 111–12. See also my *Society and Puritanism in pre-Revolutionary England* (Panther edn., 1969), p. 195. For Thomas Scott see p. 78 below.

115. See p. 37 above; Cliffe, *op. cit.*, pp. 157–8.

116. Milton, *The Reason of Church-government* (1641), in *M.C.P.W.* I, p. 820.

117. Wither, *The Schollers Purgatory* (c. 1625), p. 10, in *Miscellaneous Works*, I (Spencer Soc., 1872).

118. L.L. Peck, *Northampton: Patronage and Policy at the Court of James I* (1982), p. 138. John Davies of Hereford expected a patron to give such

protection (*The Muses Sacrifice*, 1612, p. 96, in *Complete Works*, ed. A.B. Grosart, 1878, II).
119. E. Rosenberg, *Leicester, Patron of Letters, passim*.
120. R.M. Smuts, "The Puritan followers of Henrietta Maria in the 1630s", *E.H.R.*, XCIII (1978), pp. 27, 44 and *passim*.
121. G.E. Bentley, "The Theatres and the Actors", in *Revels History of Drama*, IV, p. 79.
122. J.K. Gruenfelder, *Influence in Early Stuart Elections* (Ohio State U.P., 1981), Part IV, Chapter 1.
123. Heinemann, esp. pp. 264–83.
124. F. Edwards, "The Royal Pretenders in Massinger and Ford", pp. 30–1. Other plays which got Massinger into trouble were *The Roman Actor* (1626, printed 1629), *The Emperor of the East* (1631) and *The Maid of Honour* (1632).
125. Adams, *op. cit.*, pp. 22–3; Bentley, *Revels History*, IV, p. 113. S.R. Gardiner was as usual the first to spot "The Political Element in Massinger" (*Contemporary Review*, XVIII, 1876, pp. 495-507).
126. Philip Edwards, "Society and the Theatre", *Revels History*, IV, p. 56; G.E. Bentley, "The theatres and the actors", *ibid.*, pp. 117–18.
127. T. Fuller, *Church History of Britain*, III, p. 146; cf. Vicars, quoted on p. 38 above.
128. Dekker, *Dramatic Works*, III, p. 318.
129. Rushworth, *op. cit.*, II, p. 234. See p. 35 above.
130. A. Wood, *History and Antiquities of the University of Oxford* (ed. J. Gutch, Oxford, 1796), III, p. 684.
131. F.B. Williams, *Index of Dedications and Commendatory Verses in English Books before 1641* (1962), pp. 237–40.
132. Allen, *English Political Thought, 1603–1660*, I (1938), p. 44.
133. *Il Principe* and the *Discorsi* received no licence for publication under Elizabeth or James I, either in the original or in translation. A version of the *Discorsi* did appear in 1636: *The Prince* not till 1640. Cf. F. Raab, *The English Face of Machiavelli: A Changing Interpretation, 1500–1700* (1964), pp. 274–5.
134. See pp. 61–2 above.
135. Rushworth, *op. cit.*, II, p. 564.
136. D'Ewes, *Journal* (ed. W.H. Coates, Yale U.P., 1942), p. 164.
137. Gillett, *op. cit.*, pp. 359–71; cf. pp. 185–248 *passim*.
138. D. Masson, *The Life of John Milton* (1859-80), III, pp. 268–9.
139. M. Hunter, *Science and Society in Restoration England* (Cambridge U.P., 1981), p. 36.
140. See p. 6 above.
141. Hume, *The Development of English Drama in the late Seventeenth Century*, pp. 255, 260. For censorship of plays by Wilson, Dryden, Lee, Crowne, Tate and Southerne, see Susan Staves, *Players' Scepters: Fictions of Authority in the Restoration* (Nebraska U.P., 1979), p. 50.
142. *The Kingdoms Intelligencer*, 31 August 1663.
143. L'Estrange, *Interest Mistaken* (1662), quoted by G. Kitchen, *Sir Roger*

L'Estrange: A Contribution to the History of the Press in the Seventeenth Century (1913), p. 87.

144. L'Estrange, *Considerations and Proposals in Order to the Regulation of the Press* (1663), p. 10.
145. Fraser, *op. cit.*, p. 126.
146. Siebert, *op. cit.*, p. 267.
147. See p. 49 above.
148. A. Powell, *John Aubrey and his friends* (1948), p. 203.
149. *Reliquiae Baxterianae* (1696), p. 123; W.M. Lamont, *Richard Baxter and the Millennium* (1979), p. 15.
150. F. Bastian, *Defoe's Early Life* (1981), p. 56. For Butler and Traherne see pp. 233 and 286 below.
151. J.R. Jacob, *Henry Stubbe, radical Protestantism and the early Enlightenment* (Cambridge U.P., 1983), Chapter 4 *passim*.
152. T.P. O'Malley, "The Press and Quakerism, 1653-1659", *Journal of the Friends' Historical Soc.*, 54 (1979), p. 173; Luella Wright, *The Literary Life of the Early Quakers* (Columbia U.P., 1932), pp. 97-107.
153. O. Heywood, *Autobiography, Diaries, Anecdote and Event Books* (ed. J.H. Turner, Bingley, 1882-5), III, pp. 335-6.
154. *M.P.L.*, II, pp. 161, 164-5, 357. See p. 170 below.
155. Ed. J. Treglown, *The Letters of John Wilmot, Earl of Rochester*, p. 196.
156. See p. 271 below.
157. Baxter, *Poetical Fragments* (1681), Epistle to the Reader.
158. Hume, *op. cit.*, pp. 201, 222-3, 344-5; cf. pp. 217, 243, 343.
159. C. Grant Robertson, *Select Statutes, Cases and Documents to illustrate English Constitutional History* (3rd. edn., 1919), pp. 381, 404.
160. D.R. Lacey, *Dissent and Parliamentary Politics in England, 1661-1689* (Rutgers U.P., 1969), p. 134.
161. Rushworth, *op. cit.*, II, Sig. A; R. MacGillivray, *Restoration Historians and the English Civil War* (The Hague, 1974), pp. 2, 106.
162. See pp. 113-15 below.
163. *An Apologie for Poetrie* (1595), in *Elizabethan Critical Essays* (ed. G.G. Smith, Oxford U.P., 1904), I, p. 175. Written c. 1583.
164. Greville, *Life of Sidney*, pp. 2-3. Cf. Sidney's *Disprayse of a Courtly Life*, in *Poems*, pp. 262-4; Puttenham, in Smith, *op. cit.*, p. 40. It is remarkable that W.W. Greg, in his lengthy *Pastoral Poetry and Pastoral Drama: A Literary Inquiry, with special reference to the pre-restoration stage in England* (New York, 1959), left this aspect of pastoral virtually untouched. He thought Fulke Greville was "rash" to suppose there was "a deep philosophy" underlying *Arcadia* (p. 151).
165. Spenser, Letter to Ralegh prefixed to *The Faerie Queene* (1590).
166. See *Poems* (ed. G. Goodwin, Muses' Library, n.d.), Book I, Songs 3-5, Book II, Song I, Book III, Song 1, and vol. I, p. 180, II, pp. 89, 253.
167. I owe this point to *Ideas of the Restoration in English Literature, 1660-71* (forthcoming) by Nicholas Jose of the Australian National University, which I am grateful to him for allowing me to read before publication.
168. C. Webster, *Utopian Planning and the Puritan Revolution: Gabriel*

Plattes, *Samuel Hartlib and Macaria* (Research Publications of the Wellcome Unit for the History of Medicine, Oxford, 1979), p. 5.

169. Gooch, *op. cit.,* p. 297. But Harrington still employed dialogue.
170. Cf. Hume, *op. cit.,* p. 240.
171. Philip Edwards, "Society and the Theatre", p. 59.
172. S. Shepherd, *Amazons and Warrior Women*, pp. 137-8, 144-5, 150.
173. M.C. Bradbrook, *Shakespeare the Craftsman* (Cambridge U.P., 1979), p. 98.
174. Hobbes, *Leviathan*, Chapter 29.
175. Sprat, *The History of the Royal Society* (1667), p. 414.
176. *Op. cit.,* p. 28. I cite the 1681 reprint.
177. Hunt, *The Puritan Moment*, p. 201.
178. *C.S.P.D., 1653-4*, pp. 304-8; cf. p. 393.
179. *Thurloe State Papers* (ed. T. Birch, 1742), II, p. 46.
180. *M.C.P.W.*, VII, p. 388.
181. Winstanley, *Truth Lifting Up its Head above Scandals* (1649), in Sabine, *op. cit.,* pp. 136-44.
182. Hobbes, *Leviathan* (Penguin edn.) p. 514.
183. E.g. *Anatomy of Melancholy*, I, pp. 48-51, 61-4. For use of the classics for this purpose see Loretta Valtz Mannucci, *Ideali e classi nelle poesia di Milton* (Milan, 1976), pp. 178-9.
184. See especially *Flores Solitudinis, Of Life and Death*, and *The World Contemned*, in *The Works of Henry Vaughan* (ed. L.C. Martin, Oxford U.P., 1914), I.
185. An admirable example of what can be achieved by such an approach is J.R. Jacob's, *Henry Stubbe: Radical Protestantism and the early Enlightenment in England.*
186. L.B. Wright, *Religion and Empire: The Alliance between Piety and Commerce in English Expansion, 1558-1625* (North Carolina U.P., 1943), pp. 18-19.
187. William Browne, *Poems*, I, pp. 142, 145; II, pp. 275, 328, and *passim*; cf. M.C. Bradbrook, *John Webster, Citizen and Dramatist*, pp. 180-2.
188. *The Riverside Shakespeare* (ed. Anne Barton, n.d., ?1975), p. 445; cf. Harriett Hawkins, "The 'Example Theory' and the Providentialist Approach to Restoration Drama: Some Questions of Validity and Applicability", in *The Eighteenth Century: Theory and Interpretation*, 24 (1983), pp. 103-14. See also Briggs, *op. cit.,* p. 13.
189. P. Laslett, *The World We Have Lost* (1965), pp. 65-7.
190. *Ibid.,* p. 130.
191. Walwyn, *A Prediction of Mr. Edwards his Conversion and Recantation* (1646), in Haller, *Tracts on Liberty*, III, p. 343. Cf. pp. 85-6, below.
192. Ed. C. Webster, *Utopian Planning and the Puritan Revolution*, pp. 72-3.
193. E. Eisenstein, *The Printing Press as an agent of change* (Cambridge U.P., 1979), II, pp. 637-9, 644, 663, 666-82.
194. F. Manuel, *A Portrait of Isaac Newton*, p. 267. See a suggestive article by William Makin, "Navigating for Newton . . .", *Times Higher Education Supplement*, 16 December, 1983, p. 12.

195. McKeon, *Politics and Poetry in Restoration England: The Case of Dryden's 'Annus Mirabilis'*.

196. See pp. 233, 286 below for Butler and Traherne.

197. B.S. Capp, "William Lilly" in *Biographical Dictionary of British Radicals in the Seventeenth Century*, II, *G - O* (ed. R.L. Greaves and R. Zaller, Brighton, 1983), p. 191.

198. *M.E.R.*, pp. 406-7.

199. G. Christopher, *Milton and the Science of the Saints* (Princeton U.P., 1982), pp. 31, 53, 57.

200. Cf. A.C. Dobbins, *Milton and the Book of Revelation* (Alabama U.P., 1975). p. 133.

201. The point is Michael Wilding's: see p. 180 below.

202. *M.E.R.*, pp. 294, 138; cf. pp. 407-10, where I give other instances. Alastair Fowler's note in the Longman edition of Milton's *Poems* suggests that Milton's apparent geographical slip about Fuenterrabia in *Paradise Lost* I. 586-7 may conceal a political point (Cf. "The End of the Big Names: Milton's Epic Catalogues", in *English Renaissance Studies Presented to Dame Helen Gardner*, ed. J. Carey, Oxford U.P., 1980), p. 260).

203. *M.E.R.*, Chapter 31.

204. *Samson Agonistes*, ll. 971-2.

205. *Ibid.*, ll. 1702-7; cf. *M.E.R.*, pp. 445-6. The phoenix was often used as a political symbol after 1660; cf. *The Phoenix of the Solemn League and Covenant* (1661), which may have been composed by the Fifth Monarchist printer Livewell Chapman (Rostenberg, *op. cit.*, pp. 231-2).

II *Prose*

3. *From Marprelate to the Levellers*[1]

I am very proud to have been invited to deliver one of the
F. W. Bateson Memorial Lectures. I knew Freddie very well, and
much admired him and his work. It was very refreshing in the dark
days of the fifties, when we were allowed to read only the words on
the page, to encounter a literary critic who studied his authors in
relation to the society in which they lived. His journal, *Essays in
Criticism*, played as useful a part as Leavis's *Scrutiny*. The parallel
between the two men is interesting. Both exercised a profound
influence on their contemporaries, but their styles were very
different. Freddie never wished to found a school and was no self-
advertiser. Both could reasonably claim that the recognition which
they won in their own institutions was too little and came too late;
but whereas Leavis's grievances were known far and wide, Freddie
accepted his with a wry smile and a shrug. He was a modest man, and
didn't expect much. A man of principle, in literature as in politics, he
was never deflected by considerations of personal vanity or status.
He was a very good man, and I am glad I knew him.

So to my subject, which is radical prose, from the Marprelate
Tracts of 1588–9 to the sixteen-forties. After 1589, so long as the
censorship existed, radicals could not publish legally in England. As I
suggested in Chapter 2, the collapse of the censorship in the forties is,
in my opinion, the most important event in the history of
seventeenth-century English literature. Between 1640 and 1643 three
works by Martin Marprelate were reprinted, two in two editions
each.[2] Their influence was immediate and obvious.

The Marprelate Tracts had been the biggest scandal of Elizabeth
I's reign. For thirty years there had been rumblings from a Puritan
group inside and outside the House of Commons who pressed for
further reform of the Church of England. The compromise
settlement of 1559 seemed inadequate to those who wanted to get
back to the protestantism of the reign of Edward VI, and perhaps to
continue along the path of reformation. A learned theological

warfare between the Presbyterian Thomas Cartwright, Lady Margaret Professor of Divinity at Cambridge, and John Whitgift, had ended with the promotion of the latter to be Archbishop of Canterbury in 1583. Whitgift started a fierce campaign to root Puritans out of the church.

Suddenly, in 1588-9, a series of anonymous and illegally printed pamphlets appeared in rapid succession, baffling the authorities. They were signed by Martin Marprelate—Martin from Luther, Marprelate because the bishops were believed to obstruct reform.[3] They were not ordinary Puritan tracts. They were written in a witty, rumbustious, savage and extremely effective colloquial style. They not only denounced the upper clergy for the antichristian nature of their offices: they dwelt in personal and often painfully accurate detail on their sexual misfortunes. (Marriage of the clergy was a relatively new possibility.) They gave examples of the bishops' greed and rapacity. Their approach, in that hierarchical and deferential society was, to say the least, unusual. They shocked even some of the respectable Puritans whose cause Marprelate was defending.

> I am called Martin Marprelate. There be many that dislike of my doings. I may have my wants, I know. For I am a man. But my course I know to be ordinary and lawful. I saw the cause of Christ's government and of the bishops' antichristian dealing to be hidden. The most part of men could not be gotten to read anything written in the defence of the one and against the other. I bethought me therefore of a way whereby men might be drawn to do both, perceiving the humours of men in these times (especially of those that are in any place) to be given to mirth. I took that course. I might lawfully do it. Aye, for jesting is lawful by circumstances, even in the greatest matters. The circumstances of time, place and persons urged me thereunto. (p. 14)[4]

Marprelate's prose was taut, conversational, staccato, often dramatic, passionately serious for all its flippancy. It was also extremely democratic in its irreverence: that was what respectable Puritans most disliked. John Whitgift, Archbishop of Canterbury, Marprelate tells us, with some disapproval, claimed to be the second person in the realm. Martin addressed him as "nunckle Canterbury", "that miserable and desperate caitiff, John Whitgift, the Pope of Lambeth", "a plain Antichrist", "Neither will I say that his grace is an infidel (nor yet swear that he is much better)." The bishops, Marprelate tells us, claim to be so poor that

> their children are like to go a-begging. There is a present remedy for that. For to what end else is John of Canterbury unmarried, but to provide for the bishops' children who shall be poorly left? Though indeed, I never said in my

life that there was ever any great familiarity (though I know there was some acquaintance) between Mistress Toye and John Whitgift. And I'll defie 'em, I'll defie 'em, that will say so of me. And wherefore is Richard of Peterborough unmarried, but to provide for other men's children? O, now I remember me, he has also a charge to provide for, his hostess and cousin of Sibsan. The petticoat which he bestowed upon her within this six months was not the best in England, the token was not unmeet for her state. (pp. 15, 48)

John Aylmer, Bishop of London, was "dumb dunsical John of good London". Thomas Cooper, Bishop of Winchester: "his face is made of seasoned wainscot and will lie as fast as a dog can trot". Of Dr John Bridges, Dean of Salisbury: "I have laughed as though I had been tickled, to see with what sleight he can throw in a popish reason, and who saw him? And with what art he can convey himself from the question, and go to another matter; it is wonderful to think. But what would not a dean do to get a bishopric?' (pp. 20, 18).

We are still not absolutely certain who Martin Marprelate was, even though his printers were tortured to make them reveal his name. One suspect, John Penry, was later hanged; another, John Udall, was sentenced to death and was only released from prison to die.[5] Martin's rude, personalizing style appealed because it was subversive of degree, hierarchy and indeed the great chain of being itself. The shocking thing about his tracts was that their rollicking popular idiom, in addition to making intellectuals laugh, deliberately brought the Puritan cause into the market place. An Italian visitor about this time said that "the very women and shop-keepers were able . . . to determine what laws were fit to be made concerning church-government. . . . The most ignorant of the common people were mad for a . . . reformation of religion". Thomas Fuller later confirmed that the tracts were "greedily read, . . . and . . . firmly believed, especially of the common sort, to whom no better music than to hear their betters upbraided".[6] That was the audience to which the Levellers were later to appeal. By the Marprelate tracts, Richard Bancroft said, "the interest of the people in kingdoms is greatly advanced".[7] No more prose of that sort was printed in England for fifty years. Nashe and others hired to reply to the tracts imitated Marprelate; but they picked up only the flyting style, not the moral urgency which gives Martin's prose its bite. Marprelate helped to frighten off the successors of Leicester and Sidney from Puritanism, to reconcile them to the national church. The prose of Perkins and his school—Preston, Sibbes, Ames—lacks both the sparkle and the scurrility of Marprelate. But Martin was not forgotten. The Cambridge author of *The Pilgrimage to Parnassus* (1598–9) expected his audience to know what it meant to "buy a good Martin". A pamphlet of 1642, which purported to reprint an address of July 1589 to Queen Elizabeth complained (among many other things) of "Master Martin, . . . an overthrower of the clergy, . . . a ringleader to the rascal sort".[8]

Where we do meet radical prose in the fifty years which separate Marprelate from the Levellers is in the pamphlets of Thomas Scott, who published in the Netherlands a series of attacks on James I's foreign policy in an equally convinced, passionate and dramatic conversational style. Here is an extract from *The Belgicke Pismire* (1622), whose object was to recommend to Englishmen the frugality and industry of the bourgeois Dutch:

The tailor hath taken measure of many fair manors, and surveyed them by the yard, making that the Jacob's staff to level the nobility; who being careful to dress themselves superfluously brave care not for their country but make that naked and ragged; and the poor tenant, uncertain to stay longer than his year, is loath to build a nest for another bird; and so the land is impoverished and polled, and everything exposed to waste. But this is not all the mischief, for the poor tenant, undone also by this hard farm and outed of all (having notwithstanding his pains and providence eaten up his horse and cows and whole estate) now falls either to theft or beggary; in which lazy kind of life he soon finds such sweetness as he wonders not now that his landlord loved his ease so well. . . . For such as have nothing are without care or fear, and may sit still when others must look out.[9]

Scott's *Vox Populi* ran to five editions between 1620 and 1623. Such writings no doubt helped to keep the Marprelate tradition alive in the sixteen-twenties and thirties. They had to be smuggled in from the Netherlands, at grave risk to the smugglers. Scott's *The Interpreter* and *Essex's Ghost* were reprinted after 1640: so was *A Dialogue*, which Carlson attributed to Job Throkmorton. The pulpit style of John Everard, who died in 1641, looks back to Marprelate and forward to Richard Overton, the future Leveller. "Then comes up Dr. Reason. Oh! he is a great man, he is a learned doctor indeed! He is doctor of the chair at least; when all the rest are silenced, yet he must be heard; and he will believe nothing that you cannot bring within his bounds". Some hear echoes of Marprelate in Bastwick and Prynne.[10]

Who read Marprelate and Scott before 1640? We do not know. Some people must have done so for there to be such a rash of reprints once the censorship collapsed. Richard Overton was certainly one reader. He was echoing Marprelate from his very first pamphlet, *Vox Borealis* (1640, written 1639), printed by "Margery Marprelate".

> Martin Mar-Prelat was a bonny lad,
> His brave adventures made the prelates mad;
> Though he be dead, yet he hath left behind
> A generation of the Martin kind, . . .
> Margery Mar-Prelat, of renowned fame.

Dr Gimelfarb-Brack thinks that Overton was responsible for the Marprelate reprints of 1640–3.[11] A summary of the writings of the great Biblical chronologist and millenarian, Thomas Brightman, was at last able to be published in 1641. It contained a puff for books by "Margery Mar-Prelate": "you would admire if you knew how greedy men are of these books, and are much thought of in London". Overton may also have had a hand in this tract, which was in dialogue form, as was a summary of Napier's millenarian ideas published in the same year. From 1645 onwards Overton wrote at least six pamphlets over the names of Martin Marprelate Junior, Martin Marpriest or Martin Claw-Clergy, which suggests that he expected his public to recognize the allusion. Overton's crisp prose has all the wit and sparkle, all the moral intensity, of his model. Richard Baxter complained of the great influence of the Marpriest tracts in the New Model Army.[12]

But of course Marprelate was not the only influence shaping popular prose. Three other streams are traditionally invoked. First, Puritan plain preaching. Main-line Puritans from Perkins through Preston, Sibbes, Richard Holdsworth and Stephen Marshall to John Wilkins wanted to convince ordinary men and women of truths which they believed to be supremely important. They therefore avoided the witty rhetorical flourishes of court and university preachers, teaching a "plain, easy and familiar style".[13] When politicians and pamphleteers, on both sides in the civil war, needed to convince, they too found the plain style, and the flyting style, almost essential.

The concept of formally written prose is indeed itself academic: Milton smells of the lamp. Popular prose was transcribed speech, not formal rhetoric: M. Jourdain had grasped that point. Prose was used to instruct. Academic learning was conveyed in Latin, but prentices learnt in the vernacular. English prose was for ordinary people. Puritan sermons were intended to instruct, not—like poetry or court sermons—to give aesthetic delight or to entertain. Elizabethan and Jacobean dramatists switch to prose when low-life characters come on the stage. Poetry had its roots in community ritual, miracle plays, the songs and ballads of the peasantry. Prose was what men used in the market place.

A second stream then is craftsmen's and scientific prose, to which Thomas Sprat looked back when he said that the Royal Society aimed at "bringing all things as near the mathematical plainness as they can; and preferring the language of artisans, countrymen and merchants before that of wits or scholars".[14] In England in the three generations before 1640 far more scientific literature in the vernacular was published than anywhere else in Europe. Most of this was written in a utilitarian style designed to appeal to artisans, small merchants and yeomen—a public not dissimilar to that of the Puritan preachers. The seamen whose narratives Hakluyt printed spoke directly to this audience. William Gilbert cultivated an unadorned style on principle.[15] There were also the translators and popularizers of the classics, who like Philemon Holland aimed at "a mean and popular style".[16]

Thirdly, there are novels like those of Dekker and Deloney, written for a middle-class audience in a functionally popular style but lacking the artistic control of Marprelate and the interregnum radicals. And there is popular dramatic prose, the prose of the Red Bull and the Fortune, too little of which got into print for it to be easy to assess. Margot Heinemann has shown that the closing of the theatres in 1642 did not mean the end of the drama's influence on prose. She is certainly right in arguing that some writers for the stage took to pamphleteering after 1640, some—like Overton—on the Parliamentarian side.[17] It is of course logical as soon as one thinks about it; we were prevented from seeing it only by the stereotype assumption that anyone connected with the theatre must be a royalist, which she has done so much to disprove. Early pamphlets against Laud in dialogue form led on to Overton's, Walwyn's, Winstanley's and Coppe's more sophisticated use of dialogue.

Marprelate's radical prose was inseparable from his radical ideas. Wallace Notestein drew attention to the complicated and illogical sentence structure of lawyers, J.P.s and parsons, who thought formal documents ought to be in Latin, and so wrote a Latinized English, translating from the colloquial vernacular. Interregnum radicals, Notestein suggested, first made spoken English normal in prose dealing with serious political subjects.[18] The Levellers also insisted that the laws should be translated out of law French and Latin into the language which ordinary people could understand. They were echoing John Hare, who had called for a purge of the language as part of the overthrow of the Norman Yoke in politics and society. The radicals were less concerned about Cicero, Seneca and Tacitus than their social superiors were—or so the literary historians tell us;—and perhaps they wrote all the better English for not knowing too much Latin. University education, Defoe used to say, ruined English prose style by making gentlemen think in Latin;[19] the speech of ordinary people had broken through this academic barrier with Marprelate. It did so again, irreversibly this time, during the interregnum. First the Bible in English, then the laws in English, then prose in English.

Civil war propagandists then were speaking to a wider audience than writers who could publish in the thirties. Most of the latter had in mind a Latin-educated university or court audience; popular literature was of the trivial and ephemeral sort—like almanacs— though even these had been censored before 1640 by what Nicholas Fiske later called "the malice of the clergy". During the civil war of 1642–6 both sides had to give reasons for asking their countrymen to fight for them, or at least to pay very high taxes. So an entirely new literary form appeared—the serious pamphlet with popular appeal, intended not only for private reading but also for reading aloud to illiterate audiences.

Initially the Puritan clergy, masters of the plain style, were best at this. But nothing is more competitive than civil war. "Swelling words of vanity may tickle the ear, . . . and please in matters of discourse", wrote the Puritan Valentine Marshall, "But when it comes to push of pike they afford but little comfort".[20] Royalist and Parliamentarian journalists soon realised that arguments must be spiced with wit and raillery, not to say scurrility, if they were to sell and be attended to. Even Puritan preachers knew that that sermon is preached in vain which sends its auditory to sleep. So they had employed anecdotes, dialogue. But in the rough-and-tumble of the forties they suffered from the social inhibitions which had led their predecessors to condemn Marprelate.

On the Parliamentarian side, the conduct of the war, and attitudes to religious toleration (really part of the conduct of the war) soon came to be matters of public debate. Political issues were freely discussed, verbally and in print, by far wider circles than had ever participated in politics before. The most critical and intellectually aware members of this audience were likely to be craftsmen and yeomen. The mechanic preachers who dominated radical sects and set the tone for autobiographical writings like *Grace Abounding* came from the same class. Printers were themselves craftsmen, drawn from the social stratum to which Levellers consciously appealed. The Leveller John Jones argued that mechanic jurors should be superior to judges with ruling-class prejudices. Lilburne wanted every man to be his own lawyer; Walwyn thought a cobbler taken from his bench could judge as well as anyone. Culpeper's *Herbal* aimed at making every man his own doctor. Critics of the universities similarly contrasted the divine grace which might be vouchsafed to any craftsman with the classical education which conservative clergymen thought necessary before a man could be ordained.[21]

In the debates on how to win the war more radical groups began to express their views; and when the war had been won they intensified their attempts to mobilize public opinion behind their reforming programmes. In *Areopagitica* Milton wrote that the censor will "let pass nothing but what is vulgarly received already", and so will favour a dull conformity. But in the sixteen-forties discussion was free in an unprecedented way—in religious congregations under mechanic preachers, in alehouses and in regiments of the New Model Army where pamphlets were read aloud to the illiterate, or devoured by troopers "dispersed in their quarters" where, Baxter disapprovingly noted, "they had none to contradict them".[22]

Another contributory factor was the breakdown of the Calvinist theology, which never recovered from the unsuccessful attempt to establish a persecuting Presbyterian national church in the forties. Calvinists believed that the mass of mankind was irretrievably damned by a divine decree resulting from Adam's fall—999 out of 1000, said Thomas Shepard, the New England theologian.[23] Yet preachers had to say something to those whom they believed to be the unregenerate. Puritans evolved the Covenant theology, which emphasized that the elect cannot be known on earth, and suggested that a serious concern about a man's eternal fate was presumptive evidence that grace was at work in his heart. But in the forties the unregenerate themselves began to take a share in the talking. This must in itself have helped to extend the audience for theological writing: Diggers, Ranters and Quakers were appealing to those whom orthodox Calvinists thought irredeemable, as Levellers and Diggers appealed to those who had previously (in the opinion of their betters) existed only to be ruled.

Totally new vistas were opened up. Winstanley, Ranters and

Quakers proclaimed that all mankind might be saved. Milton opened up a wide-ranging discussion of divorce, and Ranters attacked the monogamous family. Levellers called for a big extension of the franchise, and for legal and economic reforms. Winstanley proclaimed that true freedom could be won only in a communist society. The traditional hierarchy, of whose arch the King had been the keystone, collapsed when Charles was tried and executed as a traitor to his people—a unique experience in the history of Europe. The House of Lords was abolished. A state church, a professional clergy and tithes to pay for them, were all called in question; and, as conservatives had predicted, those who questioned tithes were soon refusing to pay rent to landlords. Everything could be discussed, and nearly everything was. And it was discussed before a popular audience, the descendants of Shakespeare's groundlings as well as of the readers of Marprelate and Thomas Scott. Arguments had to be clear and simple, and had to stand up to criticism. Intense intellectual competition sharpened styles as well as arguments.

In his *History of the Royal Society* Sprat pointed out that in periods of civil war "all languages . . . increase by extraordinary degrees; for in such busy and active times there arise more new thoughts of men which must be signified and varied by new expressions". So the English language during the Revolution "was enlarged by many sound and necessary forms and idioms which before it wanted".[24] Prose was shorn of the florid circumlocutions in which scholars and courtiers had delighted. As the demand for books expanded, so the market enforced the emergence of a more direct conversational style. We see a change coming over Milton's style—from the calculated rhetoric of *Areopagitica*, aimed at winning the support of intellectuals for religious toleration and against censorship, to the simpler prose of the pamphlets of 1659–60, when he was trying desperately to rally all supporters of the Good Old Cause against a restoration of monarchy, or of the last pamphlets of 1673–4, when he was trying to unite Anglicans and nonconformists against what he saw as a threat of popery and absolutism.

This is the background against which we should see the radical tracts of the late forties and early fifties. I am only a historian, and shall say nothing about quality: the texts can speak for themselves. No doubt I let myself be influenced by the content. But I think that some Levellers, Diggers, Ranters, Quakers and other radicals of the revolutionary decades show the qualities of good prose which we usually associate with a considerably later date. All had a serious message to get across and devoted considerable literary skill to the task of presentation.

Some examples then. In April 1641 Overton replied to the defenders of Archbishop Laud, now in prison. "But the bishop was charitable: that he was indeed, to cut off men's ears, and damn them to perpetual imprisonment for speaking two or three angry words against his lawn sleeves and rochet". (The reference was to Prynne and Bastwick; Overton now switches to a drummer boy executed as a traitor after a demonstration). "But how strangely was the body of his [Laud's] charity divided when he hung it up in quarters upon four several gates, and stuck the head on London Bridge! Was he not a very merciful man, think you, to make such havoc of a poor young fellow? . . . He was took upon suspicion to be one of the company that beset his princely palace at Lambeth; this then could be no less than high treason".[25]

Overton's *Araignment of Mr. Persecution* (1645) is original not so much in its ideas as in its dramatic form: it is almost a one-act play.[26] It was dedicated to the Westminster Assembly of Divines, an impertinently ironical start to a pamphlet which attacked all that the Assembly held sacred. Overton—young Martin—pointed out that the divines had spent more time in securing their own incomes from tithes than in producing a Directory of worship. ("For he is an infidel and denieth the faith, that doth not provide for his family"). Young Martin offered himself as a candidate for a good living: "Young Martin can thunder-thump the pulpit, oh, he can stare most devoutly, rail and bawl most fervently, storm most tempestuously even till he foam at mouth most precisely; oh, how he can sputter't out! 'Oh these cursed Anabaptists, these wicked Brownists, these heretics, these schismatics, these sectaries'; Oh, Martin hath it at his finger's end, he's a university man, skilled in the tongues and sciences, and can sophisticate any text, oh he is excellent at false glosses and scholastic interpretations, he can wrest the Scriptures most neatly, tell the people it is thus and thus in the original, an excellent man to make a presbyter!"[27]

Here is a different kind of invective from a pamphlet of 1646, in which Overton discusses the alleged plots of the Parliamentarian leaders at the beginning of the civil war:

Their work was to subvert the monarchical lords and clergy. . . . But this was a mighty work, and they were no wise able to effect it of themselves.

"Therefore", say they, "the generality of the people must be engaged; and how must this be done? Why", say they, "we must associate with that part of the clergy that are now made underlings, . . . and with the most zealous religious non-conformists, and by the help of these we will lay before the generality of the people all the Popish innovations in religion, all the oppressions of the bishops and High Commission, all the exorbitances of the Council-board and Star Chamber, all the injustice of the Chancery and courts of justice, all the illegal taxations . . . , whereby we shall be sure to get into our party the generality of the City of London, and all the considerable substantial people of both nations . . ."

"But", say some, "this will never be effected without a war, for the King will have a strong party, and he will never submit to us". "'Tis not expected otherwise", say they; "and great and vast sums of money must be raised, and soldiers and ammunition must be had, whereof we shall not need to fear any want; for what will not an oppressed, rich and religious people do to be delivered from all kinds of oppression, both spiritual and temporal, and to be restored to purity and freedom in religion, and to the just liberty of their persons and estates?"[28]

Walwyn's irony is subtler, not uninfluenced by Montaigne.

Since the Scriptures are now in English, which at first were in Hebrew, Greek or Syriac, or what other language; why may not one that understands English only both understand and declare the true meaning of them as well as an English Hebrician or Grecian or Roman whatsoever? "Aye but", says some politic learned man, "a man that doth not understand the original language cannot so perfectly give the sense of the Scripture as he that doth; or as one that makes it his study for ten or twenty years together, and hath no other employment: every man being best skilled in his own profession wherein he hath been bred and accustomed". I did well to say "some politic learned man" might thus object: for indeed, what is here but policy? For if it be as such men would imply, I pray you what are you the better for having the Scripture in your own language? When it was locked up in the Latin tongue by the policy of Rome, you might have had a learned friar for your money at any time to have interpreted the same; and though now you have it in your own language you are taught not to trust your own understanding (have a care of your purses!). You must have a university man to interpret the English, or you are in as bad a case as before—but not in worse; for, for your money, you may have plenty at your service, and to interpret as best shall please your fancy".[29]

Bunyan, we recall, thought it no disgrace to "God's own, . . . most commonly of the poorer sort" that "they cannot, with Pontius Pilate, speak Hebrew, Greek and Latin".[30]

There is Walwyn's very funny burlesque pamphlet, *A Prediction of Master Edwards his Conversion and Recantation* (1646). Walwyn's description of the death-bed repentance of the great red-baiter

Thomas Edwards, written in all mock-seriousness, establishes a new genre, which looks forward to Swift's account of John Partridge's death, and to the spoofs of Defoe. Walwyn makes this fierce persecutor of sectaries confess:

There was nothing which I conceived effectual to work upon the superstitious or ignorant but I made use thereof as the prelates had done before me; yea, I strictly observed order in such things as few men consider, and yet are very powerful in the minds of many; as the wearing of my cloak of at least a clergyman's length, my hat of a due breadth and bigness, both for brim and crown, somewhat different from laymen, my band also of a peculiar strain, and my clothes *all black*, I would not have worn a coloured suit at any rate, that I thought enough to betray all, nor any trimming on my black, as being unsuitable to a divine's habit. I had a care to be sadder in countenance and more solemn in discourse because it was the custom of a clergyman, . . . though I knew full well that God was no respecter of persons, and that he made not choice of the great or learned men of the world to be his prophets and publishers of the gospel; but herdsmen, fishermen, tent-makers, toll-gatherers etc., and that our blessed Saviour thought it no disparagement to be reputed the son of a carpenter.[31]

Egalitarian irreverence affected style as well as content. The King's nephew and cavalry commander, Prince Rupert, Duke of Cumberland, was referred to as Prince Robber, Duke of Plunderland; Oliver Cromwell's red nose and alleged brewery opened up new propagandist possibilities. Political points could never have been made in such a direct way before 1640. Allegory was consequently no longer necessary as a disguise. An argument was established much more briefly and effectively by a personal insult than by a syllogism.

I might quote many other Levellers—Sexby dedicating to Oliver Cromwell the tract advocating his assassination: "To your Highness justly belongs the honour of dying for the people, and it cannot choose but be unspeakable consolation to you in the last moments of your life, to consider with how much benefit to the world you are like to leave it. 'Tis then only (my Lord) the titles you now usurp will be truly yours; you will then be indeed the deliverer of your country. . . . Religion shall be then restored, liberty asserted and Parliaments have those privileges they have fought for. . . . All this we hope from your Highness's happy expiration, who are the true father of your country: for while you live we can call nothing ours, and it is from your death that we hope for our inheritances".[32] Or Clarkson in his early, near-Leveller days, discussing Parliament: "Who are the oppressors but the nobility and gentry, and who are oppressed, if not the yeoman, the farmer, the tradesman and the like? . . . Have you not chosen oppressors to redeem you from oppression? . . . Your slavery is their liberty, your poverty is their prosperity. . . . Peace is their ruin, . . . by war they are enriched. . . . Peace is their war, peace is their poverty".[33] Or in his later more ironical style:

Now if then you had asked me, . . . my answer had plainly been this: That my God was a grave, ancient, holy old man, as I supposed sat in heaven in a chair of gold; but as for his nature I knew no more than a child; and as for the devil, I really believed was some deformed person out of man, and that he could where, when and how, in what shape appear he pleased; and therefore the devil was a great scarecrow, in so much that every black thing I saw in the night, I thought was the devil. . . . For heaven I thought was a glorious place, with variety of rooms suitable for himself and his son Christ and the Holy Ghost. And hell, where it was I knew not, but judged it a local place, all dark, fire and brimstone, which the devils did torment the wicked in, and that for ever.[34]

Or the anonymous author of *Tyranipocrit Discovered* (1649), whom some have suspected to be Walwyn. He is attacking the conventionally orthodox doctrine of justification by faith. "Man may profit man, but no man can profit God. And therefore if we will do good, we must do it to mankind and not to God without men. Now for faith, that cannot help our neighbours. . . . Faith no doubt is a comfortable thing for him that hath it, but another's faith cannot help me. But if I be poor and want food and raiment, if my rich neighbour do love me, although he do not believe as I do, yet love will cause him to help me; but if he have faith to remove mountains, and goods to build churches, yet if he do not love me, he would not help me."[35]

This leads on to the experimental prose (and punctuation) of Abiezer Coppe, almost certainly an attempt to reproduce his pulpit style. Here is the opening of his first *Fiery Flying Roll* (1649):

My dear one.
All or none.
Every one under the sun.
My own. . . .
Behold, by mine own almightiness (in me) I have been changed in a moment, in the twinkling of an eye, at the sound of the trump.
And now the Lord is descended from heaven, with a shout, with the voice of the archangel, and with the trump of God.
And the sea, the earth, yea all things are now giving up their dead. And all things that ever were, are, or shall be visible—are the grave wherein the King

of Glory (the eternal, invisible almightiness), hath lain as it were dead and buried.

But behold, behold, he is now risen . . . . and . . . . by his mighty angel is proclaiming (with a loud voice). . . .

"Be no longer so horridly, hellishly, impudently, arrogantly wicked as to judge what is sin, what not; what evil and what not. For . . . . sin and transgression is finished. . . ."

[It is still God speaking:] "Thou hast many bags of money, and behold now I come as a thief in the night, with my sword drawn in my hand, and like a thief as I am, I say Deliver your purse, deliver sirrah! Deliver or I'll cut thy throat; deliver my money . . . . to poor cripples, lazars, yea to rogues, thieves, whores and cutpurses, who are flesh of thy flesh and every whit as good as thyself in mine eye, who are ready to starve in plaguey gaols and nasty dungeons, or else by myself", saith the Lord, "I will torment thee day and night.

The plague of God is in your purses, barns, houses, horses; murrain will take your hogs (O ye fat swine of the earth), who shall shortly go to the knife and be hung up i'th roof, except . . . . Blasting, mill-dew, locusts, caterpillars, yea fire your houses and goods, take your corn and fruit, the moth your garments and the rot your sheep. Did you not see my hand, this last year, stretched out?

You did not see.

My hand is stretched out still.

Your gold and silver, though you can't see it, is cankered. . . . The rust of your silver, I say, shall eat your flesh as it were fire".

Here is his dialogue with a beggar whom he met on the road:

Art poor?

Yea, very poor, said he.

Whereupon the strange woman who flattereth with her lips, and is subtle of heart, said within me,

It's a poor wretch, give him two-pence.

But my Excellency and Majesty (in me) scorned her words, confounded her language, and kicked her out of his presence.

But immediately the well-favoured harlot (whom I carried not upon my horse behind me, but who rose up in me), said:

It's a poor wretch, give him 6d., and that's enough for a squire or knight to give to one poor body.

Besides (saith the holy Scripturean whore) he's worse than an infidel that provides not for his own family.[36]

Have a care of the main chance.

And thus she flattereth with her lips, and her words being smoother than oil, and her lips dropping as the honeycomb, I was fired to hasten my hand into my pocket, and pulling out a shilling, said to the poor wretch, give me sixpence, here's a shilling for thee.

He answered, I cannot, I have never a penny.

Whereupon I said, I would fain have given thee something if thou couldst have changed my money.

Then saith he, God bless you. . . .

Whereupon, with much reluctancy, . . . I turned my horse's head from him, riding away. . . .

And behold, the plague of God fell into my pocket; and the rest of my silver rose up in judgment against me, and consumed my flesh as with fire; so that I and my money perished with me;

and he went back and gave him all he had.[37]

Also experimental is the curiously liturgical style of the early George Fox:

Come priests, did not the Whore set up your schools and colleges, this false church whereby you are made ministers, and gave them the names of Trinity College, Jesus College, Emanuel College where you are made ministers since the true church went into the wilderness? And here have you not drunken the Whore's cup? Guilty or not guilty? And was not this Whore of Rome the first author of preaching by the hour-glass—funeral sermons ten shillings a sermon, twenty shillings a sermon, ten groats the grave, and mortuaries, and £200 a year for preaching? Is not this the Whore of Rome's cup? And have not you all drunk it? And do you not drink it daily? Are you guilty or not guilty? Did not the church of Rome first ordain the Jesuits' tribe, the order of black-coats? And was not the Whore of Rome the first setter-up of sprinkling a little water upon children's faces for money, and churching of women for money? And have not you drunken this cup? Come priests, are you guilty or not guilty?[38]

Gerrard Winstanley's seems to me prose of a higher order. Like Overton, Walwyn and Coppe, he slips into dialogue and back again effortlessly. But his radical theology helps to give his style vigour and immediacy. Winstanley believed that the external world was the manifestation of God, and so our senses are to be valued because by them we know this world, and so know God, reason, truth. Metaphors spring naturally and abundantly to Winstanley's pen, because (like Milton) he thinks of the spiritual and the physical as closely interconnected.

Here are a few examples, taken from various pamphlets:

Kingly power is like a great spread tree; if you lop off the head or top bough, and let the other branches and root stand, it will grow again and recover fresher strength.

England is a prison: the variety of subtleties in the laws preserved by the sword are bolts, bars and doors of the prison; the lawyers are the jailors, and poor men are the prisoners.

The law is the fox, poor men are the geese; he pulls off their feathers and feeds upon them.

These great ones are too stately houses for Christ to dwell in; he takes up his abode in a manger.

All your particular churches are like the enclosers of land, which hedges in some to be the heirs of life, and hedges out others.

These men make themselves ministers as a man teaches birds to speak.[39]

Nor is Winstanley just a writer of the occasional vivid phrase. He is also capable of sustained eloquence in many keys. Take his warning in 1649 to London and the Army that the civil war has not yet been won:

Therefore England beware; thou art in danger of being brought under the Norman power more than ever. The King Charles that was successor to William the Conqueror thou hast cast out: yet William the Conqueror's army begins to gather into head again, and the old Norman prerogative law is the place of their rendezvous. For though their chief captain Charles be gone, yet his colonels, which are lords of manors, his councillors and divines, which are our lawyers and priests, his inferior officers and soldiers, which are the freeholders and landlords, all which did steal away our land from us when they killed and murdered our fathers in that Norman conquest; and the bailiffs that are slaves to their covetous lusts, and all the ignorant bawling women against our digging for freedom, are the snapsack boys and the ammunition sluts that follow the Norman camp. These are all striving to get into a body again, that they may set up a new Norman slavery over us.[40]

Here is a simple descriptive piece:

Then they came privately by day to Gerrard Winstanley's house, and drove away four cows, I not knowing of it; and some of the Lord's tenants rode to the next town shouting the Diggers were conquered, the Diggers were conquered. Truly it is an easy thing to beat a man and cry conquest over him, after his hands are tied as they tied ours. But if their cause be so good, why will they not suffer us to speak, and let reason and equity, the foundation of righteous laws, judge them and us? But strangers made rescue of those cows and drove them astray out of the bailiffs' hands, so that the bailiffs lost them; but before the bailiffs had lost the cows, I hearing of it went to them and said, "Here is my body, take me that I may come to speak to those Normans that have stolen our land from us; and let the cows go, for they are none of mine"; and after some time, they telling me that they had nothing against my body, it was my goods they were to have; then said I, "Take my goods, for the cows are not mine"; and so I went away and left them, being quiet in my heart and filled with comfort within myself, that the King of Righteousness would cause this to work for the advancing of his own cause, which I prefer above estate or livelihood.[41]

Bunyan moved in Ranter circles in his youth, probably in the Army, and remembered many things he had heard there. His Mr

Badman was not the straw figure he almost certainly would have been before 1640, and this owes much to Bunyan's participation in the discussions of the Revolution. At one time he wondered whether Christianity was any better founded than Mahomedanism: the translation of the *Koran* into English in 1649 could certainly not have happened earlier. Bunyan's immediate debt to Levellers and Diggers cannot be demonstrated, but it is difficult to think that a man who had Ranter friends in the late forties and became a Baptist in the early fifties would not have read at least the Levellers. He undoubtedly read Quaker pamphlets. There is no time to argue the case now, but with some of the characterization in *The Pilgrim's Progress* compare Overton's Superstition, who spoke of "my well-beloved uncles Cardinal False-Heart, Cardinal Would-have-wit, Cardinal Want-wit, Dr Corrupt Doctrine, Dr Wrest-Scripture, Dr Canon and Dr Ambition".[42] Mr Persecution, Overton tells us, had been through "all the universities, and colleges in Christendom".[43] The immediacy of Bunyan's style constantly recalls Walwyn and Winstanley.

But it is not a matter of tracing individual influences. In the forties and fifties men and women discussed ideas that could not previously have been discussed, still less printed; debate was opened up, new techniques of persuasion were discovered. Even the restoration of political censorship in the fifties, followed by the return of clerical control after 1660, could not undo this experience.

Old-fashioned literary historians made far too much of supposed "French influences" on restoration prose. There was no need to go into exile to learn how to write easy English. Nor were the effects limited to radicals. We should perhaps now speak of "journalists'" or "publicists'" prose rather than radical. An impeccable royalist like Berkenhead learnt it in competition with a turncoat journalist like Marchamont Nedham. Nedham attacked Lancelot Andrewes's "jingling" prose style, and himself echoed Marprelate, as a contemporary pointed out.[44] The cutting edge of Hobbes's style was sharpened by his awareness of what was going on. Classical and Biblical allusions are now subordinated to the argument. Traditional techniques of controversy—following the adversary paragraph by paragraph, dissecting him at length—are becoming old-fashioned.

Of course some of this would no doubt have happened anyway, as Walwyn's reading of Montaigne suggests. It is difficult to be precise about the effects of the flood of controversial literature. But if we put ourselves imaginatively back into the sixteen-forties, we can surely see that the breakdown of the censorship must have played a vital role. Undergraduates today do not have to smuggle in illegal copies of *Ulysses* and *Lady Chatterley's Lover*, as I had to do, and that is a good thing. But the consequences of this liberation are trifling compared with those of the sixteen-forties, just as the risks I ran did not include flogging or having my ears sliced off. Free competition in a vastly expanded market helped to reduce book prices: *Areopagitica* cost 4d., *The Agreement of the People* 2d. Before 1640 there had been no cheap Bibles because printing the Bible was a monopoly.[45]

The breakdown of censorship facilitated the continuing influence of Martin Marprelate on English radical prose: Dryden was making a shrewd stylistic point when he called Marprelate "the Marvell of those times".[46] Richard Leigh was perhaps less perceptive when he associated Milton with Marprelate.[47] We might pursue the line of popular prose back behind Marprelate to earlier protestant propagandists, Crowley, Lever, Latimer, Simon Fish, perhaps to the Lollards. Martin himself claimed kinship with Langland, whom protestants wrongly associated with the Lollards. The title-page of an edition of *Piers Plowman* published in 1589 paraphrased Marprelate's *Epistle* and described Piers as "Grandsire of Martin Marprelate".[48]

I want to conclude by emphasizing Sprat's point that the sixteen-forties and fifties marked a divide in English prose, as in so many other areas of English life, which could not be wished away by pretending that 1660 was the eleventh year of Charles II's reign, and that nothing had happened between 1641 and 1660. The interregnum radicals spoke to a far wider audience for a longer period than Marprelate was able to do. In the end they too were suppressed; but not before they had established as a tradition what had previously been a nine-days wonder. They spoke especially to the artisans at whom Puritan sermons had been aimed, and whose language Sprat recommended to the Royal Society as a model.

Once men began to write like Overton, Walwyn, Coppe and Winstanley, with a direct urgency and personal appeal, when vivid description serves an artistic as well as a moral purpose, the new prose has reached maturity. The gap between ornate, scholarly fine writing and utilitarian artisans' prose has been bridged. The prose of everyday speech has spread beyond the stage and the pulpit, and we are on the high road to Bunyan, Defoe, Swift and the novel.

NOTES

1. This, the second F. W. Bateson Memorial lecture, was delivered in Oxford on 17 February 1982. It was printed in *Essays in Criticism, XXXII* (1982).
2. *A Dialogue* (1640, 1643), *Hay any Worke* (1641, 1643), *The Character of a Puritan* (1643).
3. For other suggested origins of the name see Marie Gimelfarb-Brack, *op. cit.*, pp. 171-2.
4. All my quotations are from the 1967 reprint of *The Epistle* by the Scolar Press, Leeds, in *The Marprelate Tracts (1588-1589)*.
5. The best recent book on the subject, Leland M. Carlson, *Martin Marprelate, Gentleman: Master Job Throkmorton Laid Open in his Colors* (San Marino, 1981), argues forcefully that Throkmorton was the author. For the intriguing suggestion that John Field may have had some connection with Marprelate see Collinson, *Godly People*, pp. 355, 370.
6. Izaak Walton, "Life of Mr. Richard Hooker", in *Lives* (World's Classics), p. 187; T. Fuller, *The Church History of Britain*, III, p. 99. First published 1655. For Marprelate's popularity see C. Burrage, *The Early English Dissenters* (Cambridge U.P., 1912), II, p. 26.
7. R. Bancroft, *A Sermon Preached at Pauls Crosse the 9 of Februarie 1588[-9]*, p. 87; Collinson, *The Elizabethan Puritan Movement*, p. 393.
8. Ed. J.B. Leishman, *The Three Parnassus Plays (1598-1601)* (1949), p. 113; *Asinus Onustus The Asse Overladen* (1642), pp. 11-12.
9. [T. Scott], *The Belgicke Pismire* (1622), pp. 32-3. Printed in the Netherlands.
10. Everard, *The Gospel-Treasury Opened* (1657), p. 83. I owe this reference to Mr Nigel Smith. Cf. Martin Butler, *op. cit.*, pp. 90, 95.
11. Gimelfarb-Brack, *op. cit.*, pp. 24, 89, 119-24, 134, 315-27, 548.
12. *A Revelation of Mr. Brightmans Revelation* (1641); *Napiers Narration* (1641); *Reliquiae Baxterianae*. p. 53.
13. W.T. Costello, *The Scholastic Curriculum at early seventeenth-century Cambridge* (Harvard U.P., 1958), p. 57; cf. Dryden, "A Defence of the Epilogue to *The Conquest of Granada*", in *Plays* (Mermaid Series, n.d.), I, p. 223. Professor Jordan would add Thomas Helwys as another whose style contributed to the evolution of popular plain prose (*The Development of Religious Toleration in England, 1603-1640*, 1936, p. 284).
14. Sprat, *The History of the Royal Society*, p. 113.
15. F.R. Johnson, *Astronomical Thought in Renaissance England* (Johns Hopkins U.P., 1937), esp. pp. 290-3; Dudley North, *Discourses upon Trade* (1691), in *Early English Tracts on Commerce* (ed. J.R. McCulloch, Cambridge U.P., 1952), p. 508; W. Gilbert, *On the Loadstone and Magnetic Bodies* (1600), Author's Preface. I cite from the reprint of 1893

(trans. P. Fleury Molletay). Cf. Robert Barclay, *An Apology for Christian Religion* (1676), Proposition 10, xxvii.

16. Livy, *The Romane Historie* (trans. Philemon Holland, 1600), Preface.
17. Heinemann, Chapter 13; Gimelfarb-Brack, *op. cit.*, pp. 5–9.
18. In lectures delivered in Oxford, 1949–50.
19. John Hare, *St. Edwards Ghost, or Anti-Normanism* (1647), written 1642. Reprinted in *Harleian Miscellany* (1744–6), VIII, pp. 89–101. For Defoe see p. 124 below.
20. Valentine Marshall, "To the Reader", in Richard Capel, *Remains* (1658).
21. My *Change and Continuity in 17th-Century England* (1974), pp. 161–4.
22. *Reliquiae Baxterianae*, p. 53.
23. Ed. M. McGiffert, *God's Plot: The Paradoxes of Puritan Piety, Being the Autobiography and Journal of Thomas Shepard* (Massachusetts U.P., 1972), p. 9. Cf. *W.T.U.D.*, p. 260.
24. Sprat, *op. cit.*, p. 42.
25. Quoted in Gimelfarb-Brack, *op. cit.*, p. 525.
26. *Ibid.*, p. 152.
27. Haller, *Tracts on Liberty in the Puritan Revolution*, III, p. 207.
28. *Ibid.*, II, pp. 358–9.
29. *Ibid.*, II, pp. 301–2.
30. Bunyan, *Works*, III, pp. 676, 695.
31. Haller, *op. cit.*, III, pp. 344–5. Cf. pp. 59–60 above.
32. W. Allen, *Killing No Murder* (1657), Preface. The pamphlet is generally attributed to Sexby.
33. Clarkson, *A Generall Charge* (1647), pp. 10–27.
34. Clarkson, *The Lost sheep Found* (1660), pp. 6–7. Reprinted by The Rota, Exeter, in 1974, and by Nigel Smith, *A Collection of Ranter Writings from the 17th century* (1983).
35. In *British Pamphleteers*, I, *From the Sixteenth Century to the French Revolution* (ed. G. Orwell and R. Reynolds, 1948), p. 87.
36. Cf. Richard Overton, quoted on p. 84 above.
37. Coppe, *A Fiery Flying Roll* (1649), Sig. A 2, p. 7; *A Second Fiery Flying Roule* (1649), pp. 2–5. Both were reprinted by The Rota, Exeter in 1973, and by Nigel Smith, *op. cit.*
38. G. Fox, *The Lambs Officer* (1659), pp. 3–4. The Quaker Samuel Fisher's buffooning alliterative style may also owe something to Marprelate (*W.T.U.D.*, p. 260).
39. G. Winstanley, *The Law of Freedom and Other Writings*, pp. 162–3, 170, 239, 245, 214.
40. *Ibid.*, pp. 141–2.
41. *Ibid.*, p. 139.
42. Quoted in Gimelfarb-Brack, *op. cit.*, p. 513.
43. Haller, *op. cit.*, III, p. 212.
44. D. Featley, *Sacra Nemesis* (Oxford, 1644) I owe these points to the kindness of Mr I.A. McCalman. For Berkenhead see chapter 4 below.
45. L. Miller, "Milton's *Areopagitica*: Price 4d.", *Notes and Queries*, CCXX (1975); ed. J. Gutch, *Collectanea Curiosa* (1781), I, pp. 275–6; *HMC Salisbury MSS.*, Parts XXIII–IV, pp. 282, 369.

46. John Dryden, *Religio Laici* (1682), Preface.
47. Leigh, *The Transproser Rehearsed* (1673), pp. 55, 136–7. Roger L'Estrange recalled Martin Junior in 1661 (*Interest Mistaken, or, The Holy Cheat*, p. 30).
48. Carlson, op. cit., pp. 340, 376. Professor Carlson thinks that the type is similar to that of the first four Marprelate tracts.

4. *Sir John Berkenhead, 1617-79*[1]

Sir John Berkenhead is not on the face of it the most exciting of
subjects for a biography. He was a small town boy from Cheshire, "a
poor ale-house-keeper's son", Marvell put it in the days of Sir John's
grandeur.[2] He had the good fortune to win the patronage of the all-
powerful Archbishop Laud, apparently by his skill in calligraphy.
Laud got him made a Fellow of All Souls—probably just after
Marchamont Nedham and Abiezer Coppe had ceased to be
undergraduates there. The thought of their possible meeting is
intriguing. Berkenhead's period of glory was during the civil war,
when he edited the royalist newsbook, *Mercurius Aulicus*. But this
came to an end before Berkenhead was thirty years old, and there is
nothing particularly remarkable about his later career—royalist
agent in the sixteen-fifties, never however at the centre of conspiracy;
editor, courtier, M.P., knight, F.R.S. after the restoration. In
August 1649, incongruously enough, he had obtained a grant of arms
from Charles II's exiled court.[3] It was a symbol both of his social
aspirations and of his respect for the old order, and belief in its
survival power.

Dr Thomas nevertheless contrived to make a very interesting book
out of these unpromising materials. Its excellence and its novelty
derive from two main themes. First, a radical reassessment of the
place of Berkenhead and *Mercurius Aulicus* in the history of English
journalism; and secondly a study of Berkenhead's share in the origins
of English classicism. There are many subsidiary themes, notably a
reconsideration of the role of the Laudians in English history after
the Archbishop's overthrow, but these two are the most original.

No one had studied *Mercurius Aulicus* in any depth before. Dr
Thomas shows how Berkenhead superseded the much more high-
powered Peter Heylyn as the paper's editor, primarily because of his
racy conversational style, to which the academic Heylyn could never
descend. But *Mercurius Aulicus* was not merely witty and scurrilous.
Berkenhead, who was only twenty-five at the outbreak of civil war,

had served in Laud's secretariat at Lambeth, and remained a convinced Laudian throughout his life—a significant break from the mild Puritanism of his inn-keeper and saddler father. Dr Thomas demonstrates how very close Berkenhead was to the centre of power in royalist Oxford. Through the secretaries of state, George Digby and Edward Nicholas, perhaps also through Henry Jermyn, Berkenhead received a great deal of accurate military and political information. This was suggested by the Venetian Resident in London as early as July 1643, and by many Parliamentarian newswriters. At a time when Charles I sometimes allowed Hyde and Falkland to write propaganda statements depicting him as a would-be constitutional monarch, Berkenhead "represented accurately the King's real opinions", his uncompromising intransigence, his refusal to admit any respectable motives in his opponents. This was clearly revealed in 1645, when it was discovered that "expressions and arguments in the newsbook were identical with those in one of the King's letters recently captured by Parliament".[4]

"Aulicus's accuracy was at its zenith in 1643, when its punctilious method of citing sources, giving dates and statistics, and its full descriptions of important events at once and deservedly established it as England's premier newsbook. For too long it has suffered from the stigma which S.R. Gardiner fixed upon it, but the more favourable conclusions of some recent historians will be amply supported and reinforced by the present investigation". To attempt to correct Gardiner is a bold undertaking, but Dr Thomas is as good as his word. In an England starved of reliable news, *Mercurius Aulicus's* accuracy made it respected even by sympathizers with Parliament, who often found it more reliable than its many Parliamentarian rivals; its rôle as a royal mouthpiece made its confident extremism acceptable to rank-and-file royalists until the bitter end.[5]

Dr Thomas underlines the paradox in Berkenhead's achievement. "The Court—the bastion of conservatism and privilege—refused to countenance the publication of anything but foreign and the most harmless home news before the Civil War forced its hand. . . . It was the somewhat sterile reflex of an exclusive tradition feeling itself threatened by new and encroaching social forces. Ironically, in 1643 the regime which had relied so heavily on suppression of news set about capturing a nation-wide audience with an enthusiasm and skill unprecedented in English journalism".[6] *Mercurius Aulicus* enjoyed, less paradoxically, the privileges of monopoly. It was "backed by a powerful and extensive organisation". Its sources of information were of the highest quality, and it received authoritative guidance. It was better printed than the Parliamentarian newsbooks, and it concentrated all the journalistic talent in the court at Oxford and in the university. On the Parliamentary side some twenty-two periodicals competed with each other and with *Mercurius Aulicus*. None of them had access to official sources of information, at least before 1645. The "variety of our misreporting pamphlets", one of them admitted, cast the greatest possible slur on Parliament's good name.[7]

Berkenhead himself looked back to the happier times when there had been no need for newsbooks.[8] After the restoration he supervised *The Kingdomes Intelligencer* and *Mercurius Publicus*, two overlapping official gazettes which reverted to the tradition of printing mainly foreign news with a minimum of home news.

Parliamentary Acts and Bills are merely listed; the actual debates are ignored. Most of the items are conveyed in a sort of colourless officialese, very different from *Aulicus*'s smart style. It is largely a typical product of the bureaucratic machine, reassuring the faithful, calming the restless, and denouncing waverers and all who step out of line. The intention is not to inform and entertain, but to buttress a *status quo*. Indeed, its responses are as predictable, because automatic and inflexible, as those which the Cavaliers when excluded from power had found so laughable in their usurpers.[9]

Berkenhead, now Sir John, was as solemn and boring and restrictive in the sixties as in the forties he had been lively, audacious and subversive.

Berkenhead's achievement as editor of *Mercurius Aulicus* was then not due only to his authoritative backing and the excellence of his sources of intelligence. Above all it was earned by his mastery of a colloquial, witty prose, hard-hitting and direct. Again there is paradox here, for plain prose had hitherto been a Puritan ideal. The Laudian Heylyn was a reluctant and unsatisfactory editor of *Mercurius Aulicus* largely because he could not bring his style down to the level required. He and his biographers indeed conspired to hush up his connection with *Mercurius Aulicus*, Dr Thomas tells us.[10] Berkenhead perfected a prose which in its style and stylishness is closer to that of the Levellers on the radical wing of the Parliamentarians than to anything the King's side had hitherto produced. Satire had languished under the early Stuart censorship,[11] but it was reinvigorated by the civil war. Berkenhead's political commitment gave a new ruthlessness to his satire: personal attacks were in order in the new freedom. "Scandal-mongering as a national pastime" flourished under his predecessor as editor of *Mercurius Aulicus*, and reached a peak under Berkenhead.[12]

Dr Thomas's assessment of Berkenhead's achievement as a prose stylist is so just and so favourable that his condemnation of Berkenhead as a politician is the more weighty.

The purist intransigence of *Aulicus* manifests a temper (and that not confined to the Court) which drove the nation ever deeper into war with itself. For it was a temper that made a virtue—as the embattled often do—of inflexibility. *Aulicus*'s brand of insistence upon the enormities of influential Parliamentarians might have been calculated to produce the very thing it feared. It studiously, even brilliantly, avoided conceding to the foe even a misguided idealism and common human feeling. It is that sort of blindness, so damaging to human politics, that seems to distinguish the stance of men like Berkenhead and Digby from that of Clarendon and Falkland.

"All nobles and gentry" were for the King; the rest were "such cattle as were never thought fit to die by the sword".[13] For some three years *Mercurius Aulicus* "broadcast the message that change meant anarchy, and that dissent was sedition". It helped to create the stereotype caricature of the barbarian nonconformist fanatic as well as the stereotype of "the laughing Cavalier—a being compounded of heroic loyalty and devil-may-care wit—which has endured to the present day."[14] Dr Thomas suggests that *Mercurius Aulicus* (with or without the King's encouragement) did its best to sabotage the peace negotiations at Uxbridge at the beginning of 1645. And in general, from Berkenhead's habitual extremism "the reader could only conclude that his choice lay between supporting the Revolution and obtaining no reform at all".[15] *Mercurius Aulicus* thus contributed to promoting stubborn resistance among royalists and drove moderate Parliamentarians into the hands of Army extremists.

"*Aulicus* proved that talented men could profitably be employed in writing newsbooks; and out of that realisation grew a more direct relationship between the daily shifting pattern of events and the serious literary pursuits of cultivated men and women, so that literary traditions and techniques became more deeply involved in partisan debate". Through "the entry of men like Berkenhead into the often despised trade of journalism . . . popular writing gained a new distinction. At the same time they carried over into more sophisticated letters the lessons of clarity, directness and accessi-

bility."[16] So Dr Thomas ushers in his second theme. He reminds us
that Marchamont Nedham associated *Aulicus* with the culture of the
early Stuart court, with Inigo Jones and the masque, with "Cavalier"
drama, from Beaumont and Fletcher to Shirley.[17] It seemed self-
evident to Berkenhead that culture stood or fell with the monarchy:
"Never rebel was to arts a friend". Royalists have a divine right to
eloquence and wit: their opponents must be uncivilized foes to art
and learning. Dr Thomas illustrates this theme especially from *A
Letter from Mercurius Civicus to Mercurius Rusticus*, which he
plausibly attributes to Berkenhead.[18]

In 1647 Berkenhead was prominently associated with the
publication of Beaumont and Fletcher's *Comedies and Tragedies*. The
frontispiece carried nine lines of Latin verse by Berkenhead, and he
also contributed one of the commendatory poems. This publication
was not "simply a commercial or aesthetic venture: it was also a
morale-boosting gesture of defiance, a propagandist reassertion of
the Stuart ethic at a crucial moment in the fortunes of the Court".
Berkenhead described Beaumont and Fletcher's *The Faithful
Shepherdess* as too refined for "the bold heap." He contrasted
Shakespeare's "trunk-hose-wit", which suffered from writing too
much for the "mob".

The Cavaliers' collective sense of political and ethical order conditioned
their literary theory. It acted on the form as well as on the content of their
verse, by confirming their inclination towards the technical virtues of
Classical poetry. The growing security and self-sufficiency of the couplet,
apparent in Berkenhead's usage, reflects this mounting preoccupation with
moral orthodoxy and regularity. It naturally led Berkenhead not only to
criticize Shakespeare, but also to deplore "metaphysical" excesses and
cherish the memory of Ben Jonson. In short, Berkenhead's verses afford a
glimpse into the complex of pressures behind the aristocratic, neo-classical
fashions then coming to the fore. The desire for rule, uniformity and
"decorum" was not motivated merely by some arbitrary aesthetic theory: it
images the centralizing and institutionalizing tendencies of the aristocratic
elite, tendencies only fortified by the upheaval of 1646.

The publication of Cartwright's *Comedies, Tragi-Comedies with
Other Poems* (1651) was a similar gesture of defiance. Berkenhead's
commendatory verses emphasized that inferior wits scorn serious
verse as they do bishops and kings.[19]

Dr Thomas stresses the role of the small, closely-knit Cavalier
coteries during the interregnum, which bolstered the morale of their
members by a high classicism as well as by drinking songs and healths

to the King.[20] "In the midst of mounting confusion the making of
distinctions was felt to be more than ever an imperative function.
Discrimination and refinement were duties both to nature and to
art." The concern for propriety and decorum arose from the
situation in which the Cavaliers found themselves. "Comedy in the
late 1640s was inevitable, and profoundly necessary to the Cavaliers;
necessary, that is, if they were to adjust to changing circumstances
and survive in some way more than mere brute survival. They had to
sustain a sense of identity, a self-respect, and a belief in human society
as they understood it, in a hostile, unaccommodating, and
deteriorating environment." "The laughing Cavalier was . . . a man
adapting himself (sometimes desperately and hysterically) to his new
environment".[21] This seems to me a very interesting idea, worth
dwelling on.

The Cavaliers' insistence on including politics in their poetry marks their
refusal to acquiesce (at any level) in the orthodoxies prevailing against them;
and this was one means by which the received aristocratic culture of the
Court, which had once drifted dangerously into escapist fantasy, was
brought back into vivifying contact with reality—a reality which included
philistinism, ignorance, opposition and barbarity. The interregnum
stimulated the rationalization of poetic theory, the formulation of
general standards and the emergence of a corporate criticism.

This looks forward to the restoration far more than it looks back to
Beaumont and Fletcher and Charles I's court. Both Sprat and Dryden
quoted Berkenhead with approval.[22]

His "urbane common sense" and embattled classicism offered a
refuge for those aristocrats who felt their defeat to be profoundly
unnatural, the triumph of their vulgar enemies supremely absurd and
therefore ultimately ephemeral. "To the Cavaliers, the Rebel is the
type of low-born foolish man on the make, ambitious and avaricious,
and altogether distorted by the pressures of the expansionist and
divisive forces he embodies—forces often remarked on subsequently
as characteristic of modern capitalist society." "A deep sense of
coherence and continuity confronts the anarchic and disruptive",
and gives edge to Cavalier wit.[23]

Rebel egomania is presented as a denial of that sense of knowing oneself and
belonging to one's place in society which Royalists felt so strongly (and the
question of their motives for doing so are another matter of no immediate
relevance). Cavalier comedy, like Cavalier neo-classicism, is fundamentally a
preoccupation with being properly related to other members of a community

in which an ordered hierarchy of traditional *mores* and institutions can express and preserve shared values.[24]

Dr Thomas stresses Berkenhead's contribution to burlesque, so popular in the later seventeenth century as the heroic mode collapsed.[25]

The return of court and monarchy appeared to demonstrate the validity of Berkenhead's confidence in hierarchy, though Dr Thomas sapiently observes that the royalists' own propaganda helped to blind them to the imminence of the restoration in 1659–60. His analysis throws light on post-restoration classicism in England, perhaps on classicism in general. French influences, yes: Versailles was the realization of all that Charles I and Henrietta Maria had ever aspired to, all that Charles II's court could never reach. Yet the background to Versailles was the Fronde: fear of disorder and social upset underlies the classical insistence on order, decorum and the rules. "The Great Wit's great work is to refuse", Berkenhead said.[26] It was, Dr Thomas insists, not as odd as it seems at first sight that Berkenhead sat with Cowley, Dryden, Denham, Waller and Sprat on the Royal Society's committee to reform the English language. Otherwise Berkenhead's membership of the Royal Society illustrates Mr Skinner's argument that it was a gentleman's club rather than a group of dedicated professional scientists.[27] Berkenhead jeered at Petty, and seems to have agreed with his friend and correspondent Thomas Barlow that pursuit of scientific knowledge was "a Jesuit plot, designed to infect the universities with 'novel whimsies' and to divert students from 'the severer studies of the old philosophy and scholastic divinity'".[28]

Dr Thomas enlists our sympathy for the tough and indomitable fighter during the revolutionary decades; but it is not so easy to make Sir John attractive after the restoration when he and Roger L'Estrange were, in Marvell's words, "public tooth-drawers of the press".[29] Dr Thomas however makes some valid points about the group of Laudians who because of their intransigence, their steadfastness and their cohesion, appeared far more important in 1660 than they really were. Berkenhead got his knighthood, but he had learnt and forgotten nothing. He opposed Charles II's policy of religious toleration. He thought the abolition of pluralism would mean the destruction of learning and the Church of England. Not that he seems to have been a very religious man. "What he wanted throughout was submission to the political forms of the Anglican

Establishment."[30] He even criticized the government's reliance on forms of supply like the chimney tax, which, Berkenhead thought, put the state "at the mercy of Presbyterian-dominated business and financial interests". His career culminated in his rejection in 1679 as M.P. for the cathedral town of Salisbury, showing how utterly irrelevant Laudianism had become to the political problems of restoration England.[31] (Marchamont Nedham, the only journalist of comparable abilities to Berkenhead, was able to change sides more than once because he lacked Berkenhead's confining principles.)

There is much more of value in this book. Dr Thomas has newly attributed nine pamphlets, two newsbooks and two prefaces to Berkenhead. His appendices will be very useful to students of newsbooks in the interregnum. But the main significance of his book lies in the suggestiveness of his analysis of the origins and significance of royalist classicism. Dryden has a poise, a detachment, a power of sympathetic imagination to which Berkenhead could never attain, as well as an ability to serve the winning side which recalls Marchamont Nedham. Dryden had none of the intransigence, the determination to refuse and reject, which are characteristic of Berkenhead. But Dryden was a friend of Berkenhead's, quoted him with approval, and took over many of his views on the nature of poetry and of satire, his rejection of metaphysical poetry, his preference for the heroic couplet.[32] The direct line which Dr Thomas draws from Berkenhead and his circle to Dryden offers new insights into the nature of classicism in England.

NOTES

1. A review of P.W. Thomas, *Sir John Berkenhead, 1617–1679: a Royalist Career in Politics and Polemics* (Oxford U.P., 1969), in *Essays in Criticism*, XX (1970).
2. Thomas, *op. cit.*, p. 6.
3. *Ibid.*, p. 173.
4. *Ibid.*, pp. 42–3, 66, 76–8.
5. *Ibid.*, pp. 65–6, 57–61.
6. *Ibid.*, p. 56.
7. *Ibid.*, pp. 62, 91.
8. *Ibid.*, p. 57.
9. *Ibid.*, p. 215.
10. *Ibid.*, pp. 31–4.

11. See pp. 4, 34–5 above.
12. Thomas, *op. cit.*, pp. 103–4. Cf. pp. 81, 86 above.
13. *Ibid.*, pp. 76–7.
14. *Ibid.*, p. 98.
15. *Ibid.*, pp. 76–87.
16. *Ibid.*, pp. 98, 107.
17. Dr Thomas discusses this court culture at greater length in "Two Cultures? Court and Country under Charles I", in *The Origins of the English Civil War* (ed. C. Russell, 1973), pp. 168–93.
18. Thomas, *Berkenhead*, pp. 100–3, 120–1.
19. *Ibid.*, pp. 134–6, 177.
20. *Ibid.*, p. 143.
21. *Ibid.*, pp. 167–70.
22. *Ibid.*, pp. 178–9.
23. Samuel Butler was to make similar assumptions. See pp. 286–91 below.
24. *Ibid.*, pp. 166–7, 208–9.
25. See p. 324 below.
26. Thomas, *Berkenhead*, p. 157.
27. Quentin Skinner, "Thomas Hobbes and the Nature of the Early Royal Society", *The Historical Journal*, XII (1969), pp. 217–39.
28. Thomas, *Berkenhead*, pp. 233–4. Henry Stubbe had similar theories about the Royal Society. See p. 285 below.
29. Thomas, *Berkenhead*, p. 211.
30. *Ibid.*, pp. 219–21, 231.
31. *Ibid.*, pp. 222, 237.
32. *Ibid.*, pp. 134–5, 178.

5. *Daniel Defoe (1660–1731) and* Robinson Crusoe[1]

Those who, like myself, first encountered *Robinson Crusoe* in an abridged edition are surprised when they read the original. It seems a very long time before we get to the point. An account of the hero's early life occupies the first fifty or so pages, one-seventh of Part I, before he is shipwrecked on his island. The original, moreover, looks much more like a protestant homily or moral fable—a "parable" as the Preface to Part II describes it[2]—than the abridgments which made it such a popular children's story.

Robinson Crusoe is very carefully placed socially. His father was a German immigrant who made good as a merchant at Hull, and then retired to the more genteel cathedral city of York, where Robinson was born. His elder brother joined the English army and got killed. Robinson's father had designed him for the law: but the son's head "began to be filled very early with rambling thoughts". His father lectured him solemnly on the advantages of "the middle state", "not exposed to the miseries and hardships, the labour and sufferings of the mechanic part of mankind, and not embarrassed with the pride, luxury, ambition and envy of the upper part of mankind".[3] Robinson Crusoe's later misfortunes can be seen as a series of providential judgments on him for his disobedience and neglect of his proper calling. This, his "original sin"[4], led to punishment and repentance of his "rash and immoderate desire of rising faster than the nature of the thing admitted".[5] Crusoe ultimately came to accept that greater happiness was to be found in contentment with "the state wherein God and nature had placed me".[6] Despite repeated backslidings,[7] repentance led to his rescue and to great worldly success.

Robinson Crusoe seems an exemplar of the protestant and bourgeois virtues. On the island his survival and ultimate prosperity were earned by hard work and self-discipline, asceticism and refusal to waste time.[8] He observed the Sabbath as a non-working day—though rather intermittently.[9] He came to the habit of asking God's blessing on his food.[10] He "could not abide the thought" of

nakedness, "though I was all alone". One of his first actions after
rescuing Friday was to give him a pair of linen drawers.[11] Soon after
landing on the island Crusoe drew up a balance sheet of good and evil,
profit and loss, as Defoe's *Complete English Tradesman* was
instructed to do.[12] In the best Puritan tradition Robinson Crusoe
kept a diary, which was intended at least in part as a spiritual journal
and balance sheet—as Pepys's Diary was when he started it. When
Crusoe had rescued the English captain from death at the hands of
the mutineers, he at once bargained for a lift back to England
"passage-free".[13]

So traditional protestantism is accompanied by prudential business
morality: Max Weber's "spirit of capitalism". Crusoe's attitude
towards predestination and Providence seems to fit into this pattern.
He recognizes that God uses our own actions to punish us for our
sins. "A secret overruling decree . . . hurries us on to be the
instruments of our own destruction". Alternatively, what appears to
be a calamity will sometimes work out to our advantage.[14] Providence
expresses itself for Crusoe in "secret hints, or pressings of my mind,
to doing or not doing anything that presented". He "never failed to
obey" such secret dictates, though he could not account for them.[15]

If we read *Robinson Crusoe* in this light a turning point occurs
when the hero has completed his second year on the island. He began
to realise that, by God's grace, he could find a Paradise within him,
happier far, than "the wicked, cursed, abominable life I led all the past
part of my days".[16] But apparently the moral theme, if Defoe
originally intended it, now no longer satisfied him. As Robinson
Crusoe "was going to give thanks to God for bringing me to this
place, . . . something shocked my mind at that thought . . . 'How
canst thou be such a hypocrite', said I, even audibly, 'to pretend to
be thankful for a condition which, however thou mayst endeavour to
be contented with, thou wouldst rather pray heartily to be
delivered from?'"[17]

So the moral theme is somewhat intermittent. Perhaps Defoe, like
his readers, tends to get so interested in Robinson Crusoe's here and
now that he forgets the longer perspectives, or gets new ones? Part II
perhaps attempts to restore the moral balance, and this may be one
reason for its being so much less enthralling than Part I. But Part II
was presumably written as an afterthought, in response to the success
of the original novel. Its account of Crusoe's return to his island
contains many points of interest; but after that it turns into a

conventional travel-adventure story, a narrative trot round the
world. It lacks the intense imaginative concentration of Part I. On
the island Crusoe is essentially on the defensive, trying to rescue
himself from real or imagined enemies, like the hero of Kafka's *The
Burrow*. His battles with the Indians have this object. In Part II,
where the western merchants are continually fighting against
Africans and Asiatics, they have no justification; the endless series
of engagements and the victories of superior military technology
are in consequence less gripping and ultimately become boring.

Karl Marx used Robinson Crusoe on his island to illustrate the
differences between production for use and production for exchange,
between use value and exchange value. Crusoe became crucial to
arguments about division of labour, individualism and primitive
accumulation.[18] No doubt in reaction against this approach, there
has been in the last twenty years a spate of attempts to read *Robinson
Crusoe* as a systematic and consistent allegory, religious or biographical.[19] These attempts seem to me strained. Defoe was happily
innocent of the demand that twentieth-century critics make for
"coherent and formally sophisticated narrative".[20] He certainly used
the techniques of allegory from time to time, and in his *Serious
Reflections during the Life and Surprising Adventures of Robinson
Crusoe* (1720) he hinted at all sorts of allegorical intentions. But the
disagreements of the commentators show how difficult it is to
interpret the novel as a deliberate allegory; and it seems to me very
unlikely that Defoe's (or Crusoe's) remarks in *Serious Reflections*
were part of his original plan. His main object in writing this third
part (apart presumably from making a little money) was to defend
himself against the charge of composing a mere foolish romance,
"fiction and lies".[21]

I have the advantage of coming to Defoe from the seventeenth
century. I am not as surprised as modern literary critics to find that a
man brought up to be a nonconformist minister should know a good
deal of Calvinist theology. On the other hand, approaching from the
seventeenth century, I do not necessarily expect Defoe to be
consistent in his thinking. He learnt his theology not from a few
books but from a lifetime's immersion in a cultural environment of
disintegrating Puritanism. Many of us today would have difficulty in
making a coherent philosophy out of the bits of Marx and Freud and
Einstein which we pick up in books, in bars and from the box.

So we need not perhaps be too upset by Defoe's ambiguities; but they call for investigation. Is *Robinson Crusoe* a Puritan moral story or not? Is internal grace all that matters? Must we see the conversion of Friday as "a crucial feature of Crusoe's regeneration"?[22] How important are the material conveniences of civilization? The Russian aristocrat in the Second Part, who refused Crusoe's offer of a chance to escape from exile because he might succumb to the temptations of life in the civilized world, could perhaps be seen as a foil to Robinson Crusoe's denunciation of himself as a hypocrite for thanking God for grace on a desert island. But the aristocrat did not miss the chance of sending his son to face the dangers of the great world. Which side is Defoe on?

Robinson Crusoe is far from being a protestant bigot. He works out his own version of natural religion,[23] and he finds that Friday easily comprehends the truths of Christianity when they are explained to him.[24] Friday has the "simple unfeigned honesty" as well as the physique of the noble savage.[25] Will Atkins, one of the Englishmen whom Robinson Crusoe found on his return to his island, married a pagan woman: her simple but shrewd questioning forced him to think a great deal more seriously about the Christianity which he formally accepted.[26] Crusoe expected more mercy from "the savages, who were man-eaters" than from the monopolists of the East India Company.[27]

Crusoe is a citizen of the world. The point is made from the beginning of the novel. This quintessential Englishman was the son of an immigrant—not even of a Dutch or Flemish immigrant, like William III, but of a German immigrant, like George I—and indeed from Bremen, surrounded by Hanoverian territory.[28] Defoe was certainly making a point here. In *The True-Born Englishman* he had mocked those who wished to defend English racial purity against alien immigrants:-

> We have been Europe's sink, the jakes where she
> Voids all her offal outcast progeny.

He was also making a point when he depicted the Spanish settlers of Crusoe's island as far more tolerant and far more civilized in their relations with the natives than the English castaways.[29]

As Defoe's contemporary critic, Charles Gildon, pointed out, Robinson Crusoe appears to make little of the distinction between protestant and catholic. In Brazil he conformed to the Roman church and it was a second thought that persuaded him to sell his Brazilian plantation rather than resume his residence there, as had been his first intention.[30] Crusoe as sovereign of his island "allowed liberty of conscience throughout my dominions", to protestants, papists and pagans.[31] It was a French Catholic priest, curiously, who insisted on the English settlers marrying the Indian women with whom they were living, and on the latter being baptized.[32] Such ceremonies seem to mean little to Crusoe: he never thought of baptizing Friday, though the latter came "to be such a Christian as I have known few equal to him in my life".[33] Crusoe's attempt to honour the sabbath by notching sticks so that he would always know which day of the week it was came to nothing: he soon lost count. Here again this superfluous fact must be making some sort of point. Radical protestants like Milton did not think much of observing particular times and seasons, or of ceremonies: though they would have argued that a layman was enough of a priest to baptize if the occasion arose.

What Crusoe does feel strongly about is priestcraft, whether among pagans, papists or protestants.[34] 'Disputes . . . about . . . niceties in doctrines or schemes of church-government . . . were all perfectly useless to us, as, for aught I can yet see, they have been to all the rest in the world".[35] Crusoe subjects the existence of the devil to pretty rational criticism.[36] It is surely not in complete innocence that Defoe shows Crusoe floored by Friday's question why God allowed the devil to exist. "At first I could not tell what to say, so I pretended not to hear him;" and when this failed to work he changed the subject. "It was a testimony to me, how the mere notions of nature, though they will guide reasonable creatures to the knowledge of a God, and of a worship due to the supreme being of God as the consequence of our nature; yet nothing but divine revelation can form the knowledge of Jesus Christ".[37]

We could read that as covert deism, or as Crusoe's (or even Defoe's) naiveté. But Defoe was certainly not naive in his theology. His father, like John Milton's, had intended him for the ministry. Daniel had been well drilled at the dissenting academy of Newington Green; he had studied Baxter carefully. He was theologically sophisticated enough to spot the anti-Trinitarianism in *Paradise Lost* which most critics failed to notice for another 200 years, and which some still obstinately deny. Evidence of Milton's unsoundness on the Trinity has been in print only since 1825, but Defoe may well have had access to oral traditions. He certainly read Milton with very great care and attention,[38] and admired him long before Addison taught readers of *The Spectator* that Milton was a great poet. Defoe was fourteen when Milton died.

In many ways Defoe is more a man of the Enlightenment than a traditional protestant; Professor Watt long ago pointed out that Defoe's is a modified Puritanism, modified in the direction of secularism. The ideas are the same as those of early and mid seventeenth-century Puritans, but they are held with less intensity.[39] They are no longer the ideas of a beleaguered garrison or shock troops: triumphant over adversity, Puritanism succumbed after success. *Robinson Crusoe* lends support to the point made by Weber's critics, that in arguing that "the protestant ethic" prepared for the development of capitalism he drew too much of his evidence from late seventeenth- and even eighteenth-century Puritanism. Weber's concern was to refute Marx—or perhaps rather the crude Marxists of his day who asserted the priority of the economic base over the ideological superstructure in a way that Marx was careful never to do. Weber did not claim to have produced a "religious" first cause in place of an "economic" one. But he did tend to assume that "protestantism", "Calvinism", were eternal categories. Tawney and many after him pointed out that by the late seventeenth century, Puritanism was influenced by capitalism more than it influenced it. Protestantism, Tawney thought—and I agree—, developed with and in consequence of the rise of capitalism rather than vice versa. Defoe—and Robinson Crusoe—were products of established capitalist society.

If we stress the moral purpose of *Robinson Crusoe* it could be read as a tract in favour of religious toleration, on the familiar theme of its usefulness to trade. But now this is argued not (as it was by seventeenth-century economists) because toleration would attract religious refugee merchants and craftsmen to England but on grounds of the pointlessness of persecution in a world in which international trade overrode religious divisions. Thus Crusoe on going to Brazil automatically conformed to popery, though he does not tell us this until later, as an ostensibly penitent afterthought. A Brazilian monastery looked after his financial interests in his absence as carefully as did the protestant widow in London. His conformity to popery seems to have paid dividends, handsomely; but that makes the point a different way: to be successful in business one must not have exclusive religious prejudices. The greatest profits were to be made by trading with papists, at the price of some surrender of conviction. As *Robinson Crusoe* shows, the world of the Caribbean, with its frequent shipwrecks and sea rescues, led to a mix-up of nationalities and creeds in which religious intolerance would have been extremely inconvenient, to say the least. Once the Spanish claim to an absolute monopoly of the whole area could no longer be enforced, religious toleration and free access to trade went together. One of the greatest solvents of religious intolerance was the slave trade: Catholic planters wanted the slaves which protestant English and Dutch traders supplied. Defoe gives a stirring speech in favour of religious toleration to the French Roman Catholic priest which made Crusoe say that if "all the members of his church" had "the like moderation, they would soon be all protestants".[40] In face of pagan savages, religious divisions between Christians seemed increasingly silly; far more serious things united the merchants of western Christendom than divided them.

There had indeed always been something paradoxical about anti-Catholicism in England. Those gentlemen who loudly denounced popery in the House of Commons and called for the enforcement of the laws against recusants themselves lived on friendly terms with their Catholic neighbours, intermarried and protected their relations. Even Milton, fiercely anti-papist, had cordial personal relations with a cardinal when he was in Rome, protected Edmund Spenser's papist grandson and was "intimately acquainted" with the papist William Joyner after the restoration. Anti-Catholicism was often a way of attacking absolutism. It became active, so long as the Stuarts were on the throne, whenever the international power of Spain or France seemed to threaten England's security. That is why it was minimal in the 1650s and again after 1688, and especially after the Act of Settlement finally excluded Catholics from succeeding to the English throne. Once the Hanoverian succession was secure, the easy-going tolerance which in practice existed in the closed society of the county community could without danger be extended to the whole international trading community.

From Marx onwards much has been written about Defoe as economist, as a precursor of Adam Smith. The phrase "the wealth of nations" occurs at least thirty-three times in Defoe's writings, it has been calculated.[41] Robinson Crusoe attacked the monopoly of the East India Company, which could condemn a man unheard once he had been wrongfully accused of piracy. His accusers were both his judges, from whose arbitrary sentence there was no appeal, and his executioners. This monopoly created the same insecurity for lawful traders as did "savages".[42]

More important perhaps is the clarity of some of Defoe's concepts. "All that I could make use of, was all that was valuable", Crusoe observed. "I suffered no more corn to grow, because I did not want it" [i.e. need it]; and he contrasted the world to which he returned, in which "the men of labour spent their strength in daily strugglings to maintain the vital strength they laboured with, . . . living but to work and working but to live" to produce wealth which the rich then squandered "in vile excesses or empty pleasures". On the island Crusoe's large stock of money and bullion was useless. "I would have given it all for three or four pairs of English shoes and stockings".[43] Defoe had learnt a lot from Locke (or his predecessors) about the labour theory of value;[44] and from Harrington (and the world around him) about the influence of economics on politics. ("The revolution of trade brought a revolution in the very nature of things. . . . Now we see the nobility and the ancient gentry have almost everywhere sold their estates and the commonalty and tradesmen have bought them: so that now the gentry are richer than the nobility, and the tradesmen are richer than them all").[45]

Notwithstanding his own unsuccessful commercial practice, Defoe wrote popular and successful books like *The Complete English Tradesman*. "Trade", he wrote here, "must not be entered into as a thing of light concern; it is called business very properly, for it is a business for life; . . . nothing but what are to be called the necessary duties of life are to intervene, and even these are to be limited, so as not to be prejudicial to business". A man must not "be so intent upon religious duties as to neglect the proper times and seasons of business". Defoe discusses cases of conscience such as a pious shopkeeper might encounter.[46] He was in favour of high wages and freer trade, believing that England's industrial superiority would enable her by these means to gain the advantage over all other nations.[47]

In many ways *Robinson Crusoe*, a book about life on a desert island, is a glorification of west European technology. It is thanks to the tools and commodities which Crusoe salvages from the wreck that he is able not only to survive but to prosper, drawing on the heritage of centuries of civilization.[48] But in the process he has to master many new techniques; division of labour and diversity of acquired skills, he points out, would have infinitely lightened this labour. "What might be a little to be done with help and tools was a vast labour and required a prodigious time to do alone and by hand".[49] "I believe few people have thought much upon . . . the strange multitude of little things necessary in the providing, producing, curing, dressing and finishing this one article of bread".[50] Just as man in Hobbes's state of nature brings with him many of the assumptions of bourgeois society,[51] so Robinson Crusoe has on his island much of the capital equipment and more of the mental furniture of an eighteenth-century English bourgeois. The very pointed criticisms of China in Parts II and III, though no doubt motivated by what Defoe regarded as excessive fashionable adulation of Chinese art and culture, derive ultimately from a contempt for China's technological and therefore military inferiority to western Europe.[52]

From this point of view *Robinson Crusoe* could be read, as James Joyce read it, as a tract in favour of west European imperialism in its early eighteenth-century phase. Crusoe takes possession of the island as his property.[53] He brings to it capital and technical skills, but until Friday appears he lacks labour power to develop these to the best advantage. Part II describes the much more effective solution developed by Crusoe's successors on the island. Indians are reduced, first by military defeat, then by starvation, to accept the position either of subordinate labourers or of smallholders producing under supervision. Crusoe contrasts this brutal behaviour with his own treatment of Friday, whom he had "instructed . . . in the rational principles of life". His successors failed in "civilizing and reducing them by kind usage and affectionate arguings", and so "never had them to assist them and fight for them as I had my man Friday".[54] Two approaches to colonizing, each with its advantages, each with its disadvantages.

Commentators on the later Defoe do not perhaps reflect sufficiently on his earlier radicalism. He joined Monmouth's rebellion in 1685, the last episode of the democratic English Revolution: like Milton twenty-five years earlier, he was lucky to escape a traitor's death. Defoe was a staunch supporter of the Revolution of 1688 and of William III. His later career shows no political consistency, but whose does at that period? The disappointment of radical Whigs with the Revolution settlement was intense. Some, like Wildman, continued to plot ineffectually against the régime;[55] others, like Ferguson, turned Jacobite. Defoe's *Legion's Memorial* (1701) was very radical in its appeal to the people against

Parliament, and *The Shortest Way with the Dissenters* (1702) got him into serious trouble. Here he put forward, ironically, what read like an extreme Tory position of intolerance: dissenters should be banished, their preachers hanged. The pamphlet outraged both Whigs and Tories, and Defoe was sentenced to the pillory.

He seems henceforth to have decided—unlike Milton after 1660—that there was no hope of a radical solution for England in the foreseeable future. "I have seen the bottom of all parties", he wrote in words which recall Sir Lewis Namier's analysis of the 1760s; "the bottom of all their pretences, and the bottom of their sincerity, and as the Preacher said that all was vanity and vexation of spirit, so I say of these: all is a mere show, outside, and abominable hypocrisy, of every party, in every age, under every government, in every turn of government; when they are OUT to get IN, to prevent being OUT; every sect, every party, and almost every person that we have an account of, have, for ought I see, been guilty, more or less, of the general charge, viz. that their interest governs their principle".[56]

So—protesting a little too much—he followed the universal practice and sold his pen to Harley, a man of the centre. But Defoe retained many of the principles—or prejudices—of his younger days. In *The Poor Man's Plea* (1698) "we of the plebeii" denounced the class bias of the laws promoted by the voluntary societies for the reformation of manners. "The man with a gold ring and gay clothes may swear before the justice or at the justice; may reel home through the open streets and no man take any notice of him; but if a poor man gets drunk or swears an oath, he must to the stocks without remedy".[57] Particularly interesting is Defoe's changing attitude towards "the mob". In *Legion's Memorial* he warned Parliament "you are not above the people's resentments". When he was put in the pillory for *The Shortest Way with the Dissenters* he, like Lilburne two generations earlier, was hailed as a martyr by the populace. But a more ambivalent attitude emerges in the *Hymn to the Mob* of 1708. Luther, Calvin, Knox and Cranmer were sons of the mob.

> Our mobs the reformation still pursue
> And seldom have been in the wrong till now.

For now church and king mobs rabble dissenters. The mob, Defoe thinks, has lost its creative power; its main objects have been secured with the victory of Parliamentary government over absolutism, and it has now become fickle, purposeless, destructive; its agitations can serve only the purposes of the Jacobites. Defoe prefers the prejudices of a corrupt Parliament to those of the even more purchasable London populace, soon to be bawling for Sacheverell and against the Revolution of 1688. "These new dictators of the streets" must be controlled, "and if persuasion won't the gallows will".[58] In 1724 he published *The Great Law of Subordination*, dealing with the insufferable behaviour of servants.

With some exaggeration we could see Defoe the radical as an isolated survivor: his ship had foundered, and if any of his comrades had survived he had lost contact with them. He had to make do as best he could with what he could salvage from the wreckage. His personal isolation was partly his own fault: but there were social reasons for the political impotence of ex-radicals. The settlement of 1688 had established the rule of a corrupt Parliament, representing the men of property, over a corrupt society: this is the age of *The Beggars' Opera, Gulliver's Travels, Jonathan Wild*, and Edward Thompson's *Whigs and Hunters*. Yet what alternative was there? Given the illiteracy of the majority of the population, their dependence for political ideas on landlords, employers, parsons, there was no possibility of instituting real democracy. Even if manhood suffrage could by some miracle have been introduced, it would have been more likely to lead to a restoration of the Stuarts than to a just and equal society. Maintenance of the revolution settlement of 1688 and of the Hanoverian succession of 1714, Defoe thought, was necessary to prevent a restoration of absolutism and clerical tyranny: only so could an England be preserved in which men of the middling sort go about their business freely. The gentry were an incubus in this society, as gentlemen officers were a nuisance to tarpaulins on board ship;[59] but any possible alternative to gentry rule would be something worse.

It is surely not without irony that the only one of Defoe's later books in which truly radical ideas appear is *A General History of the Robberies and Murders Of the most notorious Pyrates*, published five years after *Robinson Crusoe*. In this there are echoes of Milton and Winstanley as well as of Locke and contemporary deists. The pirates express class-consciousness, anti-clericalism, democratic principles; they oppose the slave trade and liberate slaves.[60] Defoe's object was no doubt to satirize contemporary society; but he seems to get carried away by enthusiasm for the pirates as "the scourge of tyrants and avarice, and the brave assertors of liberty".[61] This subject has since been suggestively explored by Marcus Rediker.[62]

So Defoe found himself a radical in a society in which there was no alternative to the corrupt rule of a gentry Parliament; in which the urgencies of revolutionary Puritanism had been watered down to accommodate life in a sinful commercial world. To what purposes was he to devote his "plebeian vitality"?[63] The novels seem to have been his answer—far from escapist, but retreating from the political life in which he had been ensnared hitherto. But I suspect that in choosing a different medium of communication he no more abandoned his desire to preach than Milton did after he had been "church-outed by the prelates". "Preaching of sermons is speaking to a few of mankind", Defoe observed; "printing of books is talking to the whole world".[64] It is one of the marvels of the new technology. In *Robinson Crusoe* Defoe did indeed talk to the whole world, even if what he said was often highly ambiguous.

So where are we? Our first problem is to differentiate Defoe from Robinson Crusoe. Defoe purports to be only the editor, not the author, of *Robinson Crusoe*, as of *Moll Flanders* and *Roxana*. Commentators on *Paradise Lost* have recently distinguished between John Milton and the narrator of the epic. Whether or not they are right to do so, we should certainly wrong Defoe if we attributed all Crusoe's naivetés to him. I have already suggested one or two examples. Crusoe's attitude towards slavery, cannibalism and racialism is shot through with ambiguities. The contrast between Crusoe's treatment of Friday and his successors' far more brutal attitude towards the Indians can hardly be accidental. Crusoe believes in his civilizing mission, in the white man's burden. He establishes excellent relations with Friday and his father. So do the Spaniards who succeed him on the island. It is the English castaways who ill-treat the natives. Crusoe, in alliance with the Spaniards, does much to improve the lot of the conquered Indians on his return to the island. On his subsequent journey, he is appalled by "the massacre of Madagascar", when western military superiority is used to wipe out a town and its inhabitants in revenge for the killing of an Englishman who had attempted to violate a native girl.[65] The superior European technology of which Defoe so heartily approved could put power into the hands of drunken brutes: Christianity, whose expansion seemed to him so desirable, turned out to be no less double-edged. It could civilize the natives: it could also, Crusoe learnt, be a means of instilling labour discipline, to the profit of those who introduced it.

It is to Crusoe's (and Defoe's) credit that he sees and clearly describes the two sides of western colonization, its brutal exploitation and tyranny as well as its "civilizing" role. It is, after all, the age of the South Sea Bubble: never had English merchants and speculators got rich so quickly on plunder of the rest of the world.[66] On Crusoe's initial trading voyage to West Africa he made profits of 700%.[67] He brought back some gains from the island when he returned to Europe; but his really vast wealth came from his rentier share of a slave plantation in Brazil, managed for him during his absence in part by a Brazilian monastery. Crusoe saw nothing of the no doubt brutal methods by which his profits were made: his readers may be equally inattentive.

What was Crusoe's attitude towards slavery? Before his island voyage he had sold "my boy Xury", who had helped him to escape from slavery in Salee. Crusoe was "very loath to sell the poor boy's liberty, who had assisted me so faithfully in procuring my own", and agreed only after the purchaser had promised to set Xury free in ten years' time if he turned Christian, and after Xury himself had accepted the deal.[68] This contrasts very markedly with the way in which Friday was treated, culminating in an honourable burial service when he died at sea. But Crusoe bought a slave in his Brazilian plantation, and had no scruple about participating in a voyage to bring slaves from West Africa to Brazil.[69] He afterwards expressed disapproval of this, but not because of any objection to the trade; rather he should have bought slaves "from those whose business it was to fetch them".[70] The first word he taught Friday was "Master".[71] The idle Englishmen who succeeded him on the island planned a slaving raid "so as to make them do the laborious part of the work for them". Crusoe deplored their idleness, but thought this particular scheme "not so preposterous".[72] It seemed impossible to teach disciplined labour to the Indians *en masse* without coercion.[73]

So clearly Crusoe did not disapprove of slavery as an institution. His total horror of the practice of cannibalism at first made him give God thanks that "I was distinguished from such dreadful creatures as these".[74] He for long planned to "destroy some of these monsters in their cruel bloody entertainment".[75] But on maturer reflection he realised that "these people do not commit this as a crime; it is not against their own consciences reproving or their light reproaching them", and consequently that he had no authority "to be judge or executioner upon these men as criminals". "How do I know what God himself judges in this particular case?", since God has chosen to leave them without the benefit of Christian teaching. To attack them unprovoked "would justify the conduct of the Spaniards, in all their barbarities practised in America, where they destroyed millions of these people who . . . were yet as to the Spaniards very innocent people". "The rooting them out of the country is spoken of with the utmost abhorrence and detestation, even by the Spaniards them-selves at this time".[76] So Crusoe abandoned his idea of punishing the Indians and limited his plans to capturing "two or three savages . . . so as to make them entirely slaves to me, to do whatever I should direct them".[77]

Here Defoe is participating in a most interesting manner in a discussion which had been going on for some time. The conquest and subjugation of pagan savages had been justified because of uncivilized practices like cannibalism; Crusoe's reflex accepted this. But on further consideration he rejected the argument that people should be punished for actions which to them seemed natural.[78] This under-mined much of the theory on which the initial conquest and subjugation of American Indians—and of the Irish[79]—had been justified. Defoe underlined the point by gratuitously suggesting more than once that starving Europeans might justifiably resort to cannibalism, though perhaps they should not "crave a blessing on that meat".[80]

Crusoe seems however to have taken for granted the cultural inferiority of American Indians, their child-like relationship to the superior Europeans whom they must call Master. But within these limits he lived happily side by side with Friday and got great satisfaction out of teaching him English, western techniques and the rudiments of Christianity. He deplored the provocatively bellicose racialism of his English successors on the island and atrocities like the massacre of Madagascar, which he describes with full frankness. "I thought it was a sad life, when we must be always obliged to be killing our fellow-creatures to preserve ourselves".[81] Fine sentiments; but how are they reconciled with slavery as an institution, and with European occupation of America?

Some of these ambiguities, as I have suggested, were no doubt the product of the historical situation in which Defoe wrote; he may well have been personally unconscious of them.[82] On slavery he con-tradicted himself as well as contradicting Robinson Crusoe. In *The*

Reformation of Manners (1702) he had attacked those who "barter baubles for the souls of men", and in 1724 his Captain Misson was to say that "trading for those of our own species" was unchristian.[83] But elsewhere Defoe accepted the slave trade as "the most useful and most profitable trade . . . of any part of the general commerce of the nation", asking only that slaves should not be more harshly treated than economically necessary.[84]

Defoe's starting point may have been that "the wise creator has most evidently shown to us that he designed the world for commerce".[85] In 1719, the year of *Robinson Crusoe*, he published *A Historical Account of the Voyages and Adventures of Sir Walter Raleigh*, advocating colonization of the Orinoco area in which Crusoe's island was situated;[86] and in *Serious Reflections* Crusoe suggested forcible subjection of "the barbarous and idolatrous nations of the world". This would be something very different from the "impious and unchristian" practice of forcing Christians to conform to some version of the Christian religion other than their own. But after outlining a detailed scheme for conquering and christianizing Japan, Crusoe gives the arguments for and against and leaves the question open.[87]

Perhaps Defoe was himself undecided. Slavery is both evil in itself and necessary to English commercial prosperity and greatness. European conquest did add to the wealth of the world by forcing "savages" to labour, either as slaves or in conditions of vile exploitation. We can see the consequences. Defoe saw some of them—it is difficult to say quite how many. But at the date at which he wrote some optimism was still just possible, however fallacious it turned out to be. The most revealing moment perhaps comes in Part II when Crusoe is appalled but impotent at the massacre of Madagascar and can merely dissociate himself from it. It is one of the few moments of his career when he did not claim full responsibility for what was happening. Exactly what Defoe intended to convey here is anybody's guess.

So though Defoe and Crusoe have much in common, we may suspect that Defoe was more aware of the ambiguities and contradictions in Crusoe's attitudes than commentators have always allowed. Take for instance Friday's hope that Crusoe will go to his country and "teach wild mans to be good, sober, tame mans". This was, Crusoe tells us "a thing which . . . I had not the least thought, or intention, or desire of undertaking".[88] It is a palpable hit at the reluctance of English protestants to undertake missionary work among native peoples, though this had often figured largely in seventeenth-century prospectuses of trading companies. The lack of interest in proselytizing in Defoe's time is indeed astonishing when we contrast it with the fervour of late nineteenth-century missionary movements. Since the Indians could not be blamed for their cultural inferiority (which all eighteenth-century observers took for granted) it would seem obvious that teaching them at least the rudiments of Christianity should have been the duty of Englishmen reducing them to labour. But then they might have been less docile labourers. The Society for the Propagation of the Gospel itself owned plantations in the West Indies and would not allow Christianity to be taught to their slaves lest they got ideas above their station. I fear that Calvinism (and that racialist book, the Old Testament) bears a large responsibility here. Even Milton thought that the "heavy curse" that they should be "servant of servants" had been laid on the whole "vicious race" of the descendants of Ham (*Paradise Lost*, XII, 101–5).

It was not a protestant Englishman but the French Roman Catholic priest who concerned himself with conversion. "As for me", Robinson Crusoe admitted, "I had not so much entertained a thought of this in my heart before, and I believe I should not have thought of it; for I looked upon these savages as slaves, and people whom, had we any work for them to do, we would have used as such, or would have been glad to have transported to any other part of the world".[89] Defoe is clearly distancing himself from Crusoe here, and is making two points. First, that the Indians were regarded as chattels rather than as people. This is consistent with the fact that Crusoe swept Friday away with him to Europe, without consulting him, though it meant that Friday's father was left in the lurch and in complete ignorance of his son's fate. Secondly, that conversion seems superfluous if not a little silly. Crusoe was scathing in his criticism of the mass "conversion, as they call it, of the Chinese to Christianity" by Catholics.[90] It was the statistical return that mattered, Defoe implies, not the welfare of individual souls. The priest who spoke so eloquently about converting the Indians also pledged himself to stay behind on the island to serve them. But Robinson Crusoe talked him out of this idea: he left in fact by the next boat. The irony can hardly have been unintentional on Defoe's part. Robinson Crusoe slowly, on the basis of experience, came to see that Christianity could be useful for labour discipline.[91] If my analysis is right, Defoe is once again having it both ways.

I contrasted Crusoe's sale into slavery of Xury and his acceptance of Friday as a companion, albeit one of inferior status. In the loneliness of his Kafka-like burrow, where he was terrified of his own kind no less than of wild animals, Crusoe longed for human companionship and converse. Friday was the answer to this longing: he could never be a mere chattel. Friday is Crusoe's (and Defoe's?) answer to racialism and the exploitation of man by man. He is the first Uncle Tom. The whole episode idealizes the historical role of colonialism as a system which imposes labour discipline in the interests of exploitation.

Defoe then is not just glorifying trade, colonization and the spread of the technological achievements of capitalism. There is an element of this, but it is so involved in contradictions and complexities that we can never be quite sure what Defoe's own position is. Nor is he just writing a Puritan tract. Crusoe wavered in his emphasis on divine Providence. One moment it appeared that "God had miraculously caused this grain to grow" to feed him; but his "religious thankfulness to God's providence" abated when a natural explanation was found.[92] Crusoe even queries the justice of God's Providence at the crucial point we have just been considering, in hiding knowledge necessary to salvation "from so many millions of souls" who might well "make a much better use of it than we did".[93] And if we look at the story rather than at what Crusoe tells us, we notice that "the mad rambling boy, as he calls himself", is not punished but extremely generously rewarded after all his journeyings. It is even doubtful if he ever very consistently repents—at least the point is not made as clear as it should have been in a moral tract—but he ends up very much better off than he would have been if he had followed his father's wishes.[94]

Crusoe's "strong impulses" derive from the same Puritan tradition as the "rousing motions" which led Milton's Samson to slaughter the Philistine aristocracy and priests. Some twentieth-century commentators find it difficult to accept that Milton regarded the English aristocracy and priests as enemies of God whom it was his religious duty to hate, with whom he was at war as Samson was at war with their Philistine equivalents. They argue that we must differentiate sharply between Milton and Samson. Since Milton was writing a play this is of course arguable; if Defoe had written *Samson Agonistes*, I should be convinced by the argument. But *Robinson Crusoe* is half a century later than *Samson Agonistes*. Defoe no longer hoped for the victory of God's cause on earth in the sense that Milton did. Second causes now explained many things that used to be attributed to Providence. One at least of Crusoe's "providences" appears to have been merely a coincidence.[95] The sense of sin has lost its power over those who talk about it. Crusoe keeps forgetting whether he really has repented or not, just as he forgets to notch up the Sabbath.

So I think we should keep open minds about the extent to which Defoe was conscious of the contradictions in *Robinson Crusoe*: they may have been his way of conveying a message. Professor Watt is no doubt right to warn us that often we see exquisite irony in Defoe only because our assumptions have changed: Defoe puts sentiments into his characters' mouths which strike us as deliciously and artfully naive but which Defoe intended to edify us.[96] History has perhaps been kind to him. But whenever we are too confidently taking Defoe at Crusoe's or Moll Flanders's face value, we must recall that the author of *The Shortest Way with the Dissenters* did not always make his points in the most direct and obvious way, especially when the points were unpopular or risky.

Arnold Kettle speaks of "two sorts of realism":

On the one hand there is the shrewd realism of *acceptance*—the sort of thing one associates with so many of C.P. Snow's characters who are realists in the sense of knowing their way around—on the other the more dangerous and exciting realism of *potentiality*—the realism involved in the ability to see the inner forces at work in a particular set-up. The one guides Defoe towards his unrivalled power of recording the surface of his world as it is. The other puts vitality into his book by making us see that world in terms of both its human deficiencies and possibilities.[97]

Professor Kettle uses two quotations from Governor Bradford's *Journal* to illustrate "the shift within Puritanism from the allegorical to the realist tradition" which

is bound up with the growing material success of the bourgeoisie. Because the well-to-do Puritans were now to a considerable degree in control of their situation, their interest in conscience and morality became much more practical, more bound up with action, less inward and more outward; interest in the here and now as opposed to the future; therefore, in literary terms, more realistic.[98]

Over thirty years ago I wrote about the literary tendency to isolate the hero or heroine from society, leaving him or her to work out salvation alone with God. I suggested that this was something specifically Puritan, which links *Paradise Lost*, *Paradise Regained* and *Samson Agonistes* with *The Pilgrim's Progress* and *Clarissa Harlowe* as well as with Defoe.[99] I think now that this perspective was too short, and the emphasis on Puritanism too restricting. In Marlowe's *Dr Faustus* and *Tamburlaine*, in Shakespeare's *Hamlet*, *Lear*, *Richard II* and many other Elizabethan and Jacobean plays, the individual hero is in a sense isolated even in his debates with others; and I think one should carry the tradition forward to the great romantic individualists. But *Robinson Crusoe* remains perhaps the purest in form of them all. In all the others the hero engages in dialogue—unless we assume that Satan in *Paradise Regained* represents one part of the personality of the Son of God, that the debate is wholly interior. Richardson's novels are a dialogue conducted by means of correspondence. For most of the time Crusoe talks to himself, occasionally to God. But I still think it was right to connect the Robinson Crusoe situation with the rise of individualism, of a greater self-consciousness.

The emphasis on the individual in isolation may also help to explain the absence of sex in the novel. The author of *Moll Flanders* and *Roxana* was not unaware of the existence and power of sex. Nor was he "Puritanically" squeamish. It might be in keeping with the conventions of the age not to discuss the problem in relation to Crusoe alone on the island. But women play no significant part at all in his life as related in the novel. He is perfunctorily married in a single sentence at the end of Part I; his wife is equally unceremoniously killed off in the same sentence. She could not be less relevant to the concerns of the novel. And what was Defoe up to in those marriages in Part II which the French priest insisted on? He cannot really have expected us to believe that the three desperadoes who took Indian women to live with would *all* be constant to them, and that none of the Spaniards would be interested. Professor Watt suggests, interestingly, that for Defoe sex is a commodity rather than a human relationship. Since there is no exchange on Crusoe's island there is no use for commodities. When the Englishmen came to select their Indian mates, the choice of the first man fell not on the most beautiful girl but on "the homeliest and the oldest of the five". For "it was application and business that they were to expect assistance in, as much as anything else; and she proved the best wife in the parcel".[100] The crude commercial metaphor underlines the fact that a woman is a source of labour power even more than of sexual gratification. From Brazil, "beside other supplies, I sent seven women", Crusoe tells us; and he promised "to send them some women from England, with a good cargo of necessaries".[101] The formal marriage insisted on by the French priest only confirmed the economic relationship which already existed in its own right. Defoe no doubt shared the radical protestant scepticism about the importance of mere ceremonies. The companionship and solace which Milton (and many other radical protestants) thought essential to marriage Robinson Crusoe found in Friday—who was however a pupil and an audience rather than a companion.[102] "Two Paradises 'twere in one/To dwell in Paradise alone". Crusoe gets very nearly the best of both worlds.

Finally, a few words about Defoe's style. "Easy, plain and familiar language", he wrote, is "the excellency of all writing, on whatever subject or to whatever persons they are that we write to, or speak". "A perfect style or language" is "that in which a man speaking to five hundred people, all of common and various capacities, should be understood by them all, in the same sense which the speaker intended to be understood".[103] I have suggested that we should trace the evolution of colloquial English prose back through Bunyan and spiritual autobiographies to the interregnum pamphlets of Levellers and Diggers, ultimately to Puritan sermons and the Marprelate Tracts.[104] But the question of influences and sources is very complicated. Pascal's *Lettres Provinciales* were translated into English in 1658, and their deadpan style of narrative by an apparently simple soul who praises the Jesuits for in effect abolishing Christianity certainly attracted the attention of post-restoration pamphleteers. The common factor between Pascal and the Levellers is that both were engaged in controversy, both wanted to appeal to the common man against the establishment, and so both had to be simple, direct and pungent.

We might ponder a little more on the role of the dissenting academies in the evolution of prose like Defoe's. Their teaching was in the vernacular and was oriented towards modern subjects. Those who attended them were, like Defoe himself, middle-class boys who did not go to a university. They provided a cultural alternative which gave a man like Defoe his self-confidence, his assurance. When he spoke up for Legion, he knew that he was as well-educated in useful learning as those whom he attacked. When he mocked the true-born Englishman he was deriding the pretensions of aristocrats who claimed to have come over with the Conqueror but had nothing else to be said for them.

> 'Tis that from some French trooper they derive
> Who with the Norman bastard did arrive . . .
> Wealth, howsoever got, in England makes
> Lords of mechanics, gentlemen of rakes:
> Antiquity and birth are useless here;
> 'Tis impudence and money makes a peer . . .
> These are the heroes that despise the Dutch,
> And rail at new-come foreigners so much,
> Forgetting that themselves are all derived
> From the most scoundrel race that ever lived.

Defoe's style is class-conscious in its avoidance of Latinisms. Bunyan was not ashamed of the fact that he could not, "with Pontius Pilate, speak Hebrew, Greek and Latin".[105] Defoe was not ignorant of Latin, but he observed that education at Oxford or Cambridge had a bad effect on prose style since it made men think in Latin.[106] There is here a linguistic patriotism as ardent as Milton's, and going much deeper. Defoe's prose, we are told, "contains a higher proportion of words of Anglo-Saxon origin than that of any other well-known writer, with the significant exception of Bunyan".[107] Again it is the audience to which Bunyan and Defoe appealed—lesser merchants, artisans and yeomen, and their wives—that is decisive. Many of them were accustomed to the Puritan plain style of preaching, and to the artisans' prose which Sprat cited as a model in his *History of the Royal Society of London.* None of them would have any use for the classical allusions which it flattered academics and gentlemen to be able to recognize. They would associate Latin culture with the ruling class which excluded them from the universities.

There is a curious pattern to Defoe's career. After many years of starting unsuccessful "projects" he had been driven to earn his living and pay his debts by dubious political journalism. The feel for his audience which he acquired through the trial-and-error consumer research of this journalism enabled him to end up with one of the most successful projects of all time: he invented the novel, to meet and develop the demands of a fiction-reading public which was to grow consistently during the next two and a half centuries. Here he at last found a satisfactory outlet for his most remarkable gift, his Shakespearean capacity for entering into and enjoying the most diverse personalities—Robinson Crusoe and the French priest, Moll Flanders and Captain Misson.

It started with the dramatic dialogues in *The Family Instructor* (1717) and similar didactic works, just as Richardson started with *Letters written for Particular Friends*. But personification took human flesh, as it had done in *Paradise Regained* and *The Pilgrim's Progress*. In the novels Defoe was able to cut loose from the dogmatic and rather conventional censoriousness which he felt obliged to adopt when he moralized. The ambiguities, perplexities and doubts were no longer temptations to be stamped on: they could be expressed in living human beings, each one of whom could be allowed to develop the full potentiality of his or her being. Apart from an introductory and concluding paragraph or two, men and women were their own justification. This was carrying the principle of toleration—necessary for England's commercial greatness—to its logical conclusion.

Even though Defoe did not write for the theatre, his use of prose to tell stories which served no direct moral or allegorical purpose seemed to Gildon rather a shocking lapse from the Puritan distrust of fiction. So it did to Defoe at first, but fortunately his sense of God's plenty overcame his scruples. So the democratic revolution, defeated in politics, triumphed in the novel.

NOTES

1. Published in *History Workshop Journal*, 10 (1980).
2. D. Defoe, *The Life and Adventures of Robinson Crusoe* (Oxford, 1840), Part II, p. 7. All subsequent references are to this edition.
3. I, p. 3. For Defoe's praise of "the middle station" see *The Complete English Tradesman* (1841), II, pp. 89–90: first published in 1727.
4. I, pp. 2, 15, 231–2.
5. I, pp. 44–6.
6. I, pp. 199, 231–2.
7. I, pp. 8–9, 15–16, 44, 95, 103–6, 111–14, 133–5, 155–7, 185, 189, 194.
8. II, p. 325, I. pp. 67–8: contrast the idleness and debauchery of his English successors on the islands, II, pp. 85–6. Professor Weimann points out that Crusoe still had a lot of rum left after twenty-four years (*Daniel Defoe: Eine Einführung in das Romanwerk*, Halle, Saale, 1962, p. 60; cf. pp. 62, 95).
9. I, pp. 75, 85, 123.
10. I, p. 108.
11. I, pp. 158, 247
12. I, pp. 77–8; Defoe, *The Complete English Tradesman* II, p. 121. Annual charitable gifts were part of the Tradesman's balance sheet.

13. I, p. 305.
14. I, pp. 14, 73, 215, 236, 301–2, 327, 362.
15. I, pp. 207–8, 225, 274, 299, 345; pp. 4–5, 57–8, 66, 119, 199, 331. This point is heavily stressed in Defoe's *Serious Reflections during the Life and Surprising Adventures of Robinson Crusoe* (1720), Chapter 5 (Of listening to the voice of providence) and A Vision of the Angelic World, pp. 47–57. I refer to this work henceforth as III.
16. I, pp. 132–4.
17. I, pp. 134–5; cf. 160–1.
18. Karl Marx, *Capital*, I (ed. Dona Torr, 1946), pp. 47–50; *Grundrisse* (Penguin edn., 1973), pp. 83–4. Cf. S. Hymer, "*Robinson Crusoe* and the Secret of Primitive Accumulation", *Monthly Review*, 23 (1971), pp. 11–36, and Mario Miegge, *Protestantesimo e capitalismo da Calvino a Weber: contributi ad un dibattito* (Turin, 1983), pp. 31–6.
19. See especially M.E. Novak, *Economics and the Fiction of Daniel Defoe* (California U.P., 1962) and *Defoe and the Nature of Man* (Oxford U.P., 1963); G.A. Starr, *Defoe and Spiritual Autobiography* (Princeton U.P., 1965) and *Defoe and Casuistry* (Princeton U.P., 1971); J.P. Hunter, *The Reluctant Pilgrim* (Baltimore, 1966), J.J. Richetti, *Defoe's Narratives: Situations and Structures* (Oxford U.P.,1957, pp. 18–26); D. Brooks, *Numbers and Patterns in the Eighteenth Century Novel* (1973) offers a numerological interpretation. None of these can compare in interest with E.M.W. Tillyard's pages on Defoe in *The Epic Strain in the English Novel* (1958).
20. P. Rogers, *Robinson Crusoe* (1979), p. 53.
21. C. Gildon, *The Life and Strange Surprising Adventures of Mr D . . . De F . . . of London, Hosier* (1719), p. 47.
22. Starr, *Defoe and Spiritual Autobiography*, p. 125.
23. I, p. 108.
24. I, pp. 248–9, 258–9.
25. I, pp. 244, 254. For noble savages see *A New Voyage Round the World* (Oxford, 1840), pp. 121–2: first published 1725.
26. II, pp. 162–7; cf. p. 37.
27. II, pp. 262–3. For Defoe's opposition to the East India Company's monopoly, see pp. 111–12 above.
28. I, p. 1. Oliver Cromwell in 1656–7 had aspired to annex Bremen.
29. II, p. 87.
30. I, pp. 343–4, 363. Cf. Gildon, *op. cit.*, p. 41.
31. I, p. 288, II, p. 177.
32. II, pp. 128, 132–6, 156–8.
33. I, p. 263.
34. I, pp. 258–9; cf. II, p. 180.
35. I, pp. 263–4.
36. I, pp. 183–4. Cf. Defoe's *Political History of the Devil* (1726).
37. I, pp. 260–1.
38. Cf. *M.E.R.*, p. 294. Milton lived for the last eleven years of his life a few hundred yards from Defoe's father's house.
39. Ian Watt, *The Rise of the Novel* (1957), Chapter 3.

40. II, pp. 156–8. For Defoe's impatience with religious bigotry, see *The Consolidator* (Oxford, 1840), p. 296 (bound with *History of the Plague in London*). First published 1705.
41. Junjiro Amakawa, "Defoe as an Economist", *Kwansei Gakuin University Annual Studies*, XV (1966), pp. 101–26, and p. 103 in particular.
42. Amakawa, p. 104.
43. I, pp. 67, 153, 229; II, p. 80; cf. Defoe's *The Life, Adventures and Pyracies Of the Famous Captain Singleton* (Oxford, 1840), pp. 156–7: first published 1720.
44. See John Locke, *Two Treatises of Government* (ed. P. Laslett, Cambridge U.P., 1960), pp. 304–20.
45. Defoe, *A Plan of the English Commerce* (Oxford U.P., 1928), pp. 36–8: first published 1728. Cf. *An Argument Shewing, that a Standing Army, with Consent of Parliament, is not Inconsistent with a Free Government* (1698), in *Selected Writings of Daniel Defoe* (ed. J.T. Boulton, Cambridge U.P., 1975), p. 45; *A Review*, II, No. 26 (3 January 1706), *ibid.*, p. 120; and *The Complete English Tradesman, passim.*
46. *The Complete English Tradesman*, pp. 33–4; cf. P. Earle, *The World of Defoe* (1976), pp. 295–6.
47. Amakawa, *op. cit.*, esp. p. 107.
48. I, p. 74; cf. Weimann, *op. cit.*, p. 62.
49. I, pp. 124–7, 136.
50. I, pp. 139–41; cf. pp. 144–5.
51. T. Hobbes, *Leviathan* (1651); cf. Macpherson, *The Political Theory of Possessive Individualism*, Chapter II.
52. II, pp. 272–9; III, pp. 133–49. Contrast *The Consolidator* (Oxford, 1840), pp. 211–15.
53. Esp. I, p. 366. For Joyce see *Twentieth-century Interpretations of Robinson Crusoe* (ed. F.H. Ellis, Englewood Cliffs, New Jersey, 1969), p. 15.
54. II, p. 64; *A Plan of the English Commerce*, pp. xi, 260, 268–77; cf. Hymer, *op. cit., passim.* and Miegge, *op. cit.*, pp. 31–6.
55. For Wildman, see Maurice Ashley, *John Wildman* (1947).
56. Quoted in Weimann, *Daniel Defoe*, p. 107.
57. Ed. H. Morley, *The Earlier Life and Chief Earlier Works of Daniel Defoe* (1889), p. 167. The point had been made by Fox and many Quakers in the sixteen-fifties (*The Experience of Defeat*, Chapter Five).
58. Alick West, *The Mountain in the Sunlight* (1958), pp. 67–73. In *An Appeal to Honour and Justice* (1715), Defoe denied having sold his pen (printed with G. Chalmers, *The Life of Daniel De Foe*, Oxford, 1841). In *The Consolidator* he made the same charge against Dryden (p. 225).
59. I, p. 17; cf. Defoe's "satire has no business with the crown", quoted on p. 308 below.
60. I have discussed this at greater length in "Radical Pirates?", in *The Origins of Anglo-American Radicalism* (ed. M.C. and J.R. Jacob, 1984), pp. 17–32.
61. *A General History of the . . . Pyrates* (ed. M. Schonbron, 1972), p. 588.

62. M. Rediker, "'Under the Banner of King Death': The Social World of Anglo-American Pirates, 1716–1726", *The William and Mary Quarterly*, 3rd series, XXXVIII (1981), pp. 203–27.
63. Weimann, pp. 82–3.
64. Defoe, *The Storm* (1704), quoted by Watt, p. 107.
65. II, Chapter 9.
66. Weimann, *Daniel Defoe*, p. 54; cf. pp. 62, 95.
67. I, p. 19; cf. Weimann, *Daniel Defoe*, pp. 70–1, 74–5, 89.
68. I, p. 39.
69. I, pp. 43, 45.
70. I, p. 232.
71. I, p. 245; cf. p. 254.
72. II, p. 73.
73. Cf. II, pp. 118–20.
74. I, p. 196; cf. p. 218; and III, pp. 35–6, 40; *Captain Singleton*, p. 15.
75. I, p. 200.
76. I, pp. 200–4, 257; cf. pp. 277–8.
77. I, pp. 237–8.
78. Cf. II, p. 63. Just to confuse the issue, Crusoe appears to accept this argument in III, pp. 247–8.
79. Cf. the excellent book by Nicholas Canny, *The Elizabethan Conquest of Ireland* (1978).
80. I, pp. 222–3, II, p. 182, III, pp. 40, 132. Defoe returned to the point in many other works: see Novak, *Defoe and the Nature of Man*, pp. 44–5, 65, 67, 71–2.
81. II, p. 249.
82. A. Kettle, *An Introduction to the English Novel* (1951), I, pp. 21–3, 55–62; Weimann, Chapter 2.
83. *A General History of the . . . Pyrates*, pp. 403–4; Earle (1973), pp. 68, 70. Earle quotes a moving passage from Baxter's *Christian Directory* against the enslavement of Africans (p. 67).
84. Quoted by F.H. Ellis in his Introduction to *Twentieth-Century Interpretations of Robinson Crusoe*, p. 6.
85. *A General History of Trade*, No. 1 (August 1713), p. 10, quoted by Novak, *Defoe and the Nature of Man*, pp. 7–8.
86. F. Bastian, *Defoe's Early Life* (1981), p. 267.
87. III, pp. 253–6, 264–70.
88. I, p. 271.
89. II, pp. 139–40.
90. II, p. 265.
91. II, pp. 64, 142, 171, 177.
92. I, p. 92.
93. I, pp. 248–9.
94. Cf. Weimann, *Daniel Defoe*, pp. 55–6. This point was made, interestingly enough, by Gildon in the year *Robinson Crusoe* appeared (pp. 2, 31–2).
95. I, p. 92; cf. II, pp. 9–10.
96. Watt, *op. cit.*, pp. 115–36.

97. Kettle, *Introduction*, p. 207; "Precursors of Defoe: Puritanism and the Rise of the Novel", in *On the Novel* (ed. B.S. Benedicz, 1971).
98. Kettle, *Introduction*, p. 211.
99. In my *Puritanism and Revolution* (Panther edn.), pp. 364–6; cf. III, pp. 3–17, M.A. Radzinowicz, *Towards Samson Agonistes: The Growth of Milton's Mind* (Princeton U.P., 1978), pp. 16, 346–7, Staves, *op. cit.*, p. 293, and Dollimore, *op. cit.*, p. 175.
100. II, pp. 82–3.
101. I, p. 366.
102. Watt, *op. cit.*, pp. 70–2.
103. Defoe, *The Complete English Tradesman*, I, p. 19. It is perhaps not the happiest example of "a perfect style".
104. See Chapter 3 above.
105. J. Bunyan, *A Few Sighs from Hell* (1658), in *Works* (ed. G. Offor, 1860), II, p. 695.
106. Defoe, *The Complete English Gentleman* (ed. K.D. Büllbring, 1895), pp. 197–9.
107. Watt, *op cit.*, p. 106. For the radical associations of linguistic Saxonism see "The Norman Yoke" in my *Puritanism and Revolution* (Panther edn.), pp. 79–80.

III *Seven Poets*

6. George Wither (1588–1667) and John Milton (1608–74)[1]

George Wither was born in the Armada year, twenty years before Milton. Wither published all his best poetry before he was thirty-seven, though he continued to write incessantly for the remaining forty-two years of his life. Milton published his first book of verse at the age of thirty-seven, and already had a few prose pamphlets to his credit. He too wrote far more in bulk thereafter, much of it in Latin, all of it incomparably higher quality than Wither's later writings.

Wither was a well-known, not to say notorious, character long before the civil war. He had spent some months in jail on account of his very popular satire, *Abuses Stript and Whipt*, published in 1613 and running to seven editions by 1617. He claimed that 30,000 copies of his *Motto* were sold in a few weeks in 1613. This enabled him to be independent of patrons: *Abuses Stript and Whipt* was dedicated to himself.[2] Edward Phillips, who may or may not have been repeating Milton's estimate, said that Wither was "vulgarly taken for a great poet, and by some for a prophet". Aubrey thought better of Wither as prophet than as poet: "He had a strange sagacity and foresight into mundane affairs".[3] An enormously long poem, *Brittans Remembrancer*, published in 1628, used the plague of 1625 to announce judgments to come "if repentance prevent not". Wither claimed in 1645 to have predicted the civil war, and many agreed with him.[4] Extracts from *Brittans Remembrancer* were reprinted in 1643.[5] In 1655 Arise Evans attacked Wither in the same breath as he attacked the astrologer-prophet William Lilly. Defoe thought Wither had foretold the ruin of London in 1665–6.[6]

Sir John Berkenhead, who was not naturally sympathetic to Wither, called him "a pitiful poet" and "pseudo-propheta".[7] But some of Wither's early lyrics are better than his later reputation would suggest. His sad deterioration is usually attributed to his vision of himself as an inspired prophet with a message for the English people. "God opened my mouth", he declared in 1641, "and compelled me, beyond my natural abilities, to speak."[8] But Milton's view of his relation to his Muse in *Paradise Lost* is not essentially different. I want very briefly to draw attention to the many points of similarity between the political careers and political and religious ideas of the two poets. This will do nothing to explain the greatness of Milton: but if we see how much he had in common with even the later Wither, it may help us to understand that he was no unique and lonely genius.

Wither and Milton were both self-consciously Spenserians. Milton was introduced as an imitator of Spenser in 1645; he himself told Dryden that Spenser was "his original". Spenser was associated with the radical political wing in government circles, with Leicester, Walsingham, Ralegh. The Spenserian succession—Sidney, Daniel, the Fletchers, John Davies, Drayton, Browne, Wither, Quarles, Milton—was also a political succession.[9] Many of these poets followed Spenser's example in using the conventions of pastoral poetry to make political criticisms without drawing the attention of the censor. One thinks of *Britannia's Pastorals* by Wither's friend Browne, of Wither's own *Shepherds Hunting* and *Philarete*, of *Lycidas*. Wither was patronized by Southampton and the third Earl of Pembroke, who succeeded to the political attitudes and patronage of Leicester and Walsingham. Wither regularly dedicated his most controversial poems to Pembroke, who apparently came to Wither's rescue when he was in prison in 1615.[10] On Pembroke's death Wither applied to the fourth Earl.

Wither went to Oxford, Milton to Cambridge. Both left "somewhat discontented". But Wither, being a gentleman, proceeded to an Inn of Chancery, whilst Milton—aiming then at a clerical career—returned to Cambridge. However, both retained a considerable contempt for the university curriculum and for dons.[11] Wither, like Milton, was no respecter of rank unaccompanied by virtue. From his earliest satires he attacked court luxury, extravagance, and corruption, purchase of offices and peerages, bribery, monopolies. Alterations which he made to the 1625 version of *Brittans Remembrancer* before republication in 1628 show his mistrust of Charles I growing.[12] In retrospect at least he stressed the cultural divide between King and nation, symbolized by court masques:

> He and his queen became
> So often represented by the name
> Of heathenish deities, that they at last
> Became (even when their mummeries were past)

Like those they represented: and did move
Within their sphere like Venus, Mars and Jove.[13]

Similar themes underlie Milton's pamphlets of the early 1640s, and are emphasized in *The Ready and Easy Way to Establish a Free Commonwealth* of 1660.

But it was the international situation which really alarmed Wither from the 1620s, as it did Milton: the failure to support England's natural protestant allies on the continent from Habsburg attack, the sense that protestantism was not yet secure in England. Both poets very early took up a patriotic anti-Spanish stance, shown in the poems which each wrote for the fifth of November. In 1643 Wither accused Charles of failing to protect his kingdoms against the popish menace.[14] He saw the civil war as fought against Antichrist.[15]

Hence whilst both Wither and Milton strongly favoured toleration of all protestants, they did not extend this to those whom they regarded as a Spanish fifth column in England or in Ireland. Both shared the Puritan desire to purge the English Church of popish remnants, and consequently abhorred the Laudian régime: Wither indeed had earlier shown considerable scepticism about bishops. This extended for both to a passionate anti-clericalism, a hatred of ambitious clergymen, of simony and the patronage system, of the state church, its tithes, its courts, its excommunications, its fees, its superstitious ceremonies and uneconomic observation of saints' days. Both Wither and Milton attacked censorship.[16]

Wither's quarrel with the Stationers' Company played a similar role in his development to the furore over Milton's divorce pamphlets. Wither wrote no *Areopagitica*: but long before Milton he had acquired a strong and lasting hatred of censorship as an insult to human dignity.[17] Its effects on him can be simply shown. Between 1612 and 1628 he published sixteen works in sixteen years, the last of them—*Brittans Remembrancer*—printed by himself because he could not find a publisher. Between 1641 (when the censorship collapsed) and 1666 he published fifty-six works in twenty-five years. In the intervening thirteen years, the Laudian years, he published only two translations—*The Psalmes of David* (in the Netherlands, since he could find no English publisher) and Nemesius's *The Nature of Man*—together with the politically innocuous *Emblemes* (1635). A consistent feature of the thinking of both poets was a reasoned defence of the rights of the individual conscience, a rejection of implicit faith, of reliance on the judgment of others, and of the use of force in religious affairs. A nation, Wither declared in 1648, à propos the Solemn League and Covenant, cannot vow "to pin their faith upon another's sleeve".[18] It is impossible "to force belief".[19] Persecution, he told Charles II in 1661, makes proselytes "only for the devil or Antichrist".[20] Like Milton, he came to think of persecution as both antichristian and ineffective.[21]

> 'Tis not the cutting off of one man's ears
> Will stop the voice which everybody hears.[22]

"Let truth and error fight it out together" was the Miltonic advice he gave the King in 1662.[23] Toleration, Wither thought, was the only alternative to state-imposed hypocrisy.[24] Like Milton in *Lycidas*, Wither in 1632 had hoped to see God inflicting "that vengeance which is prepared for impenitent persecutors".[25]

Wither disliked the "blind mouths" of the clergy as much as Milton did: "mute as a rich clergyman" was Wither's phrase.

> To be thy shepherds wolves are stolen in . . .
> Men use religion as a stalking-horse
> To catch preferment . . .[26]

In his comment on Psalm 68 Wither prayed that "heretics, hirelings and contentious persons may be reproved and reformed or cut off". The Miltonic "hirelings" comes between two words which could give no offence to the hierarchy.[27] Both Wither and Milton disliked the Laudian campaign against lecturers: Wither made the point by visualizing Jesus first expelling merchants from his church and then himself lecturing there.[28] "As if we could not pray", he complained in 1628, "until our preaching we had sent away."[29]

Like Milton, Wither thought that the clergy and bishops (whom Charles I "out of the dunghill had promoted") were largely responsible for the civil war. In 1628 he predicted, with remarkable accuracy, how the clergy would take the lead in polarizing society:

> If ever in thy fields (as God forbid)
> The blood of thine own children shall be shed
> By civil discord, they shall blow the flame. . . .
>
> One part of these will for preferment strive
> By lifting up the King's prerogative
> Above itself. They shall persuade him to
> Much more than law or conscience bids him do
> And say, God warrants it.

In reaction, others will preach

Rebellion to the people, and shall strain
The Word of God sedition to maintain.[30]

This sort of erastian anti-clericalism explains how Wither could have been a friend of Selden's, and of Milton's crony, Marchamont Nedham. It is very close to Milton's position in the mid forties.

Wither shared Milton's horror of idolatry. Both in consequence approved of iconoclasm.[31] Both rejected set forms of worship (as idolatry). As early as 1645 Wither spoke for "union without uniformity".

God in no need stands
Either of churches, tithes or rents on lands

he declared eight years later.[32] After 1660 he conformed to the Church of England for a short time, but found that "men have made such idols of their disciplines and formalities" that he ultimately decided—with Milton and Colonel Hutchinson—that he would not confine his "belief or practice to any one national or congregational society of Christians".[33]

Ben Jonson had sneered at Wither as the idol of apprentices, journeymen and fishwives.[34] This referred to his popularity rather than to his politics. Wither deliberately cultivated a plain style of writing. It was a style at which Milton aimed only after the defeat of the Revolution. The reliance of both was on the middling sort: virtue more than compensated for humble birth. Thomas Beedome in 1641 chose this for especial praise. Wither's

heaven-bred boldness durst control
Without respect of persons, every sin.[35]

Wither favoured the sturdy independence of the "freeborn", whom he contrasted with servants. He disliked snobbish monuments in churches.[36] Like Milton, Wither believed in human equality, but associated it with a mobile society. Wither thought beggars were wicked:[37] "indiscreet and fond compassion" for the poor could be a vice.[38] When Wither, like Milton, in 1660 advocated "the just division of waste commons",[39] he seems to have regarded this as a means of getting rid of poor squatters. Both despised "the rabble" little less than they despised courtiers.[40] Both had to recognize after the civil war that "the rabble" might be in favour of monarchy.[41]

In 1642 Wither had no hesitation in taking the side of Parliament. Although already in his fifties, he (unlike Milton) served in the Army and became Major Wither. Like Milton, he originally accepted the leadership of the "Presbyterians", though as early as 1642 he seems to have been described as an Independent.[42] He soon became a supporter of the win-the-war party. His extremism is shown by his suggestion that the estates of royalist gentlemen should be confiscated, so that they should become peasants—"a degree to which honest men are born; and too good for them, some of them being made lords and knights for attempting to enslave freemen".[43]

In 1643 Wither claimed sovereignty for Parliament ("in whose commands the King's are best obeyed"). The doctrine that the King can do no wrong means that his ministers can be called to account. In 1645 he wrote, in words that seem to echo his friend Selden,

> A king is but a substituted head
> Made for convenience.

But a new note was coming in. "The people first did make both laws and kings"—a Leveller (and Miltonic) rather than a Parliamentarian maxim.[44]

> And know there is on earth a greater thing.
> Than an unrighteous Parliament or King.[45]

In 1646 Wither accused Charles of abusing the public trust,[46] and two years later he called on the "erring and deluded King" to repent of his errors and sins.[47] By 1646 he was ominously demanding a purge of Parliament.[48]

In the late 1640s Wither became no less disillusioned with Parliament than Milton was at the time of writing *The Character of the Long Parliament.* Both experienced delays and perversion of justice by Parliamentary committees.[49] The Revolution turned out to be

> A good play spoiled
> And by unworthy actors foiled.[50]

In October or November 1648 Wither called for a fundamental overhaul of the Parliamentarian apparatus, and argued simultaneously against the enforced religious uniformity insisted on by the Presbyterian clergy. Like Milton in *The Tenure of Kings and Magistrates* slightly later, Wither urged before the event the trial and execution of justice upon the King.[51]

For Wither, as for Milton, Pride's Purge of Parliament in December 1648, the trial and condemnation of Charles I, the abolition of the House of Lords, and the proclamation of the republic seemed to offer new hope. In August 1649 he expressed unqualified jubilation at the victory of Parliament's troops in Ireland.[52] In 1650-1 he composed hymns to celebrate the anniversary of Charles's execution:

> This is the day whereon our yoke
> Of Norman bondage first was broke
> And England from her chains made free.[53]

In *British Appeals* (1651) he again praised the trial and execution of Charles "by public justice and in public place", and attacked Charles II as "the Scottish King with all his rabblement".[54] Lilburne in 1652 went out of his way to speak well of Wither—and Milton.[55] Parliament recognized the debt due to Wither and gave him a job as commissioner for sale of the King's goods.

Wither justified the dissolution of the Rump of the Long Parliament in 1653,[56] and like Milton he accepted office under the Protectorate of Oliver Cromwell. In 1657 he published a poem in which he declared that:

> We look for such a government as shall
> Make way for Christ. . . .
> His Highness hath made progress in a path
> As far forth toward it, as any hath
> Since Christ ascended.[57]

The hyperbole is exceeded only by Milton's extraordinary statement that the events of the English Revolution were "the most heroic and exemplary achievements since the foundation of the world"—not excepting apparently the life and death of Christ. ("Since the ascension" was often used by Wither's contemporaries to suggest that there had been apostasy since the time of the Apostles—an apostasy which was now ending).[58]

Towards Oliver Cromwell Wither's attitude became ambivalent. In retrospect he claimed to have been deceived by the Protector's "show of piety".[59] But earlier he had been more enthusiastic.[60] In 1655 Cromwell was "God's especial favourite".[61] Next year Wither welcomed the growing conservatism evidenced by the fact that assize juries were now being summoned "out of the eminent baronets, knights, esquires and gentlemen to serve in their respective counties". It promised greater stability. Even in 1659 Cromwell's

> virtues were enough to do
> So much as God designed him to.[62]

By his own account at least Wither was on terms of some intimacy with Cromwell, though he proved less able to influence him politically than he had hoped.[63] But, again like Milton, Wither did not shrink from warning the rulers of England of their failure to live up to the ideals of the Good Old Cause, to rebuke them for creating necessities in order to plead them.[64] Such warnings go back to 1645, when Wither spoke of the "avarice and ambition" of military men, words which were often repeated later by Milton and others.[65]

Like Milton once more, Wither disapproved of the offer of the crown to Cromwell in 1657. He was satisfied with some aspects of the Protector's foreign policy, though he did not like the aggressive wars and alliance with popish France which Oliver (and Charles II after him) entered into.[66] We may compare the Son of God's rejection of alliances in *Paradise Regained*, Book III. For Wither, like Milton, had seen the English Revolution as an opportunity for reversing Charles I's pro-papist policy and replacing it with a protestant crusade. Both thought the Pope was Antichrist, and both believed that the end of the world and the destruction of Antichrist were approaching.

As early as 1612 Wither believed that "the Lord's great day is near".[67] In 1632 he proclaimed that the "Second Coming . . . now draweth nigh"; "the worst age is come".[68] For Milton Christ was "shortly-expected King", whose kingdom "is now at hand", foreboding "hasty ruin and destruction to all tyrants".[69] Like Milton later, Wither thought of the English as the chosen people; this must have affected both poets' political attitudes when the Revolution came. It was indeed because of the special responsibilities of a chosen people that Wither, like any Hebrew prophet, had felt called upon to pronounce doom on those who failed to live up to God's high demands.[70] In 1643 he referred to the royalists as "bands and . . . confederates of Antichrist"; "his last great battery Antichrist now rears", he declared in 1645.[71] In 1659 Wither repeated that "the ruin of the Beast is now at hand".[72] Two years later he still hoped to live to see the fall of the Mystery of Iniquity,[73] although he did not expect the millennium until 1666 years after the death of Christ. Then Christ would "visibly reign upon earth with his saints, . . . according to their expectation in the main whom you call Fifth Monarchy Men".[74] Like Milton again however Wither rejected attempts to expedite Christ's coming by political violence.[75]

Like Milton, Wither soon began to realize that all was not going well with the English Revolution. In 1653 he anticipated Haslerig,

Vane, Stubbe and Milton by suggesting that liberty could be safeguarded only by a perpetual Parliament, recruited from time to time by partial elections.[76] In 1647 he was writing

> Even you, who had
> The righteous Cause . . . have made
> Defaults enough to let all see
> The best had need forgiven be.[77]

In 1655 Wither believed that it was God "which did remove the government we had" and transferred power to Cromwell. In 1659 Wither again justified Charles I's execution: kings are "the people's creatures".[78] He spoke of "the rabble/Of malcontents which that ejected King" would bring back with him.[79] Even in 1660 he had the temerity to say in print

> Once when sick to death the body lay
> 'Twas cured by taking of the head away.[80]

In August 1659 Wither had clearly seen that restoration of monarchy was imminent, but he continued, even later than Milton, to proclaim his adherence to "that which is not called amiss the Good Old Cause". Wither still asserted that

> the Cause we had
> Was very good, though we ourselves were bad.[81]

He insisted that

> It is a much more honourable thing
> To save a people than to make a king.[82]

Like Milton, Wither would have preferred even the rule of Monck to a restoration of the monarchy.[83]

He agreed with Milton that the people had been influenced by a mistaken short-run idea of their own interests, by "the vain and groundless apprehension that nothing but kingship can restore trade", and by divisions among the Parliamentarians. They had not been influenced by royalism, by

> Love unto his person or his cause
> Or zeal to true religion or the laws.[84]

"No man thought/Our Cause (it seems) worth speaking for", still less fighting for.[85] Wither shared all Milton's horror at the betrayal of the Revolution by those who had undertaken to lead it—the saints and Parliament.[86] Since men were "willing to return/To our late bondage",[87] God had deserted what both believed to be his Cause.

Milton's phrase "choosing them a captain back for Egypt" has often been praised: Wither anticipated it in 1659:

> They now rebelliously a captain choose
> To lead them back to bondage, like the Jews.[88]

Wither was eloquently ironical about the bribery and corruption which accompanied Parliamentary elections. Can we speak of a "free Parliament" when M.P.s

> By bribes, threats, fawnings or corrupted friends
> Procure their own elections for self-ends;
> When the electors likewise cheated are
> Of their free choice, by weakness, hope or fear?
> Call you that free, which was at first begot
> In bondage?

A corruptible village sends as many representatives

> as any shire
> Which doth two hundred times their burdens bear.

He called for redistribution of the franchise.[89] Wither continued to preach forgiveness and reconciliation, but had greater hopes of the King than of Parliament.[90] He resented the way in which all blame was put "on those whom they fanatics please to call."[91] But Wither made use of Verner's Fifth Monarchist rising of 1661 (which he condemned in a very half-hearted manner) to warn the government. If so small a body of dedicated men could terrorize London, what might not "the desperation of so many hundred thousands . . . amount unto?" What "if the whole body of God's elect in these nations . . . should engage all together as one man in his Cause?"[92]

The restoration was a personal catastrophe for Wither. He was financially ruined. He was imprisoned by Parliament for two years. This was the consequence of a pretty sharp attack on the Cavalier Parliament made in *Vox Vulgi*, for its failure to heal and reconcile. The thought that "the Lord's great day is near" remained some consolation even after 1660. "The saints' last Purgatory is now commencing", he declared in 1666.[93] But—already a septuagenarian —he reverted more and more to his personal grievances and his unregarded role as a prophet—not that he had ever ignored either of these subjects, but now they became obsessive.

In *Brittans Remembrancer* Wither had said that he would obey "that government (whate'er it be)" in which he had received his birth and breeding, subject to the laws of the land.[94] In 1659 he asserted

that he invariably acted on the Hobbist principle of obeying every
authority so long as it wielded effective power: and no longer—though
of course Wither put this in religious terms: the power "by God and
by this people chose".[95] After the restoration he did not fail to insist
that the relationship between King and people was reciprocal:

> Men who are much oppressed against reason
> Will not much fear to act what you call treason.[96]

This providential view fitted in with Wither's interests. He had—or
thought he had—large financial claims against the state, dating from
the sixteen-forties; and these claims could be met only by the
government in being. Yet Wither in his role of prophet could never
resist lecturing each government in turn; and this did not predispose
rulers in his favour.[97]

Since in 1660 it was clear that God no longer favoured the
Parliamentary cause, Wither was prepared to like what he got,
hopelessly and helplessly. God will do what he thinks best, whatever
our reaction.[98] It was difficult for human beings to judge God, or the
ups and downs of history.[99] Wither's absolute reliance on divine
Providence as against human instruments is shown by his repeated
advocacy of election by lot, whether of Parliaments or of the
Protector.[100] Then the decision would clearly be taken out of men's
hands and left to God.

Like Milton, though rather earlier, Wither apparently moved from
Calvinism to an undenominational Arminian position. As early as
1628 he rejected the absolute decrees.[101] In 1636 he insisted on free
will. Without it "we neither husband the gifts of nature (which is
God's common grace) nor endeavour as we ought to do according to
that ability which we have received". At the Fall "we lost indeed our
light but not our eyes". Christ would reprobate "those only who
rejected" the light, "not because they saw it not but because they loved
it not". All men "received . . . that common grace . . . so far forth as
might have enabled them to become Sons of God".[102] Nemesius, as
translated by Wither, anticipated *Areopagitica*: "either man should
have been made void of reason, or else being indued with reason and
exercised in action, he must have in him free will". God gave him
choice, as he gave it to the angels. So man can ultimately attain

> to a state that's better
> Than what he lost

—a Paradise within him, happier far. Like Milton in *Areopagitica*,

Wither held the Baconian view that knowledge could help us to recover from the consequences of the Fall. In 1662 he proclaimed free will and universal redemption.[103] Human beings must take full responsibility for their actions, including the defeat of the Revolution.[104]

Wither early rejected a fugitive and cloistered virtue: those who withdraw into "an hermetical solitariness . . . wrong their country and their friends", and are "weak, . . . slothful and unjust".

> Give me the man that with a quaking arm
> Walks with a stedfast mind though greatest harm;
> And though his flesh doth tremble, makes it stand
> To execute what Reason doth command.[105]

This is of course conventional Puritanism: trust in God *and* keep your powder dry. But it gives a courage in adversity that looks forward to Abdiel.

> Do as you please; my way to me is known,
> And I will walk it, though I walk alone.[106]

Like Milton in *Paradise Lost*, Wither saw it as his task to rally the defeated remnant of God's servants, to save them from despair. They must not repine at God's will as revealed in history. At Naseby, Wither had declared in 1649, God had shown himself on the side of Parliament.[107] In 1659 he had been able to envisage a return of Charles II only as a punishment for the English people, who had failed to take advantage of the opportunities which he had offered them. Men get the government they deserve;[108] everything that happens is in accordance with God's will:

> And he that would, and he that would not too,
> Shall help effect what God intends to do. . . .
>
> Yea they who pull down and they who erect
> Shall in the close concur in one effect.[109]

Christopher Clobery saw in the events of 1659 fulfilment of the predictions of *Brittans Remembrancer*: referring to "these nations", he took the Miltonic point that "their fall is wilful".[110] In prison after the restoration, Wither's faith was strengthened against "atheistical arguments and objections of carnal men . . . by looking back as far as the creation". All the evils from which humanity suffers are the consequence of Adam's Fall. God's "providential changing of governments and governors" was intended "to the punishment of sin, to the encouragement of virtue, to the exercising of patience, faith, humility, constancy, love and other graces of the saints". "Our sins have been the sole cause . . . that we ourselves have been destructive to ourselves". So Wither justified God's ways to men.[111] The restoration was "a test both of his [Charles II's] and our obedience to God's commands".[112]

The English people then had *freely* brought judgments on themselves.

> Repine not therefore at what God shall do
> Whate'er it be; but willingly thereto
> Submit yourselves, and heartily repent
> Your provocations.[113]

It was the task of God's servants

> to stand out all the shocks
> Of tyranny, like never-moved rocks.

whilst waiting for divisions to appear among their oppressors.[114] Although

> it to the saints pertains
> To bind in fetters and in iron chains
> Both kings and peers,

they must not attempt it "unseasonably" or

> With carnal weapons, in a carnal mode,
> Seeking their own ends when they his [God's] pretended.[115]

God "will provide deliverers", but in his own time.[116] Yet Wither died before the publication of *Paradise Lost*. The analogies derive from the historical context.

In this light Wither's attitude towards the sects is interesting. In *The Schollers Purgatory* (c. 1624) he tells us that he was much wooed by the sectaries. In 1628 he mentioned Familists and Brownists without the ritually expected horror, just as Milton was to do in 1641. As early as 1623 Wither made the classic Familist distinction between "the history" and "the mystery", and he referred more than once to "the Everlasting Gospel", a phrase associated with radical sectaries.[117] Wither used as an argument for toleration Roger William's analogy between congregational churches and trading companies—part of the City and ultimately subordinated to its government, but with their own internal constitutional arrangements.[118] Wither continued to hold the radical belief that all mankind could be saved.[119] His attitude towards the Quakers resembles Milton's.

Wither anticipated them in mocking at exaggerated social compliments, and took up the point again, explicitly in defence of
Quakers, in 1661.[120] He virtually aligned himself with Quakers as
despised "messengers of God", and spoke with admiration of their
courage under persecution and of their opposition to oaths. "They
are our Levellers new named", he wrote—a point normally made by
the Quakers' enemies.[121] "Habakkuk in his mode, and at such a time
as this, was a Quaker; so likewise was Ezekiel".[122]

Wither demanded for himself the rights of a freeborn Englishman,
whether against King or Parliament.[123] He recognized the class bias
of the English legal system.[124] He disliked lawyers, the delays and
venality of the law, and the mumbo-jumbo of law French ("this
Norman gibberish", Milton called it). He linked those traditional
enemies of the radicals, lawyers, and priests.[125] Like Milton and most
of the radicals, Wither exalted reason above precedent, experience
above authority; again he expressed these points relatively early. But,
again like Milton, he was prepared to plead precedent against both
King and Parliament when it suited him.[126]

Like Milton, Wither had not much use for the Fathers of the
church, preferring to follow his own reason and conscience. Both
thought that many disputed theological matters concerned things
indifferent, and became increasingly concerned as such squabbles
fragmented the unity of the radicals.[127] Both accepted astrology, with
reservations, but both objected to idle curiosity, to prying "into
those secrets God meant should be hidden"—for instance what God
was doing before he created the world.[128]

Like Milton, Wither thought that hell was a state of mind.[129]
Milton's heresies do not appear in Wither's writings, but then we
should not know about Milton's real beliefs if the unpublishable *De
Doctrina Christiana* had not survived. The translation of Nemesius,
and especially Wither's Preface, was one of the sources on which
Richard Overton drew for his *Mans Mortalitie* of 1643. But Nemesius
merely reports Hebrew views on the close union of body and soul,
and that "man was made from the beginning neither wholly mortal
neither wholly immortal". Wither appears to reject the mortalism
which Milton adopted.[130] There is likewise no evidence that Wither
was anything but orthodox on the Trinity, though he emphasized
the triumph of Christ's manhood at the resurrection. He recorded,
without comment, that some rejected the historical Jesus Christ who
died at Jerusalem.[131] He laid especial emphasis, as Milton did, on the

liberty to which Sons of God might attain on earth. For him, as for Milton, "the Lord's anointed" meant the elect rather than kings.[132] But in all this there is nothing as positive as the anti-Trinitarianism to which Milton in private committed himself.

Wither perhaps approaches Milton's antinomianism. He was no strict Sabbatarian. "Bodily labours and exercises" might be used on Sundays "wheresoever (without respect to sensual or covetous ends) a rectified conscience shall persuade us that the honour of God, the charity we owe to our neighbours or an unfeigned necessity requires them to be done". This is exactly Milton's position in the *De Doctrina Christiana*.[133] Neither poet was a killjoy Puritan. The creatures exist in order to be enjoyed.[134] Like Milton in 1645, Wither thought amorous poems more suitable for youthful years; both continued to enjoy a rude story, a sexual innuendo. Wither wrote, but did not publish, a mildly naughty epithalamium.[135] Both smoked, both appear to have been betting men.[136] For Wither as for Milton hypocrisy was the worst of crimes.[137]

Wither shared Milton's high ideal of love in marriage, rejecting marriage for money and enforced virginity. Both insisted that children should choose their marriage partners, but Wither shared the contemptuous (and Biblical) view that

> The woman for the man was made
> And not the man for her,[138]

which Milton expressed as "He for God only, she for God in him"; both, however, had more appreciation of the woman's point of view than most of their contemporaries. Wither's references to his own "dear Betty" are touchingly affectionate and appreciative. But Wither had no occasion to discuss divorce. When he wrote, "Nor rob I her of aught which she can miss", he was referring to a stolen kiss. When Milton apparently echoed the words, he was referring to male adultery.[139]

Wither, "our Juvenal", was a favourite with Milton's headmaster Alexander Gil, who probably made his pupils translate him into Latin. Influences are tricky things to establish, and I should not like to claim as much as some of Wither's editors. Circe occurs in *Brittans Remembrancer*, Sabrina in one of Wither's epithalamia. More interesting perhaps are parallels, uses of the same imagery. They may serve to remind us how unoriginal Milton was. Wither, for instance, often refers to Sons of Belial, and echoes, "Licence they mean when they cry liberty" more than once. The North was false for Wither in 1642 and 1660, as it was for Milton in 1648 and 1667, no doubt for political as well as Biblical reasons.[140] In 1659 Wither observed that Samson (like Wither himself) could only "be roused up to execute God's vengeance upon the enemies of his country" after he had suffered personal injury.[141] Professor Kermode suggested that the train of thought which led to the versification of *Samson Agonistes* derived from Wither's discussion of Hebrew poetry in *A Preparation to the Psalter* (1619).[142] In common with Milton, Wither exalted the Psalms above all secular poetry.[143]

A few miscellaneous coincidences. Wither, like Milton, seems to have had difficulties with his father over his choice of a poetic career: the epigram in which he explained himself foreshadows Milton's *Ad Patrem*.[144] Both Wither and Milton were devoted to music.[145] They shared a sturdy linguistic patriotism. Wither argued that the phrase Roman Catholic was "an absurd term, contradictory to itself"; Milton improved the joke, referring to "the Pope's bull", "a particular universal".[146] Wither admired Robert Gell, who probably married Milton to his third wife; Wither quoted Gell's views on the Second Coming.[147]

In *Brittans Remembrancer* Wither wrote:

> If thou forbear
> What now thy conscience bids thee to declare
> Thy foolish hope shall fail thee.

This passage may have been in Milton's mind when he wrote his famous words: "When time was, thou couldst not find a syllable of all that thou hadst read or studied to utter on her behalf."[148] Like Milton and many more of his contemporaries, Wither looked to later ages for the justification he had not found in his own day. *Brittans Remembrancer* was dedicated "to posterity and to these times (if they please)". In *Campo-Musae* he appealed to "better times to come".[149] In 1661, like Milton, he felt that he had become an exile in his own country.[150]

One respect in which Wither significantly differed from Milton was in his prophetic sense of England's historical destiny as a great trading power. In 1628 he remarked on the wealth of London and England, and saw their potential prosperity as far greater.[151] In 1645 he was apparently considered for appointment to the Governorship of the Somers Islands.[152] He wanted forests and wastes to be sold again in 1661, and he argued against a restoration of bishops' lands.[153] Among other reasons for rejecting saints' days he included their cost to the nation in loss of labouring time.[154] He favoured social mobility.

In his post-restoration years, when he was not clamouring for financial redress or bewailing imprisonment, Wither occupied himself in collecting and reprinting extracts from his former prophecies to show how right he had been, and so to convince the public that he still was right. But the old fire had gone. Wither may have claimed that the restoration made no difference, but it destroyed his role. As prophet of wrath to come before 1640 he had gained some attention. But his harping on human wickedness did not help to solve the problems which the Revolution had thrown up. Unlike Milton, Wither had no hard core of positive convictions to which he could cling in victory or defeat.

> To what place soe'er we go
> The same sins bring the same plagues too.[155]

We can do nothing to break out of this vicious circle until God decides the time has come. Wither was against sin, but there were plenty of preachers competing in that line of business. Wither's prophetic role had reached its peak in the forties. After 1660 even he realised that he had really nothing left to say. "I . . . will let the world awhile alone", he promised in *Nil Ultra* (1666).[156] He became a garrulous, self-centred and self-pitying old man, who could not stop writing and publishing. He experienced financial loss, imprisonment, and ideological confusion. Unlike Milton, he does not seemed to have learned any lessons from the experience.

One conclusion to draw might be that Wither and Milton had so much in common that a historical approach gives no help towards explaining the gulf between them as poets. But if we place them both in context, it could be argued that it was Milton's good fortune that he was just reaching the height of his poetic powers when he actively participated in "the most heroic and exemplary achievements since the foundation of the world". So far from the writings of his left hand being a waste of time, it was the hopes, the illusions, of the English Revolution, culminating in the traumatic defeat of God's cause, that transformed the intended Arthuriad into *Paradise Lost*, *Paradise Regained*, and *Samson Agonistes*. For Wither the equivalent experience was the plague of 1625; *Brittans Remembrancer* aspired to be his

Paradise Lost, justifying God's ways to men. There are powerful passages in the poem, but the event—or rather Wither's reaction to the event—would not carry the burden which he laid on it. The plague shocked and horrified Wither, but his personal involvement extended no further than to a self-righteous satisfaction that he had not fled from the City as other men did. His main concern was to use the tragedy to denounce the sins of others in a wholly traditional manner. Even when Wither recalls Marvell's "double heart", his expression of it is flat:

> But, oh my God! though grovelling I appear
> Upon the ground, and have a rooting here,
> Which hauls me downward, yet in my desire
> To that which is above me I aspire.[157]

It was therefore natural for Wither to see sin as the sole explanation for the failure of the Revolution; but he had no specific programme to offer. Wither retained his confidence that God would work things out for the best; but he did not believe that any particular institution or group was the instrument of God's purposes—neither the Army nor Parliament nor the saints.[158]

Milton, on the other hand, was totally involved in the Revolution, and felt a share in the guilt of the English people which had led God to desert his own cause. Milton's whole position, after twenty years of effort and self-sacrifice, was in ruins and had to be reconstructed, rethought, and refelt. Wither too experienced disillusionment and defeat, he too was arrested, imprisoned, and suffered financial loss at the restoration, and he too admitted his own share in "our national demerits".[159] But Wither had his glib explanation ready-made: sin, which Wither had been denouncing for forty years. Milton arrived at a theologically similar conclusion, but after travelling through hell and heaven to find it.

NOTES

1. Originally published in *English Renaissance Studies Presented to Dame Helen Gardner* (ed. J. Carey, Oxford U.P., 1980).
2. C.S. Hensley, *The Later Career of George Wither* (The Hague, 1969), pp. 30–5.
3. E. Phillips, *Theatrum Poetarum* (1674), Part II, pp. 56–7; J. Aubrey, *Brief Lives*, II, p. 306.

4. *Vox Pacifica* (1645), pp. 18–24; cf. J.M. French, "Thorn-Dury's Notes on Wither", *Huntington Library Quarterly*, XXII (1959–60), pp. 386–8. Whenever possible I quote Wither from the Spenser Society reprints, but cite the page number of the original edition when this is given.

5. [Anon.], *Withers Remembrancer: Or Extracts Out of . . . Brittans Remembrancer* (1643), Sig. A 2.

6. A. Evans, *The Voice of King Charls the Father to Charls the Son* (1655), p. 38; Defoe, *The History of the Plague in London* (Oxford, 1840), p. 23. First published 1722. Defoe's account of the plague of 1665 draws on Wither's descriptions of the plague of 1625.

7. Thomas, *Berkenhead*, p. 182.

8. Wither, *Hallelujah*, ed. E. Farr (1857), p. xxiv; cf. pp. xxxi, 384–6; *Vox Pacifica* (1645), pp. 10–12, 32 ff.; *Epistolium-Vagum-Prosa-Metricum* (1659), p. 28; *Parallelogrammaton* (1662), p. 30; *Ecchoes from the Sixth Trumpet* (1666), p. 98.

9. Wither, *Juvenilia* (1626 and 1633), I, pp. 264–5. See p. 55 above and p. 195 below; also *M.E.R.*, pp. 19, 50, 59–64.

10. I owe this point to Margot Heinemann. For Pembroke's role as patron of opposition writers see Heinemann, esp. pp. 264–82.

11. Wither, *Juvenilia*, I, pp. 2–5, 175–82; II, pp. 319–20.

12. Wither, *The History of the Pestilence*, 1625 (ed. J.M. French, Harvard U.P., 1932), p. xii; cf. *Brittans Remembrancer*, II, pp. 396, 455–60, 470–4, 520–2, 527–30, 554–5.

13. *British Appeals* (1651), p. 11. Cf. Marvell on the royal actor in the *Horatian Ode* and Milton in *Eikonoklastes*; see also P.W. Thomas, "Two Cultures? Court and Country under Charles I".

14. *Campo-Musae* (1643), pp. 53–4, 61–3.

15. *Vox Pacifica*, p. 68.

16. *Brittans Remembrancer*, p. 5. See also pp. 47–8 above.

17. Wither, *Juvenilia*, III, pp. 630–3; *The Schollers Purgatory* (?1624), *passim*; *Brittans Remembrancer* (1628), Sig. B2, p. 287. Siebert, *Freedom of the Press in England, 1476–1776*, p. 132. *The Schollers Purgatory* may have been published abroad.

18. *Prosopopeia Britannica* (1648), pp. 86, 91–3.

19. *Vox Pacifica*, p. 141.

20. *Speculum Speculativum* (1660), pp. 113–14.

21. *Meditations Upon the Lords Prayer* (1665), p. 40; *Three Private Meditations*, pp. 42–5.

22. Wither, *A Proclamation in the Name of the King of Kings* (1662), p. 68.

23. Wither, *Verses Intended to the King's Majesty* (1662), p. 11.

24. Wither, *Westrow Revived*, pp. 8–9; *Vox Vulgi* (1661), p. 17. (I quote from the reprint edited by W.D. Macray, 1880).

25. *The Psalmes of David* (The Netherlands, 1632), p. 180; cf. *Juvenilia*, I, p. 93; *Hallelujah*, pp. 76–7; *Vox Pacifica* (1645), p. 141; *Prosopopeia Brittanica* (1648), pp. 90, 95–6, and *passim*; *Westrow Revived* (1653), p. 10; *Speculum Speculativum* (1660), pp. 125–6; *Parallelogrammaton* (1662), pp. 100–1.

26. *Juvenilia*, II, p. 436; *Brittans Remembrancer*, pp. 244–5; cr. p. 191.
27. *The Psalmes of David*, II, p. 141.
28. *The Hymnes and Songs of the Church* (1623). I quote from the edition of E. Farr (1856), p. 194.
29. *Brittans Remembrancer*, p. 247; cf. pp. 244–55, *passim*.
30. *Ibid.*, pp. 262–3.
31. *Brittans Remembrancer*, pp. 133–4; *Parallelogrammaton*, pp. 111, 117; *Salt upon Salt* (1659), pp. 24–5; Milton, *Eikonoklastes*, *passim*.
32. *Vox Pacifica*, p. 145; *Westrow Revived*, p. 56; *Parallelogrammaton*, pp. 109, 117, 125; *Three Private Meditations* (1666), pp. 46–8.
33. *Parallelogrammaton* (1662), pp. 108, 116–18; *Three Private Meditations* (1666), pp. 46–8.
34. Jonson, *Works* (ed. C.H. Herford and P. and E. Simpson, Oxford U.P., 1925–52) VII, p. 659.
35. T. Beedome, *Select Poems, Divine and Humane* (Nonesuch Press, 1928), pp. 26–7, "To the excellent Poet Mr. George Withers from thy unknown well-wisher". First published 1641.
36. *Brittans Remembrancer*, pp. 133–4.
37. *Meditations Upon the Lords Prayer*, p. 114.
38. *Juvenilia*, I, pp. 19–20, 131, 265–6; II, pp. 436–8, 478–9; III, pp. 625–30, 691–2, 719–29, 733–4, 776–7; *Hymns and Songs*, p. 231; *Brittans Remembrancer*, pp. 10–11, 117; cf. p. 248; *Hallelujah*, p. xxviii; cf. *M.C.P.W.*, IV, p. 271.
39. *Fides-Anglicana*, pp. 52–4; cf. *M.C.P.W.*, VII, p. 338.
40. *Juvenilia*, I, pp. 254–5, 372–4, 383–6, 428.
41. Wither, *Prosopopeia Britannica* (1648), pp. 47–8; *Epistolium-Vagum-Prosa-Metricum* (1659), p. 20; *M.C.P.W.*, IV, p. 635.
42. Wither, *Reasons humbly offered in justification of an order granted to Major George Wither* (1642), p. 4.
43. Wither, *The Speech Without Doore* (1644), p. 5; *The Two Incomparable Generalissimos of the World* (1644), single sheet.
44. Wither, *Campo-Musae* (1643), pp. 8, 10–11, 33, 44–6, 49–50, 63–4; cf. *Tuba Pacifica* (1664), p. 20. For Selden see his *Table Talk* (1847), p. 97.
45. *Vox Pacifica*, p. 213; cf. pp. 151–2, 200–12.
46. *Opsobalsamum Anglicanum* (1646), p. 19.
47. *Prosopopeia Britannica*, pp. 7–57. The passage quoted is from p. 8.
48. *Vox Pacifica*, pp. 40–3; *Opsobalsamum Anglicanum*, p. 9.
49. G.E. Aylmer, *The State's Servants* (1973), p. 135.
50. Wither, *Amygdala Britannica* (1647), p. 9.
51. *Prosopopeia Britannica*, *passim*.
52. Wither, *Carmen Eucharisticon* (1649), *passim*.
53. Wither, *Three Grains of Spirituall Frankincense* (1651), p. 9. For Wither's acceptance of the radical theory of the Norman Yoke see further *Campo-Musae*, p. 47, and *Speculum Speculativum* (1660), p. 58. For Milton see *M.E.R.*, p. 100.
54. *British Appeals*, pp. 29–51. 26B.
55. Haller, *Tracts on Liberty*, III, pp. 291–2; D.M. Wolfe, "Lilburne's Note on Milton", *Modern Language Notes*, LVI (1941).

56. *Epistolium-Vagum-Prosa-Metricum*, p. 16.

57. Wither, *A Suddain Flash* (1657), p. 16.

58. See my *The Experience of Defeat*, pp. 297–301.

59. *A Cordial Confection* (1659), p. 25. Partially reprinted in W.M. Clyde, *The Struggle for the Freedom of the Press from Caxton to Cromwell* (Oxford U.P., 1934), pp. 338–42.

60. *The Protector* (1665), *passim.*; *Salt upon Salt* (1659), p. 38.

61. *Vaticinium Causuale* (1655), p. 3.

62. *Boni Ominis Votum* (July 1656), in *Echoes from the Sixth Trumpet* (1660), p. 115; *Salt upon Salt*, p. 44.

63. *M.C.P.W.*, IV, p. 549; Wither, *A Cordial Confection*, in Clyde, loc. cit.

64. *Westrow Revived*, p. 68. The charge was laid against Oliver Cromwell.

65. Wither, *Vox Pacifica*, p. 196; *Prosopopeia Britannica*, pp. 58–71; *Westrow Revived*, pp. 70–2; *Vaticinium Causuale* (1655), pp. 8, 14–16. Cf. *M.E.R.*, pp. 189–97; *The Experience of Defeat*, pp. 281–2.

66. *Salt upon Salt*, pp. 9–10; *Parallelogrammaton*, pp. 5, 35. In 1664 Wither was in favour of union with the Dutch (*Tuba Pacifica*, 1614, pp. 11–12; *Sigh for the Pitchers*, 1666, *passim.*) To his great credit, Wither disapproved of slavery and the slave trade (*Sigh for the Pitchers*, pp. 29–30).

67. *Juvenilia*, II, p. 406.

68. *The Psalmes of David*, II, pp. 184, 145; cf. *Campo-Musae*, pp. 25, 66, 68; *Westrow Revived*, pp. 54–5; *Parallelogrammaton*, pp. 98, 123, 137.

69. *M.C.P.W.*, I, pp. 706–7; III, pp. 210, 256, 316, 536, 598–9. Milton held these views in 1649 no less than in 1641, Wither in 1612 no less than in 1662 (*Prince Henries Obsequies*, 1612; *Parallelogrammaton*, pp. 48–58).

70. *Brittans Remembrancer*, pp. 18, 22, 24, 31–2, 162–5.

71. *Campo-Musae*, p. 64; *Vox Pacificae*, p. 68.

72. *Epistolium-Vagum-Prosa-Metricum*, p. 18; cf. pp. 25–6.

73. *The Prisoners Plea* (1661), p. 30; *Parallelogrammaton*, pp. 56–7; cf. *Vaticinia Poetica* (1666), pp. 6, 8–9; *Ecchoes from the Sixth Trumpet* (1666), p. 53.

74. *Parallelogrammaton*, p. 54; cf. *A Memorandum to London* (1661), p. 72.

75. *A Suddain Flash*, p. 16; *Epistolium-Vagum*, p. 25.

76. Wither, *The Dark Lantern* (1653), pp. 1, 37–74. Wither spoke with cautious enthusiasm of the Venetian constitution.

77. *Amygdala Britannica* (1647), p. 9.

78. *Vaticinium Causuale* (1655), p. 11; *A Cordial Confection* (1659), pp. 8–9, 31.

79. *Epistolium-Vagum*, p. 22.

80. *Speculum Speculativum*, p. 17—written, Wither tells us, "immediately after his Majesty's restoration".

81. *Furor Poeticus* (1660), pp. 19–20; cf. *Vox Vulgi* (1661), p. 17. I quote from [the reprint of 1880, ed. W.D.] Macray's edition.

82. *Furor Poeticus* (1660), p. 7; cf. *Ecchoes from the Sixth Trumpet*, p. 143.

83. *Furor-Poeticus*, pp. 4–7.

84. *Speculum Speculativum*, pp. 81–3; *M.C.P.W.*, VII, p. 461.

85. *Speculum Speculativum*, p. 59.

86. *Ibid.*, pp. 25, 30, 58; *Furor-Poeticus*, p. 20.

87. *Furor-Poeticus*, pp. 4–7.

88. *Epistolium-Vagum*, pp. 24–5; *Speculum Speculativum* (1660), pp. 42–3, 69–75; *M.C.P.W.*, VII, p. 463.

89. *Furor-Poeticus*, pp. 15–16; *Opsobalsamum Anglicanum*, pp. 12–13; *Verses Intended to the King's Majesty*, pp. 5–6.

90. *Speculum Speculativum*, pp. 24–34; *Vox Vulgi*, pp. 14, 16; *The Prisoners Plea*, pp. 45–51.

91. *Vox Vulgi*, p. 19; *Ecchoes from the Sixth Trumpet*, pp. 89, 94–6.

92. *Fides-Anglicana* (1661), pp. 21–5.

93. *Speculum Speculativum*, pp. 128–34; *An Improvement of Imprisonment*, p. 44; *The Prisoners Plea*, p. 30; *Parallelogrammaton*, pp. 7, 22, 138; *A Memorandum to London*, p. 72; *Vaticinia Poetica*, pp. 6, 8–9, 20; *Ecchoes from the Sixth Trumpet*, Sig. B 4—B 4v, Cv, pp. 51–2.

94. *Brittans Remembrancer*, II, p. 268.

95. *Epistolium-Vagum*, pp. 2, 15–16; *Salt upon Salt*, pp. 12–13, 46; *A Cordial Confection*, pp. 6–7; cf. *Speculum Speculativum*, p. 56; *Fides-Anglicana*, pp. 4–5, 27–8; *Furor-Poeticus*, pp. 12, 19, 33; *Parallelogrammaton*, pp. 68–73, 87 ("I never refused the oath of allegiance to any possessionary power or person"); *A Proclamation in the Name of the King of Kings*, pp. 51–4; *Verses Intended to the King's Majesty*, p. 9.

96. *Tuba-Pacifica*, p. 20. Since Wither was arguing against a Dutch War, this might have sounded ominous.

97. His attempt to use Venner's rising to frighten the government came as part of his unremitting struggle for financial redress (*Fides-Anglicana*, pp. 21–5).

98. *Furor-Poeticus*, pp. 7–15, 23, 37.

99. *Speculum Speculativum*, Sig. A 2v, pp. 18, 78.

100. *Salt upon Salt*, p. 43; *Furor-Poeticus*, pp. 18–19. Wither expressed considerable scepticism about the process by which Richard Cromwell emerged as Oliver's designated heir (*ibid.*, pp. 39–40).

101. *Brittans Remembrancer*, pp. 39–40, 52–9, 249–52; cf. *The Psalmes of David*, II, pp. 168, 303–4.

102. Nemesius, *The Nature of Man*, Englished by George Wither (1636), Sig. A3–5. William Haller noted the importance of this passage (*Liberty and Reformation in the Puritan Revolution*, Columbia U.P., 1955, p. 177). *The Nature of Man* was reprinted in 1657.

103. Nemesius, *op. cit.*, pp. 568–9; Wither, *Vaticinia Poetica* (1666), p. 27; *Parallelogrammaton*, pp. 61–5; cf. *Juvenilia*, I, pp. 263–4; *M.C.P.W.*, II, pp. 366–7.

104. Ed. French, *The History of the Pestilence*, p. xiii; *Brittans Remembrancer*, pp. 52–3; *Emblemes* (1635), Book IV, No. xliii; *A Cordial Confection*, p. 26; *Parallelogrammaton*, pp. 68–9; *Meditations upon the Lord's Prayer*, p. 79; *Vaticinia Poetica*, pp. 26–7; *Fragmenta Poetica* (1669), pp. 123–4.

105. *Juvenilia*, I. p. 281; *Brittans Remembrancer*, p. 62, cf. pp. 286–7.

106. *Campo-Musae*, pp. 64–5; cf. *Brittans Remembrancer*, pp. 13, 44, 54, 59–72, 78, 82, 98–9; *Opobalsamum Anglicanum*, p. 6.

107. *Carmen Eucharisticon* (1649).

108. *Epistolum-Vagum*, pp. 16, 19–23, 29; *Vox Vulgi*, pp. 25, 35; cf. *Furor-Poeticus*, pp. 16–17.

109. Wither, *The Dark Lantern*, pp. 18–19.

110. J.M. French, "Thorn-Dury's Notes on Wither", *Huntington Library Quarterly*, 22 (1959–60), pp. 386–8. A glance at *Brittans Remembrancer*, pp. 245–52, will show how right Clobery was. Cf. *Juvenilia*, I, pp. 49–52.

111. *Parallelogrammaton*, pp. 46, 68–9; *A Cordial Confection*, p. 26.

112. *Parallelogrammaton*, pp. 74–5.

113. *Ecchoes from the Sixth Trumpet*, pp. 97–8.

114. *A Memorandum to London*, pp. 56, 58.

115. *Speculum Speculativum*, pp. 55–6. This poem was dedicated to Charles II.

116. *Parallelogrammaton*, pp. 46, 68–70, 74; cf. pp. 28, 38, 45.

117. *Hymnes and Songs*, p. liii; *Vox Vulgi*, p. 19; *A Memorandum to London*, p. 52; *Ecchoes from the Sixth Trumpet*, pp. 89, 96; *M.C.P.W.*, I, pp. 783–8, II, p. 178.

118. *An Improvement of Imprisonment*, p. 103; *Parallelogrammaton*, pp. 104–5. For Williams see *W.T.U.D.*, p. 101.

119. *Parallelogrammaton*, pp. 61–5; *Meditations on the Lord's Prayer*, pp. 78–96, 120–6, 132–3; *A Memorandum to London*, pp. 52–3.

120. *Hymnes and Songs*, p. xxxvii; *The Prisoners Plea* (1661), p. 27.

121. *Speculum Speculativum*, pp. 51–2; *Parallelogrammaton*, pp. 43–4, 88–93; *Vaticinia Poetica*, pp. 10–12.

122. *Parallelogrammaton*, p. 44.

123. *Juvenilia*, III, pp. 629, 896; *Prosopopeia Britannica*, pp. 29–33.

124. *Emblemes*, Book III, No. xxxiii.

125. *Juvenilia*, I, pp. 198–200; *Brittans Remembrancer*, pp. 30, 107, 129, 186–9; *Speculum Speculativum*, p. 67.

126. *Juvenilia*, III, pp. 679–80, 700; *Brittans Remembrancer*, pp. 234–6; *Vox Vulgi*, pp. 14, 30; *Parallelogrammaton*, p. 101.

127. *Juvenilia*, III, p. 679; *Carmen Expostularium* (1647), *passim; Ecchoes from the Sixth Trumpet*, p. 19. Cf. *M.E.R.*, pp. 199, 212, 369.

128. *Brittans Remembrancer*, p. 47; *Juvenilia*, I, pp. 300–1. Cf. *M.C.P.W.*, I, pp. 293, 319–20; *Paradise Lost*, VIII. 188–97, *Paradise Regained*, Book IV.

129. Wither, *Meditations upon the Lords Prayer* (1665), p. 96.

130. Nemesius, *op. cit.*, pp. 23–6, 82–93; cf. pp. 242–3; *Westrow Revived*, p. 37.

131. *Hymnes and Songs*, pp. 206–7; *Hallelujah*, pp. 244–6; *Ecchoes from the Sixth Trumpet*, p. 121.

132. *The Psalmes of David*, II, p. 246; Preface to Nemesius, *op. cit.*, Sig. A5; *Fides-Anglicana*, p. 22.

133. *Hymnes and Songs*, p. 216; *Emblemes*, II. 15, IV. 26; *Parallelogrammaton*, pp. 49–56; *M.C.P.W.*, VI, pp. 353–4, 537–41, 639–40, 708–14.

134. *Hallelujah*, p. 45.

135. *Juvenilia*, I, pp. 236–42, 258–62; Milton, *Prolusion VI, Defensio Secunda, passim*; French, "Thorn-Dury's Notes on Wither", pp. 383–5.

136. Wither, *An Improvement of Imprisonment* (1661), pp. 98–100. Contrast

the diatribe against tobacco in *Juvenilia*, I, pp. 222–4—written perhaps with an eye on James I. For betting see *Juvenilia*, III, p. 751; *Brittans Remembrancer*, p. 4; *M.E.R.*, p. 59.

137. *Brittans Remembrancer*, pp. 19, 134–9; *Campo-Musae*, p. 66; *Westrow Revived*, p. 8 ("Hypocrisy / Is worse than error") *Furor-Poeticus*, p. 43; *Vox Vulgi*, p. 17; *Paradise Lost*, III. 682–5, IV. 121–2, 744–7.

138. *Juvenilia*, II, pp. 480–3; *Hallelujah*, pp. 309–19; *Parallelogrammaton*, p. 34.

139. *An Improvement of Imprisonment* (1661), pp. 81–8, 92–5, 105–7, 120; *A Memorandum to London* (1665), p. 72; *Juvenilia*, III, p. 920; *M.C.P.W.*, III, p. 674.

140. *Campo-Musae*, p. 52; *Furor-Poeticus*, p. 24; *M.E.R.*, pp. 371–2.

141. *Epistolium-Vagum*, pp. 23, 27.

142. F. Kermode, "*Samson Agonistes* and Hebrew Prosody", *Durham University Journal*, New Series 14 (1952), pp. 59–63.

143. Cf. Wither, *Halleluiah, or Brittans Second Remembrancer* (1641), to the Reader.

144. *Juvenilia*, II, pp. 361–3.

145. *Emblemes*, II. 3. We have Percy Scholes's authority for Wither's keen interest in and competent knowledge of music (*The Puritans and Music*, Oxford U.P., London, 1934, p. 156). Scholes referred especially to *A Preparation to the Psalter*.

146. *Juvenilia*, I, p. 22; *Parallelogrammaton*, p. 105; *Three Private Meditations* (1665), p. 46; *M.C.P.W.*, VIII, p. 422.

147. *Ecchoes from the Sixth Trumpet*, pp. 8–9.

148. *Brittans Remembrancer*, p. 7; *M.C.P.W.*, I, p. 804.

149. *Campo-Musae*, pp. 2, 48; cf. *M.C.P.W.*, VII, pp. 462–3, VIII, p. 4. *Brittans Remembrancer* was reprinted in 1689 to celebrate the Glorious Revolution.

150. *An Improvement of Imprisonment*, p. 101.

151. *Brittans Remembrancer*, pp. 16–18, 39, 237–8.

152. J.M. French, "Four Scarce Poems of George Wither", *Huntington Library Bulletin*, II (1931), pp. 94–5; A. Pritchard, "George Wither and the Somers Islands", *Notes and Queries*, CCVI (1961), pp. 428–30. French lists other economic offices for which Wither was considered.

153. *Fides-Anglicana*, pp. 35–54.

154. *Parallelogrammaton*, pp. 123–4.

155. *Ecchoes from the Sixth Trumpet*, Sig. Dv.

156. *Three Private Meditations*, p. 32; cf. pp. 28–40 *passim*.

157. *Emblemes*, IV. 1.

158. *Speculum Speculativum*, pp. 30, 35, 55–8.

159. *Furor-Poeticus*, pp. 19–20; *Vox Vulgi*, p. 17.

7. John Milton (1608–74) and Andrew Marvell (1621–78)[1]

Fifty-odd years ago I sat at school in York working for School Certificate, the then equivalent of O-levels. My English Literature texts included the poems by Milton, Marvell and Dryden in *The Golden Treasury*. Those who drafted the School Certificate syllabus had good precedent for linking Milton, Marvell and Dryden. On 7 September 1658 the three of them walked, as employees of the Protectorate, in the procession at Oliver Cromwell's funeral.[2] Dryden soon abandoned the convictions—or interests—which led him, like Marvell, to write celebratory poems to Cromwell: but Milton and Marvell remained true to the beliefs which had united them in the sixteen-fifties and which, I shall argue, continued to unite them until Milton's death in 1674.

At first sight Milton and Marvell seem far apart—the metaphysical, lightly-elegant wit, and the organ-voiced inspired bard. On closer examination we find greater similarities of theme and treatment. Marvell was more serious than some of the books suggest; Milton—thank God!—a great deal less serious than the image. In their political outlook, in their dislikes, they had much in common.

Politics was an essential part of the experience of both poets. Throughout the eighteenth century Marvell was renowned primarily as a courageous partisan of liberty, though his poems were never as neglected as we used to assume from the fact that Samuel Johnson did not include him in his *Lives of the Poets*. Milton's politics as well as his poetry inspired Thomson, Blake, Shelley, the Chartists and countless others. Wordsworth's "Milton, thou shouldst be living at this hour" is matched by Thomas Moore's "Is there none/To act a Marvell's part?"[3] I have no sympathy for the gentlemanly aestheticism which mars even so good a book as Leishman's *The Art of Marvell's Poetry*. Leishman contrasts writing for cultivated gentlemen with Marvell's "rather philistine and ill-informed . . . post-restoration activities", devoting "a disproportionate attention to matters which wisdom would dismiss with, at the most, a weary smile".[4] Such a view suggests a lack of imagination horrifying in one who sets up to be a critic of poetry. If it is impossible for this sort of critic to conceive the cultural consequences of living under a tyranny, there are many parts of the world today to which he could turn for education. Marvell's activities which Leishman's "wisdom would dismiss with a weary smile" included keeping Milton alive and free to write *Paradise Lost*, *Paradise Regained* and *Samson Agonistes*, as well as trying to shield dissenters from persecution and his country from becoming a French puppet state.

I sympathize much more with those critics who see even Marvell's apparently unpolitical verse as shot through with consciousness of living at a great historical turning-point—such as informs "An Horatian Ode" and "The First Anniversary of the Government under O.C.": even "To his Coy Mistress" is full of witty allusions to political and religious happenings of Marvell's day which are missed by many critics.[5] The conversion of the Jews, for instance, was a subject of current controversy in the sixteen-forties and sixteen-fifties. It was agreed to be a necessary antecedent of the overthrow of Antichrist, the Pope. One favoured date for this event, based on the careful calculations of the best mathematicians of the time, was 1656. Since Noah's Flood took place in the year 1656 from the Creation, the next cataclysmic event might be expected in AD 1656. So in

>   I would
> Love you ten years before the Flood:
> And you should if you please refuse
> Till the Conversion of the *Jews* (ll. 7–10)

the two periods follow logically from one another. If the lady continues to refuse "Till the Conversion of the *Jews*" she may find that the time is shorter than she thinks.[6]

There remains the traditional problem of why Marvell's best poetry, like Vaughan's, seems to date from the early sixteen-fifties, as though it relates to the tensions of his politically undecided period, and could not be recovered once Marvell was committed. Such an evaluation underestimates Marvell's satires, now fortunately being more carefully assessed.[7] And there may be optical illusions here, since few of Marvell's poems can be confidently dated. I shall quote from time to time from pieces doubtfully attributed to Marvell, like "Britannia and Rawleigh" and the "Dialogue between the Two Horses". I do not wish to argue for their authenticity; but since some contemporaries believed them to be by Marvell it is reasonable to suppose that they express views not very dissimilar to his.[8]

We do not know when Milton and Marvell first became acquainted. The record starts in February 1653 with a letter from Milton to John Bradshaw, president of the court which had condemned Charles I in 1649, and in 1653 President of the Council of State. Milton (aged 44) had recently gone completely blind, which clearly hampered his efficiency as the republic's Secretary for Foreign Tongues. In this letter Milton pushed the thirty-one-year-old Marvell as a possible assistant to him, and praised him in generous terms as "a man whom both by report and the converse I have had with him is of singular desert for the state to make use of: who also offers himself, if there be any employment for him". ("The forward youth that would appear / Must now forsake his Muses dear / Nor in the shadows sing / His numbers languishing".) Milton mentioned Marvell's father, lately the Puritan minister of Hull—one of those who had swung Hull to support Parliament in the civil war, Bishop Hacket thought.[9] Milton also referred in 1653 to the fact that Marvell had spent four years abroad in Holland, France, Italy and Spain, "to very good purpose as I believe, and the gaining of those four languages; besides he is a scholar and well-read in Latin and Greek authors". As an added recommendation Milton reminded Bradshaw that Marvell "comes now lately out of the house of the Lord Fairfax who was General", where he was language tutor to Mary Fairfax. Marvell's French was good enough for him to act as interpreter at French-speaking courts when he was secretary to the embassy of the Earl of Carlisle in 1663–4, as well as translate speeches into Latin. Like Milton, Marvell wrote Latin poems.[10] "It would be hard to find a man so fit every way". Milton concluded in 1653, hinting that Marvell had the makings of a man who might rise to ambassadorial rank.[11]

This letter gives us some information about Marvell's early career which we should not otherwise have; and it poses some interesting problems. Why should Milton push this young man so hard? He was not *prima facie* Milton's type. Marvell as a Cambridge undergraduate had had a brief connection with the Jesuits, though it did not lead to lasting conversion as in the case of that other son of a Yorkshire Puritan minister, Richard Crashawe. The fact that Marvell was sent down from Trinity may charitably be attributed to non-residence following the death of his father when Marvell was nineteen. Milton we recall had himself been rusticated. Marvell's four years abroad had been between 1642 and 1646: so he appears to have opted out of the civil war which had meant so much to Milton. Marvell's connections in the sixteen-forties seem to have been royalist rather than parliamentarian. Biographers have perhaps made too much of Marvell's alleged royalism: the only poem which Margoliouth calls "unequivocally royalist" is, he agrees, of doubtful attribution. Marvell's poem to Lovelace no more commits him to Lovelace's royalist politics than Milton's help to the imprisoned Davenant in 1652 (if he did help him) committed Milton to Davenant's.[12]

The opening stanza of the "Horatian Ode", although of course ironical, suggests an uncommitted person consciously moving towards commitment, rather than a change of allegiance.[13] The poem distinguishes between Charles I's personal virtues and the historic force which Oliver Cromwell personifies. I find it difficult to believe that "Tom May's Death", with its sneers at May as a turncoat from courtier to propagandist for Parliament, was written when May died, only a few months after the "Horatian Ode" was composed. There are in fact many echoes of May in the Ode.[14] It seems to me more likely that at any rate the final version of the poem on May was written after the restoration; lines 85–90 appear to refer to the exhumation of May's body from Westminster Abbey in September 1661. It may well be that Marvell had some personal grudge against May, who like Marvell seems to have had connections both with Hull and with Fairfax;[15] but a post-restoration date makes it a less unpleasant poem than if it was written immediately after May's death in November 1650, and opens up the possibility of all sorts of ironical overtones. Post-1660 turncoats included ex-Parliamentarians whose enthusiastic new-found royalism could not be openly attacked. ("Coward churchmen", for instance.)

In 1653 or early 1654 Mrs Anne Sadleir told Roger Williams that Marvell had helped Milton in writing *Eikonoklastes*, his demolition of *Eikon Basilike*. *Eikonoklastes* was published in October 1649, so if Mrs Sadleir was right, Marvell must have got to know Milton not later than the summer of 1649. French and Parker assumed that she was mistaken, and that if Marvell did help Milton with anything it should be the *Defensio* (February 1651) or John Phillips's *Responsio* of December 1651. But it is always rash to be wiser than a contemporary; Mrs Sadleir was the aunt of Cyriack Skinner, the mutual friend of Milton and Marvell; Marvell's father dedicated a sermon to her: and her reference to "that most accursed libel" sounds more like *Eikonoklastes* than either of the other two tracts.[16] Mrs Sadleir's remark that Milton "had two or three wives living" when he wrote his divorce tracts is inaccurate; but it may well be a distortion of correct information. Milton believed polygamy to be lawful, and during his first wife's absence he had a "design of marrying one of Dr Davis's daughters". He was "in treaty" for this marriage when his wife returned, we are told by the anonymous biographer whom Parker believed to be Cyriack Skinner.[17]

There are other possible links between the two poets. Marvell was born fifteen miles outside Hull, and all his life he was associated with the town of which his father had been minister; in 1658 and from 1659 to his death he was its M.P.. Cyriack Skinner, Milton's pupil in the mid-sixteen-forties and his very special friend, came from Barrow-on-Humber. Marvell mentioned him in a letter to Milton of 2 June 1654. The Skinners were close friends of the Marvell family. Andrew's father had been drowned in 1640 whilst crossing the Humber with "Madam Skinner", probably Cyriack's sister.[18] Margoliouth plausibly suggested that Marvell's poem "The Picture of little T.C. in a Prospect of Flowers" was written about Theophila Cornewall, Cyriack's niece. Margoliouth indeed supposed that Marvell's foreign travels might have been undertaken as tutor to Edward Skinner, Cyriack's brother, and conjectured that Cyriack introduced Marvell to Milton.[19] Aubrey, in listing Milton's "familiar learned acquaintance", named Andrew Marvell first and Skinner second. Wood called Marvell "some time one of John Milton's companions".[20]

Now from 1648 to 1655, and again in 1659–60, the governor of Hull was Robert Overton, himself born at Easington in Holderness, just outside Hull. Milton in 1654 referred to Overton as an intimate friend over many years, and Marvell in a letter to Milton of the same year spoke with "an affectionate curiosity" about "Colonel Overton's business", his arrest for republican activities.[21] Overton's chaplain at Hull in the sixteen-fifties was John Canne, who must have been known to Milton since both were propagandists for the republic and Canne often echoes Milton in his writings. Skinner, Overton or Canne might have introduced Marvell to Milton. So might the regicide John Alured, an East Yorkshireman active in the Parliamentarian county committee during the forties; or his brother Colonel Matthew Alured, also associated with Hull.[22]

Another possible link is Fairfax, in whose household Marvell lived, probably from the beginning of 1651 until just before Milton's letter to Bradshaw of February 1653. Milton wrote a sonnet to Fairfax in 1648, must have known him as a member of the Council of State until Fairfax retired in 1650, and still praised him warmly in 1654.[23] This still leaves the problem of how Marvell came to be employed by Fairfax. Apart from the possibility that Milton had a hand in it, there were traditional links between the West Riding and Hull, which had been strengthened during the civil war when these were the two main Parliamentarian areas in Yorkshire. Fairfax was often in Hull.

Milton failed to get Marvell a job in the government service in 1653; instead the younger poet went to Eton as tutor to Cromwell's ward, William Dutton, no doubt on Milton's recommendation. At Eton Marvell lived in the house of John Oxenbridge. Milton knew Oxenbridge well enough to send him a copy of the *Defensio Secunda* in 1654.[24] Oxenbridge is believed to have been the source of Marvell's knowledge of Bermuda, whither Oxenbridge had fled as a religious refugee under Laud. It would be nice to know more of Oxenbridge's influence on Marvell. The sour Antony Wood described him as "a person noted to be of no good principles". In 1634 he was deprived of his tutorship by Laud, Chancellor of Oxford University. Oxenbridge's offence was organizing student participation in moves to democratize the government of Magdalen Hall. He sought refuge in Bermuda, "safe from the storms and prelates' rage", as Marvell put it, "an isle far kinder than our own". In 1641 or 1642, he returned, when "liberty of conscience had returned". I quote from Marvell's epitaph on Jane Oxenbridge. Oxenbridge preached "very enthusiastically", apparently for some years as an itinerant. After the Battle of Marston Moor he settled at Beverley, very near Hull, where he remained until the early sixteen-fifties. His second wife was the daughter of Hezekiah Woodward, whose name was often associated with Milton's in the sixteen-forties. In 1660 Oxenbridge emigrated again, this time to Surinam, then to Barbados, ending up in Boston, New England. At Magdalen Hall, Oxenbridge had been tutor to John Bidle, the main exponent of anti-Trinitarianism in England in the sixteen-forties and fifties. Milton was an anti-Trinitarian: Marvell was accused of the same heresy. If he held it, he was as careful as Milton was never to proclaim it publicly; like Milton, Marvell defended Arians.[25]

Masson suggested, plausibly enough, that the Latin poems which Marvell wrote in 1653–4 may have been intended to keep himself and his literary skills before the eyes of officialdom. The first was "A Letter to Doctor Ingelo", a Fellow of Eton who had accompanied Bulstrode Whitelocke as chaplain on his embassy to Sweden. This is in effect "a political poem celebrating the Protector's alliance with Sweden"; it was followed by two epigrams on Cromwell's portrait given to Queen Christina.[26] The eulogy on Christina in "A Letter to Doctor Ingelo" recalls Milton's extravagant praise of her in his *Second Defence* in 1654.

Not later than January 1656 Marvell took William Dutton to France. He may have circulated Milton's *Pro Se Defensio* at Saumur.[27] In September 1657 Marvell at last became Latin Secretary to the Commonwealth—through Milton's influence, Samuel Parker alleged. We catch glimpses of Marvell in August 1658 trailing ambassadors around.[28] In July 1659, under the restored Rump of the Long Parliament, he occupied lodgings in Whitehall.[29] We recall that Milton had lost his lodgings there in 1651. If, as would appear, Marvell was promoted by the restored Rump, this throws a light on his political attitudes which deserves emphasis. The deposition of Protector Richard Cromwell and the restoration of the republic were moves to the left, short-lived though they proved to be. Colonel Overton returned from jail to political influence; Marvell's conservative superior John Thurloe disappeared from the scene. The radical John Canne for a short time replaced Marchamont Nedham as editor of *Mercurius Politicus*. Milton, who had gradually withdrawn from political activity with the growing conservatism of the Protectorate, returned hopefully to the fray in 1659 with a series of pamphlets in which he tried (vainly) to reunite the radicals in face of the return to monarchy which above all things he abhorred. If Marvell was promoted by the Rump, it looks as though they thought he too supported them. Early in 1653 (almost certainly) Marvell had in "The Character of Holland" lauded the English Commonwealth as the "darling of heaven, and of men the care".[30]

This is important evidence for our assessment of Marvell's attitude towards Oliver Cromwell. Some biographers, including Professor Wallace, have seen "The First Anniversary" as a plea for Cromwell to accept the crown. Others, like Professors Zwicker and Patterson in this century, and Marvell's opponent Bishop Samuel Parker in the seventeenth century, saw it as an *attack* on kingship, and a warning to Oliver not to accept the crown, similar to those which Milton uttered in the *Second Defence*.[31] Although I cannot argue the case here, the latter view seems to me correct: re-read lines 15–16, 22–4, 103–30, 249–58, 387–94 (and Margoliouth's note on line 106) with an open mind, a nodding acquaintance with the Bible, and an awareness of the historical situation. Marvell promised kings that, if he was given time, he would "with graver accents shake / Your royal sloth, and your long slumbers wake". For Marvell, as for Milton in the first *Defence*, and again in *Samson Agonistes*, "matchless Gideon" was an example of a great leader who refused the crown.[32] In 1659 Marvell was associated with James Harrington's republican Rota Club, whose president was Cyriack Skinner. There are many traces of Harringtonian ideas in Marvell's writings, some of them dating from before Harrington published.[33]

In 1660, when forward youths were competing to write panegyrics on Charles II and Monck, Milton and Marvell were conspicuous by their silence. Yet Marvell never publicly attacked the Stuarts with the venom Milton had shown in *Eikonklastes* and the *Ready and Easy Way*. In consequence he was in a position to help Milton at the restoration, when by some miracle, still not fully explained, the latter was saved from the hanging, disembowelling and quartering which befell so many of his friends and associates. Sir William Davenant and the Boyle family no doubt helped; but Marvell had Fairfax's ear, and Fairfax was an important man in 1660. (His role had been more decisive in making the restoration possible than that of anyone but Monck: Monck took a dukedom, and many other old Parliamentarians were given peerages, but Fairfax accepted no honours and returned again to retirement in Yorkshire). Not only was Milton saved from execution, he was released from prison and received an official pardon. Marvell even had the audacity to raise in the House of Commons (December 1660) the fact that Milton had been charged excessive fees by his jailer. Marvell's motion was seconded by Colonel Edward King, whose wife was the daughter of Bridget Skinner, Cyriack's niece.[34]

After 1660 Milton was silenced. It was for a long time impossible for him to publish. He turned from pamphleteering to perfecting his radically heretical theological treatise, the *De Doctrina Christiana*, and to those intensely political poems *Paradise Lost*, *Paradise Regained* and *Samson Agonistes*. Not until 1673 was there enough of a political thaw for him to risk pamphleteering again, and then he returned to battle with a series of tracts which I shall discuss later.

We know little about the political activities of either Milton or

Marvell in the sixteen-sixties. Milton lay very low. Some young men, including Samuel Parker, "haunted his house day by day", taking part in seditious discussions. Marvell first met Parker there; the latter was then discussing how long the restored monarchy would last.[35] We have traces of Marvell's activities in the House of Commons in 1667 in Milward's *Diary*. He defended the old Parliamentarian civil servant Phineas Pett against attempts to make him a scapegoat for the disasters of the second Dutch war.[36] He even came to the rescue of Clarendon when M.P.s tried to saddle him with responsibility for the war (which in fact he had opposed), though Marvell did not miss the opportunity to stress Clarendon's alleged remark that "the King was an unactive person and indisposed for government". Marvell remained loyal to his old political associates—James Harrington, John Owen, John Howe and Richard Baxter as well as Milton. In 1668, though in a minority, Marvell spoke up against the Conventicles Act.[39] He accused the government of truckling to France, and was "most sharp" against Arlington and some of the Council. He is alleged to have said that the Duke of Lauderdale deserved a halter rather than a garter. Defoe tells us that Marvell invented the nickname "Cabal" to describe the government of Clifford, Arlington, Buckingham, Ashley-Cooper and Lauderdale, which has stuck.[38]

The famous republican conspirator, Colonel Blood the crown stealer, in 1670 mentioned Marvell as one of his associates.[39] Marvell described Blood admiringly as "a most bold and yet sober fellow", who "astonished the King and the court with the generosity and wisdom of his answers".[40] Professor Haley has produced evidence to suggest that Marvell shared in the clandestine plotting organized by Peter du Moulin in the sixteen-seventies, in contact with the Dutch government. In 1662–3 Marvell had been in the Netherlands for nearly a year on unidentified "business". He was reported there again early in 1674, at a time when there is a gap in his correspondence. These visits may have been entirely innocent; but the Netherlands was the natural refuge of English republican exiles, and Marvell was a close friend of at least one Dutch agent. A list of conspirators' code names in 1674 includes Marvell's, and he was denounced more than once to the authorities by informers.[41] Marvell may have been writing pamphlets for this group, and perhaps helping with others; the ironical style of its most significant tract, du Moulin's *England's Appeal* (1673), seems to me strongly reminiscent of Marvell.[42] Marvell's own major pamphlet, *An Account of the Growth of Popery and Arbitrary Government in England* (1667), is an elaboration of *England's Appeal.*

Professor Haley was interested mainly in the connection with the Dutch republic, the natural ally of the English opposition. But for our purposes even more interesting is Marvell's association with what in 1671 was referred to as "Marchamond . . . and Milton with their junto".[43] Marchamont Nedham was a professional journalist who in the sixteen-forties wrote first for Parliament, then for the King. In his first Parliamentary phase, Nedham seems to have shared many of Milton's views—his insistence on religious liberty, his Erastian rejection of clerical domination, his dislike for Dr Featley.[44] After Nedham's first arrest in 1649 Milton (it seems) persuaded him to revert to the Parliamentarian allegiance. So thorough was the transformation that in May 1650 Nedham published a book, *The Case of the Commonwealth*, defending the republic in terms which endeared him to eighteenth-century republicans; and in June Nedham was appointed editor of a semi-official weekly newspaper, *Mercurius Politicus*, under Milton's supervision. At the restoration Nedham fled to the Netherlands until the Act of Oblivion was passed. Despite republishing some of the earlier pro-royalist writing in 1661, Nedham remained, in Antony Wood's words, "a great crony of Milton's, the latter's disciple".[45]

They were closely linked in the public mind. In 1652 the Leveller John Lilburne joined Nedham and Milton in praise. Seven years later the arch-regicide, John Bradshaw, a month before his death, altered his will so as to leave a legacy of £10 each to Milton and Nedham. In 1660 the royalist propagandist Roger L'Estrange associated Milton and his "brother" Nedham as possible authors of a pamphlet which "runs foul, tends to tumult".[46] Edward Phillips referred to Nedham as one of Milton's "particular friends", along with Andrew Marvell, "young Lawrence" and Cyriack Skinner. So the friendship between Milton and Nedham lasted for twenty years. But the reference in 1671 to the "junto" of Milton and Nedham suggests that they may have resumed active political co-operation as opposition to Charles II's government grew.

Pamphlets arising out of Marvell's controversy with Samuel Parker frequently associate the former with Nedham and Milton. In his posthumous *History of his own Time* (1728) Parker refers to "that vile fellow Marvell" as "one of the cabal of 1660, a remnant of the rebellion, who had bound themselves by oath from the beginning to embarrass the King. If he was not the conspirators' secretary, yet he was admitted to all their seditious consultations on account of the old friendship between them"; and Milton was Marvell's patron. Richard Leigh said Milton and Nedham served as models for Marvell, who was Milton's "fellow journeyman" and lickspittle. He linked "a Martin Marprelate, a Milton" with Marvell. Dryden seized on this perceptive recognition of the ancestry of Marvell's prose and ideas by calling Martin Marprelate "the Marvell of those times", who used railing and scurrility to "hedge in a stake amongst the rabble". L'Estrange and several other pamphleteers suggested that Milton guided Marvell's pen. Some hinted that there was a homosexual relationship between them.[47] Echard associated Marvell and Nedham as "both pestilent wits and noted incendiaries". The attacks of Parker and his satellites so incensed Milton that he proposed to reply himself. But his friends dissuaded him, his nephew tells us. Those friends must certainly have included Marvell, whose dignified defence of Milton appeared in the second part of *The Rehearsal Transpros'd.*[48]

We can see two tactics pursued by this junto. The first was that of *The Rehearsal Transpros'd* (1672), to try to isolate the high Tories and high-flying Anglicans like Samuel Parker, and to persuade Charles II to act as heir to Oliver Cromwell, building up his own tolerationist party in opposition to the persecutors who dominated the House of Commons. This tactic succeeded at least to the extent that the King, who issued his Declaration of Indulgence in 1673, was amused by Marvell's book and protected its author—thanks to the mediation of Milton's old friend the Earl of Anglesey. It is probably to this period that we should relate the stories that both Milton and Marvell were approached by government agents who invited them to sell their pens to the government—as Nedham in fact did after 1675; Milton and Marvell refused. Or they may refer to the period in 1670 when efforts were being made to persuade Charles II to divorce his childless and papist queen in order to marry a protestant. The divorce case of Lord Roos, in which the King was very interested, offered a possible precedent; Milton may have been consulted as a well-known expert on divorce. Marvell also took note of the Roos case, drawing his nephew William Popple's attention to the fact that all but three of the bishops voted in the Lords with the Duke of York and "all the papist Lords" against the Roos divorce.[49]

When this failed, the second tactic was that of Marvell's *Growth of Popery and Arbitrary Government in England.* Here perhaps Milton can help us to understand Marvell. In 1673 Milton found it possible to resume pamphleteering, which would earlier have been dangerous for a marked man like him. Charles II's Declaration of Indulgence had opened up possibilities of liberty for protestant dissenters, whilst at the same time exciting fears that the King's main aim was to secure toleration for Roman Catholics, for sinister political purposes. Until this date Milton had not spent much energy on attacking popery; he did not like it, but he had more immediate enemies. But by the sixteen-seventies it seemed quite possible that the King might declare himself a papist—for political purposes which Milton understood. Charles had close relations with Louis XIV, the personification of the union of popery with absolutism. Here was an international Catholic absolutist menace, analogous to the régime of Laud and Henrietta Maria, the object of Milton's first political assaults. He saw an issue on which it was possible for him to appear in print again.

In 1673 he published *Of True Religion, Heresy, Schism, Toleration, and what means may be used against the Growth of Popery.* "The increase of popery is at this day no small trouble and offence to [the] greatest part of the nation", declared the opening sentence. Milton's stated object was to unite "all true protestants" against the national enemy. He even quoted the 39 Articles in an attempt to embrace Anglicans as well as dissenters in this alliance. How right was his assessment of the possibilities of uniting protestants is shown by the fact that when in April 1675 Danby's friends in the House of Commons wanted to head off a motion of censure against the minister, they decided (rightly) that the best diversion would be to encourage a wide discussion of the dangers of popery. What was different about *Of True Religion* was Milton's daring attempt to use conventionally accepted anti-popery as a lever to win a remarkably wide tolerance. The poet assumed that "Anabaptists, Arians, Arminians and Socinians" were all protestants, who should be tolerated equally with Lutherans and Calvinists. He devoted more space to Arians and Socinians than to any other sect.[50]

Milton was not alone in using anti-popery for political purposes. William Dell had tried in 1667 to break a similar long silence by publishing a pamphlet entitled *The Increase of Popery in England*, but it was "seized in the press", and did not appear until the greater liberty of 1681. Marvell, I suggested, may have had a hand in Peter du Moulin's *England's Appeal*, which also appeared in 1673. In the same year Traherne published *Roman Forgeries*, a scholarly but severe critique; and Benlowes reprinted *Papa Perstrictus*, a twenty-eight-year-old attack on the Pope.[51] William Penn's *One Project for the Good of England* (1679) had the same aim of uniting English protestants.

Marvell shared Milton's dislike of absolute monarchy, and like Milton attacked the absolutist tendencies, as he saw them, of Charles II's government, under cover of attacking popery. "There has now for divers years a design been carried on to change the lawful government of England into an absolute tyranny, and to convert the established protestant religion into downright popery": so the opening sentence of *An Account of the Growth of Popery and Arbitrary Government in England* makes explicit the theme of Milton's *Of True Religion, Heresy, Schism* of 1673. Marvell ended by stressing "the tendency of all affairs and counsels in this nation towards a revolution".[52] Marvell virtually quoted Milton when he wrote "Popery is such a thing as cannot, but for the want of a word to express it, be called a religion". Marvell, like Milton, referred to the papal agent Rinuccini "assuming the temporal as well as spiritual power in Ireland" at the head of the rebels in the sixteen-forties: "all of which ended in the ruin of his Majesty's [Charles I's] reputation, government and person".[53] Marvell had hinted to the mayor of Hull that papists were responsible for the Fire of London. He reported in February 1671 on the House of Commons' concern about "the dangerous growth of popery". In his private letters to William Popple he is much more concerned with the dangers of absolutism: popery is not mentioned.[54] "The Statue in Stocks-Market", uncertainly attributed to Marvell, mocks the statue which had originally been designed for John Sobieski but was adapted for Charles II, who was incongruously depicted trampling on a Turk. It recalls Milton's translation of *Letters Patents* for the election of John Sobieski as King of Poland in 1674. The point about Sobieski was that he was an *elected* and patriotic monarch, who was to pursue a forceful foreign policy with great success.[55]

The Growth of Popery was something very different from *The Rehearsal Transpros'd*. Apart from its greater seriousness, there is a difference in attitude towards Charles II, whose personal policy Marvell was in fact attacking, though the pretence of respect for the King is kept up. The government offered £100—a sizeable sum in those days—as a reward for the discovery of the author of *The Growth of Popery.* No more royal protection! The very elaborate precautions which Marvell took to prevent his authorship becoming known remind us of the serious risks which those who publicly attacked the government took. The printer of the unlicensed *Mr. Smirke* was imprisoned in 1676.[56] It was an act of great courage when Marvell put his own name to the second part of *The Rehearsal Transpros'd.* Sir John Coventry had his nose slit for a light-hearted reference to Charles II and actresses, and Dryden was cudgelled at the orders of a duke. The blind Milton feared assassination in the sixties. Marvell was threatened with assassination in the next decade. His remark, recorded by Aubrey, that he would not drink in any man's company to whom he would not entrust his life, may have been grim rather than facetious. There were rumours that his death at the age of fifty-seven was not due to natural causes.[57]

I have argued that we must always bear the censorship in mind when considering the literature of this period.[58] Even Marvell's letters to his constituents have to be read with this in mind. In October 1675 he wrote to the mayor of Hull: "I desire that what I write down to you may not easily or unnecessarily return to a third hand at London". Next month "it seems . . . that there is some sentinel set both upon you and me"; he repeated the warning not to "do, say or write anything but what we care not though it be public". If we compare Marvell's private letters to his nephew with his official letters to Hull we get an interesting gloss on the deadpan style of the latter.[59]

Literary historians I fear do not always bear sufficiently in mind the subterfuges which writers necessarily had to adopt in order not to expose themselves to danger. Marvell's urbane flattery of Charles II in *The Rehearsal Transpros'd* is not "naive", as Professor Wallace suggests; nor is it merely "opportunistic" or "insincere", the only alternatives he is prepared to consider.[60] It is part of the accepted discourse of the time, deriving partly from the censorship but also from agreed conventions of this post-revolutionary society. If you wanted to put forward a serious political argument which would be listened to by your opponents—as opposed to writing a libellous lampoon—you had to assume, or pretend to assume, that the King could do no wrong, that if wrong was done it was the ministers' fault, and that the only problem was getting information through to the King.[61] Nor should we take Marvell literally when in April 1677 he said "the three kingdoms are like to be in good hands" because

Ormonde was to govern Ireland and Lauderdale Scotland.[62] He meant the opposite.

Outspoken anti-monarchism like that of "Britannia and Rawleigh" and the "Dialogue between the Two Horses"—whether or not they are Marvell's—was possible only in anonymous satires which circulated privately and illegally. The technique of attributing perfection to the King and all errors to his ministers is demonstrated in *An Account of the Growth of Popery*.[63] In his official correspondence with Hull Marvell always treated Charles with respect. But in private letters to his nephew he did not keep up the pretence that the King is never to blame. The very funny mock "royal speech" of 13 April 1675 shows that Marvell did not fail to hold Charles personally responsible for his actions. In *Last Instructions to a Painter* he cites the fate of Charles I as a warning to his son.[64] "As none will deny that to alter our monarchy into a Commonwealth were treason, so by the same fundamental rule, the crime is no less to make that monarchy absolute". "For one man's weakness a whole nation bleeds"—words which recall those for which the Long Parliament sent Henry Marten to the Tower in 1643.[65]

During the last years of his life Marvell had business-political relations with a couple of relatives both of himself and his Hull friends the Thompsons. One at least of these was a dissenter, probably an Independent; both were allies of Shaftesbury. They were fierce opponents of the ruling clique in the City, and when they were bankrupted Marvell may have been convinced "that they were the victims of a persecution provoked by their stand for the religious and civil liberties of the City". At all events, he sheltered them in his house when they had to go to ground, as Milton had been sheltered in 1660. The political associations of the group extend backwards to Agitators of the New Model Army and forward to Rye House plotters.[66]

Marvell was continually trying to unite the opponents of absolutism. Milton had tried to unite all other protestants against bishops in 1641–2, all opponents of censorship in 1644, opponents of monarchy in 1649 and 1659–60; in 1673, as we saw, he quoted the 39 Articles in an attempt to bring together as many protestants as possible against the danger of popery and absolutism. This no more meant Milton's conversion to Anglicanism than Marvell's praise of the independent royalist gentry meant that he idealized them or shared all their views: in each case a short-term alliance seemed possible.

Marvell's famous phrase about the Good Old Cause in *The Rehearsal Transpros'd* must be read in this light. Marvell wanted his book to unite the broadest possible opposition to the high-flyers; and so, though Part I of the pamphlet is unsigned, he wants not to be provocative. His severest criticisms are aimed at the Laudian clergy and their Romanizing tendencies. It was they who led Charles I to "that imaginary absolute government, upon which rock we all ruined".[67] Five years later he said that it was Cardinal Rinuccini's assumption of temporal as well as spiritual power in Ireland "which ended in the ruin of his Majesty's reputation, government and person".[68] His words in 1672, "the Cause was too good to have been fought for. Men ought to have trusted God; they ought and might have trusted the King with the whole matter" cannot be interpreted as a rejection of the Good Old Cause.[69] If the cause was too good to have been fought *for, a fortiori* it was too good to fight *against*—as Charles I had done. Samuel Parker saw this point clearly enough: so did the author of *A Common-Place Book out of the Rehearsal Transpros'd*.[70] "In this world a good cause signifies little, unless it be as well defended", Marvell wrote in 1671.[71] His famous phrase meant that the war *should* not have been fought because it *need* not have been fought, because the victory of Parliament was inevitable, war or no war. In *The Rehearsal Transpros'd* Marvell continued with considerable irony,

The King himself, being of so accurate and piercing a judgment, would soon have felt where it stuck. For men may spare their pains when nature is at work, and the world will not go faster for our driving. Even as our present Majesty's happy restoration did itself come, all things else happen in their best and proper time, without any need of our officiousness.[72]

Here Marvell was following the historical and political theory of his friend James Harrington. Worshippers of the Royal Martyr would again note Marvell's implied criticism of Charles I's intransigence.

In the sixteen-fifties Marvell had been very sharp against the Levellers, the radical democrats, whom like Oliver Cromwell he probably deliberately confused with the communist Diggers:

> this naked equal Flat,
> Which *Levellers* take Pattern at. . . .
> The World when first created sure
> Was such a Table rase and pure.
> Or rather such is the *Toril*
> Ere the Bulls enter at Madril.[73]

This seems a reference to Hobbes: the egalitarian state of nature necessarily leads to the state of war until political authority is established to tame the many-headed monster. Milton was much less hostile to the Levellers. In 1649 he ignored the Council of State's instructions to attack them, though he acted immediately on an order to attack Irish loyalists. Levellers continued to speak sympathetically of Milton as late as 1657. But Marvell, though opposed to Cromwell's acceptance of the crown, seems never to have committed himself against monarchy as an institution with the virulence of Milton in 1649 and 1660—unless "Britannia and Rawleigh" is by Marvell.

So perhaps we can put the relation between the two poets in perspective. Marvell was originally pushed forward by Milton, and almost certainly got his position in government service through Milton; he retained—as Masson stressed—a deference for Milton which was almost servile. He was a member of Milton's circle in the sixteen-sixties, of his "junto" in the sixteen-seventies. Both retained their convictions of the sixteen-fifties: neither was to be bought, though overtures were apparently made to both on behalf of the government. Both died poor.[74] So Marvell's dignified defence of Milton in *The Rehearsal Transpros'd*, and his poem before the second edition of *Paradise Lost*, are the culmination of over twenty years of discipleship and friendship.

There are, it seems to me, continuing parallels between the political attitudes of the two men, from their first co-operation in 1649 or the early fifties till Milton's death in 1674. They shared a libertarian Puritanism, for instance.[75] Both were facetious at the expense of the liturgy.[76] Both hated bishops and the whole hierarchy of the church. Like Milton, Marvell saw Constantine as the villain of the early history of Christianity, since he endowed the church with property and confirmed the political power of bishops. Marvell speaks of "the ambition of bishops", and—in the decent obscurity of a Latin poem—asks if a prelate can be innocent (*"insons"*). In 1678 he even opposed a bill "for securing the protestant religion" because it gave too much power to bishops. He more than once hinted at the desirability of secularizing the property of the hierarchy. At least the incomes of the lesser clergy should be augmented at the expense of rich pluralists.[77] It was probably Milton's nephew John Phillips who responded most severely to Parker's denunciation of nonconformists as seditious. Like Marvell, he represented it as an attack on the trading part of the nation: "as good have no people as those that will not pay tithes".[78]

Both Milton and Marvell believed that priests "from the time of the Apostles onwards" had been responsible for persecution. Both resented the distinction between clergy and laity. Marvell even likened some clerics to the devil:

there have never been wanting among them such as would set the magistrate upon the pinnacle of the temple, and showing him all the power, wealth and glory of the kingdoms of the earth have proffered the prince all, so he would be tempted to fall down and worship them.[79]

(We recall *Paradise Regained*.) We must not be deceived by the apparent mildness of Marvell's irony, as when he advised the bishops that "it were not amiss" if parsons were to be asked to give "some account of their Christianity: for the world has always hitherto been so uncivil as to expect something of that from the clergy".[80] Marvell's contemporaries had no doubt where he stood. Nonconformists have mightily bought up the original *Rehearsal Transpros'd*, declared Henry Stubbe. "If at any time the fanatics had occasion for [Marvell's] help", Samuel Parker agreed, "he presently issues forth of his cave like a gladiator or wild beast".[81] Like Milton, Marvell declared firmly against religious intolerance—from "Bermudas", where the exiles were escaping from "the prelates rage", to *Mr. Smirke* in 1676. "One that is a Christian in good earnest", Marvell wrote, "when a creed is imposed, will sooner eat fire than take it against his judgment".[82] We recall Milton on being a heretic in the truth. We do not know whether Marvell shared Milton's more outrageous heresies—as we should not know about Milton if the *De Doctrina Christiana* had not survived. Marvell defended Arianism, and was himself accused of Socinianism.[83] The only hint of antinomianism in the younger poet comes in the *Poem upon the Death of O.C.*: "to the good / . . . All law is useless".[84] We are just beginning to realise how much millenarianism there is in Marvell. Here too he links up with Milton, for whom Christ was "shortly expected King" in 1641, whose return would remove all earthly tyrannies, he declared in 1649. Milton saw the sentence on Charles I as an anticipation of the last Judgment, and continued to the end to look forward to the reign on earth of Christ and his saints.[85]

It is I hope superfluous to explain that there were many millenarians in the forties and early fifties, expecting the coming of Christ in the near future, who are to be distinguished from the small

Fifth Monarchist group of the years after 1653, which strove to expedite that coming by military violence. Marvell illustrates the distinction in *The First Anniversary*, which is a millenarian poem whose author attacks Fifth Monarchists.[86] Like Milton's in *Paradise Regained*, Marvell's millenarianism does not call for immediate political action to establish the rule of the saints; on the contrary, the magistrates themselves must become godly. Marvell's praise of Cromwell in millenarian terms—"if these the times, then this must be the man"—uses the Protector's virtues to suggest that the millennium may be approaching. It has nothing to do with advocating kingship for Oliver. Marvell (like Milton) sees the monarchy as a later and less satisfactory period of Jewish history than the rule of the judges, though superior to the rule of the priests.[87] By the time he came to write *The Rehearsal Transpros'd* Marvell no longer had the millenarian expectations of the fifties.[88] But he had not returned to a traditional cyclical conception of history. Things will change, even if not so fast as he had once hoped. His mood was that of Adam at the end of *Paradise Lost*:

> By small
> Accomplishing great things, by things deemed weak
> Subverting worldly strong, and worldly wise
> By simply meek. (XII, 566–9)

Marvell also shared a millenarian internationalism with Milton and his friends, Lady Ranelagh, Henry Oldenburg and John Dury, and with Lady Ranelagh's brother Robert Boyle. Cromwell "to all states not free / Shall climacteric be".[89] I have argued elsewhere that in the increasingly secular climate of the sixteen-sixties and seventies the concept of the chosen nation, as modified by Harringtonianism, could become a doctrine justifying colonial and commercial expansion based on sea power. Marvell went some way in this direction in his Cromwell poems. In 1664 he told the Tsar that England's "navies do carry a moveable frontier to all the habitable world".[90] Like Milton, Marvell held that human actions are directed by Providence. Milton carried this to the extent of believing that his muse was divinely inspired; Marvell said, apropos of *The Rehearsal Transpros'd*: "I am (if I may say it with reverence) drawn in, I hope by a good providence, to intermeddle in a noble and high argument which therefore by how much it is above my capacity I shall use the more industry not to disparage it".[91]

A problem which Marvell encountered earlier than Milton was that of coming to terms with history. After the failure of the Revolution to which he had sacrificed twenty years of his life, and (he thought) his eyesight, Milton faced the task of justifying to men the ways of a God who appeared to have spat in the faces of his most devoted servants. *Paradise Lost, Paradise Regained* and *Samson Agonistes* were the result. Marvell's problem was less tragic; but he too in "An Horatian Ode" records the impact of an impersonal historical force, apparently transcending good and evil, "The force of angry Heavens flame", which led Cromwell

> To ruine the great Work of Time
> And cast the Kingdome old
> Into another Mold.
>
> Though Justice against Fate complain,
> And plead the antient Rights in vain:
> But those do hold or break
> As Men are stronger or weak. (ll. 34–40)

Charles I died with dignity; but Cromwell was the instrument of Providence; the Revolution cannot be wished away. In his Cromwell poems Marvell was asserting eternal Providence against a history that was often perplexing; in *Upon Appleton House* he contrasted public life with the better fortitude of patience.[92] Marvell came to terms with history, as Adam did in the last two books of *Paradise Lost*, and as Samson did in *Samson Agonistes*. This was perhaps less of an effort for Marvell than acceptance of the restoration was to be for Milton. "The world will not go the faster for our driving", but neither will it go the slower for our regrets. It would have been useless for Charles I to call "the *Gods* with vulgar spight / To vindicate his helpless Right". Like it or not, history had to be accepted.[93] Wisdom is "to make their *Destiny* their *Choice*". "We must nevertheless be content with such bodies", Marvell wrote, "and to inhabit such an earth, as it hath pleased God to allot us".[94]

But Marvell's sense of historic destiny is part of a wider outlook, which informs his poetry as well as his prose. Earl Miner has suggested that the underlying theme of "The Nymph complaining for the death of her Faun" is the loss of innocence in the face of historical violence, a loss which is regrettable but inevitable.[95] We recall the many poems in which "Fate does Iron wedges drive, / And alwaies crouds it self betwixt"; "her Decrees of Steel / Us as the distant Poles have plac'd". "Necessity", Marvell wrote in 1672, "drove the great iron nail through the axle-tree of nature".[96] Marvell had Milton's sense—a conception surely born of the agonies and triumphs and sufferings of the Revolution?—of good attained through evil, of the impossibility of good without evil, of the pointlessness of rejecting good because of concomitant evil. The English Commonwealth was founded on a bleeding head, just as the Roman state had been, just as Shakespeare's Henry IV was "full of woe / That blood should sprinkle me to make me grow".[97] It was from the rind of one apple tasted in a garden that knowledge of good and evil came into the world. "In a sense", wrote Dr Chernaik recently, Marvell "has only one subject: the fall of man".[98] Tearing our pleasures "with rough strife / Thorough the iron gates of Life" makes them greater, not less. The highest praise of Cromwell was that he

> "as the *Angel* of our Commonweal,
> Troubling the Waters, yearly mak'st them Heal".

Or as Endymion, who wanted the moon, said to Cynthia:

> Though I so high may not pretend,
> It is the same so you descend.

In a lengthy simile in *The First Anniversary* primitive man, terrified by the setting of the sun and the shadows, continued to look for light in the west, and was beginning to despair—

> When streight the Sun behind him he descry'd,
> Smiling serenely from the further side.[99]

It is impossible not to be struck by the recurrence in Marvell of the linked themes of liberty and necessity, of innocence crushed by or learning from external violence (the Mower Poems, "The Nymph"), of the pressures of time or passion, of love and beauty inevitably giving rise to tyranny and war, once the garden state of childhood innocence has passed. Love is defined as begotten upon impossibility by "Magnanimous Despair": the conjunction of the mind faces the opposition of the stars; lovers kept apart by Fate's "Decree of Steel" can never come together "Unless the giddy Heaven fall, / And Earth some new Convulsion tear". In the "Dialogue between the Soul and Body", the soul is "Shipwrackt into Health again". In "The Match" a self-immolating explosion is the answer to time.[100] There are various ways in which time can be outwitted—"Thus, though we

cannot make our Sun / Stand still, yet we will make him run", in the
"Coy Mistress"; by a contemplative withdrawal or philosophic
ecstasy ("The Garden"), or by the power of an heroic historical agent
like Cromwell, who—unlike "heavy Monarchs"—

> "the force of scattered Time contracts.
> And in one year the work of Ages acts".[101]

To make your destiny your choice is the reverse of "necessitarianism".
Wither, in his translation of *The Nature of Man* (1636) made
Nemesius say that man had "a greater power than destiny because he
maketh it his choice".[102] The Matchless Orinda likewise thought "he
can best command his fate" who "makes his necessity his choice".[103]
So did Almanzor in Dryden's *Conquest of Granada* (Part II, IV, iii).
Marvell's political choices were also moral choices.[104]

Milton wrestled with similar paradoxes: absolute freedom was
essential, but so was self-discipline and co-operation with God's
purposes; the Son of God in *Paradise Regained* rejected violence, but
Samson slaughtered God's enemies later in the same volume. Adam
chose death with Eve rather than life alone in Paradise, in one of the
finest passages of romantic love in the English language; a few lines
later Milton dismissed him as "fondly overcome with female charm".
True glory is rejection of glory: this conclusion of *Samson Agonistes*
repeats a theme of Marvell's "The Coronet" and "A Dialogue
between The Resolved Soul and Created Pleasure". The man whom
his contemporaries called "learned Mr. Milton" in *Paradise Regained*
rejected learning as a Satanic temptation, in words which recall
Marvell's "Dialogue" again:

> "None hither mounts by the degree
> Of Knowledge, but Humility (ll. 73–4)

So—very different though they seem at first sight—the two poets
have a great deal in common. They were both devoted to music: the
most serious temptation the Resolved Soul had to face was love of
music: compare "The Fair Singer". Both admired Spenser and
inherited the Spenserian poetic tradition.[105] Both admired Ralegh.
From at least 1649 their lives were linked. Marvell owed his career to
Milton, and remained very deferential. "I shall now study it even to
the getting of it by heart", he wrote of Milton's *Second Defence of the
People of England.* The words sound exaggerated; but Marvell's *The
First Anniversary* has been described as almost a versification of the

Second Defence.[106] Thirteen references to Milton's 1645 *Poems* have been noted by Marvell's editors, and many more to Milton's prose, in *Last Instructions to a Painter* as well as in *The First Anniversary*—and in *Britannia and Rawleigh*. In *The Rehearsal Transpros'd* Marvell derided Bishop Bramhall, formerly the victim of Milton's controversial pen; his treatment of the sex life of Samuel Parker's curate at Ickham strongly recalls Milton's rollicking savagery at the expense of Alexander More in his *Defence*. A powerful case has recently been made for Milton's borrowings from Marvell.[107] In 1660 and 1672 Marvell was able to protect his former patron. In 1674 his "On Mr. Milton's *Paradise lost*" was designed to sell the second edition of the epic to the London public.

A curious thing about "On Mr. Milton's *Paradise lost*" is its reference to Samson. On first reading the epic Marvell was worried lest Milton would ruin

> The sacred Truths to Fable and old Song,
> (So *Sampson* groap'd the Temples Posts in spight
> The World o'rewhelming to revenge his Sight.) (ll. 8–10)

But Milton's Samson in *Samson Agonistes* did not "grope the temple's posts in spite". The notion that personal revenge is a main motive is present in the Book of Judges, but not in Milton's poem.[108] Marvell must have known this, must have read *Samson Agonistes*, and was better fitted to understand *Paradise Lost* than most. What is he up to? Marvell's "misdoubts" about the theme of *Paradise Lost* remind me of what Milton's old friend and fellow-translator, Theodore Haak,[109] told his compatriot Benthem about *Paradise Lost*. When Milton's friends heard the poem's title, they feared that it would be a lament for the loss of England's happiness with the downfall of the revolutionary régime. But when they read it, they saw that Milton had dealt only with the fall of Adam; reassured, they withdrew their objections to publication. But, Benthem says, "so far as I understand from what Haak told me and what I read for myself", although at first sight the epic's subject was indeed the fall of our first parents, in fact "this very wily politician [*dieser sehr schlau Politicus*] concealed under this disguise exactly the sort of lament that his friends had originally suspected".[110] Haak was likely to know about Milton's intentions: Marvell even more so.

Marvell may have been afraid that Milton would give the game away too easily; or he may—as he expressly says—have feared that

Milton would trivialize his theme, "to show it in a play". (We recall the "memorable Scene" of the "*Royal Actor*" on "the *Tragic Scaffold*", his execution applauded by the "bloody hands" of the "armed Bands"; it parallels Milton's "masking scene" as a description of the same occasion).[111] Charles had not called on "the *Gods* with vulgar spight", as Samson "groaped the Temples posts". Yet Marvell's Samson is not after all the Samson of Judges but of *Samson Agonistes.* Marvell's anxiety

> Through that wide Field how he his way should find
> O're which lame Faith leads Understanding blind (ll. 13–14)

proved to be unjustified. Marvell accepted Milton's own belief that heaven rewarded with prophecy "thy loss of Sight"—as it rewarded Samson.

Mr Wilding I think is right to argue that many of Milton's allusions to himself in *Paradise Lost* are intended to remind his readers of his political past, and to stress that he is "unchanged . . . though fallen on evil days . . . and evil tongues". In particular his claim to exalted status as the blind bard is a defiant riposte to royalist propagandists who suggested that God had so afflicted him as a punishment for his defence of regicide. On the contrary, Milton and Marvell implicitly claim: Milton had been rewarded for deliberately sacrificing his eyes in the service of God's cause.[112] God led the blind Samson on to successful political action, victory won after coming to terms with defeat.

Milton and Marvell have in common profound political convictions, shared for twenty-five years, and the belief that—like Abdiel, like Samson, like Marvell and Milton themselves—it is impossible to cease to struggle for what one believes to be right. Both poets were confident that in the long run the world can be changed by human effort.[113] Both owed a great poetic debt to the English Revolution. His immersion in politics saved Milton from isolation and escapism; Marvell's acceptance of the republic saved him from the sort of dilettantism of which Leishman approved.[114] Both were remembered not only as poets but as fighters for liberty. But they also have in common a sense of humour. Burnet called Marvell "the liveliest droll of the age".[115] There is no space to illustrate Marvell's gay and Milton's sarcastic wit, but Marvell makes the point in "On *Paradise Lost*" by aligning himself with Milton against the "tinkling Rhime" of "the *Town-Bays*", who "tires without his Bells": and then recalls that his own condemnation of rhyme is made in rhymed couplets.

Rhyme in drama and long poems was a political issue; favoured by Charles II and his court, rhyme was attacked by Buckingham in the Epilogue to *The Rehearsal* which Marvell "transprosed".[116] Milton claimed to have liberated his compatriots from the "bondage" of rhyme. Did the two poets remember the 1658 procession in which Dryden took part? Milton must have smiled with grim appreciation when in "On *Paradise Lost*" his political ally praised England's most notorious defender of regicide not only as a prophet but in terms appropriate to a king—"That majesty, which through thy work doth reign". It was rather a good joke, if you think about it, especially if we take it as coming from one republican to another. But of course the majesty is not inherent in John Milton personally. What reigns in him is the will of God, the God of Milton and Marvell who is also history, fate, which—as even the blind Samson came to recognize—"Tis Madness to resist or blame".

NOTES

1. Originally published in *Approaches to Marvell: the York Tercentenary Lectures* (ed. C.A. Patrides, 1978).
2. *C.S.P.D.*, *1658-9*, p. 131.
3. T. Moore, *Corruption* (1808).
4. J.B. Leishman, *The Art of Marvell's Poetry* (1972), pp. 20-2. First published 1966.
5. In my "Society and Andrew Marvell" (*Puritanism and Revolution*, Panther edn., 1968, pp. 324-50) I may have over-argued the case; but I remain convinced that there is a case to argue.
6. I have made this point at greater length, and documented it, in *Antichrist in Seventeenth-Century England* (Oxford U.P., 1971), p. 181. Contrast John Crowe Ransom, in *Andrew Marvell* (ed. J. Carey, Penguin, 1969), p. 213—a classic case in which a little historical knowledge would have saved a critic from writing nonsense and grossly misleading his readers about the skills of a great poet. Even less knowledge would have been necessary to prevent him objecting to "the tide of Humber" as periphrastic poetic diction. Marvell's father was drowned in these tidal waters. See also my "Till the Conversion of the Jews", in *Millenarianism in English Thought and Literature* (ed. R. Popkin, California U.P., forthcoming).

7. See Farley-Hills, *The Benevolence of Laughter*, 1974 (esp. Chapter 4).
8. Contrast J.M. Wallace, *Destiny His Choice: The Loyalism of Andrew Marvell* (Cambridge U.P., 1968), pp. 146, 185-6. Having attributed "loyalist" monarchist views to Marvell, Professor Wallace uses these views as a yard-stick for rejecting some anti-monarchical poems from the canon. Whether they are to be rejected or not, these arguments seem to me inadequate. When *Britannia and Rawleigh* accused the Church of England of adopting Hobbes's philosophy, this may be a reference to Samuel Parker—and so perhaps evidence for Marvell's authorship.
9. J. Hacket, *Scrinia Reserata* (1693), II, p. 186.
10. G. Miège, *A Relation of Three Embassies* (1669), pp. 361, 415, 451. Carlisle, whom Marvell had known as Charles Howard, Cromwellian Major-General, courtier and peer, "hath no language, and so must wholly trust his secretary". The comment is that of George Downing, another Cromwellian civil servant who survived the restoration (S. Konovalov, "The English in Russia: Three Embassies, 1662-5", *Oxford Slavonic Papers*, X, 1962, esp. pp. 65-7).
11. *M.C.P.W.*, IV, pp. 859-60.
12. *M.P.L.*, I, pp. 429-36. Marvell's "defence of Richard Lovelace in his censorship difficulties with the Commonwealth may well have reflected Milton's influence" (R. Zaller, in *Biographical Dictionary of British Radicals*, II, G-O, p. 222).
13. Contrast Elsie Duncan-Jones, "Marvell: A Great Master of Words", *Proceedings of the British Academy*, LXI (1975), p. 284.
14. Cleanth Brooks, "Marvell's Horatian Ode", in ed. Carey, *Andrew Marvell*, pp. 180-2; cf. Judith Richards, "Literary Criticism and the Historian: Towards reconstructing Marvell's meaning in "An Horatian Ode", *Literature and History*, 7 (1981), p. 41; contrast W.L. Chernaik, *The Poet's Time: Politics and Religion in the work of Andrew Marvell* (Cambridge U.P., 1983), pp. 174-82, 206-8.
15. Contrast E. Duncan-Jones, *op. cit.*, pp. 282-3, who favours the earlier dating; and p. 285 for Hull and Fairfax.
16. J.M. French, *Life and Records of John Milton* (Rutgers U.P., 1949-58), III, p. 396; W.R. Parker, *Milton: A Biography* (Oxford U.P., 1968), II, pp. 964, 1022. Professor Le Comte thought that *An Horatian Ode* quoted Milton's *Defence of the People of England*, and suggested that Marvell must have seen the manuscript before publication (E. Le Comte, *Poet's Riddles*, Port Washington, N.Y., 1975, p. 158).
17. Parker, *op. cit.*, II, p. 926. Cf. Mrs Duncan-Jones's suggestion that Marvell may have helped Milton with the Latin version of the *Declaration of the Parliament of England* of March 1649 (*op. cit.*, p. 287).
18. Parker, *op. cit.*, I, pp. xiv-xv, 248; II, p. 1022; *M.C.P.W.*, IV, p. 864; Masson, *Life of Milton*, IV, p. 623.
19. Leishman, *op. cit.*, p. 182; *M.P.L.*, I, p. 293, II, p. 377.
20. H. Darbishire, *Early Lives of Milton* (1932), p. 7; A. Wood, *Athenae Oxonienses* (ed. P. Bliss, Oxford U.P., 1813-20), IV, p. 230.
21. Parker, *op. cit.*, I, p. 452, II, p. 837; *M.C.P.W.*, IV, pp. 670, 864.

22. *Biographical Dictionary of British Radicals*, I, *A–F* (1982), pp. 12–13.
23. *M.C.P.W.*, IV, pp. 669–70.
24. Parker, *op. cit.*, I, p. 451; cf. II, p. 861.
25. Wood, *op. cit.*, III, p. 593, 1026–8; Marvell, *Mr. Smirke*, in *Complete Works* (ed. A.B. Grosart, 1872–5), IV, pp. 65–6. Katherine Philips, the Matchless Orinda, was Oxenbridge's niece.
26. Masson, *op. cit.*, IV, pp. 623–5; *M.P.L.*, I, pp. 104–8, 314–19.
27. P. Legouis, *Andrew Marvell* (Oxford U.P., 1965), p. 106.
28. Parker, *op. cit.*, II, p. 1062; *Thurloe State Papers*, VII, pp. 298, 373.
29. G. Davies, *The Restoration of Charles II, 1658–1660* (Oxford U.P., 1955), p. 104.
30. A letter from Marvell to George Downing, English ambassador in the Netherlands, dated February 1659, in which Marvell speaks disparagingly of the republicans, and of the partisans of Richard Cromwell as "our side", was written in Marvell's official capacity; it need not necessarily represent his personal feelings (*M.P.L.*, II, p. 294).
31. Wallace, *op. cit.*, pp. 108–14, 122–3; S. Parker, *History of his own Time* (1728), p. 215; S.N. Zwicker, "Models of Government in Marvell's 'The First Anniversary'", *Criticism*, XVI (1974), pp. 1–12; Annabel Patterson, "Against Polarization: Literature and Politics in Marvell's Cromwell Poems", *English Literary Renaissance*, V (1975), pp. 264–8; Chernaik, *op. cit.*, pp. 6–7, 88, 101; M. McKeon, "Pastoralism, Puritanism, Imperialism, Scientism: Andrew Marvell and the Problem of Mediation", *Yearbook of English Studies*, 13 (1983), pp. 58–9.
32. Ll. 249–58; cf. *On the Victory obtained by Blake*, ll. 6–8; contrast ll. 139–40.
33. For Marvell's friendship with Harrington, see Aubrey, *Brief Lives*, II, p. 54.
34. W.R. Parker, *op. cit.*, I, p. 576, II, p. 1088.
35. *Ibid*, I, p. 631.
36. *The Diary of John Milward* (ed. C. Robbins, Cambridge U.P., 1938), p. 108. Cf. the famous lines on Pett in *Last Instructions to a Painter* (ll. 165–90).
37. Robbins, *op. cit.*, pp. 86, 116, 128, 185, 225, 238.
38. D. Defoe, *A Tour through England and Wales* (Everyman edn.), I, p. 51.
39. *C.S.P.D., 1671*, p. 496.
40. *M.P.L.*, II, p. 326.
41. K.H.D. Haley, *William of Orange and the English Opposition, 1672–4* (Oxford U.P., 1953), pp. 57–9, 63, 97–8, 166, 196; D. Davison, "Marvell and Politics", *Notes and Queries*, CC (1955), p. 202; L.N. Wall, "Marvell and the Third Dutch War", *ibid.*, CCII (1957), pp. 296–7.
42. Cf. esp. the passages quoted in Haley, *op. cit.*, p. 103; cf. p. 222.
43. *The Correspondence of Henry Oldenburg* (ed. A.R. and M.B. Hall, Wisconsin U.P.), VII (1970), pp. 439–41. Oldenburg was a friend both of Milton and of Cyriack Skinner (W.R. Parker, *op. cit.*, II, P. 1047).
44. I owe these points to Mr Ian McCalman.
45. Wood, *op. cit.*, I, p. 484; Darbishire, *op. cit.*, pp. 44, 74.

46. See *M.E.R.*, pp. 225-6. Others who linked Milton and Nedham in 1659-62 include William Prynne, *A True and Perfect Narrative* (1659), p. 50; [Richard Watson], *The Panegyricke and the Storme* (1659); Colonel Baker, *The Blazing Star* (1660), p. 5; [Anon.], *A Third Conference between Oliver Cromwell and Hugh Peters* (1660); [Anon.], *The London Printers Lamentation* (1660); Henry Foulis, *The History of the Wicked Plots* (1662), p. 24. I owe all these references to the kindness of Mr McCalman.

47. [Richard Leigh], *The Transproser Rehearsed* (Oxford, 1673), p. 55; Dryden, *Religio Laici*, Preface.; Legouis, *op. cit.*, pp. 122, 199-200.

48. [S. Parker], *A Reproof to the Rehearsal Transprosed* (1673), p. 212 and *passim*; S. Parker, *A History of his own Time*, pp. 214-15; [Anon.], *S 'Too him, Bayes* (Oxford, 1673); [Anon.], *A Common-Place Book out of the Rehearsal Transpros'd* (1673); [Leigh], *op. cit.*, pp. 32, 52, 131-2, 135-7, 146-7; cf. pp. 9, 30, 41-3, 55-6, 72, 98, 110, 113, 126-9; *Works of Andrew Marvell* (ed. Capt. Edward Thompson, 1776), III, p. 486; W.R. Parker, *op. cit.*, I, p. 630. Cf. *C.S.P.D.*, *1667-8*, pp. 121-2—which reads to me like a forgery or a provocation; and *C.S.P.D.*, *1678*, p. 373. For innumerable other references to Marvell's association with and dependence on Milton see J.M. French, *Life Records of John Milton*, I, pp. 37-8, 49, 52, 55ff., 72, 110, 126, 131-7, 146-7).

49. *M.P.L.*, II, p. 315; cf. Marvell, *The Rehearsal Transpros'd* (ed. D.I.B. Smith, Oxford U.P., 1971), pp. 137-8 and *M.E.R.*, p. 223.

50. *The Diaries and Papers of Sir Edward Dering. . . 1644 to 1684* (ed. M.F. Bond, 1976), pp. 61-3; *M.E.R.*, pp. 218-19.

51. See pp. 203, 228-30 below. Cf. Marvell's *Short Historical Essay touching General Councils, Creeds and Impositions in Matters of Religion*, first printed with *Mr. Smirke* (1678), separately published in 1680.

52. Grosart, *op. cit.*, IV, p. 412.

53. Grosart, *op. cit.*, IV, p. 248; cf. pp. 250, 259-60.

54. *M.P.L.*, II, pp. 53, 132, 315-17; cf. I, p. 402.

55. A poem dubiously ascribed to Rochester was similarly facetious about this statue; *M.P.L.*, I, p. 395; *M.E.R.*, pp. 219-20.

56. Legouis, *op. cit.*, p. 205.

57. Aubrey, *op. cit.*, II, pp. 53-4. Cf. Jacob, *Henry Stubbe*, p. 138: was Stubbe murdered?

58. See Chapter 2 above.

59. *M.P.L.*, II, pp. 92-3, 166, 169-70, 313-18, 321-2, 341-3, 346-8.

60. Wallace, *op. cit.*, p. 207.

61. Contrast Donal Smith, "The Political Beliefs of Andrew Marvell", *University of Toronto Quarterly*, XXXVI (1966-7), pp. 55-67, who takes Marvell's profession of respect for Charles seriously and rejects the evidence of the satires—partly because of uncertainties of attribution, partly because there is "a high degree of convention in the court lampoons". If illicit publications were by "convention" anti-monarchical, this throws doubts on the seriousness of official laudation of the monarch.

62. C. Robbins, "Six Letters by Andrew Marvell", *Etudes Anglaises*, XVII (1964), p. 55.
63. Grosart, *op. cit.*, IV, p. 249; cf. pp. 307–8.
64. *Ibid.*, p. 231; *M.P.L.*, II, pp. 267, 286; cf. p. 269, I, pp. 170–1.
65. Grosart, *op. cit.*, IV, p. 261; *M.P.L.*, I, p. 221 ("An Historical Poem").
66. F.S. Tupper, "Mary Palmer alias Mary Marvell", *Proceedings of the Modern Language Association*, LIII (1938), pp. 368–92; L.N. Wall, "Marvell's Friends in the City", *Notes and Queries*, CCIV (1969), pp. 204–7. The publication of Marvell's *Poems* in 1681 was a by-product of this affair (Legouis, *op. cit.*, pp. 148–9, 241, and references there cited).
67. *The Rehearsal Transpros'd*, p. 134 and pp. 127–35 *passim*; cf. p. 223.
68. Grosart, *op. cit.*, II, p. 259.
69. *The Rehearsal Transpros'd*, p. 135.
70. [S. Parker], *A Reproof to the Rehearsal Transpros'd*, p. 443; *a Common Place Book*, pp. 51–2; Edmund Hickeringhill, *Gregory Father Grey-Beard, With his Vizard off* (1673), pp. 135–6.
71. *M.P.L.*, II, p. 324.
72. *The Rehearsal Transpros'd*, p. 135. Cf. Isaac Barrow's suggestion that "letting the world move on its own hinges" ensures stability both in the natural world and in politics (quoted in Margaret C. Jacob's *The Newtonians and the English Revolution, 1689–1720*, Cornell U.P., 1976, p. 62).
73. *Upon Appleton House*, ll. 449–50, 445–8 (*M.P.L.*, I, p. 76; cf. pp. 21, 115).
74. Though himself incorruptible, Marvell was prepared to use bribery on behalf of Hull (*M.P.L.*, II, p. 239, 246, 289). How else did you get anything done in restoration England?
75. As is well argued by Chernaik, *op. cit.*, pp. 129, 133, 138–9, 144.
76. *The Rehearsal Transpros'd*, p. 28; *M.E.R.*, p. 454. Cf. Quarles, p. 196 below.
77. *The Rehearsal Transpros'd*, pp. 237, 380; *Mr. Smirke*, in Grosart, *op. cit.*, IV, pp. 41, 105; II, pp. xxix–xxx; cf. *M.P.L.*, I, pp. 388, 404.
78. [Phillips], *Samuel Lord Bishop of Oxon., his Celebrated Reasons for Abrogating the Test . . . answered by Samuel, Archdeacon of Canterbury* (1688), p. 16; cf. p. 14. This was in reply to Parker's *Reasons for Abrogating the Test* (1688).
79. Grosart, *op. cit.*, IV, pp. 94–8, 129–30, 152; *The Rehearsal Transpros'd*, pp. 44, 94, 135–42, 239.
80. Grosart, *op. cit.*, IV, p. 9.
81. [H. Stubbe], *Rosemary and Bayes* (1672), pp. 12–13, 18–19; S. Parker, *A History of his own Time*, p. 214.
82. Grosart, *op. cit.*, IV, p. 126.
83. *Ibid.*, IV, pp. 65–6, 115–24; [Stubbe], *Rosemary and Bayes*, p. 10; [S. Parker], *A Reproof*, p. 78.
84. Ll. 221–2.
85. *M.E.R.*, Chapter 22.
86. *M.P.L.*, I, p. 116, ll. 297–320; cf. Chernaik, *op. cit.*, p. 46. I would not

wish to associate Marvell—as Professor Wallace does—exclusively with millenarian nihilists like Anthony Ascham. For the distinction between millenarianism and Fifth Monarchism see the unpublished Ph.D thesis of J.P. Laydon, *The Kingdom of Christ and the Powers of the Earth: The Political Uses of Apocalyptic and Millenarian Ideas in England, 1648-1653* (Cambridge, 1976), *passim*.

87. That Marvell (like Milton) thought monarchy antichristian was one of the charges made against him by Richard Leigh (*The Transproser Rehearsed*, pp. 95-6).

88. R. Nevo, *The Dial of Virtue: A Study of Poems on Affairs of State in the Seventeenth Century* (Princeton U.P., 1963), p. 118.

89. J.R. Jacob, "Boyle's Circle in the Protectorate: Revelation, Politics and the Millennium", *Journal of the History of Ideas*, XXXVIII (1977), p. 136. A similar revolutionary internationalism is preached in *Britannia and Rawleigh*.

90. *The Experience of Defeat*, Chapter 6, section 4; G. Miège, *A Relation of Three Embassies*, p. 170. Marvell translated Carlisle's speech into French.

91. *M.P.L.*, II, p. 328. This is the traditional Puritan position: we must keep our powder dry *because* we are fighting God's battles (cf. my *God's Englishman*, Penguin edn., 1972, Chapter 9).

92. See the excellent article by R.B. Waddington, "Milton among the Carolines", in *The Age of Milton: Backgrounds to Seventeenth-Century Literature* (ed. C.A. Patrides and R.B. Waddington, Massachusetts U.P., 1980), pp. 357-9.

93. See my *Puritanism and Revolution*, pp. 344-5.

94. *The Rehearsal Transpros'd*, p. 231.

95. Earl Miner, "The Death of Innocence in Marvell's 'Nymph Complaining for the Death of her Faun'", *Modern Philology*, LXV (1967); *The Metaphysical Mode from Donne to Cowley* (Princeton U.P., 1969), pp. 246-71.

96. *The Rehearsal Transpros'd*, p. 230.

97. Shakespeare, *Richard II*, V, vi, ll. 45-6. Cf. p. 12 above.

98. Chernaik, *op. cit.*, p. 26.

99. *M.P.L.*., I, pp. 28, 119, 126, 117.

100. Cf. Ann E. Berthoff, *The Resolved Soul: A Study of Marvell's Major Poems* (Princeton U.P., 1970), pp. 77-9, 87, 100, 125, 132-3, 143; R. Selden, "Historical Thought and Marvell's Horatian Ode", *Durham University Journal*, LXV (1972), pp. 44-5.

101. Nevo, *op. cit.*, pp. 91, 98, 109, 178; Berthoff, *op. cit.*, pp. 152-3; cf. pp. 106, 114, 122-3; McKeon, *Politics and Poetry in Restoration England*, pp. 184-5.

102. Nemesius, *The Nature of Man* (1636), p. 520.

103. Saintsbury, *Caroline Poets*, I, pp. 523, 564, 567; cf. 599, and my *God's Englishman*, p. 219.

104. C.A. Patrides ("'Till prepared for longer flight': The sublunar poetry of Andrew Marvell", in *Approaches to Marvell*, p. 39) attributes to me the idea that Marvell "endorsed a necessitarian view of history". Any-

one who refers to the passage which Professor Patrides cites will agree, I think, that this is not the case. Cf. Nevo, *op. cit.*, pp. 91–106.

105. M.C. Bradbrook and M.G. Lloyd Thomas, *Andrew Marvell* (Cambridge U.P., 1940), pp. 49, 54; cf. *Britannia and Rawleigh*, ll. 42–54.
106. Patterson, *op. cit.*, p. 266. There are possible reminiscences of *Eikonklastes* in *An Horatian Ode* and *The First Anniversary* (ll. 99–158) as well as in *The Statue in Stocks-Market*. *Last Instructions to a Painter* also recalls Milton's *Defence* (Patterson, *op. cit.*, p. 264; Nevo, *op. cit.*, p. 182; cf. p. 160 above). Margoliouth heard echoes of Milton's first *Defence* in *Britannia and Rawleigh* (ll. 149–52) and of *Paradise Lost* in *Last Instructions* (ll. 142–6, 788). Cf. "An Historical Poem", ll. 101–2.
107. *The Rehearsal Transpros'd*, p. 154; R.B. Waddington, "Milton among the Carolines", pp. 357–9. With *Paradise Lost*, IX. 1000–1, cf. *The First Anniversary*, ll. 203–5.
108. Cf. S. Fish, "Question and Answer in *Samson Agonistes*", *Critical Quarterly*, IX (1969), p. 256.
109. W.R. Parker, *op. cit.*, I, pp. 250, 295; II, pp. 972, 1186; P.R. Barnett, *Theodore Haak, F.R.S. (1605–1690)* ('S Gravenaghe, 1962), *passim*, esp, pp. 156, 162–3.
110. H.L. Benthem, *Engelaendischer Kirch- und Schulen-Statt* (Lüneburg, 1694), p. 58.
111. Cf. *The Statue in Stocks-Market*, ll. 34–41; "scaffold, . . . masquerade, . . . equipage of this vile scene".
112. Michael Wilding, "Regaining the Radical Milton", in *The Radical Reader* (ed. S. Knight and M. Wilding, Sydney, 1977), pp. 126–7, 143.
113. See the penetrating analysis of *Paradise Regained* in Irene Samuel's "The Regaining of Paradise", in *The Prison and the Pinnacle* (ed. B. Rajan, 1973), pp. 123–4, 132–4.
114. I. Rivers, *The Poetry of Conservatism, 1600–1745: a study of poets and public affairs from Jonson to Pope* (Cambridge, 1973), pp. 78–83, 113.
115. Burnet, *History of My own Time*, (ed. O. Airy, Oxford U.P., 1897), I, pp. 467–8. For Milton see *M.E.R.*, pp. 453–5.
116. Buckingham, Fairfax's son-in-law, was another great Yorkshire figure. He corresponded on amicable terms with Sir Henry Thompson of York, Marvell's friend and political crony, a "cousin" of the Thompson conspirators whom Marvell protected. (*The Works of . . . George Villiers, Duke of Buckingham*, 1775, II, pp. 210–16). This Yorkshire interest deserves further study. See pp. 161–2 above.

8. *Francis Quarles (1592–1644) and Edward Benlowes (1602–76)*[1]

I

Quarles and Benlowes were linked by friendship in their lifetime, and shared a posthumous reputation as bad poets. They also shared a Calvinism of the type represented by most Elizabethan and Jacobean bishops, and by Archbishop Ussher under Charles I, to which many nonconformists looked back nostalgically after 1660. It was the Calvinism of Spenser and the Spenserian poets, of Henry Vaughan. But this Calvinism did not prevent Quarles and Benlowes opposing Parliament during the civil war, though with moderation and in Benlowes's case belatedly.

Quarles was perhaps the most popular English poet in the seventeenth century.[2] He first made his reputation in the sixteen-twenties and early thirties by a series of paraphrases of Biblical stories interspersed with meditations. He wrote a "vain amatory poem", *Argalus and Parthenia* (1629), based on an episode in Sidney's *Arcadia.* A volume of *Divine Fancies* was followed by the prodigiously successful *Emblemes* (1635), its successor *Hieroglyphikes of the Life of Man* (1638) and a number of shorter poems. From 1640, like Milton, he turned to prose: *Enchyridion* (1640), political aphorisms; *Barnabas and Boanerges* (1644), politico-religious meditations; and finally three more directly political tracts published anonymously in 1644-5. Quarles died in 1644. *The Shepheards Oracles* (eclogues) was published in 1646; his comedy, *The Virgin Widow*, in 1649.

We are fortunate now to have Dr Höltgen's full biography, which places Quarles firmly in his London and Essex environment. The family was conveniently if distantly related to Lord Burleigh; James Quarles, the poet's father, enjoyed a profitable career at court as Clerk of the Green Cloth, Purveyor of the Royal Household and Surveyor of the Navy. Naturally he profited by holding such offices; and he married an heiress. So Francis was born into a substantial landed family. His elder brother was knighted by James I in 1608.

But Francis was a younger son, and though he went to Cambridge and Lincoln's Inn he never obtained the court office which he might reasonably have expected. At the age of twenty-four he accompanied Princess Elizabeth and her new husband, the Elector Palatine, to Germany in the train of the Earl of Arundel, one of four noblemen appointed to escort her. But nothing came of this connection: Quarles dedicated none of his many works to Arundel, nor indeed ever referred to him at all.[3] There is a mystery here. Quarles was a man of intelligence, who clearly thought a good deal about politics. His widow said that "his mind was chiefly set upon his devotion and study",[4] but this sounds like a rationalization for her husband's failure to make good at court. He tried. In 1626 Quarles was a partner in an unsuccessful patent for making saltpetre. He also held "a lease in reversion of the impositions on tobacco and tobacco pipes to be imported into . . . Ireland". In 1631 he petitioned Charles I for some recognition of his father's services.[5] Three years later Edward Benlowes tried to help his friend with a long and unreadable laudatory Latin poem, *Quarleis*, with introductory verses to Charles I asking for advancement for Quarles.[6] But despite Pope's sneer at "pensioned Quarles" there is no evidence that he was successful, and by the late thirties he was in financial straits.

One possible explanation is that Quarles moved in the wrong circles. His godfather was the Essex magnate Sir Francis Barrington, and throughout his life Quarles was a dependant of this great Puritan family whose ramifications included the Cromwells, the Hampdens and the St Johns. In the sixteen-twenties and thirties the Barringtons were out of sympathy with the politics of the court; Sir Francis and his son-in-law Sir William Masham suffered imprisonment in 1628 for refusing forced loans. Both families were closely associated with John Winthrop, Governor of the Massachusetts Bay colony; Roger Williams had been Masham's chaplain.[7] The younger Sir Thomas Barrington was a member of the Providence Island Company. If Quarles had court aspirations the Barrington connection was not wholly advantageous.[8] The conservative Arundel would have been a safer patron, but clearly he and the poet did not take to one another. Apart from rather optimistic dedications to James and Charles, Quarles chose patrons like the Earls of Pembroke, Leicester and Holland, or the Scots Marquis of Hamilton and Sir James Fullerton. The Earl of Essex, commander-in-chief of Parliament's armies in the civil war, owned a copy of Quarles's *Argalus and Parthenia*.[9]

Everything that we know about Quarles fits him into this protestant and patriotic background. The church courts noticed his mother in the dangerous year 1589 as a favourer of conventiclers. The Presbyterian cleric William Tichbourne spoke of her as "my special and most kind friend", and left her in his will "my clock now standing in her house", as well as 6s. 8d. apiece to Francis and his brother to "buy either of them a book withall"; he may well have been their tutor. Quarles went to the Puritan and Ramist Christ's College, the College of William Perkins and William Ames, and to Lincoln's Inn, where the famous Puritan Thomas Gataker was preacher.[10] Among his friends, perhaps from Cambridge days, was the quintessential Puritan, Richard Sibbes.

Most important for Quarles was his relationship to James Ussher, the great ecclesiastical historian, whom the poet almost certainly got to know through the Barringtons. Ussher was quite out of sympathy with the Laudian innovations in the Church of England: the only promotion he received was in the semi-exile of Ireland. In the sixteen-forties the Long Parliament invited Ussher to become a member of its Westminster Assembly of Divines, and his proposed "reduced episcopacy" was much in favour in circles like that of the Barringtons. Ussher was a close friend of William Crashawe, the very Puritan father of the poet, and preached the funeral sermon for Mrs Crashawe. Ussher's was the only effective patronage Quarles found, though in 1634 he was appointed Chronologer to the City of London—an office which Middleton and Ben Jonson had held before him. Quarles became Ussher's secretary and accompanied him to Ireland. In 1640 he dedicated his *Enchyridion* to Ussher's daughter Elizabeth. Quarles shared Ussher's dislike of Laudianism. In the last year of his life he was supporting an Ussher-like scheme for the nomination of bishops by "the whole clergy and freeholders" of the diocese, and for a great increase in the number of bishops so that their power might be reduced.[11]

Quarles and George Wither are often compared—by Coleridge among others. Both published emblems in 1635, both were patronized by the Earl of Pembroke. Winthrop praised Wither; Quarles approved of Winthrop.[12] Both have been called Puritans. Yet when civil war came Wither took up arms for Parliament; Quarles took up his pen for the King. How are we to explain this?

Quarles was always a staunch middle-of-the-road Calvinist Anglican, satisfied with the Jacobean church which Professor

Collinson has recently eulogized, wishing to see no change in the direction of popery (or Arminianism) or of sectarianism.[13] But we should not be surprised that he was no opponent of monarchy. Everybody who could express himself in print or in Parliament during these years was a "royalist": Sir John Eliot, John Pym, William Prynne and Wither no less than Quarles. Quarles's conventional echo of James I: "A lawful King/Is God's lieutenant" does not imply support for divine right or for absolutism. On the contrary: in the same poem Quarles assumes that England is a "mixed monarchy".[14] Even in his posthumous *The New Distemper* (1645) Quarles agreed that absolute monarchy was "apt to fall into the distemper of tyranny". He looked back "into the blessed days of Queen Elizabeth"—the traditional way of criticizing her successors.[15]

Like George Herbert, who really did choose not to be a courtier, like Wither, Quarles was critcal of "the apish congies of th'unconstant court".[16] In his *Divine Fancies* (1632) there are epigrams against courtiers as well as against precisians. Quarles's relations with the Massachusetts Bay colony under the Barrington's friend John Winthrop suggest that—again like George Herbert—he may have thought that under Laud true religion might be forced to take refuge on the other side of the Atlantic.

In 1638 John Josselyn, son of neighbour of Quarles's and possibly brother of a Lincoln's Inn contemporary, went to New England. He took with him, for John Cotton's approbation, six of Quarles's English translations of the Psalms. Josselyn was soon afterwards an officer in the Parliamentary army: he was a botanical expert who later dedicated his work to the Royal Society.[18] The incident throws light on Quarles's attitude at this late date to Cotton and Governor Winthrop.

Quarles was hostile to sectaries. But he was aggressively protestant and anti-Catholic. In one of his "royalist" pamphlets he praised "the happy days of Edward VI, when all the Roman rubbish and trumpery was scavenged out of this (the new reformed) church". He acclaimed "the precious memory of . . . thrice famous Luther", who exposed the Roman Whore of Babylon; and Nicholas Ridley, who stood for "England's faith" against "Rome's cursed cruelty", as well as Foxe's "high immortal pen". The question in *The Virgin Widow* "Who would have conceived that Sir Walter Ralegh's blood should have cured Gondomar's *fistula in ano*?" might have come from Middleton's

A Game of Chess. On his deathbed Quarles refused a prescription
from a Catholic doctor.[19]

Whether Quarles acquired his faith at Christ's or earlier, he
remained firmly Calvinist, hostile to Schoolmen and monks. He
believed that grace cannot be lost, and supported the doctrine of
Christ's most famous Puritan theologian, William Perkins, that God
"counts it as done, what we have willed to do".

> We must expect the call
> . And, being called, must move and rise withal.

Again with Milton, Quarles preferred the authority of the Bible
to that of the church.[20] Quarles was always hostile to Laudianism,
specifically because of its compliance with Catholicism. He criticized
not only lecturers who became too dependent on their paymasters,
the people, but also bishops who merely suppressed them rather than
replacing them with more orthodox preachers. He saw schismatics as
alienated intellectuals, on the look-out for money. With Ussher,
Quarles rejected the divine right of episcopacy. The delay between
the registering of Quarles's *Emblemes* with the London Stationers'
Company in May 1634 and its final publication in 1635 with the
imprimatur of the Vice-Chancellor of Cambridge, may have been due
to the necessity of circumventing the Laudian censorship in
London.[21]

There is indeed impressive consistency in Quarles's position
throughout his career. "The true protestant religion stands like a
virtue between two vices, popery and separatism". "I am no papist
nor sectary, but a true lover of reformation and peace", he
proclaimed in 1643. To be in favour of "reformation" marked a man
as anti-Laudian.[22] "If I reprove the vanity of the times", Quarles
acknowledged, "it derides me with the style of Puritan". "Deride not
him whom the looser would call Puritan". He criticized the theatre,
but only for playing on Sundays.[23] The fact that he wrote a play for
performance at the Barringtons' home in 1641 is one of the many
examples Margot Heinemann gives in her convincing denial of the
"Puritanism" of such Puritans.

The main thrust of the posthumous *The Shepheards Oracles* (1646)
is anti-Catholic, with Laudianism a secondary target.[24] Quarles's
reference to the clergy being exposed to "the scorn/ Of every base
mechanic"[25] may help to explain why he expressed a steady
constitutionalist-royalist position in the sixteen-forties, when many

who shared his religious views supported Parliament. From about 1639 Quarles lived at Terling in Essex, a village with a long-standing sectarian tradition which appears to have gained the upper hand in the sixteen-forties, to Quarles's social as well as theological disgust. In 1644 a petition circulated against the poet upset him very much by accusing him of popery. Quarles was, I suspect, an example of Brian Manning's "party of order"—those who had been extremely unhappy about the rule of Laud in the thirties, who welcomed the prospect of moderate reform by Parliament in 1640, but who were then alarmed by uncontrolled direct action by the lower classes.[26] This would be especially true of a radical centre like Terling. In *The Virgin Widow* mechanick preachers are criticized. Schismatics are a subsidiary target of *The Shepheards Oracles*. Quarles relies on Parliament to restore religious order.[27]

These considerations throw light on Quarles's pamphlets of the sixteen-forties. *Enchyridion* (1640) is a pre-Harringtonian study: Quarles emphasizes that the gentry need a king just as King Charles needs the gentry. Quarles warns against letting "new gentry multiply too fast": similarly "the lower sort of people" must be kept in place.[28] The clergy should never be dependent on either the people or a foreign power (i.e. Rome).[29] The tract is strongly influenced by Machiavelli, sometimes to the extent of unacknowledged quotation. Machiavelli had long been known to constitutional monarchists like Ralegh and Bacon, and had been used by James Bovey to attack the policies of Laud and Strafford: Quarles's dependence on him is one more piece of evidence that he was no divine right of kings man.[30] It makes better sense to think of him as trying to work against the influence of what he would regard as extremists on both sides.

Quarles's political pamphlets of 1644-5, published anonymously and apparently in Oxford, still express a middle-of-the-road position.[31] The Oxford imprint may be spurious: *The Loyall Convert* of 1644 at least appeared in London simultaneously. Much of it might have been written by a reasonable non-party arbitrator or neutral commentator. *The Whipper Whipt* (1644) ingeniously defends Cornelius Burges, the well-known Presbyterian member of the Westminster Assembly, and another protégé of Pembroke's, who had in the past expressed strong monarchist views. What Quarles defends is mixed monarchy, with the power of the Laudian bishops reduced by Parliament to a "primitive episcopacy" on Ussher's model.[32] The King is the supreme authority when all else fails, as Sir John Eliot had argued: he *must* be trusted. But Quarles continued to hope against hope that moderate men on both sides would come together to end the war and restore order. In dedicating to Charles *Judgment and Mercy for Afflicted Souls* (1646) "in these bad, sad times", Quarles's publisher audaciously associated Ussher with the King as joint "instruments of good to this distracted, distempered church and state".[33] The "loyal convert" had not been converted to Laudianism: he was trying to convert royalists to the Barringtons' policy. Quarles would have approved of the settlement of 1660, when Parliament recalled King and bishops but did not restore the Court of High Commission. The title given to the posthumous collected reprint of 1645, *The Profest Royalist*, was in all probability not Quarles's.[34]

In 1641 Quarles, addressing Lady Barrington, referred to "this noble family, which hath always merited the utmost of my service and shall for ever challenge the best of my endeavours". In 1641–2 Sir Thomas Barrington and Quarles were united in welcoming Comenius to England. All of the poet's last tracts in fact were in sympathy with the views of Sir Thomas at that time. They "gave both sides occasion to take offence", and justified Anthony Wood in applying the epithet "Puritanical" to Quarles.[35] They are closer to the thinking of Philip Hunton than to that of most royalists.

David Lloyd, twenty-four years after Quarles's death, had a story about the poet "going to his Majesty at Oxford". There is no other evidence for this. Dr Höltgen suggests that Quarles had been driven out of Terling by the dominant sectaries there, and wrote his tracts —at least in part—in Oxford.[36] But when Quarles died on 8 September 1644 he was buried as a pauper in London three days later. The poet's reference in *The Loyall Convert* to the King as one of the three estates of the realm suggests that he was not in Oxford when he wrote it. This Parliamentarian position had been adopted briefly by one section of the King's advisers in 1642, but was firmly rejected by almost all of them by 1644.[37]

If Quarles did go to Oxford because he was driven out of Terling, his death in Terling or London, his burial in London, and his widow's subsequent residence in Terling, all call for explanation. Residence in Oxford and support for the King would render him liable to penalties from Parliament; yet there is no mention of him or his widow in the *Calendar of the Committee for Compounding with Delinquents*. Was he exempt as a pauper? If Quarles went to Oxford, why did he leave? Did he, like Chillingworth, find the royalist publicans and sinners as unattractive as the Parliamentarian scribes and Pharisees? Quarles had apparently been in dire financial straits from the late sixteen-thirties. He had to accept tips of £3 and £5 from Lady Barrington. Fuller suggested that Quarles suffered "great losses" in connection with the Irish rebellion. But his poverty dates from well before 1641.[38]

Quarles fits neatly into the line of poets investigated by Miss Grundy in *The Spenserian Poets* (1969). They include Sylvester, Drayton (who shared with Quarles the patronage of the Countess of Dorset and whose epitaph Quarles wrote),[39] Browne, Wither, Giles and Phineas Fletcher. The latter was a special friend of Quarles, who called Fletcher "the Spenser of this age" and said "my genius jumps with thine".[40] One characteristic of this line of poets—which could be extended to include Milton—is shared political attitudes. All were strongly protestant, strongly patriotic in a rather old-fashioned way, looking back to the days of Good Queen Bess. Ussher, himself a poet in his youth, spoke of "my old friend Edmund Spenser".[41] Quarles and Milton have in common Christ's College, Ramism, anti-Catholicism, tolerance of most protestants but refusal of toleration to papists. Both wrote long religious poems, both were interested in Samson, both invoked Urania, both employed the engraver William Marshall. Quarles echoes *Lycidas* in his *Threnodes.* Their portraits may have been confused.[42]

Quarles's most popular book was his *Emblemes.* There are interesting problems about the emblem as a genre. Its apparent relation to images in churches suggests Catholicism. But critics may have tended too easily to associate emblems with the sensitivity informing the counter-reformation. Perhaps ordinary people in protestant countries needed a substitute for images? (Edward Phillips, Milton's nephew, described Quarles as "the darling of our plebeian judgments"). Emblems are not the exclusive property of the counter-reformation, or of Jesuits, whom Quarles likened to wolves.[43] The Huguenot Georgette de Montenay and the Dutch Calvinist van der Noot both come into the story. Emblems appeared in the works of the Familist Hendrik Niclaes, translated into English in the fifteen-seventies, many of them reprinted during the Revolution.[44] The first English emblem-book, published in 1586, was by Geoffrey Whitney, a good protestant and student at Leiden. Andrew Willet (who published in 1592) was a famous anti-Catholic propagandist. George Wither (1635) and the Scot Robert Farley (1639) were staunch protestants. Quarles consciously and deliberately protestantized emblems that he took over from Catholic sources.[45] Bunyan was soon to write in the same genre. One of Quarles's emblems got into the Methodist hymn-book, and Dr Höltgen tells us that the *Emblemes* was still popular with nineteenth century Evangelicals.[46]

There is certainly room for further thought and enquiry about a literary form which could appeal alike to Jesuits and to fiercely anti-Catholic protestants. It might lead to the useful conclusion that form and content are separable. Catholics and protestants shared a common classical culture which made it easy to think of Cupid as a god.[47] More worthy of investigation are the Hermeticist and alchemical overtones of much of the emblem imagery. The mode of thought of the emblematists derived from the world of correspondences, analogies and signatures rather than from that of traditional Catholicism.[48] Quarles called his second volume of emblems *Hieroglyphikes of the Life of Man*, and appealed directly to the *prisca theologia*: "it is an Egyptian dish". Quarles had already told the reader of his *Emblemes* that "before the knowledge of letters God was known by hieroglyphics. And indeed, what are the heavens, the earth, nay every creature but hieroglyphics and emblems of his glory?" Coleridge noted the antithesis between "the thinking of . . . a Quarles and . . . of a Bacon".[49] It was the scientific revolution which in the long run undermined the emblematic as well as the Hermeticist mode of thought.

Quarles was neither a great poet nor a significant thinker. His forte was an ability to express epigramatically the safe commonplaces of his age and class. That is why he was so soon and so completely outmoded. But one aspect of his verse deserves more comment than it has received. Although Quarles could be guilty of a smug pietism, he could also on occasion show an unexpected sense of fun—as in his occasional Byronic rhymes ("checks his/vexes", "linen/skin in").[50] Quarles's play, *The Virgin Wife* was a romp, and a pretty unpuritanical romp; but some of its jokes made it suitable for performance in the Barrington household—e.g. the reference to a surfeit of duck at Canterbury (i.e. Sir Arthur Duck, Laud's right-hand man), and the malapropism about Lady Temple (the Church of England): "the common people think she is troubled with a liturgy". "A lethargy, you mean".[51] The popular anti-sectarian song, "Hey then up go we!" was "noised by the ballad-singers about the streets of London". It is a splendid combination of accurate reporting, malicious wit and knockabout humour.[52] In *The Shepheards Oracles* and in *Barnabas and Boanerges* Quarles shows a real dramatic talent for entering into the mode of thought of those whom he is pillorying: his caricatures have the sort of plausibility which was to get Defoe into trouble. In this sense Dr Höltgen is right to deny Anthony Wood's charge that Quarles was puritanical.[53] But then very few "Puritans" were.

II

Benlowes was the friend, admirer and disciple of Quarles. The younger poet influenced Quarles no less than did Phineas Fletcher: Quarles recognized this in dedicating his *Emblemes* to Benlowes. It is possible that Benlowes—himself interested in Hermeticism—introduced counter-reformation models of emblem-writing to Quarles. If this is so, it would add a little irony to the fact that in 1643 Benlowes appealed to Quarles's patron, the Puritan Sir Thomas Barrington, for protection against the Puritan county committee of Essex.[54]

Like Quarles, Benlowes was a member of the non-courtier, just-royalist gentry. He too, like so many of this class, was in grave financial difficulties in the mid-century. The completeness of his bankruptcy was even more spectacular than that of Quarles, who died mercifully early. Benlowes began as head of a landed family worth over £1000 a year: he died the recipient of charity. Unlike Quarles, Benlowes does not seem even to have tried to obtain a job at court—that source of windfall wealth for the lucky few, of accelerated ruin for the many. Benlowes was as severe on courts as George Herbert, or as the Earl of Derby, pattern of royalism.[55] Wood attributed Benlowes's ruin to reckless generosity and lavish patronage. He also suffered from the heavy taxation, sequestration, composition fines, plunderings and unpaid rents which accompanied the civil war.[56] Perhaps equally important was the poet's failure to attend diligently to cultivating his estates on up-to-date business lines. The anagram of his name which he favoured was Benevolus, and whilst his wealth lasted he was indeed a generous patron and friend. He expressed strong disapproval of depopulating enclosures.[57] He failed to keep accounts, to take any personal interest in estate management, to rack rents until it was too late—when he did it viciously.[58] Despite his episcopalianism he bought bishops' lands when Parliament put them up for sale: another of his unsuccessful investments.

Since Dr Thirsk's magisterial articles in the early nineteen-fifties we have all tended to assume that most royalist landowners emerged unscathed from the revolutionary decades.[59] The cases of Quarles and Benlowes show that for some improvident royalist landowners the interregnum was a terminal catastrophe. We have no idea how many suffered their fate during or after the interregnum. But if they are statistically insignificant, they help us to realise how devastating was the lot of the exceptions.

The story of Benlowes's economic decline and fall has been carefully told by Harold Jenkins. It is classic in its simplicity. Benlowes had begun to mortgage property in 1645, four years before he paid his composition fine of £600. In 1653 his house was burnt down. Many charitable endowments made by the family in its more affluent years, which had fallen into arrears, had to be met. In 1655, with a magnificent gesture, Benlowes mortgaged his whole estate to pay his debts and raise a dowry of £6000 for his niece. The decimation tax of the same year was the final blow. Benlowes decided to sell his lands outright. This, however, was the beginning, not the end, of his troubles. The prospective purchaser, Nathan Wright, was a London merchant, accustomed to efficient business habits. He at first showed pardonable irritation at Benlowes's failure to produce documentary evidence for his titles, at the "emcumbrances" on the estates and the dilapidated condition of the buildings. But he soon realised that he could take advantage of the poet's incompetence. Benlowes valued the properties at £22,000. Wright paid £1000 on account, got possession, and then beat the price down to £15,315. Of this sum it appears that Benlowes received in cash only just over £1000: the remainder went in clearing the mortgage and other debts, and in interest payments. The small sums which the poet did obtain cost him twelve years' litigation against the purchaser and his son, Sir Benjamin, whose baronetcy marked the family's successful arrival in the county society which Benlowes was leaving.[60]

To complete the picture there is the traditional fraudulent steward, to whom Benlowes entrusted the running of his estates, and who swindled him. The only original twist to this familiar story is that the steward did not enrich himself by his master's ruin. John Schoren, a papist printer whom Benlowes had picked up in the Netherlands during his youthful grand tour, died in penury as great as his employer's, and seems to have been nearly as financially incompetent. Nevertheless Schoren wrung an excessive annuity out of Benlowes in lieu of wages, got it secured by a bond for £200, and subsequently produced earlier bonds which Benevolus, in his casual way, had thought were cancelled. Schoren left his master's service at the beginning of the civil war, probably with some of the poet's money in his pockets. By 1645 Benlowes's finances were in such chaos that he took Schoren back. The latter supervised the sale of what was salvaged after the fire at Benlowes's house, and decamped with every penny of the proceeds. During the Protectorate Schoren was blackmailing the former royalist officer, and until his death in 1665 continued to bewilder him with a series of law-suits for alleged arrears: a practice which Mrs Schoren continued until she was awarded nearly £200 out of money owed to Benlowes by Wright. From him that had not was taken away even that which he had.

Quarles was already going the same way, and there were many in a similar pass. Benlowes's story is remarkable only for the fullness of the documentation, the completeness of his ruin: and for the fact that he was a poet. But this economic background may throw some light not only on his own poems, but on the type of poetry which he wrote: poetry which to the next age would seem as empty as Benevolus's pockets, as irrelevant as his claims on Sir Benjamin Wright.

One other feature of Benlowes's background must be mentioned. Unlike Quarles, he came of a Catholic family. (Recusancy fines may indeed have begun to shake the family fortunes before he succeeded to the property.) His relations intended that Benlowes should retain the family estates by a nominal conformity to the state church. But he became a genuine convert, a bitter anti-papist. Nevertheless, when Benlowes made his continental tour his religious position was ambiguous, and the Catholic baroque influences in his poetry are obvious. He shared the erotic religiosity of Crashawe, another unmarried poet with Catholic connections.[61] Benlowes's Anglicanism was Calvinist, anti-Laudian, hostile to priestly pretensions. He wrote a commendatory poem for *The Soules Conflict* of Richard Sibbes, the famous Puritan preacher, friend of Quarles and John Pym; but Benlowes never had any sympathy with the Presbyterianism of the vicar of his parish, Stephen Marshall. His Anglicanism had neither the decorativeness of the Laudians nor the moral fervour of the Puritans. A religion whose main positive tenet was hatred of popery seems stony soil for poetry; but it was the religion of the Fletchers, Quarles and Vaughan as well as of Benlowes. And it was a religion that survived, hoping for a non-Laudian Church of England:

> Weigh things; life's frail, pomp vain; remember Paul,
>   (The way to rise will be to fall)
> In's High Commission low, in's low conversion tall.[62]

Theophila, Benlowes's *magnum opus*, marks the end of a tradition. Much of it might be bad Herbert or bad Crashawe, inferior Vaughan, Randolph or Cleveland. It was a type of poetry which may have appealed to men whom a smattering of classical education had left with modest literary aspirations and tastes—country gentlemen rather than sophisticated courtiers. (Benlowes took up arms, for the first time, with typical maladroitness, in 1648, in what was in effect a local quarrel. Vaughan acted similarly, with equally unfortunate consequences; both thereafter expressed consistent dislike of war).[63]

Benlowes was steeped in English poetry, and he used it with cheerful eclecticism. Like Quarles, he exchanged commendatory poems and dedications with Phineas Fletcher.[64] From Spenser and the Spenserians Benlowes inherited the moral earnestness without the passion and humanity of Milton; from Donne and his courtly successors he inherited everything that Johnson criticized as "metaphysical", but not much else. Direct echoes of Donne in his poems are few, none from the love poems.[65]

It was characteristic of the mid-century "metaphysical" decadence that its practitioners borrowed sentiments and images from their predecessors as freely as T.S. Eliot was to do. They were all living on capital: but Benlowes's literary indebtedness was as excessive as his financial.[66] Samuel Butler was final on this subject, in that character of "A Small Poet" some of which is explicitly drawn from Benlowes. "Whatsoever he lights upon either in books or company, he makes bold with as his own. . . . As those that have money but seldom are always shaking their pockets when they have it: so does he when he thinks he has got something that will make him appear. . . . Bar him the imitation of something he has read, and he has no image in his thoughts". Over and above this derivative bookishness, Benlowes imitated all the technical tricks which had been modish in his youth —anagrams, echoes, rebuses, chronograms. "As for altars and pyramids in poetry, he has outdone all men that way".[67] The whole elaborate production of *Theophila*, each copy slightly different from the others, seems like an attempt to reproduce a medieval manuscript in print, for private circulation.

Benlowes compares with Quarles and other emblem poets, whose medieval affection for material symbols contrasts strikingly with the more abstract thought favoured by most Puritans. "Dangerous as have been some of Benlowes's acrobatics with concrete symbols, nothing could better show Benlowes's unphilosophic mind than the flagging of inspiration when concrete symbols are denied".[68] It all appears very old-fashioned in the age of Milton, Marvell and Waller. Yet Benlowes also lacks the passionate intensity, the sense of conflict, which characterizes the best "metaphysical" poetry from Donne to Marvell. One of the innumerable introductory passages to Benlowes's principal poem is headed "THEOPHILA'S Spiritual Warfare". But it is precisely this sense of inner conflict that is missing in Benlowes. Instead he gives us mechanical antitheses like "Darts of intolerable sweets her soul did wound", which recall Crashawe at his worst.[69] Benlowes was right to choose for the sub-title of his poem not "Love's Spiritual Warfare" but "Love's Sacrifice". Passivity in suffering is his ideal, not the militancy of "the true wayfaring Christian".

Benlowes's attitude towards the new science was characteristically ambivalent. In 1635 he helped to found the Goulston lectures in anatomy at the College of Physicians.[70] Like Vaughan, Benlowes accepted the Hermeticist cosmology. Celestial beings situated above the moon, he believed, "impart innumerable rare virtues and influential efficacies to things below". But he believed that nature was decaying; his close friend Alexander Ross was attacking the new astronomy from 1634 onwards. Like Vaughan, Benlowes compensated for social decline by complacent references to the vanity of all earthly goods.

Seeing then that happiness consists not in the affluence of exorbitant possessions, nor in the humours of fickle honour, all external splendours being unsatisfactory, let Christians neglect terrestial vanities, and retire into the recesses of religion, nothing being so great in human actions as a pious knowing mind, which disposeth great things, and may yield such permanent monuments as bring felicity to mankind above the founders of empires.[71]

The sentiments are conventional enough; but they earn pathos from their expression by a once-prosperous landowner now on the verge of bankruptcy, who left no monument of a permanence commensurate with his aspirations.

We are living in the last times, Benlowes declared, and they were the worst: atheism, profaneness and superstition prevailed oppressively. The world's favourites ("who are of past things mindless, of future regardless, having different opinions, yet but one religion, money; one God, Mammon")[72] think themselves safe in their numbers, and laugh at those who cling to older ideals.[73] But there is consolation in the next world for economic disaster in this:

> Imagine not to swim in worldly pomp,
> And afterwards to reign with Christ in bliss;
> Earth must be gall, that God may honey prove.

> His pursy conscience opens now. 'I've run
>   On rocks' (he howls) 'too late to shun,
>   Lost use and principal! Gold, I'm by thee undone!'[74]

"If we contemplate what unspeakable torments are for *ever* there, we should have no cause to envy [worldlings'] prosperity, but rather wonder that their portion on earth is not greater. . . . All the play and pageantry of earth is ever changing, and nothing abides but the stage of the world, and the spectator, God".[75]

I have quoted Benlowes's prose more than his poetry. It is no doubt the echoes of the Bible and the Prayer Book that give it dignity; but for all its carefully-balanced cadences it sometimes has a directness which contrasts remarkably with his verse. This sentence, for instance: "The number of our transgressions surpasseth our skill in arithmetic; their weight is insupportable, depressing us even to the abyss; their guilt more extense than anything but thy mercy".[76]

In 1652 the height of Benlowes's ambition had been "an estate balanced between want and waste, pity and envy";[77] he ended up in want, an object of charity. But his last years of utter penury, spent reading in the Bodleian Library and publishing Latin poems in praise of Oxford, may well have been not the least happy period of his life. Vaughan, who also looked to the after life to compensate for economic catastrophe, also found consolation in the Bodleian.[78] In *Theophila* Benlowes had thanked God that "in this general combustion of Christendom" he had veen vouchsafed "a little Zoar, as refuge;. . . the managing of public actions less agreeing with my disposition" than did contemplation.[79] After his final ruin he was freed from the onerous responsibilities of landownership which he had been so incompetent to discharge, and which he had vainly tried to shift on to his steward.

Benlowes's fate was shared by other improvident landowners, who, unless they had inherited very great wealth, were unfit to survive the grim selective decades of the middle of the century. Among men of lesser rank, those who could adapt themselves to the worship of Mammon retained their position. Other ex-Cavalier gentlemen, ruined in the King's service, ended their days eating the bread of charity, though few enjoyed the inner resources which enabled Benlowes to face pauperism with equanimity. But the cultural tradition which Benevolus continued to cherish in his Oxford garret was utterly and completely dead. His last Latin poems were unread and unreadable. *Theophila* fared little better. Benlowes was already being mocked at (not in print) by Samuel Butler, a more adaptable ex-royalist whose own poetical method Saintsbury shrewdly described as "often only that of Benlowes changed from unconscious indulgence to conscientious and deliberate utilization for comic effect".[80] Wood's succinct epitaph was: "much noted in his time, but since not, for the art and faculty of poetry"; for Pope he was "Benlowes, propitious still to blockheads". Yet all these, in their different ways, were conservatives: so completely had the standards of taste and value which prevailed before the great divide of the Interregnum been rejected. The old poetry was no more restored with our most religious King in 1660 than was the old constitution.

Quarles and Benlowes are more interesting today for their lives and their ideas than for their poetry. The tradition of fiercely protestant Anglicanism which they shared was continued by Henry Vaughan and Thomas Traherne, each of whom had poetic gifts denied to Quarles and Benlowes—though Quarles at least influenced Traherne.[81] In 1673, when anti-popery came in fashion again, Benlowes joined in the fray by refurbishing a twenty-eight-year-old Latin attack on the Pope. But that was his last moment.

NOTES

1. I have drawn on reviews of K.J. Höltgen, *Francis Quarles, 1592–1644* (Tübingen, 1978), in the *Times Literary Supplement* of 23 May, 1980; and of Harold Jenkins, *Edward Benlowes (1602–1676): Biography of a Minor Poet* (1952) in *Essays in Criticism*, III (1953).
2. Höltgen, *op. cit.*, p. 1.
3. *Ibid.*, pp. 43–6; J. Horden, *Bibliography of Francis Quarles to the Year 1800* (Oxford, 1953).
4. Ursula Quarles, *A Short Relation of the Life and Death of Mr. Francis Quarles*, in her husband's *Solomons Recantation* (1645), Sig. A 2v.

5. Höltgen, *op. cit.*, pp. 50–1, 62.
6. Quarles, *Complete Works* (ed. A.B. Grosart, 1880), I, pp. lxxix–xv; Jenkins, *op. cit.*, pp. 80–2, *Quarleis* was appended to Quarles's *Emblemes* in 1635.
7. Höltgen, *op. cit.*, pp. 153, 159, 162, 274.
8. Interestingly enough, in view of Quarles's unsuccessful patent, Barrington and Masham refused in the sixteen-thirties to help the Admiralty's saltpetre work in Essex.
9. Höltgen, *op. cit.*, pp. 49, 58–9, 108, 111, 154; *Complete Works*, II, p. 252.
10. Höltgen, *op. cit.*, pp. 23, 26, 36.
11. *Complete Works*, II, p. 252; Höltgen, *op. cit.*, pp. 52, 271, 288, 324–5.
12. Höltgen, *op. cit.*, pp. 2, 73, 329. See p. 191 above.
13. P. Collinson, *The Religion of Protestants, passim*.
14. *Hadassa* (1621), *Complete Works*, II, pp. 50–3, 66. The poem was dedicated to James. Cf. Höltgen, *op. cit.*, pp. 97, 285, 290, 341.
15. *Complete Works*, I, pp. 151, 156–71; cf. pp. 172, 174. See p. 57 above.
16. *Ibid.*, III, p. 263; cf. Ursula Quarles, *op. cit.*, Sig. A 2v. For Herbert see p. 216 below.
17. Herbert, "The Church Militant", in *Poems* (ed. R.A. Willmott), p. 209.
18. Höltgen, *op. cit.*, pp. 156–9. But in the posthumous *Shepheards Oracles* Quarles suggests that schismatics go to New England (*Works*, III, pp. 222–3).
19. *Complete Works*, I, pp. lxii–iii, 149; III, pp. 222–6, 304; Höltgen, *op. cit.*, p. 291.
20. *Complete Works*, I, pp. 47, 122; II, pp. 223, 236; Höltgen, *op. cit.*, pp. 85, 259.
21. *Complete Works*, I, pp. 151–6, III, pp. 217–23; Höltgen, *op. cit.*, pp. 189, 288, 324–5. *The Soules Conflict* (1636) of Quarles's friend the Puritan Richard Sibbes suffered an even longer delay (Jenkins, *op. cit.*, p. 126).
22. *Complete Works*, I, pp. xxii–iv, 53, 138–9; cf. p. 142.
23. *Ibid.*, I, pp. 27, 125; II, p. 227.
24. *Complete Works*, III, pp. 203–8, 217–20, 227–33; cf. *Divine Fancies, ibid.*, II, pp. 249–50.
25. *Ibid.*, III, p. 233.
26. B.S. Manning, *The English People and the English Revolution* (1976), *passim*; Höltgen, *op. cit.*, pp. 269–71, 288. For Terling see K. Wrightson and D. Levine, *Poverty and Piety in an English Village: Terling, 1525–1700* (1979), *passim*.
27. *Complete Works*, III, pp. 222–6, 233–6.
28. *Ibid.*, I, pp. 14–16, 59–61.
29. *Ibid.*, I, pp. 13–16, 59–61.
30. G.S. Haight, "Francis Quarles in the Civil War", *Review of English Studies*, (1936), pp. 154–6; F. Raab, *The English Face of Machiavelli*, Chapter 3; Höltgen, *op. cit.*, pp. 294–6.
31. These pamphlets are analysed in a valuable article by I.M. Smart, "Francis Quarles: Professed Royalist and 'Puritanical' Poet", *Durham University Journal*, New Series, *LXX* (1978), pp. 187–92.
32. For Burges see Heinemann, pp. 277–8.

33. *Complete Works*, I, p. 11, 67, 151; Höltgen, *op. cit.*, pp. 283-4.
34. Höltgen, *op. cit.*, p. 350.
35. Quarles, *Hosanna . . . and Threnodes* (ed. J. Horden, Liverpool U.P., 1960), pp. xxviii-ix, 25, cf. p. xxi; Höltgen, *op. cit.*, pp. 274-6.
36. Höltgen, *op. cit.*, pp. 271, 283, 288-9, 343.
37. C.C. Weston, "The Authorship of *The Freeholders Grand Inquest*", *E.H.R.*, XCV, pp. 83-4.
38. Höltgen, *op. cit.*, pp. 276-8; Horden, *Hosanna*, p. xii.
39. *Complete Works*, I, p. lxviii; Höltgen, *op. cit.*, pp. 49, 130, 271-2.
40. Giles and Phineas Fletcher, *Poetical Works* (Ed. F.S. Boas, Cambridge U.P., 1909), II, pp. 8, 11, 284. See pp. 55, 134 above.
41. Höltgen, *op. cit.*, pp. 59, 179-80.
42. *Ibid.*, pp. 36, 67, 70, 77; W.R. Parker, *Milton, A Biography*, II, p. 725.
43. *Complete Works*, III, p. 203; Höltgen, *op. cit.*, pp. 155, 186, 233-4, 308.
44. J.H. Hessels, "Henrick Niclaes - The Family of Love", *The Bookworm* (1869), pp. 81-91, 106-11, 116-19, 131-3, 180. I owe this point, and this reference, to Nigel Smith's Introduction to *A Collection of Ranter Writings*, pp. 35, 267. Mr Smith suggests that Abiezer Coppe's "imagination is emblematic."
45. B.K. Lewalski, *Protestant Poetics and the Seventeenth Century Religious Lyric* (Princeton U.P., 1979), Chapter 6.
46. Höltgen, *op. cit.*, pp. 202, 208-10, 241, 247, 299, 310.
47. *Complete Works*, III, pp. 83, 90, 100; Höltgen, *op. cit.*, pp. 226-7.
48. Peter M. Daly, *Literature in the Light of the Emblem* (Toronto U.P., 1979), pp. 40-2, 52; Höltgen, *op. cit.*, pp. 215, 231.
49. *Complete Works*, III, pp. 45, 186; Höltgen, *op. cit.*, p. 328. See p. 326 below.
50. *Complete Works*, II, pp. 83, 210. Did Samuel Butler learn something from Quarles here?
51. *Ibid.*, III, pp. 308-9.
52. *Ibid.*, pp. 200, 235-6.
53. Wood, *Athenae Oxonienses* (ed. P. Bliss, 1813-20), III, p. 192; Höltgen, *op. cit.*, p. 308.
54. Höltgen, *op. cit.*, pp. 184, 192.
55. Jenkins, *op. cit.*, pp. 75, 98.
56. *Ibid.*, pp. 138-45, 179.
57. *Theophila*, canto i, stanza 138, in *Caroline Poets* (ed. G. Saintsbury), I.
58. Jenkins, *op. cit.*, pp. 84-7, 240-3.
59. J. Thirsk, "The Sales of Royalist Land during the Interregnum", *Economic History Review*, 2nd series, V. (1952), pp. 188-207; "The Restoration Land Settlement", *Journal of Modern History*, XXVI (1954), pp. 315-28.
60. Jenkins, *op. cit.*, Chapters 21, 23.
61. See, for example, *Theophila*, canto iv, stanzas lxi-xxvi.
62. *Theophila*, canto x, stanza 73. By omitting capitals Saintsbury obscured the allusion to the Court of High Commission, of which Benlowes would be unlikely to approve (*Caroline Poets*, I, p. 431).
63. See p. 215 below.

64. G. and P. Fletcher, *Poetical Works*, II, pp. 3, 5, 287, 317, and illustrations opposite pp. 173, 223.
65. Jenkins, *op. cit.*, p. 115.
66. *Ibid.*, pp. 113–22, 162–4, 210, 309–13 for Benlowes's borrowings from Milton; cf. Maren-Sofie Røstvig, *The Happy Man: Studies in the Metamorphoses of a Classical Ideal, 1600–1700* (Oslo, 1954), p. 224. Benlowes's "two-handed sword is the Word and Spirit" may or may not recall *Lycidas* (Saintsbury, *Caroline Poets*, I, p. 321). Ms. Røstvig suggests that Benlowes anticipated Marvell in his symbolic use of the Mower (*op. cit.*, p. 233).
67. S. Butler, *Characters and Passages from Note-Books* (ed. A.R. Waller, Cambridge U.P., 1908), pp. 47–53.
68. Jenkins, *op. cit.*, p. 203.
69. *Theophila*, canto iv, stanza 82.
70. Jenkins, *op. cit.*, pp. 90–1.
71. *Theophila*, Preface; cf. canto iii, Upon the Vanity of the World.
72. Saintsbury obscured the sense of this long and complicated sentence by omitting to close a bracket (I, p. 316).
73. Canto x, stanza 79, makes it clear that Mammon's worshippers supported Parliament:

> Gold is the fautress of all civil jars,
> > Treason's reward, the nerve of wars,
> Nurse of profaneness, suckling rage that kingdoms mars.

The pun in "fautress" is one of Benlowes's better efforts.

74. Saintsbury, I, p. 425; cf. *Theophila*, canto x, stanza 97.
75. *Theophila*, Preface.
76. *Theophila*, The Author's Prayer (Saintsbury, I, p. 343).
77. *Ibid.*, I. p. 344.
78. See p. 222 below.
79. Saintsbury, I, p. 345.
80. *Ibid.*, I, p. 311.
81. See Chapters 9 and 10 below. It is interesting that Fuller dedicated the sixth part of his *History of the University of Cambridge* to Benlowes in 1655.

9. Henry Vaughan (1621 or 1622? — 1695)[1]

Like that of most metaphysical poets, Vaughan's thought tends towards opposites, conflicts. In his case the key words are "dust", "clay", "dirt" on the one hand, and the rhyming trio "white", "bright", "light" on the other. (Cf. Crashawe's "nest/breast", "womb/tomb", "blood/flood"). We can quote almost at random:

> The mighty God, th'eternal King,
> Doth grieve for dust, and dust doth sing. (p. 473)[2]

> How shall thy dust thy praises sing? (p. 431).

> Dust and clay,
> Man's ancient wear! . . . .
> Who will ascend must be undressed. (p. 482)

"To clothe the morning star with dust" was the effect of the incarnation, until finally

> Here in dust and dirt, oh here,
> The lilies of his love appear. (p. 643: cf. p. 455 for the contrast between lilies and dust.)

> I saw eternity the other night
> Like a great ring of pure and endless light. (pp. 466–7; cf. pp. 419, 524, 526–8, 530, 533, 541, 639, 656)[3]

What do these words mean for Vaughan? Dust is what man is made of, and what he must return to. ("The dust whereof I am a part"—p. 449). But it is also a symbol for the world, its gaudy offerings, its bustle and business, as contrasted with the divine to which man should aspire:

> He gropes beneath him, and with restless care
> First makes, then hugs, a snare,
> Adores dead dust, sets heart on corn and grass. (p. 469)

Vaughan too had to live and move in the dusty world:

> Dust that would rise and dim my sight. (p. 413)

> And though (while here) of force I must
> Have commerce sometimes with poor dust (p. 452),

he nevertheless prayed

> Suffer no more this dust to overflow
> And drown my eyes. (p. 435)

> The lucky world showed me one day
> Her gorgeous mart and glittering store,
> Where with proud haste the rich made way
> To buy, the poor came to adore.

> Serious they seemed and bought up all
> The latest modes of pride and lust,
> Although the first must surely fall,
> And the last is most loathsome dust. (p. 507)

> And shall I then forsake the stars and signs,
> To dote upon thy dark and cursed mines?
> Unhappy, sad exchange! What, must I buy
> Guiana with the loss of all the sky? (p. 617)[4]

Everywhere "dust" and "dirt" are equated with the noise of the business world, with gold, with usury. In one of his early poems Vaughan expressed contempt for

>   that famished slave,
> Beggared by wealth, who starves that he may save. (p. 42)

> The fearful miser on a heap of rust
> Sate passing all his life there, did scarce trust
> His own hands with the dust. (p. 467)

Usurers

> Guard the dirt, and the bright idol hold
> Close, and commit adultery with gold. (p. 45. For "damned usury"
> cf. pp. 43, 46, 525.)

In his translation of the Jesuit Nierembergius's *Discourse of Temperance* Vaughan inserted a sentence saying that "gold and silver are no ransom for unrighteousness" (p. 264). Another insertion declared "We must not give our strength unto the world, that is to say, we must not seriously affect it. In all our negotiations with it, we must stand at a distance, and keep our affection" for God. (p. 273). In an early poem he congratulated himself that he was not rich, and so could not

> eat orphans, and suck up
> A dozen distressed widows in one cup.

He assumed that

> I (had I been rich) as sure as fate
> Would have been meddling with the King or state. (p. 14)

Against the wickedness of cities (p. 642) Vaughan continually sets the virtues of rural simplicity and poverty, the "natural" life.

> I will not fear what man
> With all his plots and power can;
> Bags that wax old may plundered be,
> But none can sequester or let
> A state that with the sun doth set
> And comes next morning fresh as he. (p. 505)

(The reference is to the Parliamentary sequestration committees, which leased out the sequestrated estates of delinquent royalists). Salvation comes to the poor and outcast, for whom God has a special regard. In the vain world of "silk perfumes and glittering coaches",

> The ragged, mean and humble throng
> Are still on foot, and as they go
> They sigh and say: "The Lord went so". (p. 651)

Adversity brings redemption for the few penitent survivors in the wilderness:

> If my way lies through deserts and wild woods;
> Where all the land with scorching heat is cursed;
> Better, the pools should flow with rain and floods
> To fill my bottle, than I die with thirst. (p. 498)

> If this world's friends might see but once.
> What some poor men may often feel,
> Glory, and gold, and crowns and thrones
> They soon would quit and learn to kneel. (p. 510).

> O thorny crown
> More soft than down!
> O painful cross, my bed of rest! (p. 536)

> Let wits,
>   Smile at fair eyes
> Or lips; but who there weeping sits,
>   Hath got the prize. (p. 43)

> With true tears wash off your mire. (p. 396)

Suffering becomes almost an end in itself:

> And sweeter airs stream from a groan
>   Than any arted string. (p. 418)

> Give me, O give me crosses here. (p. 403)

> Were all the year one constant sunshine, we
>   Should have no flowers. (p. 460)

> Blest be thy dew, and blest thy frost. (p. 464)

> Let nightingales attend the spring,
>   Winter is all my year. (p. 447).[5]

One day the meek shall inherit the earth:

> Here is their faith too, which if you will keep
> When we two part, I will a journey make
> To pluck a garland hence, while you do sleep
> And weave it for your head against you wake. (pp. 490-1)

Victory follows defeat, as light follows darkness:

> And all thy saints do overcome
> By thy blood and their martyrdom. (p. 517)

Revelation is to the humble, like the shepherds who came to Bethlehem:

> The first true worship of the world's great King
> From private and selected hearts did spring. (pp. 527-8)

> To the wild woods I will be gone
> And the coarse meal of great St. John. . . .
>   And in the desert blooms the rose. . . .
> Is not fair nature of herself
> Much richer than dull paint or pelf?. (pp. 652-3)

> Leave then thy foolish ranges;
>   For none can thee secure,
> But one who never changes,
>   Thy God, thy life, thy cure.

But this country where "grows the flower of peace" is "far beyond the stars" (p. 430).

In view of the frequent political references in Vaughan's poems, I find it difficult not to link up this general outlook with his own social circumstances. Consider who he was: a small Welsh squire, anti-Puritan rather than royalist, his loyalties primarily local (he lived nearly all his life in his Breconshire village), his hostility most intensely directed against the business world of the City and Parliaments, whose power was extending into the hitherto un-commercial areas of the land, disrupting the old social structure, the old certainties of worship. Vaughan's resentful references to usury suggest that he himself may have been a victim of money-lenders, as so many in his position necessarily were. He has nothing but hatred and contempt for the upstart Parliamentarian victors; yet because he cannot understand their power he can only oppose it blindly. So we get the fierce despair of the political poems, the escapism of many of his religious lyrics.

> So mild a lamb can never be
> 'Midst so much blood and cruelty.
> I'll to the wilderness, and can
> Find beasts more merciful than man. . . .
> Search well another world; who studies this,
> Travel in clouds, seeks manna where none is. (pp. 406–7)

The ultimate refuge is death, which Vaughan frequently invokes. His reaction to his brother William's death in 1648 was the poem beginning "Come, come, what do I here?"

> I would be
> With him I weep
> Abed, and sleep
> To wake in thee. (p. 420)

> The good man lies
> Intombed many days before he dies. (p. 439)

> Dissolve, dissolve! Death cannot do
> What I would not submit unto. (pp. 643–4)

> Graves are beds now for the weary,
> Death a nap, to wake more merry. (p. 457)

> They are all gone into the world of light!
> And I alone sit lingering here;
> Their very memory is fair and bright,
> And my sad thoughts doth clear. . . .

> I see them walking in an air of glory,
>   Whose light doth trample on my days:
> My days, which are at best but dull and hoary,
>   Mere glimmering and decays . . .
>
> Dear, beauteous death!. (pp. 483–4)
>
>   All things teach us to die,
>   And point us out the way
>   While we pass by
>   And mind it not; play not away
>   Thy glimpse of light. (p. 444)

Death gives the defeated victory over this world's victors:

>   Dear night! This world's defeat;
>   The stop to busy fools; care's check and curb;. . .
>
>   There is in God (some say)
>   A deep, but dazzling darkness; as men here
>   Say it is late and dusky, because they
>   See not all clear;
>   O for that night! where I in him
>   Might live invisible and dim. (pp. 522–3)

In his translation of *Of Temperance and Patience*, where Nierembergius mentioned hope, Vaughan added "that troublesome tympany" (p. 225). Truth flourishes in darkness and in death (p. 656).[6]

Vaughan's nostalgia for childhood is akin to the death-wish. He wants to escape backwards, into a safer world:

>   Happy those early days! When I
>   Shined in my angel-infancy.
>   Before I understood this place
>   Appointed for my second race,
>   Or taught my soul to fancy aught
>   But a white, celestial thought. . . .
>   O how I long to travel back! (pp. 419–20).
>
>   Were now that chronicle alive,
>   Those white designs which children drive. . . .
>   Quickly would I make my path even,
>   And by mere playing go to heaven. (pp. 520–1).

Vaughan is often compared to Traherne in this respect. But they are in fact very different. Traherne hoped and intended to recapture the childlike vision on earth; he thought we all could, by an effort of will and discipline.[8] Unlike Traherne, Vaughan could look back to his childhood only across the black chasm of the Revolution. He was trying to recapture a world which could not have survived. It is part of his nostalgia of defeat.[9] Martin quotes Earle's *Character of a Child*, which he rather cruelly says "Vaughan may have read":—"the elder he goes, he is a stair lower from God; and, like his first father, much worse in his breeches" (pp. 695–6).[10] Exaltation of childhood was not unknown, but it raised problems about the fate of those who died in infancy. This was especially troublesome for believers in original sin, including Lollard heretics and New England divines. Lodowick Muggleton, who believed that all were predestined from the womb to salvation or damnation, nevertheless managed to hold that those dying in infancy would be saved.[11]

The other mood of *Silex Scintillans* is the hope for redemption through blood and suffering, for victory brought about by divine intervention. The storm of affliction will bring "sunshine after rain" (pp. 412–13; cf. p. 468).

> So shall that storm purge this recluse
>   Which sinful ease made foul,
> And wind and water to thy use
>   Both wash and wing my soul. (p. 424)

> What calms can be
> So fair as storms, that appease thee? (p. 642)

Vaughan wrote two poems entitled *The Day of Judgment* (pp. 402–3, 530–1; cf. pp. 428, 486, 501–5, 609–12); he awaited it with a confident hope more common among radical Puritans than royalists.

> By all signs
> Our fullness too is now come in. (pp. 499–500)

> The fields are long since white. (pp. 530–1)

"The end of this world truly draws near", he asserted in 1654, "if it be not at the door" (p. 338). Was he thinking of 1656?[12]

> Arise, arise!
> And like old clothes fold up these skies. . . .
> O seeing thou hast paid our score,
> Why should the curse reign any more?
> Only let not our haters brag,
> Thy seamless coat is grown a rag. . . . (pp. 541–3)

There is a shade of anxiety present in the consolation.

The darkness of total corruption was for Vaughan relieved by "glimpses" of better things—either a return to the vision of childhood or a sense of community with nature. For early man

> Still Paradise lay
> In some green shade or fountain.
> Angels lay lieger here. (pp. 440–1)

> All things here show him heaven; waters that fall
>   Chide and fly up; mists of corruptest foam
>   Quit their first beds and mount; trees, herbs, flowers, all
> Strive upwards still, and point him the way home. . . .

> And seeds a kindred fire have with the sky. . . .

But our corruption rejects these glimpses:

> Yet hugs he still his dirt; the stuff he wears
>   And painted trimming takes down both his eyes
>   Heaven hath less beauty than the dust he spies,
> And money better music that the spheres. (p. 461; cf. pp. 296, 443–4, 447, 496–7, 500, 513, 528–30, 534–6, 645–6)

It is this sense of transience, this intangibility of what men once possessed more securely, that gives their force to poems like *Anguish*, with their overwhelming sense of frustration:

>   O God, disperse
> These weights, and give my spirit leave
> To act as well as to conceive!

> O my God, hear my cry;
>   Or let me die! (p. 526)

Only through death will the vision be finally recovered.

We can date most of Vaughan's best poetry with reasonable precision to the years between 1646 (when *Poems* were published) and 1655 (Part II of *Silex Scintillans*). If, as is probable, *Olor Iscanus* (1651) was completed by December 1647, when its dedication is dated,[13] then we could cut the period of his great poetry down to the years 1648–55. Most of the poems in *Thalia Rediviva* (1678) are much more placid and empty. The few exceptions—*The Revival*, for example—may plausibly be dated early. It is probable that Marvell, an almost exact contemporary of Vaughan's, also composed his greatest non-satirical poems in these years; but dating is more doubtful in his case. Vaughan, curiously, anticipates Marvell in praising those who "make that rigid necessity their pleasant choice" (p. 216).[14]

Vaughan seems to have undergone some sort of crisis in or around 1648, one consequence of which was the sudden and brief flowering of his best poetry. It had been a brutal time for the poet. His dearly-loved younger brother William died in July 1648, possibly as a result of participation in the second civil war. We do not know whether Vaughan himself fought in the first civil war, or whether he took up arms for the first time in 1648—as improvidently as Benlowes. It has been conjectured that he fought for the King in the last months of 1645.[15] But in either case, in 1648 he experienced the final catastrophe of royalism, followed by the execution of the King and a far more effective Parliamentarian occupation of Wales. "We have seen princes brought to their graves by a new way, and the highest order of human honours trampled upon by the lowest. . . . The ruin of the most goodly pieces seems to tell that the dissolution of the whole is not far off".[16] In 1650 Wales was subordinated to the Commission for the Propagation of the Gospel, whose activities seemed to many Welsh royalists to be those of a foreign occupying force imposing an alien ideology. "Mine enemies . . . have not only robbed me of that portion and provision which thou hadst graciously given me, but they have also washed their hands in the blood of my friends".[17] Henceforth Vaughan seems to have had a horror of further bloodshed (for example, pp. 517, 523).

His financial affairs were already in a bad way. His father had long been in debt, and was accused in 1649 of misappropriating charitable funds. "No honester than he should be", was the verdict of Aubrey.[18] Henry's twin brother Thomas, long the absentee rector of Llansantffraed, was evicted in 1650: others of Vaughan's friends suffered the same fate. He took up the practice of medicine in the fifties, no doubt for financial reasons in view of the family's broken fortunes.[19] The frequent references to his poverty in *Silex Scintillans* (for example, p. 422) may exaggerate; but he was less well-off than he might reasonably have expected.

All these factors must have had a bearing on his "conversion" at about this time: economic decline, political defeat, the subjection of his country to those whom he despised as alien upstarts. "I write unto thee out of a land of darkness, out of that unfortunate region where the inhabitants sit in the shadow of death: where destruction passeth for propagation and a thick black night for the glorious day-spring". So Vaughan in April 1652. The hyperbole may fairly represent his own feelings (p. 217; cf. p. 406). These experiences were accompanied by powerful impressions derived from "blessed Mr. Herbert", first mentioned in *The Mount of Olives* (1652) (p. 186); borrowings from or imitations of George Herbert are everywhere in *Silex Scintillans.*

Why did Herbert have this overwhelming effect on Vaughan? What had he to give the younger poet in the late forties? Herbert was in many ways a kindred spirit. Of Welsh origin, a member of the family of the oppositionist Earls of Pembroke, brother of the Master of the Revels, Herbert surprised and shocked his friends by becoming a country parson, "missing his design" of a court career.

> Were it not better to bestow
>   Some place and power on me?

Herbert asked God. It seemed a reasonable expectation. But the poet concluded that

> Perhaps great places and thy praise
>   Do not so well agree.[20]

He was told that "he had disparaged himself by so dirty an employment" as a country parsonage; it was "too mean an employment, and too much below his birth".[21] Herbert in effect replied by telling a friend, on the night of his induction to the living of Bemerton, "I can now behold the court with an impartial eye, and see plainly that it is made up of fraud and titles and flattery".[22] "The blessings in the holy Scripture", he had reminded his mother many years earlier, "are never given to the rich, but to the poor".[23]

Poems like "Peace" and the strongly anti-papist "The Church Militant" make clear Herbert's distaste for Charles I's court. The adjective in the title of *The Country Parson* may convey a point. Herbert contrasts country parsons with university divines and private chaplains to the nobility. He insists that the country parson must stand up to "any of the gentry or nobility of that parish"[24]—a task which would be easier for a Herbert than for humbler clerics. "Gold and grace did never yet agree".[25] The opening poem of *The Temple*, "The Church Porch", extols the bourgeois virtues; the country parson considered idleness to be "the great national sin of this land".[26] "The parson's yea is yea, and nay, nay", like the Quakers.[27] Herbert adopted what Patrick Grant calls "a radical political ecclesiology which emphasizes a spiritual church of the elect rather than the solidarity of a corporate institution".[28] On more than one occasion he warmly praised the incomparable Francis Bacon.[29]

There is not much about bishops in Herbert's writings. He had indeed few good words to say for "the dignified clergy"; he hoped rather bleakly that those "which teach temperance would avoid surfeiting, and take all occasions to express a visible humility and charity in their lives".[30] Under the Laudian persecution Herbert—provocatively again—saw religion standing

> on tiptoe in our land
> Ready to pass to the American strand.[31]

These lines, which worried the censor, clearly aligned Herbert against the dominant Laudians and with the critics of his régime. Vaughan spoke of Herbert as

> A seer, that observed thee [Christian religion] in
> Thy course, and watched the growth of sin, . . .
> and foretold
> That westward hence thy course will hold. (pp. 654–5; cf. p. 169)

Vaughan may have thought that the westward course of religion would lead it to Wales.

Herbert showed that the church could be distinguished from the court, and gave Vaughan a cause in which he could whole-heartedly believe in the dark days after 1648. In his earliest poems Vaughan—intended by his father for the law[32]—had accepted the values of the court without qualification, though he can hardly have had access to it himself. But he held no clear-cut political position. He seems to have been hostile to Parliament, and especially to popular demonstrations, but he was scathing about monopolies (p. 14). Even in *Silex Scintillans* he pilloried

> young gay swearers, with their needless loud
> Retinue,

and their "compliments", their "spruce, supple cringes" and the painted faces of their ladies. These sound more like Cavaliers than Roundheads (pp. 408–9), as do the "trimmed gallants" in *Thalia Rediviva* (1678), boasting "this lady was their friend, and such a lord" (pp. 612–13). Earlier he had attacked the "foreign fashions" of "French apes" with a vigour reminiscent of Samuel Butler on the same theme later (p. 45).[33] Vaughan's royalism was of the spirit of Edward Hyde. Like Milton, Vaughan disliked "the lascivious compositions" of some profane poetry (pp. 589–90).

The civil war destroyed the court, and made nonsense of its values. Vaughan's *Poems* (1646) concluded with "The Tenth Satyre of

Juvenal Englished", in which these values are called in question,
though Vaughan seems to have nothing to put in their place.[34] In
Olor Iscanus (probably completed in 1647) Vaughan has an elegy on
the death of Mr R.W., slain in the battle of Rowton Heath, in which
he stresses the inadequacy of poetry to cope with death (pp. 49–51).[35]
It was a theme with which a greater poet had grappled eight years
earlier. But even in 1637 Milton had found consolation for Edward
King's death, had seen how the resurrection of Lycidas could dispel
the horror of the dismembering of Orpheus; and had set himself a
programme of political action.[36] Somewhere between 1648 and 1650
Vaughan found his consolation and course of action through reading
Herbert. He became, like Quarles and Benlowes, fanatically loyal to
the national church. His foolishly belated decision to take up arms in
1648 may have been due to his (apparently) new convictions. He
never showed anything like as much devotion to monarchy as to the
church.[37]

The Church of England had been central for Herbert, though
bishops were not. The church was everywhere (or should be)
subordinated to the gentry, and was in their eyes part of the English
constitution. The anglicizing Welsh gentry had an especial need for
the Church of England, most of all in the sixteen-fifties. They were
in process of distinguishing themselves from the papist and pagan
natives: the church was their symbol of civilization. Yet in the fifties
the institutional church as Vaughan knew it had collapsed: its tithes
were taken by itinerant preachers of great enthusiasm but no respect
for the defeated royalist gentry. The Propagators of the Gospel
appealed over the heads of "the natural rulers" to the Welsh
peasantry: it was the first glimpse of the later split between
nonconformist Welsh people and their anglicizing gentry. Through
Herbert, Vaughan was able to see his own oppressed condition
reflected in that of the church. His self-chosen epithet, "Silurist",
may draw attention to the Welsh patriotic myth—that the pristine
purity of the Celtic church had been preserved when the Britons
retreated westwards to the mountains to escape the pagan Anglo-
Saxon invaders.[38] Vaughan's nostalgia for his own childhood
paralleled his nostalgia for the primitive church. The analogy gave
him consolation and a programme: practising the Christian virtues of
patience and humility, enduring sufferings quietly in a raucous
world.[39]

Herbert had had a keen sense of human degeneration, of decline from earlier, better days when men had easy access to God. For Vaughan this slow decline had become sudden catastrophe. The radicals and the Propagators of the Gospel hailed their take-over of the church as a sign of the coming millenium. Vaughan's eschatology has no place for the rule of the saints, but all the signs for him too pointed to the approaching end of the world (pp. 338, 486). The church as an institution was lost, but individuals could and must hold on grimly till the end. This sense of impending apocalypse increases between 1650 and 1655, between Parts I and II of *Silex Scintillans*[40]

The consequences of the Revolution which most offended Vaughan were those affecting religion. It had been tainted, poisoned, had become "instead of physic, a disease". The church had been despoiled and religion exiled (pp. 404-6, 654-5).

> The children chase the mother, and would heal
> The wounds they give by crying zeal.

They need to be "taught obedience" (p. 470). "Thy ministers are trodden down and the basest of the people set up in the holy place" (p. 166; cf. p. 170). The populace is "sensible of nothing but private interest and the base ways of acquiring it". Who could expect virtue or humanity from "a Masaniello, or some son of a butcher?" (p. 363). "Popular politic persons live always by events" (p. 265; cf. p. 288). "God himself died by the multitude" (p. 527; cf. pp. 487, 519, 523, 606).

Vaughan's was the church of Grindal, Abbott, Ussher, of Spenser, Quarles and Herbert: stoutly protestant, with no more sympathy for protestant sectaries than for popish recusants.[41] Vaughan cites equally the Geneva Bible and the Authorized Version; Latin he quotes from Béza's New Testament and from Tremellius rather than the Vulgate.[42] Vaughan accepted the protestant emphasis on the importance of preaching in bringing salvation; the ear became even more important than the eye when the visible church was driven underground.[43] He is one of the very few poets who feels Calvinist predestinarianism on his pulses. He has a powerful sense of the total vileness and corruption of the mass of mankind. A few only are vicariously redeemed by God's inscrutable Providence. Even Vaughan's tears are sent by God: "for I till dawn came not to thee" (pp. 528-30; cf. pp. 448-9, 472-4, 567). In poem after poem Vaughan returns to and harps upon his sinfulness.

Perhaps Hermeticism, with which Vaughan flirted for a time, was

an attempt to escape from the iron laws of predestination. His twin
brother Thomas was one of England's leading Hermeticists, satirized
as Anthroposophus by Samuel Butler.[44] Henry studied Hermes
Trismegistus, Paracelsus, Agrippa, Fludd (pp. 296, 305, 548).[45]
Rifling "through all the creatures", including himself, Henry
Vaughan found

> A piece of much antiquity,
> With hieroglyphics quite dismembered
> And broken letters, scarce remembered,

which he hoped to unite "to find out/ The mystery" (pp. 418-19).
Is this a hint at the *prisca theologia*?

Vaughan attributes feeling to herbs, trees, flowers and stones, and
seems to believe that they will share in the resurrection (pp. 432, 497,
501, 515, 531, 540). This animistic pantheism recalls Winstanley and
other interregnum radicals.[46] Vaughan would rather be "a stone, or
tree, or flower", a bird or a bee, than a straying, roaming human being
(pp. 432-3), for whom

> God ordered motion, but ordained no rest. . . .
> He knows he hath a home, but scarce knows where,
>   He says it is so far
> That he hath quite forgot how to get there. (p. 477)

Vaughan's interest in Hermeticism seems to have come *via*
medicine, the practice of which he took up in the fifties. In 1655 he
translated Nollius's *Hermetical Physick; or, The right way to preserve,
and to restore Health*. One thing that Vaughan liked about the
Hermeticists was that all their knowledge "proceeds from a laborious
manual disquisition and search into nature", whereas "the Galenists
insist wholly upon a bare received theory, . . . and will not be
persuaded to inquire further than the mouth of their leader" (p.
550—Vaughan's insertion). Hermeticism was thus Vaughan's way
into experimental medicine. "Not omitting his own observations",
was another insertion into the translation of Nollius (p. 588). It was
apropos Hermeticism that Vaughan pronounced in favour of the
Moderns against the Ancients (p. 548)

Perhaps Vaughan came to Hermeticism too late. By the sixteen-
fifties other approaches to modern science were being explored in
Oxford and London, of which he may have been unaware in
Breconshire. He ultimately came to reject "my false magic, which I
did believe/ And mystic lies" (p. 616). But there is much safety in that

word "false". He still spoke up for astrology in 1680 (pp. 672-3). Though never a full-blown Hermeticist like his brother, Henry Vaughan certainly found some of its insights appealing at the time he wrote his greatest poetry. For Thomas Vaughan the soul "doth elect" "to be made one with the higher soul", and can then separate itself from the body and all its evils. A human soul can attain to a sense of divinity and then there is nothing it cannot accomplish by its own power without external help.[47] This position was incompatible with Henry's Calvinism: what he got from Hermeticism was the close feeling of identity with nature which shines in his best poetry.

Many Hermeticists were religious radicals of a kind which Vaughan detested: so there are problems about his Hermeticism, and his relationship to Boehme, which have not yet been satisfactorily solved. As in the very different case of Milton, some of those who discuss Vaughan's Hermeticism seem more interested in defending their client's orthodoxy than in elucidating his relationship with the unorthodox. The word "mystic" creates a useful confusion for these purposes.[48]

Vaughan's religious prejudices are closely connected with his social prejudices. He assumed that "stiff-necked Brownists" would be lower-class weavers (p. 54). He condemned "this rash and impious practice" of mechanic preaching (pp. 348, 354). He disliked "the seditious and schismatical" (p. 389). His *Solitary Devotions* (1652) are addressed to a leisured audience who can refrain from "any worldly business" for three days before receiving communion (p. 157). He deplored taking communion in the sitting position (p. 456). But in translating Nollius's reference to the godly rich who "not only feed upon and live by the sweat, the slaughter and the blood of the poor oppressed but esteem them (of all others) their choicest dainties", Vaughan added, gratuitously, "for they are swallowed without much chewing, and there is none to deliver them" (p. 554; cf. p. 652: "the rich eat the poor like bread").

From his Calvinism, perhaps, Vaughan retained a horror of idleness, of waste of time; a yearning for effort, activity, which was not always easy to satisfy. "With what Christian thrift and diligence", he asked, "should we dispose of every minute of our time that we might make our calling and election sure?" (p. 180). "Nothing hath commerce with heaven but what is pure; he that would be pure, must needs be active: . . . virtue is never absent but when we are idle". The words are Vaughan's insertion in the text of

Of Temperance and Patience (p. 266). He gave vivid impression to his restless desire for action in "Misery", though here he regards it as evidence of "a peevish heart", a mutiny (pp. 472-4; cf. pp. 477, 526).

"Dust" and "dirt", then, were symbols for the world of commerce and politics, the world in which the Welsh squire, the defeated royalist, was left standing, both by the cunning of men and by the mere development of social forces. Yet he believed that "none would with more advantage use . . . the world's loved wisdom" than he (p. 520). He seems indeed to have been pretty successful as a doctor: but one suspects that he can hardly have been happy with the tone of restoration England. Fortunately he did not have to live in London. He visited Oxford, where in the Bodleian Library he found consolation in reading classical authors, among them the satirist Lucilius:

> And in this age, as sad almost as thine,
> Thy stately consolations are mine, (pp. 613-14)[49]

But his later life was racked by family quarrels. He had to be sued to provide maintenance for his disabled daughter—a depth to which Milton never sank. His son also sued him. None of it was very dignified.

Yet "in that land of darkness and blind eyes" Vaughan still had "white Sundays", memories of happy childhood days, and could still escape to his relatively untouched countryside, and pretend that because the colour scheme was the same the social relationships had not changed. Pristine purity, unsullied by the dust and heat of the real world, could be recaptured in glimpses. (Vaughan, one suspects, would have praised a fugitive and cloistered virtue). He is a poet of splendid openings and endings; his lyrics sometimes flounder after a breathtaking start, and then recover to a dying fall which haunts the memory. At its earlier best, the contrast between the humdrum reality of the poet's economic decline, the dusty world that has defeated him, and the glimpses of a white eternity, the intensity of his agony of consolation and triumph, creates a true poetry, a temporary equilibrium of stability and assuredness:

> *The Waterfall*
> With what deep murmurs through time's silent stealth
> Doth thy transparent, cool and watery wealth
>   Here flowing fall,
>   And chide, and call,
> As if his liquid, loose retinue stayed

Lingering, and were of this steep place afraid,
>> The common pass
>> Where, clear as glass,
>> All must descend
>> Not to an end:
But quickened by this deep and rocky grave,
Rise to a longer course more bright and brave. (p. 537)

The Timber
Sure thou didst flourish once! and many springs,
Many bright mornings, much dew, many showers
Passed o'er thy head: many light hearts and wings
Which are now dead, lodged in thy living bowers.

And still a new succession sings and flies;
Fresh groves grow up, and their green branches shoot
Towards the old and still enduring skies,
While the low violet thrives at their root. . . .

But these chaste fountains flow not till we die;
Some drops may fall before, but a clear spring
And ever running, till we leave to fling
Dirt in her way, will keep above the sky.

> Rom. Cap. 6 ver. 7.
> He that is dead, is freed from sin. (pp. 497-9)

NOTES

1. This piece bears a distant relationship to a review of Ross Garner's *Henry Vaughan: Experience and the Tradition* (Chicago U.P., 1959), in *Science and Society*, XXV (1961).
2. All my quotations, unless otherwise indicated, are from *The Works of Henry Vaughan* (ed. L.C. Martin, Oxford U.P., 1914). The pagination of the two volumes is continuous.
3. See F.E. Hutchinson, *Henry Vaughan: A Life and Interpretation* (Oxford U.P., 1947) for the special significance of "white" in Welsh, probably Vaughan's first language. Cf. also S.L. Bethall. *The Cultural Revolution of the 17th Century* (1951), p. 130, for Welsh technical influences on Vaughan's poetry.
4. Cf. also pp. 13-14, 19, 414, 418-19, 425-9, 436-7, 441, 443-5, 447-8, 454-6, 459, 463, 468, 471, 473, 475, 479, 486, 499, 504, 506, 512, 515-16, 520, 523, 534-5, 540, 611, 613-16, 647-8, 650. This is not an exhaustive list of uses of "dust", "dirt", etc. But it will serve to suggest their frequency.
5. Cf. pp. 40, 393-5, 399-401, 405-7, 416, 427-8, 430-2, 437, 449, 451, 459,

464, 468-9, 472-6, 478-9, 481-2, 486-8, 491, 499-501, 512, 516, 518, 526-7, 534, 537-9, 618, 642-3, 647, 656.

6. All the love songs in *Poems* are about death. Cf. *Man in Darkness, or A Discourse of Death*, in *The Mount of Olives* (Martin, pp. 168-90), and pp. 4-5, 41-2, 444, 474, 526, 533, 609-11.

7. Cf. pp. 450, 483-4, 640.

8. For Traherne see p. 232 below.

9. L.C. Martin, "Henry Vaughan and the Theme of Infancy", in *Seventeenth Century Studies Presented to Sir Herbert Grierson* (Oxford U.P., 1938), p. 245: Vaughan's civil war experience "did much to induce in him a state of depression, favourable . . . to nostalgic exaltations of nature and childhood". Cf. pp. 213-17 above. See Leah S. Marcus, *Childhood and Cultural Despair: A Theme and Variations in 17th Century Literature* (Pittsburgh U.P., 1978), Chapter 4, *passim*. Idealization of childhood, Dr Marcus suggests, can be correlated with cultural breakdown (*ibid.*, p. 246). See also Lewalski, *op. cit.*, p. 352.

10. J. Earle, *Microcosmography, or a Piece of the World Discovered in Essays and Characters* (1934), p. 6. First published 1628. Cf. Herbert, "Holy Baptism", which Vaughan certainly had read; also Owen Felltham, *Resolves* (1628, and many later editions), Martin, *op. cit.*, pp. 247-52.

11. C. Hill, B. Reay and W. M. Lamont, *The World of the Muggletonians* (1983), p. 86.

12. For 1656 see pp. 158 above, 231 below. Vaughan clearly attached significance to this date, often predicted for the end of the world. Cf. *Works*, p. 645.

13. H.R. Walley, "The Strange Case of *Olor Iscanus*", *Review of English Studies*, 18 (1942); Hutchinson *op. cit.* pp. 72-80.

14. Cf. p. 255, Vaughan's insertion in his translation of *Of Temperance and Patience*: "The strength of her [Fortune's] prerogative lies betwixt willingness and constraint. . . . Man plays with his stars until they hurt him". The Matchless Orinda, who wrote a poem to Vaughan, used Marvell's phrase. For Marvell see pp. 176-8 above.

15. Hutchinson, *op. cit.*, pp. 60-3, 97-9; cf. p. 200 above.

16. *The Mount of Olives* (1652), in *Works*, I, pp. 170-1.

17. *Ibid.*, I, p. 167.

18. Aubrey, *Brief Lives*, II, pp. 268-9. Aubrey was a cousin of the Vaughans.

19. Hutchinson, *op cit.*, pp. 90, 96, 98, 141, 193-4, 199, 201.

20. Herbert, *Works* (ed. R.A. Willmott), pp. 94-5.

21. Izaak Walton, *The Lives of John Donne, Sir Henry Wotton, Richard Hooker, George Herbert and Robert Sanderson* (World's Classics edn.), pp. 305, 277.

22. *Ibid.*, p. 289.

23. *Ibid.*, p. 282.

24. *Works*, pp. 218-9, 227. Cf. p. 255 below for the risks of criticizing "the pride and luxury of apparel" of the wife and daughter of a gentleman.

25. *Works*, p. 209.

26. *Ibid.*, p. 281.

27. *Ibid.*, p. 221.

28. P. Grant, *The Transformation of Sin: Studies in Donne, Herbert, Vaughan and Traherne* (McGill – Queen's U.P., 1974), pp. 128–9, 202.

29. *Works*, pp. 459–61.

30. Walton, *op. cit.*, p. 304.

31. *Works*, p. 209. Herbert's widow fought for Parliament.

32. Aubrey, *op. cit.*, II, p. 269.

33. See pp. 288–9 below.

34. J.F.S. Post, *Henry Vaughan: The Unfolding Vision* (Princeton U.P., 1982), Chapter 1.

35. *Ibid.*, 35–7, 43.

36. Cf. J. Martin Evans, *The Road from Horton: Looking Backwards in "Lycidas"*, English Literary Studies, Monograph Series, No. 28, *passim.*

37. But he took advantage of the eclipse of church courts to marry his deceased wife's sister around 1655 (Hutchinson, *op it.*, p. 198).

38. As is argued in Post, *op. cit.*, Chapter 5.

39. Post *op. cit.*, pp. 181–5, 207.

40. *Ibid.*, pp. 98–9, 188–9, 198.

41. Vaughan was connected by kinship or friendship with many recusant families, as was almost inevitable in Wales. He translated works by Catholics, just as Benlowes—staunch protestant of recusant origins—and Wither drew on Catholic emblems (Hutchinson, *op. cit.*, pp. 7, 131, 284); see pp. 199–201 above.

42. Hutchinson, *op. cit.*, p. 122.

43. Post, *op. cit.*, pp. 159–60.

44. *Hudibras*, Part I, canto i, l. 535. Thomas Vaughan wrote *Anthroposophia Theomagica* (1650).

45. L.C. Martin, "Henry Vaughan and Hermeticism", *Review of English Studies*, 18 (1942).

46. For the resurrection of animals see K.V. Thomas, *Man and the Natural World: Changing attitudes in England, 1500–1800* (1983), pp. 139–41. It appears to have been a belief more commonly held by radical separatists, though it had its attractions for any pet-lover.

47. *The Works of Thomas Vaughan: Eugenius Philalethes* (ed. A.E. Waite, 1919), p. 102; cf. p. 48.

48. A.W. Rudrun's "Vaughan's 'The Night': Some Hermetic Notes", *Modern Language Review*, 64 (1969) is helpful, especially on Vaughan's knowledge of Boehme. I also found useful the older writings of Elizabeth Holmes (*Henry Vaughan and the Hermetic Philosophy*, New York, 1932, esp. p. 40), and L.C. Martin ("Henry Vaughan and the Theme of Infancy", esp. pp. 247–8, 253, as well as his "Henry Vaughan and Hermeticism"). F. Kermode, "The Private Imagery of Henry Vaughan", *Review of English Studies* (New Series, 1, 1950) is refreshingly brisk in rejecting "mysticism". So is Barbara Lewalski, who insists that Hermeticism is not central to Vaughan's thought, which is steadfastly protestant (Lewalski, *op. cit.*, pp. 332, 339–40, 351).

49. Benlowes also found a refuge in the Bodleian. See p. 202 above.

10. *Thomas Traherne, 1637–74*[1]

The label "metaphysical" attached to a poet tends to identify him as "royalist". Thus Marvell is credited (if that is the word) with a royalist phase before he accepted the Commonwealth and (as used wrongly to be thought) ceased to write good poetry. Traherne is assimilated to Vaughan and Crashawe and (a more dubious "royalist") George Herbert. These clichés sometimes stop us looking seriously at the evidence.

The metaphysical lyric reflects the tensions of divided minds. The "conceit" lays incompatibles side by side, drags the apparently incongruous or indeed the logically contradictory into unity, forces things different in kind on to the same plane of reference. I have suggested that this tension, from Donne to Marvell, this consciousness of a contrast between subjective and objective, desire and possibility, idea and reality, relates, however indirectly, to the tensions of a divided society.[2]

Traherne comes late in this succession. He is writing after the Revolution has ended in compromise. The balanced rhymed couplet is replacing the metaphysical lyric; tortured conceits are out of fashion. Traherne's manner is metaphysical, but his content is less troubled, less paradoxical, less ironical and self-mocking than, for instance, Marvell's. Traherne proclaims the unity of apparent opposites, thanks to his claim to a new intellectual vision:

> He that cannot like an angel see,
> In heaven itself shall dwell in misery.[3]

> We plough the very skies, as well
> > As earth.[4]

> Corn for our food springs out of very mire.

> From clay, and mire, and dirt, my soul,
> > From vile and common ore,
> Thou must ascend.

This lesson derives from the fact that

Bells are but clay that men refine
　　And raise from duller ore;
Yet now, as if they were divine,
　　They call whole cities to adore.[5]

The opposites now balance neatly, without the inward struggles of metaphysical conflict. We may compare Peter Sterry: "We have the principle of life in us, for the most part in sensual pleasures; as a piece of gold in the dirt, as the sun in a cloud; as the brain or fancy in a mist or fume. Wipe the dirt off the gold, scatter the cloud from before the sun, the mist on the fancy; chase vain delights out of the soul; all these will shine in their proper beauties".[6]

Traherne has a splendid appreciation of wide open spaces:

The heavens were the richly studded case
　　Which did my richer wealth enclose;
　　No little private cabinet
　　　　In which my gems to set
Did I contrive: I thought the whole earth's face
　　　　At my dispose;
　　　　No confines did include
What I possessed, no limits then I viewed;
　　　　On every side
　　All endless was which then I spied.

'Tis art that hath the late invention found
　　Of shutting up in little room
　　One's boundless expectations: men
　　　　Have in a narrow pen
Confined themselves: free souls can know no bound;
　　　　But still presume
　　　　That treasure everywhere
From everlasting hills must still appear.[7]

Yet for this poet of nature "the most populous and flourishing cities" reveal "the fairest prospects".[8] The idea of nature, or of childhood, seems more important than nature or childhood themselves. So far as we know, Traherne had no children himself: there is not much evidence that he (or Vaughan) was particularly fond of them.[9]

Traherne is a poet of very intense but limited vision. He reacted fiercely against the Calvinist doctrine of original sin, and believed that in his infancy he had a pure vision which later became contaminated but could be recaptured. (Infants know by instant intuition, like the angels).[10] God created the universe for his creatures to enjoy, and rejoices in their happiness; it is therefore their duty to regain the primal vision.[11] At its best this produces magnificent poems like *Wonder, Desire, Solitude, Shadows in the Water.* But Traherne has really only one theme: a recall of the vision, an insistence that stars are better than gold, wheat than gems, water than pearls. Natural goodness is to be found in the fields, or in cities among children. At their worst, Traherne's poems can degenerate into boring catalogues, punctuated by ecstatic exclamations of delight. The repeated rhymes become monotonous: "pleasures" always anticipate "treasures"; "divine", "shine", "mine", and "skies", "eyes", "prize", "toys", "joys", "boys", are other regular occurrents.

But at his best, in his verse and in his prose, Traherne can startle and delight. My only reason for venturing to discuss him is that I believe he has not been placed in quite the right context. Miss Gladys Wade's biography is in general admirable; but in some respects she took a slightly blinkered view of seventeenth-century society and thought. Thus she sees Traherne's ancestors as Thomas Aquinas, neo-Platonists, Lancelot Andrews, Donne.[12] She mentions virtually no one who lived and wrote in Traherne's own lifetime: yet these years (1637–74) were among the most intellectually stimulating and exciting in the whole of English history. It is very difficult to imagine, *a priori*, that Traherne was not influenced by the ferment of discussion that was going on around him in his childhood and young manhood: it is even more difficult when we compare the content of some of these discussions with Traherne's themes. I shall try to suggest some respects in which he clearly was influenced by them.

Secondly, Miss Wade says "Traherne appears constantly as an enthusiastic High Anglican". She has to admit that his ordination was Presbyterian, based on "a sheaf of testimonials from the leading Puritan divines in Herefordshire" who—unlike Traherne—resigned their livings rather than conform after 1660.[13] Traherne had obtained his first benefice from a Puritan patroness.[14] Presumably he had to be reordained to retain it. Miss Wade was embarrassed by the only work which Traherne himself published after 1660. *Roman Forgeries*, for whose subject she expects us to have "a pre-conceived aversion".[15] It is indeed hardly the book one expects from a "High Anglican". Miss Wade rightly stresses that *Roman Forgeries* is based on massive scholarship, and she suggests that its publication in 1673 was "a telling bit of propaganda in support of Bridgeman's anti-Catholic principles". Sir Orlando Bridgeman, Traherne's patron, had resigned his office as Lord Keeper of the Great Seal in 1672 rather than seal the Declaration of Indulgence.[16] Just before this time Bridgeman was being reported on by government spies; he seems to have been caballing with Buckingham and Wilkins.[17] His dismissal may possibly have given Traherne his immediate incentive to publish. But he had not undertaken years of research with that end in view. We must see his book in historical perspective, not in the light of twentieth-century oecumenical assumptions.

From the sixteenth century, protestantism had come to be inextricably bound up with the continued existence of the English state; even in the early seventeenth century protestantism still did not seem secure. The threat came from the advance of Catholicism in Europe during the Thirty Years War, combined with the apparent readiness of the dominant faction in the church, the Laudian "High Anglicans", to meet Catholicism half-way. We too easily equate Laudianism with "Anglicanism". As we have seen, Quarles, Benlowes and Vaughan were devoted churchmen who would have no truck with either popery or sectarianism;[18] it is likely that such men formed a majority of articulate Anglicans. Protestantism and patriotism were closely linked: fear of an international Catholic plot persuaded men like Richard Baxter to support Parliament in the sixteen-forties. Even Lord Henry Spencer, who died fighting for the royalists, believed that victory for the King would mean that the papists would prevail and England would be "in sad condition".[19] In the fifties the conviction—absurd though it seems to us—that papists had infiltrated the sects, especially the Quakers, and were using them to undermine the English protestant community—this conviction helped to persuade many of the gentry and clergy that a restoration of King and bishops was necessary in 1660. Again Baxter is a case in point. But in the seventies a new threat to protestantism appeared in the manifest desire of Charles II and his brother James to promote absolutism and popery in subordination to the greatest European power, Louis XIV's France.

Defence of protestantism and counter-attack on popery thus had a century-long history in England: it was a patriotic duty in the eyes of all but the "High Anglican" wing in the Church of England. For over a century protestant scholars, all over Europe, had been studying the early centuries of Christianity, and had unearthed a great deal that was unfavourable to papal claims. Traherne's very detailed and well-documented *Roman Forgeries* was in this tradition of polemical scholarship, without whose clearing of the way no critical history of the early church would have been possible. Traherne cites the familiar Calvinist authorities—Bishop Jewell, Dr Reynolds, Dr James and "the learned Crashawe", father of the poet.[20] He works up to a vitriolic but measured conclusion: "the mother of lies hath espoused the father of lies. . . ."[21]

Additional urgency was given to the unmasking of Rome in the sixteen-seventies by the drift of court policy, symbolized by the dismissal of Bridgeman, who would rather have seen Presbyterians comprehended within the church than toleration for protestant and catholic dissenters derived from the royal prerogative. Alarm intensified when the Duke of York, heir to the throne, revealed himself a papist. "All were united against popery", wrote Burnet, with some exaggeration.[22] A spate of books warning against Catholicism and absolutism appeared. Samuel Butler thought the bishops would take England back to popery in order to conserve their wealth.[23]

So there is nothing surprising about Traherne's research interests, once we abandon the assumption that he was a "High Anglican". It would indeed have been surprising if he had been. When he died, Sir Edward Harley, former Parliamentarian and opponent of the court, spoke of "my worthy friend Mr. Thomas Traherne".[24] Traherne's ideas were formed at Oxford in the fifties, where many exciting intellectuals had been intruded by the Parliamentarian commissioners—John Wilkins, William Petty, Vice-Principal of Traherne's college, Brasenose, John Wallis, Seth Ward, Jonathan Goddard. Thomas Sydenham was a Fellow of Wadham alongside Thomas Sprat, future historian of the Royal Society. There is plenty of evidence for Traherne's scientific interests, which he presumably acquired at Oxford.[25] But there were other intellectual stimuli radiating to Oxford from the discussions that had gone on in London and the Army in the forties and were not yet extinct in 1653. The Army may indeed have carried radical ideas to Herefordshire, as it did to Wales and the North. Miss Wade grasped that Traherne had gone through a period of scepticism, perhaps before he went up to Oxford and during his years there from 1653 onwards. He had doubts about the authority of the Bible, and consequently about Christianity itself.[26] What she fails to remind us is how many other earnest young men and women were going through a similar crisis at about this time—Mrs

Baxter, John Bunyan, George Fox, Isaac Penington, Abiezer Coppe, Jacob Bauthumley, and countless others. It was not something personal to Traherne.[27] Traherne seems never to have relied on the Bible, miracles or apparitions, those stand-bys of orthodoxy, "to show us the certainty of true religion"—though he had seen a phantom or two himself.[28] Like very many others Traherne was looking for a new kind of rational certainty.

Traherne underwent a "second crisis",[29] which may perhaps be dated to 1656 by *Thanksgivings for the Beauty of his Providence*. The belief that 1656 years had elapsed between the Creation of the world and Noah's Flood led to anticipations of similar exciting events in 1656 A.D.—perhaps the conversion of the Jews and the beginning of the millenium. Matthew's gospel had said "as the days of Noah were, so shall also the coming of the Son of Man be".[30] Traherne associated the end of 1656 years with the renewed covenant. God saved both Noah and Traherne "in an ark by water" and so "dispelled the fogs of ignorance and atheism that else would have benighted and drowned my soul".[31] In *Christian Ethicks* (published posthumously in 1675) he was still arguing back against Ranters, those who most systematically questioned "the certainty of true religion" in the early sixteen-fifties.[32] He must I think have known their ideas and have been influenced by them.

Traherne—like Milton—reproduces many ideas which could not get into print before 1640 but were current in the world of radical speculation which flourished in the decade and a half when the press was relatively free. Not all of these ideas perhaps are incompatible with orthodoxy, but their presence in combination suggests that Traherne knew what had been going on in the world about him during his formative years. Patrick Grant perceptively noted resemblances between Traherne's doctrine of man and that of Servetus.[33] Traherne and Milton shared other ideas with more radical thinkers. Traherne believed for instance that all men were Sons of God, "in greatness and glory", just as Christ had been; some at least of them (of whom he was one) could partake of the divine nature upon earth.[34] "Every man/ Is like a God incarnate on the throne", like Adam before the Fall.[35] "An earthly man is a mortal God",[36] "a meeter dwelling place for his everlasting Godhead than the heaven of heavens".[37] We can arrive on earth "to the estate of immortality".[38] Traherne seems sometimes to have believed that all men would be saved.[39]

Traherne's conviction of the sanctity of childhood was part of his rejection of the Augustinian and Calvinist doctrine of original sin. "I shall keep within the compass of the first 420 years" of the church, Traherne stated precisely. Professor Grant points out that Augustine's anti-Pelagian treatises were mostly written after 420 A.D.[40] Familists had rejected original sin; so had Milton and most other interregnum radicals.[41] Traherne's anti-Calvinism distinguishes him from Vaughan. An infant soul is like an empty book, a *tabula rasa*.[42] To become like a little child was to become like Adam in Paradise before the Fall.[43] Man could attain on earth to a Paradise within happier far, as Ranters and Milton believed: "this world was far better than Paradise had men eyes to see its glory".[44] Traherne's theory involves a triple vision—the pure unspoilt vision of childhood, the corrupt vision of the fallen world, and the vision of Adam in Paradise which by strenuous effort we might recapture on earth. It is an entrancing idea, looking forward to Wordsworth. But it had been anticipated by some of the radicals of the interregnum. Isaac Penington, later a Quaker, wrote in his Ranter period:

To the creature, in the present state of the creature, under the present law of the creature, according to the judgment of the eye of the creature, everything is unlovely; and he that sees them not to be so, falls short of the perfection of the creaturely eye. But come deeper, beyond this state, beneath this Law; look with a true eye, and then you shall find all this unloveliness pass away, and an excellency appear, that the creature could never so much as imagine or dream of. And now come back with this eye into the present state of all things, and behold them through the true glass, and you shall see them all new here also, and as far differing from what you did or could take them to be in your creaturely apprehension.[45]

"The fault is in ourselves", John Everard had written, "not that miracles are ceased, but our eyes are blinded, and we cannot see them".[46] The Behmenist John Pordage claimed in 1655 that members of his community at Bradfield had recovered "that inward spiritual eye which hath been locked up and shut by the Fall".[47] We might also cite George Fox: "Now was I come up in spirit . . . into the Paradise of God. All things were new; and all the creation gave another smell unto me than before, beyond what words can utter. I knew nothing but pureness and innocency and righteousness, being renewed unto the image of God by Jesus Christ. The creation was opened to me".[48] Fox seems to have experienced this as a sudden conversion. Or take Peter Sterry, celebrating the perennial splendour of the visible universe, "a new world of glories". "Each dust . . . a beautiful star, each star . . . an heaven".[49] "O what a heaven doth he continually walk in to whom all things round about him are hung with these curtains of Solomon, the living brightnesses of a divine light; the flower of light springing from the face of God! In what lovely images doth this light, as the looking-glass of eternal truth and love, present him to himself, his company, all things round about him, to him!"[50] Sterry associated with Ranters,[51] believed that all men could become Sons of God and that God was potentially in all men, that all were perfectible and could attain on earth to a Paradise within.[52] It is the possibility of recapturing this vision on earth, steadily, not in occasional glimpses, which differentiates these radicals from Vaughan and makes them close to Traherne.[53]

Traherne reminds us of Winstanley as well as of Penington, Fox and Sterry. God is "a consuming fire, whose love is compared to everlasting burnings".[54] "The world is both a Paradise and a prison to different persons".[55] Like Winstanley, Traherne associated "curs'd and devis'd proprieties, . . . hedges, ditches, limits, bounds" with the Fall, and with growing up.[56] "It is not our parents' loins so much as our parents' lives that enthrals and blinds us". Sin is not inherited, but is absorbed from the world in which we live. Hence, as for Winstanley and Milton, the importance of education.[57] Growing up in the fallen world meant acquiring false values; we are "more fools at twenty years than ten".[58] "After distracting objects out they run",[59] accounting scarce things like jewels and gold more valuable than such useful but common things as air, water, the sun, trees, men and women.[60] Traherne concentrated more on the pre-lapsarian than the post-lapsarian virtues which appealed to Milton.[61]

It was traditionally orthodox to associate private property with the Fall of Man. But it was not orthodox—it was indeed highly dangerous—to suggest that it was possible to get back behind the Fall in this life, to escape from "the dirty devices of this world".[62] Some of the extreme radicals of the sixteen-forties and fifties had preached such ideas: I know of no one who expressed them explicitly in print after 1660. This may perhaps be one reason why Traherne's *Poems* and *Centuries* were not printed in his lifetime.[63] *Christian Ethicks*, which he did prepare for the press, is much more cautious. Once Traherne is put in his proper historical perspective anxiety about the censorship is at least worth considering as one reason for his failure to publish.

I am not of course arguing that Traherne was a political radical himself: far from it. I am talking only about the associations that his ideas might have for his contemporaries. Traherne believed that small children start with no sense of property or of sin. We can, with a great effort, think ourselves back into their position. Then, Traherne says, "all is mine". This recalls the vision of the Ranter Abiezer Coppe: "here hast thou wells, which thou diggedst not, houses which thou buildest not, vineyards and olive yards which thou plantedst not, corn that thou sowedst not, etc. All is given, freely given thee. Here thou hast wine and milk and honey, without money, without price".[64] But Coppe, like Winstanley, thought that all things should be held in common. Traherne's attitude to property is very different. He is urging us to attach greater importance to things of real but neglected importance—the sun, the seas, the beauties of nature. This is an attractive idea, which underlies some of Traherne's finest writing:

> Eternity doth give the richest things
> To every man and makes all kings. . . .[65]

"He that conceits nothing in the world to be his own but his low cottage and coarse diet will think it needless to praise his Maker, and will deny himself to be happy in those narrow and mean enjoyments. He that thinks all wealth is shut up in a trunk of gold will little regard the magnificence of the heavens, the light of the sun or the beauty of the universe".[66]

But the attraction is greatest to those who already have a competence: it is no consolation to a starving beggar to offer him the beauties of nature. And Traherne's starting-point itself is dubious. Young children may have no sense of limits or bounds; but if they help themselves to apples from someone else's orchard the landlord is likely to eject them from their Paradise as swiftly as Adam was ejected from his. "All things are mine" in more than a metaphorical sense only if other people recognize them as mine—unless I already have access to all the necessities of life. I once referred to Traherne's as a "communism of the imagination": to make it more than imaginary social change would be necessary.[67] It is idealistic in the philosophical sense:

> Thoughts are the angels which we send abroad,
> To visit all the parts of God's abode. . . .
>   The honey and the stings
> Of all that is, are seated in a thought.[68]

Traherne never came to grips with this. He recognized the importance of society: "To be alone in the world was to be desolate and miserable".[69] "He that thinks the sons of man impertinent to his joy and happiness can scarcely love them. . . . All mankind are my friends. And everything is enriched in serving them". "All men would be brothers and sisters throughout the whole world".[70] So every man was to be treated "as the representative of mankind . . . as if the man were Christ".[71]

> The bliss of other men is my delight
> (When once my principles are right).[72]

>> We must unite
>> If we delight
> Would yield or feel, or any excellence.[73]

"Never was anything in this world loved too much, but many things have been loved in a false way".[74]

If all men came to feel like that we should have a situation analogous to that envisaged by Winstanley, when the rising of Christ in all sons and daughters would make them see the rational necessity of establishing an egalitarian society in which there would be no private property.[75] "True goodness removes all envy and contention out of the world", wrote Traherne in *Christian Ethicks*.[76] But he discusses everything in terms of individual ethics, personal relations.[77] Beggars remain as recipients of the charity of the rich. For all his personal conviction, and his longing above all things to "be a blessing to mankind",[78] Traherne was incapable of Winstanley's insight: "the inward bondages of the mind, as covetousness, pride, hyprocrisy, envy, sorrows, fears, desperation and madness, are all occasioned by the outward bondage that one sort of people lay upon another".[79] Winstanley ultimately came to see that legislation would be necessary to promote real equality, backed up in the last resort by coercion.

Self-love is the basis of *Christian Ethicks*.[80] Traherne has to argue against "that arrogant *Leviathan*", who shared this starting-point, that "it is impossible to love ourselves without loving other things".[81] In his other works too Traherne is ultimately entirely self-absorbed, self-regarding. The world is mine, everything exists for me. The Ranters had said "All is ours", and that points a difference. Traherne does not suggest directly that the world might be everyone else's as well as his. There is no suggestion at all of how it might become theirs except by listening to Traherne and following his example carefully. He sees himself as a privileged teacher,[82] much as John Reeve, Wither and other "enthusiastic" prophets of the interregnum had seen themselves as uniquely called by God.

Traherne assumes the relatively privileged position in society of himself and those for whom he is writing. He makes a good deal of his own early poverty ("rags and cottages, . . . my father's poor house, . . . so poor"; "to live upon £10 a year and to go in leather clothes").[83] But there is enough internal evidence in his writings, confirmed from other sources, to show that he had the upbringing of a moderately well-to-do boy in the difficult civil war decade. His shoemaker father died when he was very young, and he seems to have been brought up in the household of his rich inn-keeper uncle. He had a nurse;[84] and Miss Wade plausibly conjectures that he was taught by a private tutor.[85] When Traherne was private chaplain to Sir Orlando Bridgeman he was well placed to win high preferment in the church. It was a remarkable feat for the shoemaker's son. Even his patron's loss of office could hardly have held him back if he had lived. Unlike Vaughan, he was rising in the world. Like those for whom he wrote, he was sufficiently well-off to be able to despise money.[86] They were householders, assumed to have servants.[87] "Courts of judicature stand open for our preservation", Traherne wrote; interregnum radicals had seen the law and its courts as instruments of ruling-class oppression.[88] Traherne's audience, and those who could possibly benefit by his teaching, were thus very limited in numbers. He speaks of "thousands in the world . . . who enjoy communion with God".[89] But they are a small minority.[90]

By implication Traherne justifies the pursuit of *moderate* wealth.[91] "The end of riches is that we may be beloved".[92] He accepts social rank and hierarchy. If we keep "an exact hand over all our passions and a diligent eye to extravagant actions, . . . we shall be admitted to the society and friendship of great men",[93] as Traherne himself had been. "Actions of love and honour belong in a peculiar manner to a plentiful estate. . . . Soft and tender affections are more in the court than in the shop or barn", or than among "clowns and peasants". "The love of a king is naturally more delightful than the love of a beggar".[94] Traherne accepts the facts of life in his world with the insouciance of Elizabethan poets: "Queens have died young and fair". But he is anxious for this society to be moralized. "The avaricious humour and love of property" and "the communicative humour, whereby we desire to have companions in our enjoyments to tell our joys" are reconciled in God.[95] It all depends on the motive by which we are impelled to action.[96] The optimism and confidence which naturally flowed from his comfortable position in society allowed Traherne after his "beatific vision" to feel "withdrawn from all endeavours of mending outward things. They lay so well, methoughts, they could not be mended: but I must be mended to enjoy them".[97] That is poles apart from Winstanley or Coppe—or indeed from Milton. It has more in common with the Latitudinarians.[98]

So we must not make too much of the insights which Traherne shared with interregnum radicals. They perhaps helped to give his poetry the blissful rapture which is its enduring claim to our admiration. But much of his theology is traditionally conservative. Traherne thanks God for bishops, cathedrals, tithes and the "liberal maintenance of our Saviour's clergy."[99] Interregnum radicals had denounced parsons who would accept almost any change so long as it did not affect their tithes. There is "little sense of the church in Traherne", but in *Christian Ethicks* he attacks schismatics and heretics who rail against magistrates and revile bishops.[100] He disliked "holy but ignorant zeal" which "would abolish order and beauty in the world for fear of superstitition".[101] *Christian Ethicks* is indeed very much a public performance. It operates entirely at the level of undefined abstractions—virtue, knowledge, truth, wisdom, goodness, justice, etc., etc.

Reference is often made to Traherne's "neo-Platonism", and rightly: he had read Plato, Plotinus, Pico della Mirandola and Ficino.[102] But—like Quarles, Benlowes, Vaughan and Milton—Traherne had also carefully studied Hermes Trismegistus, many of whose works were published in English translation during the liberty of the revolutionary decades and were widely drawn upon by the radicals.[103] Traherne's reference to "the secrets of nature" and his vision of infinity in a grain of sand[104] suggest the magical Hermeticist tradition. Winstanley spoke of the Creation as "the clothing of God", and said that man needs no other teachers than "the objects of creation", the natural world[105] He had anticipated Traherne in his approach to pantheism. Reason "will bring you into community with the whole globe", with God.[106] "How do we know", Traherne asked, "but the world is that body which the deity hath assumed to manifest his beauty?" God is "wholly everywhere". "This visible world is the body of God".[107] He asserted

> That all the earth is one continued globe,
> And that all men thereon are living treasures,
> That fields and meadows are a glorious robe,
> Adorning it with sweet and heavenly pleasures.[108]

Another respect in which Traherne recalls Winstanley and other radicals is in his repeated insistence that "contemplation without action is not sufficient".[109] "Practice and exercise is the life of all".[110] "To have no principles, or to live beside them, is equally miserable. . . . Philosophers are not those that speak but do great things".[111] " 'Tis death my soul to be indifferent".[112]

> Contentment is a sleepy thing! . . .
> A quiet mind is worse than poverty!
> Unless it from enjoyment spring! . . .
> Life! Life is all![113]

Life is motion.[114] Although, like Milton, Traherne on occasion makes use of scholastic method (especially in *Christian Ethicks*), he also, like Milton and other interregnum radicals, can be very critical of university scholasticism.[115] And he has a taste for dialectical paradox: "an excess of goodness [is] the fountain of all evil".[116] "By infusing the principle of self-love" God "hath made a creature capable of enjoying all worlds".[117] "Want itself is a treasure in heaven".[118]

I have suggested parallels between Traherne's ideas and Milton's. There are more. Insistence on human dignity, on man's freedom to choose good or evil, even to the extent of deliberately flouting God's will, pervades Traherne's thought as it does Milton's, from *Areopagitica* to *Paradise Lost*. Traherne thanks God that "thou didst adventure into our hands a power of displeasing thee".[119] Traherne's poem *Innocence* tries to liberate us from the Calvinist sense of sin, just as does Milton's anger at "the superstition of scarecrow sins".[120] Milton too thought that man should "love himself next to God and seek his own temporal and eternal good"; "a pious self-regard" was a "requisite and high point of Christianity".[121] Traherne's *The Circulation* expresses Milton's Hermeticist concept of a physical circuit of energy in the universe.[122] That heaven and hell are internal states is common to Traherne, Winstanley, Ranters and Milton.[123] Traherne's "Christian Epicureanism", the idea that God intended men to enjoy the material good things of life, including the joys of the senses, is integral to Milton's thinking, culminating in *Paradise Lost*, where Adam and Eve make love before the Fall, "whatever hypocrites austerely talk".[124] In *Christian Ethicks* indeed the picture of Eve in Eden is so close to *Paradise Lost* as to suggest that Traherne might have read the epic, published seven years before his death. Traherne quotes Milton's favourite Lactantius to the effect that the temple of God is built of men bearing the image of God—an idea which some have found in *Paradise Regained*.[125]

In a larger sense Traherne is engaged on Milton's task of justifying God's ways to men, at a time when God's justice and goodness were being called in question. "God is suspected and hated", Traherne tells us in *Christian Ethicks*; "enmity against God and atheism being brought into and entertained in the world. . . . Religion appears like a sour and ungrateful thing to the world, impertinent to bliss and void of reason. . . . If we cannot see some reason in His ways, we are apt to suspect there is no Deity, or if there be, yet He is malevolent and tyrannical". That was the atmosphere of post-revolutionary defeat: Traherne, like Milton, wanted "to reconcile men to God".[126] But "in strict justice we must render hatred to whom hatred is due, and love to whom love". This recalls the duty of hating God's enemies which Milton explains, and which justifies Samson's slaughter of the Philistine aristocracy and clergy in *Samson Agonistes*.[127] This emphasis on the duty of self-love and hatred for God's enemies would not I believe be acceptable to twentieth-century writers on Christian ethics. It tells us much about Traherne's highly individualistic and competitive age, when the bonds of traditional communities were breaking down. Twentieth-century literary critics get into muddles here when they read the words on the page with only their quite different modern assumptions to help them.

There are other similarities between Milton and Traherne. "Avarice and ambition", the sins which in Milton's view had led to the betrayal of the English Revolution by its leaders, frequently occur in conjunction in *Christian Ethicks*. "It is the glory of man that his avarice is insatiable and his ambition infinite". "Avarice and ambition" are not "evil in their root and fountain;" they create the dissatisfaction which leads men to God.[128] Galileo is just about the only modern whom either of them mentions.[129] In *Christian Ethicks* Traherne appears to hint at Milton's unorthodox doctrine that the world was created *ex deo*;[130] but in Century III.16 the universe was "made out of nothing for me".[131] Milton proved the existence of God by arguing that it was "intolerable and incredible that evil should be stronger than good".[132] Traherne "knew there was a deity because I was satisfied": his desires were "so august and insatiable that nothing less than a deity could satisfy them".[133] Milton is concerned with life in society: Traherne is turned in on himself.

Some of what I have written about Traherne may seem carping. I am anxious only to show that some of his ideas can be better appreciated in the light of those of the radicals of the interregnum. Seeing Traherne against this background helps to differentiate him from Vaughan, with whom he is traditionally coupled. Vaughan, like Herbert, had a stronger sense of the church than Traherne. For Vaughan the church was at bay under the persecution of the last times; for Traherne it was once again part of the state. Vaughan retained a powerful sense of original sin from which Traherne had escaped. Vaughan had no conception of the possibility of there being something divine in all men: his elect were few. In consequence Vaughan totally lacked Traherne's belief that we might recapture the innocence of childhood on earth: the occasional glimpses which Vaughan was vouchsafed were of another world. He lacked Traherne's sense of obligation to serve mankind.[134] We can be certain that Vaughan was uninfluenced by radical ideas; he would despise those who held them. Whether they directly influenced Traherne or not we do not know. But his ideas formed after theirs had circulated widely. Traherne was a man with the prejudices of his time—as Milton was. Neither is a lesser poet for not being a modern democrat or a modern liberal Christian. The fact that when we discuss Traherne's poetry we think of Blake,[135] Wordsworth, Theodor Storm,[136] and Rilke[137] as well as of Pascal[138] shows that Traherne transcended his age.

His experimental prose style must also owe something to his predecessors. His concern with the most effective spacing of words on the page reminds us of Abiezer Coppe no less than of Lancelot Andrewes.[139] I would argue indeed that his prose as well as his thought needs to be seen against the background of the vast experimentation which was going on in the first two decades of his life. Traherne was, as Miss Wade stresses, anxious to get his message through to the widest possible audience, "to make his learning available for the unlearned" (like Milton again).[140] Traherne describes what he believes to be his plain verse style in *The Author to the Critical Peruser:*

The naked truth, . . .
A simple light, transparent words, a strain
That lowly creeps yet maketh mountains plain,
Brings down the highest mysteries to sense
And keeps them there. . . .
No curling metaphors . . . nor painted eloquence. . . .
An easy style drawn from a native vein.[141]

Traherne's imagery has the vivid here-and-nowness of Winstanley.[142] I think it is more helpful to link him with the popular prose
of Levellers, Diggers, Ranters and early Quakers than with Tillotson,
Stillingfleet, South, Barrow and Cowley.[143]

Traherne died before he had published his major works, perhaps
before he felt free to publish them. We cannot know how he would
have revised them, or what he would have omitted altogether. His
intricate stanza forms, never repeated from one poem to another,
suggest a great deal of conscious artistry. He did prepare *Christian
Ethicks* for the press, and its long lists of subordinate clauses in
apposition to one another do not represent him at his best. But that
was a work designed to popularize an emasculated version of his
thinking so as not to shock—or so I suspect. What he failed to
publish reveals him not only as the last of the metaphysicals but also
as a thinker who inherited much from interregnum ideas.

Note
Traherne's *The Author to the Critical Peruser* seems to me to contain
echoes of Marvell's *Coy Mistress* which have not I believe been
noticed.

On shining banks we could nigh Tagus walk;
In flowery meads of rich Pactolus talk;
Bring in the Druids, and the Sybils view;
See what the rites are which the Indians do. . . .
          [The soul] can understand
The length of ages and the tracts of land
That from the zodiac do extended lie
Unto the poles, and view eternity.[144]

NOTES

1. Printed in *Feuillets*, No. 8 (Fribourg, Switzerland).
2. See pp. 22-4 above.

3. Traherne, *Poems, Centuries and Three Thanksgivings* (ed. A. Ridler, Oxford U.P., 1966), p. 110.
4. *Ibid.*, p. 43.
5. *Ibid.*, pp. 103–4.
6. P. Sterry, *The Appearance of God to Man in the Gospel* (1710), quoted in V. de Sola Pinto, *Peter Sterry: Platonist and Puritan, 1613–1672* (Cambridge U.P., 1934), p. 170.
7. *Poems*, pp. 131–2.
8. *Ibid.*, p. 291.
9. But see *ibid.*, p. 98; cf. pp. 212–13 above.
10. *Ibid.*, pp. 35–6; cf. p. 9.
11. *Ibid.*, pp. 49–52.
12. Gladys Wade, *Thomas Traherne* (Princeton U.P., 1944), pp. 140–1, 246.
13. Traherne wrote epitaphs for one of his sponsors, and for his daughter (*Poems*, pp. 161–2).
14. Wade, *op. cit.*, p. 65.
15. *Ibid.*, p. 116.
16. *Ibid.*, p. 102.
17. *C.S.P.D., 1670*, p. 45.
18. See pp. 190, 195, 199, 218–19 above.
19. Quoted by John Adair, *By the Sword Divided: Eyewitnesses of the English Civil War* (1983), pp. 37–8; cf. Caroline Hibbard, *Charles I and the Popish Plot* (North Carolina U.P., 1983), pp. 168–247.
20. Traherne, *Roman Forgeries: Or a True Account of False Records* (1673), Sig. B 6. Thomas Comber's *Roman Forgeries in the Councils during the first four centuries* was also published in 1673. Crashawe's title was *Romish Forgeries and Falsifications* (1606).
21. *Ibid.*, p. 297.
22. Burnet, *History of My Own Time*, II, pp. 8, 17.
23. See pp. 284–5 below.
24. Ed. T.T. Lewis, *Letters of the Lady Brilliana Harley* (Camden Soc., 1854), p. 249. On Traherne's place in the protestant tradition see Lewalski, *op. cit.*, pp. 35, 37–9.
25. See e.g. *Poems*, pp. 29, 218, 274, 282, 284.
26. Wade, *op. cit.*, pp. 43–6.
27. See *W.T.U.D.*, esp. pp. 171–3; *M.E.R.*, pp. 351–3.
28. Wade, *op. cit.*, p. 57; *Poems*, p. 287; Aubrey, *Miscellanies upon various subjects* (1890), p. 90. Aubrey claimed to have got this information at first hand from Traherne—"a learned and sober person".
29. Wade, *op. cit.*, Chapter 6.
30. Matthew, XXIV, 37, For 1656 see pp. 158, 213 above.
31. *Poems*, pp. 409–10. On p. 413 Traherne prays for the restoration of the Jews.
32. Ed. M. Bottrall, *The Way to Blessedness: Thomas Traherne's Christian Ethicks* (1962), p. 179. An editorial note here identifying the Ranters would have been helpful.
33. P. Grant, *The Transformation of Sin: Studies in Donne, Herbert, Vaughan and Traherne*, p. 186. Professor Grant suggests that both got

the doctrine from Irenaeus, "though Traherne provides little acknowledgement of his sources". He could have found the doctrine in many sources of the sixteen-forties, without going back to Irenaeus.

34. *Poems*, pp. 6, 29, 35, 39, 49, 71, 96, 191, 206, 211-13, 295, 313-14, 317, 328-9, 348, 382; *Christian Ethicks*, pp. 62, 71; *A Serious and Pathetical Contemplation Of the Mercies of God* (1699), pp. 59, 119.

35. *Poems*, p. 35; cf. pp. 210, 326, 348-50.

36. *Christian Ethicks*, p. 246.

37. *A Serious and Pathetical Contemplation*, p. 22; cf. pp. 77-8; *Poems*, p. 115, and *Meditations on the 6 Days of the Creation* (1717) (ed. G.R. Guffery, Augustan Reprint Soc., No. 119, Los Angeles, 1966), p. 75.

38. *Poems*, p. 329.

39. *Ibid.*, pp. 260, 275: *A Serious and Pathetical Contemplation*, pp. 115, 123. Further elaboration of these doctrines will be found in *W.T.U.D.* and *M.E.R.*

40. Grant, *op. cit.*, p. 179.

41. *Poems*, pp. 7-8, 10, 32-4.

42. *Ibid.*, p. 167.

43. *Ibid.*, pp. 263, 266-7, 320.

44. *Ibid.*, pp. 64, 73, 82-3, 87, 98-9, 110-11, 326, 331, 340; *Christian Ethicks*, p. 158.

45. I. Penington, *Light or Darkness* (1650), p. 3; cf. *Divine Essays* (1654), p. 126. See *The Experience of Defeat*, pp. 119-20. Traherne shared Penington's dislike of the smug cruelty which underlay conventional belief in hell; cf. his *Meditations on the Six Days of the Creation*, p. 5, with Penington's *A Letter impleading a Conversion*, bound with *Light or Darkness*.

46. Everard, *The Gospel-Treasury Opened* (2nd. edn., 1659), II, p. 340.

47. Pordage, *Innocencie Appearing, Through the dark Mists of Pretended Guilt* (1655), p. 73. For Pordage see my *The Experience of Defeat*, Chapter 8 section 1.

48. Fox, *Journal* (8th edn., 1902), I, p. 28.

49. Pinto, *op. cit.*, pp. 115-16.

50. *Ibid.*, 80; cf. pp. 97, 149-50, 182, 195.

51. *Ibid.*, pp. 26, 108-9.

52. *Ibid.*, pp. 73, 82-3, 92-101, 110-11, 127, 192; cf. John Davies of Hereford (Traherne's county), "A Thanksgiving for our Being", in *The Muses Sacrifice* (1612), "Divine Meditations", pp. 25-6, in *Poems* (ed. A.B. Grosart, 1876), II.

53. Cf. Marcus, *op. cit.*, pp. 199, 246.

54. *A Serious and Pathetical Contemplation*, p. 128; cf. my *The Religion of Gerrard Winstanley (P. and P.* Supplement, No. 5, 1978), p. 3 and references there cited.

55. *Poems*, p. 180.

56. *Ibid.*, pp. 8, 78; cf. p. 264: "churlish proprieties. . . . All proprieties and divisions were mine".

57. *Ibid.*, pp. 267-71; cf. pp. 9-13, 24, 284, 363.

58. Cf. Earle, quoted on p. 213 above.

59. *Poems*, p. 77. This almost echoes Winstanley on the Ranters: see Sabine, *op. cit.*, p. 399; G.E. Aylmer, " 'Englands Spirit Unfoulded . . .'. A newly discovered pamphlet by Gerrard Winstanley", *P. and P.*, 40 (1968), p. 15.

60. *Poems*, pp. 25, 291. Traherne had not got quite so far as to distinguish between use value and exchange value.

61. *Christian Ethicks*, p. 43.

62. *Poems*, p. 264.

63. Miss Wade shrewdly observed that "the time was coming fast when no English prose-writer would . . . use such 'enthusiastic' expressions" as Traherne did (*op. cit.*, p. 200). Perhaps it had already come.

64. Coppe, *Some Sweet Sips, of some Spirituall Wine* (1649), in Smith, *Ranter Writings*, p. 68.

65. *Poems*, pp. 39, 115; cf. pp. 171–2, 177, 180, 215–16, 242–3, 249, 260, 327–8. "Everything is mine", Luther had said in his *Table-Talk*. Traherne may have known of the English translation by H. Ball published in 1650. Laud would not permit a translation of this work to be published.

66. *Christian Ethicks*, p. 82; cf. p. 217. This is more neatly balanced socially than usual with Traherne: perhaps because he had publication in mind.

67. *The World Turned Upside Down*, p. 414. Cf. p. 234 above.

68. *Poems*, pp. 67–8.

69. *Poems*, p. 275.

70. *Ibid.*, pp. 323–6.

71. *Ibid.*, 328–9. The point is made less "enthusiastically" in *Christian Ethicks*: "How useful and comfortable men were ordained to be to one another" (p. 69).

72. *Poems*, p. 75.

73. *Ibid.*, p. 105.

74. *Ibid.*, p. 244.

75. *The Religion of Gerrard Winstanley*, pp. 28–46.

76. *Christian Ethicks*, p. 95.

77. *Ibid.*, p. 174 and *passim.*

78. *Poems*, pp. 329–30. Even here Traherne's impulse was self-regarding: "he that is a blessing to mankind must be blessed that he may be so" (p. 330). Cf. *ibid.*, p. 243; "when you love men the world quickly becometh yours".

79. *The Law of Freedom and other Writings*, p. 296.

80. *Christian Ethicks*, Chapter XIX, *passim*, pp. 186, 282. "Though there be self-love", wrote Winstanley in *Fire in the Bush*, "yet there is no hatred towards others in it, but a quiet content to let others live too" (*The Law of Freedom and other Writings*, p. 251).

81. *Christian Ethicks*, p. 283.

82. *Poems*, pp. 263, 281–2.

83. *Ibid.*, pp. 217, 287; Wade, *op. cit.*, p. 29.

84. Wade, *op. cit.*, p. 30. This was not merely a wet-nurse: she had conversations with him.

85. *Ibid.*, p. 39.

86. *Poems*, p. 217; cf. pp. 287, 339–41.
87. *Christian Ethicks*, pp. 175–6; *Poems*, p. 327. Cf. Harrington's "people" who are distinguished from servants; Locke's "people" have servants in the state of nature.
88. *Poems*, p. 384; cf. *W.T.U.D.*, Chapter 12.
89. *Poems*, pp. 279–80; cf. pp. 416–17.
90. *Ibid.*, p. 326.
91. *Poems*, pp. 321, 327, 331, 333, 369; *Christian Ethicks*, pp. 25, 38, 237,
92. *Poems*, p. 241.
93. *Christian Ethicks*, pp. 189–90; *Poems*, pp. 360–4.
94. *Poems*, p. 253; cf. *Christian Ethicks*, pp. 25, 38, 237, 241, and Wade, *op. cit.*, p. 95.
95. *Poems*, pp. 249–50.
96. Cf. *ibid.*, pp. 9, 234; *Christian Ethicks*, pp. 72–3, 165.
97. *Poems*, p. 295; cf. pp. 263, 325–6.
98. See p. 302 below.
99. *Poems*, p. 415.
100. Grant, *op. cit.*, p. 195; *Christian Ethicks*, p. 305.
101. Meditation: *How the Holy Ghost Descended upon the Apostles at Pentecost*, in Wade, *op. cit.*, p. 241.
102. *Christian Ethicks*, p. 9; Wade, *op. cit.*, pp. 218, 256; cf. *Poems*, pp. 248–9, 252–5.
103. *Christian Ethicks*, p. 251. Traherne used Everard's translation of the Hermetic writings—as did Boyle (Lewalski, *op. cit.*, p. 498). Cf. Carol L. Marks, "Thomas Traherne and Hermes Trismegistus", *Renaissance News*, XIX (1966), p. 118–31, and R.D. Bradford, *The Defence of Truth: Herbert of Cherbury and the seventeenth century* (1979), p. 103. No translation of Hermes had been printed before 1640 (see pp. 45–6 above). For Quarles, Benlowes and Vaughan and Hermeticism see pp. 196, 201, 219–21 above.
104. *Poems*, pp. 284, 142; cf. pp. 10, 224, 267–71, 327, 363.
105. *The Law of Freedom and other Writings*, p. 219; cf. p. 77, and Sabine, *Works of Winstanley*, pp. 224–5.
106. Winstanley, *The Saints Paradice* (1648), Sig. B, E, pp. 54–7; cf. J. Bauthumley, *The Light and Dark Sides of God* (1650), pp. 4, 14 (reprinted in Smith, *A Collection of Ranter Writings*).
107. *Poems*, pp. 221–3; *A Serious and Pathetical Contemplation*, p. 124.
108. *Poems*, p. 35.
109. Wade, *op. cit.*, p. 243.
110. *Poems*, p. 363; cf. pp. 55, 215, 237, 337, 404–5. Cf. Winstanley: "action is the life of all, and if thou dost not act thou dost nothing". *The Law of Freedom and other Writings*, pp. 127–8; Sabine, *op. cit.*, p. 193. Cf pp. 221–2 above.
111. *Poems*, p. 316.
112. *Ibid.*, p. 59; cf. *Christian Ethicks*, pp. 34–6, 45, 75, 77–8, 87.
113. *Poems*, pp. 146–7.
114. *Ibid.*, pp. 224–5, 274–6; cf. *W.T.U.D.*, p. 293.
115. *Poems*, pp. 270, 273.

116. *Ibid.*, p. 334.
117. *Ibid.*, pp. 336–8; cf. pp. 341–3.
118. *Ibid.*, p. 282.
119. *A Serious and Pathetical Contemplation*, p. 36.
120. *Poems*, pp. 10–12; cf. pp. 32–4, 333–42; *Christian Ethicks*, pp. 39–40, 103–5, 164, 201; *M.C.P.W.*, VI, pp. 155–9, 506.
121. *M.C.P.W.*, I, pp. 882–4, 883; cf. *W.T.U.D.*, pp. 333–4, for Coppe's attack on this idea.
122. *Poems*, pp. 45–7; *M.E.R.*, pp. 327–8.
123. *Christian Ethicks*, pp. 110–11, 145; *M.E.R.*, pp. 308–11.
124. *Paradise Lost*, IV. 744; Wade, *op. cit.*, pp. 144, 149, 234.
125. *Christian Ethicks*, pp. 160–1, *Meditations on the Six Days of the Creation*, p. 75; cf. *M.E.R.*, pp. 419–20.
126. *Ibid.*, pp. 19–20, 43; *Poems*, pp. 379–80; cf. Wade, *op. cit.*, pp. 43, 55, and my *The Experience of Defeat*, pp. 307–9.
127. *Christian Ethicks*, p. 108; *M.C.P.W.*, VI, pp. 675, 743; *M.E.R.*, p. 445.
128. *Christian Ethicks*, pp. 65, 190, 235, 283; cf. *M.E.R.*, pp. 193, 195–6. In *The Experience of Defeat* I discuss contemporary use of the phrase at greater length (pp. 281–2).
129. *Poems*, p. 284. Galileo is mentioned three times in *Paradise Lost.*
130. *Christian Ethicks*, p. 156; *M.E.R.*, Chapter 26.
131. In *Poems*, p. 271.
132. *M.C.P.W.*, VI, pp. 131–2.
133. *Poems*, p. 294.
134. See pp. 212–14 above.
135. "Desire satisfied is a tree of life" (*Poems*, p. 183); infinity in a grain of sand (*ibid.*, pp. 142, 177, 244, 273; *Christian Ethicks*, p. 199); cf. *Poems*, pp. 169–70, 263.
136. Deeming that sure beyond the seas,
     Or else in something near at hand
     Which I knew not, since nought did please
     I knew, my bliss did stand (*Poems*, p. 80). Cf. Storm, "Verloren".
137. "This is very strange that God should want" (*Poems*, p. 183; cf. p. 241).
138. With *Poems*, p. 207, cf. "Jésus sera en agonie jusqu'à la fin du monde; il ne faut pas dormir pendant ce temps-là"; with p. 275, cf. "Tout le malheur des hommes vient d'une seule chose, qui est de ne savoir pas demeurer en repos, dans une chambre". (*Pensées*, ed. L. Brunschvigg, Paris, 1904, Nos. 553 and 139).
139. Cf. Wade, *op. cit.*, pp. 147, 152.
140. *Ibid.*, p. 229.
141. *Poems*, p. 3.
142. Cf. especially examples given by Wade, *op. cit.*, pp. 203–4, 210, with Winstanley, *The Law of Freedom and other writings*, pp. 62–6.
143. Cf. Chapter 3 above; contrast Wade, *op. cit.*, pp. 198–200.
144. *Poems*, pp. 3–4. Marvell's poem was not published until 1681.

IV *Two Diarists*

11. *John Evelyn (1620–1706)*[1]

Evelyn's Diary was first published in 1818, Pepys's in 1825. That was unfortunate for Evelyn, who lacks all Pepys's humanity and charm. Yet Evelyn too has somehow become an English institution. In E.S. de Beer's monumental edition of the Diary,[2] Evelyn is treated with the seriousness and devotion normally accorded to a major literary classic. Evelyn's deletions and afterthoughts are recorded with scrupulous editorial exactness. Even the various symbols which he used to conceal the name of Mrs Godolphin have been reproduced as faithfully as is possible in type. The amount of information contained in the notes is quite staggering. To take only one example: how much editorial labour, or specialized editorial knowledge, must lie behind the footnote to a passage where Evelyn records a sermon on 1 Kings 21.20, preached by "Dr.   "! Mr de Beer has identified a sermon on this text, "corresponding closely to Evelyn's report", in the *Select Sermons* of Nicholas Brady, published in 1713, nine years after the entry in Evelyn's Diary (V. 556).

It is monumental: it is technically superb; but does Evelyn really deserve all this? It sounds ungrateful even to ask such a question when reviewing what has clearly been the labour of love of a lifetime; but it can hardly be avoided. Evelyn is not a great literary figure, not a Bunyan, a Milton or a Marvell, to cite authors who have already appeared in the series of Oxford English Texts. Nor is he a Pepys. Evelyn's Diary contains much matter of historical interest, but nearly all of this is already available in Bray's edition of 1819. Indeed, ironically, de Beer's edition increases our respect for Bray. He printed slightly more than half the Diary, but excluded practically nothing of real interest.

Mr de Beer identified virtually every character mentioned, or recorded his inability to identify in the rare cases where he failed. He also whenever possible identified Evelyn's source—for example when he takes a news item from a journal, or copies out information from a guide book. In vol. II, which contains Evelyn's youthful journeyings on the continent, this is really carried to excess. Note after note gives at full length the original passages from travel books which Evelyn translated and copied. Mr de Beer's ingenuity and industry are admirable; but are they not superfluous? Could we not just have been told in general that most of the diarist's topographical notes and rhapsodies are cribbed; what guide books were used for which town; and then have had our attention drawn (as Mr de Beer does draw it) to the occasional point of his own which Evelyn makes? Any scholar studying continental travel will have to refer to the originals; no one else can conceivably be interested in Evelyn's errors of transcription.

Wherein lies the value of Evelyn's Diary for historians? Not in what it tells us of his life, for that was uneventful. Not in Evelyn's political career, for that was undistinguished. Not even in his vivid account of the Fire of London, nor in his set characters—of Charles II, Clarendon, Clifford, Arlington, Danby, Somers—justly famous though these are. Much more valuable is the cumulative effect of the Diary in conveying political atmosphere; it is where Evelyn is least self-conscious that he most helps us to understand the times in which he wrote. He uses, for instance, the phrase "prime minister" in 1677, and reveals casually that in 1684 there was no public library in London (IV. 118, 368).

Evelyn's grandfather was principal gunpowder manufacturer to Queen Elizabeth, and his uncle continued to enjoy a virtual monopoly until 1637. The diarist's father was a landed gentleman whose income Evelyn estimated at £4000 a year. He was "wonderfully prosperous in all his Undertakings, the more remarkable, as without the accession of any lucrative Office, he pass'd his whole time in the Country, & in good husbandry" (I. 2). When sheriff of Sussex and Surrey in 1633, he was attended by 116 liveried servants in green satin doublets, nearly four times the normal retinue (II. 11). Evelyn entered Balliol as a fellow-commoner in 1637, where his main occupations were dancing and music, though "Fellow-commoners in Balliol were no more exempted from [academic] exercise than the meanest scholars there" (II. 16–18). As befitted a gentleman, Evelyn left without taking a degree; but in 1669 the university awarded him an honorary D.C.L.

In the civil war Evelyn was a royalist, appropriately enough for a descendant of monopolists. But his royalism, though we hear much of it in the Diary, was not that of the warriors or the martyrs. He spent a day or two with the royal army at the beginning of the war, but did not follow its retreat to Gloucester. For this would have "left both me and my brothers expos'd to ruine, without any advantage to his Majestie", their estates being in areas controlled by Parliament (II. 79). From November 1643 till February 1652 Evelyn was abroad. He then returned to compound for his estates, "there being now so little appearance of any change for the better, all being intirely in the rebells hands" (III. 58-9). In December 1659 he played a small part in politics, trying to persuade Colonel Morley, then Lieutenant of the Tower, to declare for the King, "to the greate hazard of my life; but the Colonel had been my Scholefellow, & I knew would not betray me". Morley however waited too long to see how the cat would jump: five months later Evelyn had to help him to purchase a pardon for £1000: "ô the sottish omission of this gent!" (III. 237-8, 241, 245).

Mr de Beer's skill has established that nothing in the Diary before about 1684 is necessarily what Evelyn wrote down at the time. This deprives it of the freshness of Pepys's; we never quite know when we are reading the wisdom that comes after the event. It is also difficult to distinguish political disapproval from Evelyn's own reluctance to accept the responsibilities of office. He "industriously avoided" becoming a J.P. (III. 434). The most important post he ever held was that of commissioner for the sick and wounded in the two Dutch wars, though he was also employed to write against the Netherlanders (IV. 41). In February 1690 he thought he might have been made a Commissioner of the Privy Seal "had I thought it seasonable, & would have ingaged my friends" (V. 7). His outlook was probably typical of that of many inadequately rewarded ex-royalists. In retrospect at least he was very critical of Charles II, "govern'd by wicked favorits" (I. 14). The Diary is non-committal about the events of 1688; and Evelyn's attitude towards William III tended to vary with the latter's military success. In July 1693 the diarist was asking God to avert "the deserved consequence" of "our folly & precipitous Change &c.", and such comments continued into 1694 (V. 148, 152, 166, 169, 205, 402-3). But as the government won through Evelyn's acceptance became less grudging. His loyalty was to church, order and property rather than to the person of the King. Old royalists with this outlook could gloomily accept 1688 as the lesser evil, just as Evelyn had formerly been prepared to accept the Commonwealth. What indeed could one do when "all the eminent nobility & persons of quality throut England declare for the Protestant Religion & Laws, & go to meete the Prince"? (IV. 609). In

1705 Evelyn sent "my Grandson with his party of my freeholders to vote for Mr. Hervy of Come", a Jacobite (V. 595).

For men of Evelyn's station the interregnum remained as a horrifying recollection, a time when "people Mechanic" had risen against their betters; when "Levellers & other of that dangerous rabble . . . would have all alike" (V. 263). Even Shaftesbury assured Evelyn, in confidence, that he would support monarchy "to his last breath, as having seene & felt the misery of being under a Mechanic Tyrannie &c." (IV. 328). Evelyn was properly contemptuous of and horrified by the Mendip miners and poor cloth workers who supported Monmouth's rebellion ("no Gent: of account being come into him"). Its defeat was an "absolutely most signal" deliverance (IV. 452, 460). Yet, strongly though Evelyn believed in "the Lawfulnesse, decentness & necessitie of subordinate degrees & ranks of men & servants" as against the Levellers (III. 543), the Diary records many facts which show how times were changing. In 1695 Evelyn's conviction of "the wonderfull prodigality & decay of Families" was confirmed by the number of bills passed "for unsettling Estates" (V. 209). On many earlier occasions he had noted the financial difficulties which brought old families into dependence on new wealth. Sir Josiah Child, "most sordidly avaricious", made enough from East India trade to marry his daughter to the eldest son of a Duke "with £30,000 portion at present, & various expectations" (IV. 306). Sir Stephen Fox, after enjoying the office of Paymaster to the Forces, was able to redeem "my Lord Cornwallis's intangl'd estate . . . by marrying his Eldest Daughter with a vast Portion". When, in 1681, Lord Sunderland was "much sunke in his Estate, by Gaming & other prodigalities", Evelyn tried to persuade Sir Stephen that "it would be his glory to set up the Earle of Sunderlands family againe" by marrying his younger daughter to Sunderland's son, despite the latter's "early inclinations to vice". But Sir Stephen, "who I am sure might have had his choice in any of the best families in England", was too wily to be caught (IV. 245-7).

Money already mattered more than rank. The Duke of Norfolk told Evelyn "he would part with & sell any thing for mony", excepting his wife. The diarist noted that the Duchess was within earshot when this was said, and added with a rare glimmer of humour that he would have sold her first if the choice had been his (IV. 312). Evelyn's views on the peerage in general may be deduced from his aside in 1680 that the Earl of Essex was "not illiterate beyond the rate of most noble-men in this age" (IV. 201). To his own elder daughter Evelyn "freely gave her her own Choice" in matrimony: but this seems to have been limited to "foure Gent: of Quality" and influenced by his confidence in her discretion (IV. 425). The less discreet younger daughter found no such tolerance when she eloped with "a young fellow . . . in no condition sortable to hers". She was cut out of her father's will (IV. 460–2).

Even in spheres where Evelyn had first-hand experience the Diary is often disappointing. He might have told us much about the Royal Society and its members, but in fact we get very little. Evelyn refused to be President of the Society, hinting in 1690 that his reasons were political. But he had already rejected the office in 1682 (IV. 296; V. 39)—probably from the same ineffective diffidence as prevented him having a successful political career. The impression one gets is that Evelyn—like Pepys—was at best an amateur dabbler in science and philosophy. He believed that a fast might change the weather, and that comets "may be warnings from God" (III. 312; IV. 235; cf. V. 2, 133). When he met Hobbes in 1651, all Evelyn has to record—at great length—is that from the philosopher's window they had a view of "the whole equipage & glorious Cavalcade" of Louis XIV celebrating his majority. The only other reference to a meeting with Hobbes is even less informative (III. 41–3, 163).

Evelyn was much more interested in religion than science. In 1682 he listened to "an incomparable discourse", showing that "the end of the world could not now be long" (IV. 271). A year later his curate was reproving people who paid more attention to "calculating times when the world was to end" than to keeping their own accounts (IV. 308). The sixteen-nineties had attracted the attention of Biblical chronologers as a possible date for the end of the world. On 18 June 1690 Bishop Lloyd of St Asaph explained to Evelyn, Boyle and Lady Ranelagh how Brightman, Mede and other experts had gone wrong in plumping for the sixteen-fifties (V. 26). But there was no revival of the political millenarianism which had been so powerful in the fifties: this was a quiet scholarly discussion among virtuosi. Sir Isaac Newton was pursuing researches into the same subject at the same time.

The main respect in which de Beer's edition of Evelyn's Diary differs from that of Bray is in its inclusion of Evelyn's notes of sermons. From the early sixties these notes get progressively longer. We thus have a sort of index of the type of sermon that was preached to wealthy congregations. It is of course highly selective, and we should not read too much into what Evelyn happened to record of the sermons he happened to hear. But some trends are perhaps worthy of comment.

First, Evelyn confirms the accepted picture of the evolution of sermon styles from "Bishops Andrews's method, full of *Logical* divisions, in short & broken periods, & latine sentences, now quite out of fashion" to "the plaine & practical" preaching, which had originally been the hallmark of Puritans. The only surprising thing is the lateness of the comment (July 1683; but compare the entry for March 9, 1673—IV. 330, 5). V. 9. Secondly, we note the extent to which the pulpit was still used as a vehicle for political propaganda. This was especially true, naturally, of the special services on 5 November, 30 January and 29 May. In 1684 the last-named date was used by a preacher at the Temple for "a Theologico-political sermon, in order to obedience & Union, . . . perstringing our present dissenters" (IV. 381). In 1692 Bishop Tenison thought that "the monstrous wicckednesse of mens lives in this nation ever since" 30 January, 1649, was the result of Charles I's execution which "did still lie heavy on this Nation" (V. 87). But here we can detect a change. In 1680 Evelyn first complained that the congregation at Deptford on the anniversary of the restoration was so thin that the vicar did not preach: "so soone do we slight & forget Gods benefits" (IV. 204). By 1692 "no manner of notice" was taken of this anniversary (V. 102). In 1702 the special service for 5 November similarly failed to produce a congregation at Deptford, and was postponed till the following Sunday (V. 520).[3] In 1689 the services for King Charles the Martyr "were curtailed & mutilitated" (IV. 620); by 1700 William Stephens went so far in preaching before the House of Commons on this anniversary as to argue that "the observation of that day was never intended out of any detestation of his Murder, but to be a document to other Kings & Rulers, how they ought to behave themselves towards their Subjects, lest they came to the like End" (V. 378).

Many sermons gave "the reasons of the preference of *Monarchical* above all other formes of Government", most of them based on Filmer's patriarchal theory (IV. 135, 336; V. 165–6). In 1665 the Master of Emmanuel preached against Levellers and for social subordination (III. 543). Social themes seem to have greatly pre-occupied preachers. "That it was lawfull to be rich", "that Sanctified Riches were marks of favour from God", and that "Piety

& religion contributed to thriving & happiness even in this world"
were familiar themes, laboured alike by an Anglican in exile in 1650,
by Evelyn's vicar at Deptford twenty-two years later, by a London
schoolmaster in 1688 and by a future bishop in 1690 (III. 11, 600–1;
IV. 585; V. 18, 73, 479; cf. IV. 73). The vicar of St Martin in the Fields
in 1701 told the very poor that it became them "to be humble, not to
murmur, to labour & worke": the rich he reminded of their
charitable duty "of reproving dissolute persons, & the punishment of
incorrigible lazy beggers &c," (V. 444, 451).[4] It is hardly surprising,
in a society of this sort, that a particularly despicable assassin declared
on the scaffold that he "hoped & believed God would deal with him
like a Gentleman" (IV. 274). Certainly gentlemen were more likely to
get a reprieve from the King in such cases (IV. 401).

But ministers had to tread warily. At Wotton Dr Bohun upset
Evelyn by a sermon "Concerning the pride & Luxury of Apparell,
which could be applyed to none save my Wife & Daughter, there
being none in all the Parish else, but meane people, who had no more
than sufficient to cloth them meanly enough". Evelyn took this ill,
and hard words passed between him and the rector (V. 542).

Particularly noticeable in Evelyn's notes of sermons after about
1690 is an emphasis on atheism, in both sexes, and especially among
the young (V. 160, 328, 331, 408). Since "atheism" apparently
included not only doubting the immortality of the soul (V. 114) but
also believing that one might be saved merely by leading a moral life
(V. 415), we need not take this too seriously; it presumably relates to
the greater freedom of expression and of the press which were
possible after 1689. But it is the background to the societies for the
reformation of manners which date from this period (V. 366, 391).
Whether the enthusiasm with which ministers put the fear of hell
into their congregations was a new development of the sixteen-
nineties, or merely increasingly recorded by Evelyn, cannot be said.
But, for example, between 3 July and 10 August, 1692, Evelyn heard
ten sermons "shewing the miserable condition of the damned", "the
greate danger of not taking warning by others Calamities", etc. (V.
107–13). Life cannot have been very cheerful for those who took their
ministers seriously. Let us hope they were not too many. In the
following year, between 30 July and 1 October, there were again nine
sermons on "the perpetual stingings of Gilt, no way to be alaied"; on
"the terrors & terrible effects of the end of irrepentant sinners"; "the
horror & perpetuity of the Torment & slavery under which all

sinners are even in this life"; "a lively description of the day of Judgement"; "a very terrible description of the tremendous Sentence & Misery" (V. 149–54). One is rather relieved that in his later years Evelyn was protected by deafness, and that on innumerable occasions he has to record "drowsinesse suddenly surprised me". This habit, "which I formerly censured in some others" (IV. 280), was one which the curate at Deptford seems to have induced more regularly than his ecclesiastical superiors.

What of Evelyn himself? The charitable Pepys thought well of him, allowing "a little for a little conceitedness". Evelyn read some of his poems to the younger diarist, "though with too much gusto", and part of a play—"very good but not as he conceits them, I think, to be" (5 November 1665). But even in his diary Evelyn does not figure as an entirely admirable character. His snobbery must have been displeasing even in that age of deference. In the depth of his grief at the death of his beloved eldest daughter he was still able to name all the "noble persons who honor'd her Obsequies" by sending coaches (IV. 430). He prayed God to forgive his sister-in-law when she cut off an entail to the profit of her second husband and to the disadvantage of her first husband's family (V. 86). When the lady died who had "had a most tender care of me during my childhood", Evelyn smugly congratulated himself on his feeling of sorrow, even though by her death "I was eased of a rent charge of £60 per ann." (III. 25).

More difficult to assess is the diarist's spasmodic humanity. He would without compunction turn an inn-keeper's daughter out of her bed in the middle of the night when he wanted it (II. 519), but so no doubt would nearly all seventeenth-century gentlemen (Evelyn caught smallpox in consequence). Mrs Godolphin, he tells us ecstatically, went out to minister to the poor "in the midst of winter, when it was hardly fit to send a servant out".[5] But was the pity which Evelyn expressed for the galley slaves at Marseilles in 1644 genuine, or an academic exercise? (II. 165). He went to see public torture at Paris in 1651, "but the spectacle was so uncomfortable, that I was not able to stay the sight of another" (III. 29). (Here at least the comment sounds unfeigned.) He was reluctant to give evidence against a highwayman who had robbed him, because it might lead to his execution (III. 73). He objected strongly to public baiting of horses for profit (III. 492). Snob though he was, he dined (in the safe company of the Earl of Ossory, it is true) at the marriage of two of their servants (IV. 194). He undoubtedly showed great courage during the Plague, though it was moderated by a sensible refusal to go to church when the disease was at its height (III. 413, 447–8, 462). He appears to have had little sense of humour: yet one hesitates in assessing the following passage: "Dr. Jessup . . . preached . . . the shortest discourse I ever heard: but what was defective in the amplitude ᴏf his sermon, we found supplied in the largenesse, & convenience of the Parsonage house, which the Doctor (who had in spiritual advancements, at least £600 per Annum) had new-built, fit for any person of quality to live in" (IV. 593).

On the evidence of the Diary alone we might just give Evelyn the benefit of the doubt on such marginal issues: we might continue to think of him as an agreeably sententious snob with a soft heart. But the Diary is not a naïve self-revelation, a record of spiritual struggles and defeats, like the journals of Puritan ministers or of Pepys. It is a carefully compiled semi-public document, in which we see Evelyn as he wished posterity to see him, warts removed. Unfortunately for Evelyn, Mr Hiscock has now revealed something of what the Diarist really was.[6] By a most skilful reconstruction from the correspondence, the Diary and Evelyn's *Life of Mrs. Godolphin*, Mr Hiscock has shown us the horrifying story which lies behind the moral platitudes of Evelyn's apotheosis of Mrs Godolphin. A married man in his fifties, Evelyn established himself as a sort of spiritual mentor to the young and beautiful Margaret Blagge, and exploited this situation ruthlessly in an attempt to prevent her marrying the man she loved. After reading Mr Hiscock's careful analysis one can never feel real respect or affection for Evelyn again. It is a pity that Mr de Beer's edition of the Diary, whose solemnity would have delighted Evelyn, comes at a moment when Evelyn's private reputation has been so finally blasted: it is bad luck for Mr de Beer, who abets Evelyn even to the extent of suppressing some "indelicate" lines in a poem which he published in 1652 (I. 66, II. 355). Perhaps Pepys appreciated them.

NOTES

1. Published in *History*, XLII (1957).
2. *The Diary of John Evelyn* (ed. E.S. de Beer, Oxford U.P., 1955, 6 vols.). My references in this chapter are to this edition.
3. Pepys was observing a similar neglect as early as the sixteen-sixties: see p. 263 below.

4. Cf. Pepys, p. 267 below.
5. Evelyn, *The Life of Margaret Godolphin* (1907), pp. 146-7. (First published 1847, but written soon after Mrs Godolphin's death in 1678).
6. W.G. Hiscock, *John Evelyn and his Family Circle* (1956).

12. *Samuel Pepys (1633–1703)*[1]

It is an interesting coincidence that two of the most famous of English diarists, Samuel Pepys and Robinson Crusoe, were born into families of the middling sort in the same year—Pepys on 23 February 1632-3, Crusoe "in the year 1632". There is a further similarity: those of us who were brought up on an abridged children's edition of *Robinson Crusoe* know nothing of the hero's life before his shipwreck. In fact Defoe sketches Crusoe's background in some detail, and in the course of the novel frequently refers to his early life.[2] Readers who know Pepys only through the Diary find him ready-made at the age of twenty-seven.

We know him—or we think we know him—better than almost any historical character of comparable importance. Thanks to the Diary we are more intimate with him than with our colleagues, neighbours and friends. But we tend to allow the endearing young man of the sixteen-sixties to obscure not only the earlier Pepys but also the man who was one of England's greatest civil servants, "the saviour of the navy" and President of the Royal Society. Normally historians can see only the public faces of civil servants—the official despatches, the minutes, the public portrait; they are fortunate if an occasional private letter survives. The great self-revealers of the past—Montaigne, Rousseau, Casanova, De Quincey—show us a carefully prepared persona. None expose themselves so nakedly as the young Pepys does.

He is not concerned to create an image of himself. He is not writing for a public but for himself;[3] and he knows what he is like. So there are no explanations, no justifications, only a dialogue between different aspects of his own personality. The Diary does not put before us a single rounded personality, but a broken bundle of mirrors. It is genuine because it is utterly inconsistent. Each of us can select his own Pepys. His Diary, like Crusoe's, reveals the course of his adaptation to the new world in which he finds himself thrown up. Crusoe succeeded on his island not only because of his resourcefulness and determination, but also because of the stores and tools which he salvaged from the wreck, and the heritage of ideas and experiences which he brought from his previous life; without these he could not have survived as successfully as he did. Let us start with Pepys before the Diary.

On 30 January 1649 Samuel Pepys, then within a few weeks of his seventeenth birthday, was present at the execution of Charles I (13.10.60).[4] We do not know whether he had played truant from St Paul's school, or whether the boys had been given a holiday. Pepys clearly did not regard it as a tragic occasion, nor the King as a martyr. He said: "Were I to preach upon him, my text should be 'The memory of the wicked shall rot' ". He remembered this with some alarm in October 1660, when he met an old schoolfellow who reminded him that "I was a great Roundhead when I was a boy". Fortunately he discovered that Mr Christmas had left St Paul's before Charles I's trial. The fact that Pepys bothered to find this out illustrates his concern (1.11.60)—understandable in the circumstances.

So when in May 1660 a naval Council of War adopted a loyal address to Charles II, just about to return to England, Pepys eagerly signed it, "that if it should come in print my name may be at it". No man at the Council of War, he observed, "seemed to say No to it, though I am confident many in their hearts were against it" (3.5.60). Nearly everyone who had been in the public service in the sixteen-fifties had a great deal to live down: political prudence was the order of the day. Fortunately for Pepys, the address was printed, "and my name at the bottom of it" (8.5.60).

For Pepys had been a servant of the republic: it was not just his schoolboyish remark on the day of the King's execution, nor his youthful "Roundhead" ideas that he needed to worry about. He came from a family of Puritans. His mother was apparently a sectarian, and he had Quaker relations.[5] In 1663 Pepys was embarrassed by Aunt James, "a poor, religious, well-meaning good soul, talking of nothing but God Almighty". She was accompanied by "a parson among the fanatics" who had prayed for Samuel, at his father's request, when the young man was operated on for the stone in 1658—a dramatic event whose anniversary he never failed to record in the Diary: he was less good at remembering his wedding-day. At the request of his brother William, Samuel tipped the minister a crown, but clearly he did not wish to be reminded of that world from which he had escaped (16.1.63). Cousin Roger was a Puritan too, friend of Presbyterians. Another cousin, Thomas, made Samuel ashamed by still crying "Gad!" and talking "of popery coming in, as all the fanatics do" (24.11.62). But on 29 June 1667 Samuel sat talking "an hour or two of the sad state of the times" with this cousin, who thought a permanent settlement was possible only if Presbyterians were brought back into the state church. The cousins "bewailed ourselves and the kingdom very freely to one another", a freedom of speech for which Samuel later blamed himself, though he agreed about the Presbyterians. (Cf. 13.6.67).

The whole family seems to have been socially highly mobile, and Parliamentarian in sympathy. Samuel's father John, first cousin of the great Edward Montagu but a younger son, was a not very prosperous London tailor who retired in 1661. Cousin Richard was made Lord Chief Justice of Ireland and knighted by Cromwell. Uncle Robert, Captain in the militia, had been receiver and commissioner for assessments in Huntingdonshire in the forties and fifties. Pepys was surprised and impressed by the efficiency of his accounting (31.1 and 5.2.64). Great-uncle Talbot and another cousin Thomas (different from the one cited) had been members of various county committees.[6] Many members of the family, as befitted dependants of Edward Montagu, created Earl of Sandwich at the restoration, had received jobs under the Protectorate.

In 1658 Samuel and his wife lived in Montague's house while the latter was at sea commanding the Protector's navy. They occupied a little room where Mrs Pepys used to make coal fires and wash Samuel's dirty clothes. They looked back at this phase of their life with amusement later, but it marked a beginning on the upward climb (29.2.64, 24–5.2.67; cf. 19.2.64). Pepys knew at least by sight "my Lord Falconbridge" and his wife, "my Lady Mary Cromwell", who on 12 June 1663 "looks as well as I have known her". On 22 April 1661 he won a bet on her Christian name. He enjoyed talking to Mrs Hunt, who was related to the Protector's family, and whose nonconformist husband continued to serve in the excise after 1660. Pepys knew Jeremiah White, Oliver's chaplain, pretty well, and gossipped with him about the Protector's family on 13 October 1664.

His acquaintance among leading Parliamentarian figures who survived the restoration included Sir William Batten, Colonel John Birch, Edward Byllynge, William Clarke, George Downing (who had been Pepys's superior in the Exchequer before 1660),[7] James Harrington, Samuel Hartlib, Sir Samuel Morland (his old tutor at

Magdalene College, Cambridge), Martin Noell, Sir William Penn,
Thomas Povey (who was to sponsor Pepys as Fellow of the Royal
Society), William Prynne, and John Wilkins. There was Major
Tolhunt, "one of my old acquaintance in Cromwell's time and
sometime of our club"—a weekly club of government servants in Pall
Mall which Pepys frequented as a young man (9.1.63, 4.10.66).
Among those whom he saw often, apart from Batten and Penn, were
Sir William Warren, Captain Anthony Deane and John Creed (who
married into the Montagu clan), all three Cromwellians, not to say
fanatics; and Simon Beale, "one of Oliver's and now of the King's
guards" (26.9.68). There were Mr and Mrs Noakes, the former of
whom Pepys had known at the Exchequer. Tom Hayter was an
Anabaptist, arrested in 1663 for attending conventicles. Many others
of his friends were dissenters. His bookseller was an Anabaptist. John
Bunyan died in 1688 at the house of John Strudwick, a grocer at the
sign of the Star on Snow Hill. This may be a relation of Thomas
Strudwick, Pepys's cousin by marriage, a confectioner who also lived
on Snow Hill, at the Three Sugar Loaves.

So it is hardly surprising that Sir Joseph Bunce said to Pepys, on 15
December 1665, "this is the time for you . . . that were for Oliver
heretofore; you are full of employment and we poor Cavaliers sit still
and can get nothing". It was "a pretty reproach", Pepys thought;
"but answered nothing to it for fear of making it worse". When he
went to visit John Lambert in gaol in 1683 Pepys still referred to him
as "my Lord Lambert".[8]

On 13 October 1660 Pepys saw the hanging, disembowelling and
quartering of the regicide Thomas Harrison. It reminded him of
Charles I's fate eleven years earlier. It was "a sad sight to see . . . the
limbs of some of our new traitors set upon Aldersgate", he observed,
with possibly a certain emphasis on "new"; until very recently some
of these men had been ruling England. A week later he "found good
satisfaction" in reading accounts of the regicides' trials: one wonders
whether these were government accounts, or the last speeches of the
victims. On 19 April 1662 he watched Barkstead, Okey and Corbet
on the way to execution, remarking that they "all looked very
cheerful". He referred to Downing, who had shanghaied them back
to England from the Netherlands as "a perfidious rogue, though the
act is good".[9] But he found it "very strange" that the regicides all died
"defending what they did to the King to be just." His chief interest
was in the execution of Sir Henry Vane, formerly head of the navy.

Vane's courage "is talked on everywhere as a miracle". Pepys thought that Vane deserved this praise (18 and 30.6.62).

There is plenty of evidence for Pepys's continuing acquaintance with enemies of the court, though naturally he was cautious. In the Diary, whose very existence he concealed, he carefully records what they were saying—in June and July 1662, for instance, on the eve of the ejection of the Presbyterian clergy. In the last week of August he went to hear the farewell sermons of Presbyterian ministers, not without sympathy for them. On 7 February 1660 he had shown pity for Quakers roughly used by soldiers, and on 7 August 1664 he was touched by the sufferings of conventiclers. In conversations with his friends Robert Blackburne, Jack Cole, Tom Hayter, William Swan and his cousin Thomas Pepys he heard many seditious remarks. On 27 June 1662 he reported to Sandwich on conversations with the "fanatic" Swan, and in return was told of Sandwich's talk with Dr Dell—presumably the famous radical critic of the universities, now extruded from his Mastership of Gonville and Caius and from his living at Yelden. On 29 May 1663, when the anniversary of the King's coronation was celebrated as a holy day, Pepys noted that "the ill temper of the City at this time, either to religion in general or to the King", was shown by the fact that "in some churches there was hardly ten people in the whole church, and those poor people". Three years later Pepys contrasted the apathy then with the enthusiasm in 1660[10]. On 24 July 1663 Pepys had a long talk concerning "several matters of state" with Joseph Hill, extruded Fellow of Magdalene College, Cambridge, a man of large acquaintance "especially among Presbyterians and Independents". "I was not unwilling to hear him talk, though he is full of words".

On 22 February 1664 Pepys spent an hour with Timothy Alsopp the King's brewer, "talking and bewailing the posture of things at present". They feared that military rule threatened. On 17 August 1666 Sir Richard Ford reminded Pepys of the deplorable consequences of Charles I's seizure of the bullion in the Tower in 1640: "the thing will never be forgot". Two years later Pepys wrote apropos Ben Jonson's *Bartholomew Fair*, "the business of abusing the Puritans begins to grow stale, and of no use, they being the people that, at last, will be found the wisest" (4.9.68). He took great pleasure in recording favourable remarks about Oliver Cromwell. In 1663 he was reading and praising Rushworth's *Historical Collections*; later he enjoyed Marvell's satires.

Pepys welcomed every opportunity to express or report disapproval of the morals of the post-restoration world in general, and in
particular of young ex-émigré Cavaliers who thought "there were
none fit to be courtiers, but such as had been abroad and knew
fashions" (9.12.61). He was delighted when he heard how
indispensable stay-at-home Parliamentarians were to the efficient
running of government business (4.10.61; 24.6.63, and *passim*), how
inferior gentlemen captains were to tarpaulins in the navy (10.1.66,
16.12.66, 29.1.67, 19.1.68, 1–3.4.68). This attitude expressed itself in
political cynicism (e.g. 1.12.61), and in an initial dislike of Samuel
Butler's *Hudibras*.[11] The tailor's son admired Sir Christopher
Mings's refusal to conceal the fact that he was the son of a shoemaker,
or to reject his old friends as he rose in the world (25.10.65). In a
confidental moment a week later Pepys confessed to the merchant
Thomas Hill "how little merit do prevail in the world, but only
favour; and that, for myself, chance without merit brought me in, and
that diligence only keeps me so".

All this must be set against what most strikes readers of the Diary—
Pepys's acceptance of and adaptation to the post-restoration world and
his determination to prosper in it. We see him advancing from buckles
on his shoes (22.1.60) through a "white suit with silver lace coat"
(2.2.60) to "my new silk coat, the first that ever I wore in my life"
(9.7.60) and a velvet coat (14.8.60). On 12 November it was diaper
napkins, "the first that ever I bought in my life", followed by a sword
(3.2.61), dancing for the first time (27.3), though by May 1663 dancing
had become "a thing very useful for a gentleman". In November 1661 he
paid his first visit to a gaming house. "My first new lace-band" appeared
on 19 October 1662, a velvet cloak and a wig in October 1663, gold
lace on his sleeves in May 1669. The culminating grandeur was his own
coach with two fine black horses, and "a spare bed for friends" (8.8.66).

When the Diary opened Pepys possessed £25. He advanced from
being worth nearly £100 on 3 June 1660 till he stopped bothering to
add up after he reached £6200 in May 1667. He had probably topped
£10,000 before the Diary ends.[12] An important consideration was
always keeping up with the Battens. Pepys did his best to prevent his
wife knowing too much about his financial situation, lest she should
advance too fast. In November 1660 she received Samuel's reluctant
permission to wear the then fashionable black patches on her face,
though she had started wearing them in August. Her progression
from washing Samuel's clothes herself to employing a maid-servant,

a cook, and then a waiting-woman was acceptable because it testified to his rising status. On 11 October 1660 Pepys had noted that drinking healths was "a thing which Mr. Blackburne formerly would not upon any terms have done". Pepys himself had thought "drinking of the King's health upon their knees in the streets" in May 1660 was "a little too much".

All this social climbing is significant. But we must not forget the survivals from the formative years of his life, his respect for Commonwealth men and methods. Pepys was always a moderate man of the centre, with an eye to the main chance. He was certainly no radical. His patron, Edward Montagu, had been Cromwell's instrument for purging radicals from the fleet. Pepys's membership of Harrington's Rota Club is almost certainly to be explained by current intellectual fashion rather than political commitment. One feels that Pepys could have adapted equally well to either régime, either life style. "Though I am much against too much spending", he wrote on 20 May 1662, "yet I do think it best to enjoy some degree of pleasure now that we have wealth, money and opportunity, rather than to leave pleasures to old age or poverty, when we cannot have them so properly". This is part of the dialogue between the two aspects of his personality.

Diaries are a familiar Puritan aid to godliness, a spiritual profit-and-loss account. Thomas Goodwin "kept a constant diary . . . of observations of the case and posture of his mind and heart towards God".[13] So did Johnston of Wariston and Vavasor Powell: the latter permitted Christian friends to read his.[14] Henry Newcome started a diary in 1646, following the example of Samuel Ward, the renowned Puritan Master of Sidney Sussex College. "How strangely I took pains to set down my sins every day and usually still the same. . . . Yet it was some restraint unto me sometimes, through fear of my own tribunal".[15]

Why, one wonders, did Samuel Pepys start keeping a diary on 1 January 1660? He must have recognized that England was passing from one age to another. Pepys was very aware of the social issues at stake, and his comments are often shrewd and illuminating. He understood by 3 April 1660 that control of the militia by gentry and merchants made rule by "the fanatics" impossible; by 1667 he was assuring himself that "religion will not so soon cause another war".

We must note too Pepys's residual Puritanisms, some of them funny, some serious. His good resolutions, reinforced by solemn vows, helped him to keep play-going and drinking under control, and so to concentrate on his work and on his finances. He paid money into the poor box when he broke his vows. This led to comical evasions and self-deceptions. "Though my oath against going to plays do not oblige me against this [play-] house, because it was not then in being, yet believing that at the time my meaning was against all public houses, I am resolved to deny myself the liberty of two plays at Court, which are in arrear to me for the months of March and April, which will more than countervail this excess, so that this month of May is the first that I must claim a liberty of going to a Court play according to my oath". When he was taken to a play at someone else's expense, "I look upon it as no breach to my oath" (8.5.63, 8.3.64, 4.8.64; cf. 5.4.64, 30.6.64). Four days later he went to another play with his wife, "she giving me her time of the last month, she having not seen any then, so my vow is not broke at all, it costing me no more money than it would have done upon her, had she gone both her times that were due to her". But only five days after that he got Mr Creed to take them both to a play, "lending him money to do it, which is a fallacy that I have found now once, to avoid my vow with, but never to be more practised, I swear". So far as the evidence of the Diary goes, he kept this oath. But he resorted to drinking brandy "as an evasion, God knows, for my drinking of wine (but it is an evasion which will not serve me now hot weather is coming, that I cannot pretend, as indeed I really have done, that I drank it for cold), but I will leave it off, and it is but seldom, as when I am in women's company, that I must call for wine, for I must be forced to drink to them" (29.4.67).

From the beginning to the end of the Diary, Pepys normally refers to Sunday by its Puritan name, "the Lord's Day"—though there are three "Sundays" in September 1660. But he did not always respect the sanctity of the day. On 22 July 1660 he hired a boat on the Sabbath, noting that it was the first time he had done such a thing. On 21 October he asked God to forgive him for stringing his lute on the Lord's day; by the following 9 February he was composing airs on the Sabbath. It seems to have been Pepys's habit to read prayers to his household on Sunday evenings, though on 29 September 1660 he was so drunk that he dared not read them "for fear of being perceived by my servants in what case I was" (cf. 15.11.65). On 12 January 1664 he made a vow to say prayers twice weekly: on 20 November 1668 he promised his wife to pray each night. In the crisis of September 1666

Pepys's office had to work on Sundays, "which Mr. Hayter had no mind to, it being the Lords day, but, being told the necessity, submitted, poor man".

In words at any rate Pepys was a firm believer in the Puritan work ethic. "It is want of work", he observed in relation to his wife, "that do make her and all other people think of ways of spending their time worse". He had already made a similar comment about "the effect of idleness and having nothing else to employ their great spirits upon" on the King and the Duke of York (cf. 3 and 13.11.62). It was, Pepys said on 20 August 1663, "against my nature to owe anything to anybody".[16] On 21 May 1663 he made a great scene about his wife using the word devil, though five days later he referred innocently to "my devilish jealousy".

Complicated equivocations enabled him to deny accepting bribes —"not looking into it till the money was out, that I might say I saw no money in the paper, if ever I should be questioned about it" (3.4.63). This is indeed the homage that vice pays to virtue—or the post-restoration civil servant to the standards set during the interregnum.

Bishop Wilkins became one of Pepys friends, and the Latitudinarians' adaptation of Puritanism to the needs of a business society no doubt appealed to him.[17] On 23 August 1668 he expressed unusual praise of "an excellent and persuasive, good and moral sermon", on a familiar theme in restoration Anglican pulpits. The preacher "shewed, like a wise man, that righteousness is a surer moral way of being rich than sin and villainy". Pepys thought the Presbyterian and Independent styles were the best for preaching, "contrary to the design of the book" he had been reading on the subject, *Five Sermons in Five Several Styles or Waies of Preaching* (6.9.68).

Pepys was at this period of his life resolutely hostile to popery and papists. As early as 18 February 1661 he was worried about the possible succession of James, Duke of York, "he being a professed friend to the Catholics". On 15 December 1662 he recorded his dislike of the idea of a Catholic Governor being appointed for Tangier, "where all the rest of the officers almost are such already". When on 19 February 1663 Charles II promised that no papists would ever be admitted to any offices or places of trust, Pepys commented: "but, God knows, too many have" (cf. 3 and 15.5.69). He would have been prepared to accept a French maid for his wife, on the sole condition that she was a protestant (23.8.64). He worried about his wife's leanings towards popery (e.g. 19.3.64). Ironically enough, he was himself later to be accused of Catholicism.

Pepys's hostility extended to the bishops and clergy of the Church of England. "I do not like that the clergy should meddle with matters of state", he commented when Bishop Henry King of Chichester (the poet) "preached before the King and made a great flattering sermon" (8.7.60). He was shocked ("if true") to be told that "many of the religious Fellows of Colleges" had been ejected from Cambridge in favour of the drunkards they had originally replaced (21.8.60). "The bishops are so high", he wrote on 20 March 1661, "that very few do love them"—a note that recurs. On 31 August 1661 the clergy are "so high, that all people that I meet with do protest against their practice" (cf. 16.2.68: "hatred" had been the word on 9.11.63). He spoke approvingly of the Calvinist Archbishop Grindal's defence of prophesyings to Queen Elizabeth,[18] and disapprovingly of Laud (4.8.62, 29.11.68). Heylyn's Life of the latter (*Cyprianus Anglicus*) he thought "a shrewd book, but that which I believe will do the bishops in general no great good, it pleads for so much popish" (10.9.65). Pepys had not much use for his own parish minister: "a cunning fellow" who evaded eviction in 1662 by gradual compromises on the issue of wearing a surplice. "I love him as I do the rest of his cloth" (5 and 25.10.62). But ultimately, after keeping him out of his house for five years, Pepys appears to have become reconciled to his existence (15.9.67). Perhaps his failure to acknowledge him had been noticed.

Pepys first heard Montagu's "indifference" and "perfect scepticism" in matters of religion with some surprise, but he soon seems to have found it acceptable (15.7; 7 and 21.10.60; 15.6.63). Mr Ollard notes that during the nine and a half years in which he kept the Diary Pepys never received the sacrament.[19] On 8–9 April 1661 Pepys was "somewhat afeard" of sleeping in a haunted chamber, but he did not let on to Sir William Batten. Next month he was listening to Biblical criticism from Jonas Moore (23.5.61). He was unimpressed by an alleged miracle urged from the pulpit (27.12.61), and on 15 June 1663 was sceptical about the appearance of the devil in Wiltshire. He revealed an interesting combination of wishful credulity with scientific scepticism in his attitude towards a hare's foot as a cure for colic. It seemed to do him good, but he was not sure how (10.1.65). Joseph Glanvill's argument for the existence of witches did not convince him (24.11.66), any more than it convinced Samuel Butler.[20] The whole bent of his inquisitive mind was away from superstition, towards science, for the Moderns against the Ancients. In his thirtieth year Pepys began to learn the multiplication table. Twenty-four years later, as President of the Royal Society, he gave his imprimatur to Isaac Newton's *Principia*. In between he praised "mathematick Admirals" and was the moving spirit in founding (with government money) the mathematical school at Christ's Hospital as a nursery for navigators. Pepys was just the sort of enlightened, curious amateur to whom the Royal Society was designed to appeal: his delight in its meetings and especially in his conversations with Wilkins and Hooke is very attractive (e.g. 1.5.65).

Was Pepys an anti-Trinitarian, like Milton, Locke, Newton, Stubbe and so may more? On 12 October 1668 he bought "William Penn's book against the Trinity", *The Sandy Foundation Shaken*. Pepys had a low opinion of Sir William's son; he found this book so well written that "it is too good for him ever to have written it; and it is a serious sort of book, and not fit for everybody to read" (12.6.69). The last comment is very ambiguous. Pepys owned a copy of *Paradise Lost* as well as of Milton's 1645 *Poems*. [21]

Two questions remain about Pepys. Why did he never achieve the knighthood which in the early days of his marriage he set as a target? Many men far less distinguished, and far less well-placed, obtained the honour. At any time between 1684 and 1688, at least, it ought to have been his for the asking. Another mystery is why he never remarried after his first wife's death. He lived with Mary Skinner for the last thirty years of his life, and she was socially accepted even by so priggish a man as John Evelyn. Yet in the Diary Pepys had criticized others for precisely this sort of liaison. The great-grand-daughter of Lord Chief Justice Coke was at least the social equal of the tailor's son. Relevant perhaps is the fact that Mary's uncle was Cyriack Skinner, Milton's friend and a former president of the radical Rota Club; and that her brother had got into very hot water indeed in 1676 for trying to publish Milton's desperately heretical *De Doctrina Christiana*. But these prudential arguments no longer applied after 1688.[22] It remains a mystery. Does Mary Skinner account for his failure to receive a knighthood?

Pepys's Diary could provide evidence for an analysis of the position of middle-class wives in this society. The unfortunate Mrs Pepys, who married Samuel when she was fifteen, had nothing to do, apart from looking after the house and the servants: she had no role in her husband's affairs. She was less fortunate than Mrs Bland, who was "as good a merchant as her husband" and "talked like a merchant in her husband's business" (3.12.62, 8.9.64), or another of Pepys's acquaintances, Mrs Pley, who supplied sailcloth to the navy and was "as famous a merchant as you have met with in England". She told Pepys that business was her "sole delight in this world".[23] Elizabeth Pepys was typical of many wives who had lost the self-respect due to a junior partner in the family firm without gaining any real independence as her husband rose in the social scale. Even the jealous Samuel gives no evidence that she was unfaithful to him, as he was regularly to her, even with her servants. The clothes and the patches which Samuel grudgingly allowed her were small compensation for her cooped up, showpiece existence. "Dancing and other pleasures" took her mind off "pleasing of me" (21.5.63). It became increasingly difficult for the poor man "to get down her head again" after "giving her too much head heretofore for the year past" (4.8.63). He had the sense to recognise that "want of work" was her trouble (p. 267 above). But how was that to be remedied? Mrs Pley was to tell him "it is charity to be kept full of employment",[24] but Elizabeth could hardly share Samuel's work. He continually tried to find pastimes for her, provided they did not cost too much. But when she brought her painting teacher to dinner, they had a flaming row, and Pepys, getting the worst of the argument, "resoved all into my having my will done, without disputing, be the reason what it will; and so I will have it" (4.5.66). One can see exactly how the exaggerated patriarchal theories of, for instance, the Marquis of Halifax, grew out of this situation; and why some women reacted vigorously when the press became freer in the sixteen-nineties.[25] Mary Skinner was perhaps wise to remain Pepys's mistress. Defoe's Roxana made a philosophy out of the observation that "a wife is looked upon as but an upper servant, a mistress is sovereign".[26] (Halifax however also makes clear the perils of the competitive jungle which was restoration society. Pepys would have been as powerless as Leantio in *Women Beware Women* if some aristocratic wolf had taken a fancy to Elizabeth).

Without his Puritan background Pepys would have got nowhere: it was his diligence that made him, as he recognized. The one thing that the "natural rulers" whom 1660 restored ought to have been able to do was to rule: for centuries it had been their function and their justification. But ruling had got so complex that only the most talented could cope. Even fighting, the traditional job of the aristocracy, had become too professional and—especially at sea—just too hard work. It called for new men, driven by ambition, with a work ethic, self-selected by a career partially open to the talents (like that in Cromwell's New Model Army). The doors were not so wide open that there were no jobs for "the gentlemen that could never be brought to order, but undid all" (8.12.67); but open enough for the tarpaulins to be able to make the navy the fighting force which Britain's aggressive foreign policy demanded, and for Pepys and his like to be there to get and account for the vast sums of money that the navy spent. Pepys's greatest contribution to English history lay in convincing his superiors that naval wars could be won only if the officer class as a whole was professionalized. After 1677 anyone aspiring to hold a lieutenant's commission must have served for three years at sea, one year at least in the lowly rank of midshipman, and must satisfy three senior officers by "solemn examination" of his mastery of the theory and practice of navigation. Naturally these conditions were not always rigorously enforced; but the standards set were such, Mr Ollard observes, as "people may resist but . . . will never dare to rescind". The captains, gentlemen or not, were subordinated to the bourgeois civil servants.[27] The successes of the navy in the next century and a half vindicated Pepys. He was less successful in getting regular pay for seamen, lack of which in 1667 made many desert to the Dutch.

Pepys's Diary was of course unpublishable in his own time. He wrote it in cypher, and even so kept its existence hidden from everybody except Sir William Coventry, another diarist (9.3.69); and regretted having told him. Yet the care with which he preserved it suggests that Pepys had envisaged the possibility of others ultimately reading it. The Diary first appeared in 1825, in the year when Milton's *De Doctrina Christiana*—unpublishable for different reasons—at last saw the light of day. When the world crashed around the republicans at the end of the sixteen-fifties, Pepys was young enough, uncommitted enough, shallow and brash enough to flow with the stream, to adapt himself to a scene which Milton completely rejected. Pepys lived fully and intensely whilst Milton stood apart and put all his life into his last great poems and his *De Doctrina*. Like Milton, Pepys thought he had sacrificed his eyes in the course of duty. But Milton believed he was working for the realization of God's kingdom on earth. For Pepys the whole accent was secular: neither life after death nor the kingdom of heaven on earth interested him much. It was life as it is—corrupt, competitive, cruel, exclusively male-centred; but within these limits it was for him rich, sensuous, rewarding in every sense. Pepys came to terms with reality, with a zest that comes near to being its own justification. He aimed lower, but he achieved his aim—if we can give any precise meaning to "lower" in this context. Elizabeth fared less well: she died in 1669, at the age of twenty-nine.

NOTES

1. I reviewed vol. VIII of the 11-volume edition of Pepys's *Diary* edited by R. Latham and W. Matthews (1970–83) in the *New Statesman*, 27 September 1974; and vols. X and XI in *The New Republic*, 4 July 1983.
2. See p. 105 above.
3. But see p. 271 above.
4. To facilitate reference to the various editions of the Diary I cite by date rather than by volume and page number.
5. Ed. Latham and Matthews, *Diary*, X, *Companion*, p. 319.
6. Where no precise reference is given for a name, see vols X and XI (Index) of Latham and Matthews, *op. cit.*
7. G.E. Aylmer, *The State's Servants: the Civil Service of the English Republic, 1649–1660* (1973), p. 100.
8. Richard Ollard, *Pepys: A Biography* (1974), p. 270.
9. Downing had been Okey's chaplain, and "like Judas betrayed his master", as Andrew Marvell put it (H.G. Tibbutt, *Colonel John Okey, 1606–1662*, Bedfordshire Historical Record Soc. Publications, XXXV, 1955, p. 139).
10. Cf. Evelyn, p. 254 above.
11. See p. 292 below.
12. Ed. Latham and Matthews, *Diary*, X, pp. 131–7.
13. T. Goodwin, *Works* (Edinburgh, 1851–63), II, p. lxviii: memoir by his son.
14. [Anon.], *The Life and Death of Mr. Vavasor Powell* (1661), Sig. A 3v, p. 12.
15. Newcome, *Autobiography* (ed. R. Parkinson, Chetham Soc., 1852), pp. 14–15. Cf. A. Macfarlane, *The Family Life of Ralph Josselin: A Seventeenth-Century Clergyman* (Cambridge U.P., 1970), pp. 4–10.
16. This is confirmed by the entry for 30.6.64, and by his scurry to pay outstanding debts at the end of each month or year.
17. For Latitudinarians see p. 302 below.
18. The reference must be to Grindal, not to Cranmer, which is a slip of Pepys's pen.
19. Ollard, *op. cit.*, p. 111.
20. See p. 282 below.
21. *M.E.R.*, p. 216.

22. Mary Skinner receives no entry in either the *Companion* or the *Index* of the Latham and Matthews edition of the *Diary*.

23. Quoted in Helen A. Kaufman, *Conscientious Cavalier: Col. Bullen Reymes, M.P., F.R.S., 1613–1672: The Man and his Times* (1962), pp. 182–4.

24. *Ibid.*, p. 183.

25. I owe many of these points to discussions with Bridget Hill. See her forthcoming book on Mary Astell.

26. Defoe, *The Fortunate Mistress* (Oxford, 1840), pp. 140, 158–62. First published 1724. Moll Flanders felt differently: "a woman should never be kept for a mistress that had the money to make herself a wife" (*Moll Flanders*, Shakespeare Head edn., I, p. 60. First published 1721).

27. Ollard, *op. cit.*, pp. 216–17, 223, 281, 285.

V Two radical royalists

13. *Samuel Butler (1613–80)*[1]

Hudibras is more quoted than read. Butler had a magnificent gift of phrase, and no power of construction whatsoever. He jotted down lines of verse as they occurred to him, incorporating them later in a new canto of *Hudibras* or some other poem: many of these fragments he never published. The brief prose *Characters* show him at his best, and the passages from his notebooks which have been published contain a series of isolated and thought-provoking epigrams. But there are long tracts of *Hudibras* which are of the greatest tedium, not even of historical interest; and these increase in Part III, published in 1677, long after the sensational success of Parts I and II in 1662–3. One suspects that by this time the link passages had got more and more perfunctory.

For these and many other reasons Butler perplexes the critics. Not all are as severe as Barbara Everett, who speaks of his "reductive and mean-minded work".[2] Mr Farley-Hills, for instance, sees Hudibras as "nearly the one great farcical poem of the language".[3] It is indeed difficult to write Butler off. There is a gusto, an energy in his work at its best that forces us to admire him. And the prose shows him to have been no indifferent thinker.

One difficulty with *Hudibras*, as has been said of *Hamlet*, is that it is so full of quotations. Many have now become household words:

> And made them fight, like mad or drunk
> For Dame Religion as for punk. (I. i. 5–6)[4]

> And pulpit, drum ecclesiastic,
> Was beat with fist, instead of a stick. (I. i. 11–12)

> As if divinity had catched
> The itch, on purpose to be scratched. (I. i. 163–4)

> Prove their doctrine orthodox
> By apostolic blows and knocks. (I. i. 197–8)

'Tis a dark lanthorn of the spirit,
Which none see by but those that bear it. (I. i. 499–500)

And every hamlet's governed
By's holiness, the church's head. (I. iii. 1209–10)

He that complies against his will,
Is of his own opinion still. (III. iii. 547–8)[5]

Such lines are so familiar that it is difficult to imagine the shock of their original impact. The jaunty colloquial style, when ostensibly recording noble exploits, must have seemed intriguingly novel. The splendid set pieces descriptive of crowd action are still effective—the Skimmington ride (II. ii. 592ff.), or the satirical account of popular support for Parliament in the early sixteen-forties:

No sow-gelder did blow his horn
To geld a cat, but cried "Reform!"
The oyster-women locked their fish up
And trudged away, to cry "No bishop!" (I. ii. 537–40)

Or the long passage about women supporters, with its double entendres:

What have they done, or what left undone,
That might advance the Cause at London?
Marched, rank and file, with drum and ensign,
T'entrench the City, for defence in;
Raised rampires, with their own soft hands,
To put the enemy to stands;
From ladies down to oyster-wenches,
Laboured like pioneers in trenches,
Fell to their pick-axes, and tools,
And helped the men to dig like moles? (II. ii. 799–808)

Such lines bustle with life and vigour. And the throw-away bathetic asides still make their point.

For brevity is very good,
When w'are, or are not, understood. (I. i. 663–4)

And dashed his brains (if any) out. (I. ii. 863).

A viler noise than swine
In windy weather when they whine. (II. ii. 624–6)

Conveying straight-faced the logic of the upside-down world is one of Butler's peculiar strengths. Here he is making satirically a point Berkenhead had made in all seriousness:[6]

> As gifted brethren, preaching by
> A carnal hour-glass, do imply
> Illumination can convey
> Into them what they have to say,
> But not how much. . . . (I. iii. 1061–5)

> Why should not conscience have vacation
> As well as other courts o'th' nation? (II. ii. 317–18)

The well-known single lines or couplets can be found in any of the three parts of *Hudibras*. But in every other way Parts II and III are vastly inferior. It would be wrong to speak of the "structure" or "plot" of *Hudibras*, but at least there is some coherence in Part I. The satire on the Parliamentarians is done skilfully enough, by using the Presbyterian gentleman and scholar Hudibras to denounce the doctrines of the Baptist tailor and Hermeticist Ralph. Hudibras has been trained in useless university scholasticism: Ralph is a mechanic preacher, relying on the inner light and decrying university education. The knight is an Aristotelian, who tells the time by algebra; his squire is a neo-Platonist and Behmenist, as so many of the radical sectaries were. Butler's technique not only shows weaknesses in the intellectual positions of Hudibras and Ralph but also exposes the precariousness of their unity, which is restored only when self-interest tells them they must hang together rather than hang separately. On the whole one feels that Ralph gets the better of the exchanges, because Butler profoundly dislikes Presbyterians (drawn from his own social class), whatever contempt he may have for sectaries. At this stage the action of the poem, with its burlesque of heroic poetry, has the effect of making the participants and their causes ridiculous, as well as the conventions of epic, as when "Pallas came in shape of rust" to prevent Hudibras's pistol going off (I. ii. 781–5).

> But as for our part, we shall tell
> The naked truth of what befell . . .
> And never coin a formal lie on't,
> To make the knight o'ercome the giant. (I. ii. 34–42).

Although Butler implied the existence of a Part II when he published "The First Part," there is no real unity; the poem is a set of loosely connected episodes. The pursuit of the lady starts quite a new theme in canto i of Part II. It is the occasion of a prolonged satirical discussion of marriage for money and the relation of the sexes, which bears no organic relation to the events and discussions of Part I, though it does continue the process of debunking heroic poetry, love and honour.[7]

The knight and the squire vie with one another in casuistry about oaths and vows, but the connection with their previous discussions is tenuous. In canto iii the totally new figure of Sidrophel introduces astrology as a subject for satire. This is only remotely connected with what has gone before in that astrologers were thought to have favoured the Parliamentary cause: Ralpho in Part I was interested in astrology.

Part III, published many years later, is also a hodge-podge. Marriage and sexual relations are the main themes of cantos i and ii; and in canto ii long and boring speeches are given to a Presbyterian and an Independent politician, unnamed but clearly not Hudibras and Ralph. There are good moments, and some quotable lines (see p. 281 below); but they relate to the politics of the late seventies rather than to the period of the civil war.

There is the question of genre: critics find *Hudibras* difficult to place. It is an anti-poem as well as a mock epic. Butler guys all the poetic conventions, and the artificiality and pretentiousness of contemporary heroic verse. The imagery, among other things, parodies the metaphysical conceit:

> The sun had long since in the lap
> Of Thetis taken out his nap,
> And like a lobster boiled, the morn
> From black to red began to turn. (II. ii. 29–32)[8]

Not that the rhymed couplet fared any better:

> For one for sense, and one for rhyme,
> I think's sufficient at one time. (II. i. 29–30)

But in his hostility to inspiration—shared with Davenant and Hobbes—Butler seems to equate poetry with fanaticism, one of his principal enemies, as it was one of Hobbes's.[9]

The animus and wit of the first two parts of *Hudibras* were directed against Presbyterians and sectaries impartially, and against the common people—women as well as men—who during the revolutionary decades had been impudent enough to intervene in matters of church and state which should have been left to their betters. By 1677 Butler's political emphasis had shifted. He received no royal pension until 1678, when he was sixty-five years old—too late and even then irregularly paid.[10] The famous lines on the old royalists could be read as a reminder:

> For loyalty is still the same,
> Whether it win or lose the game:
> True as a dial to the sun,
> Although it be not shined upon. (III. ii. 173–6).

The reference to "some under door-keeper's friend's friend" (III. i. 1392) suggest a similar disillusion.[11] So does

> Money, th'only power
> That all mankind falls down before;
> Money, that like the swords of kings,
> Is the last reason of all things. (III. ii. 1327–30)

The Parliamentarians are no longer his only target. Fragments published posthumously see faults on both sides:

> What else does history use to tell us,
> But tales of subjects being rebellious,
> The vain perfidiousness of lords,
> And fatal breach of princes' words?

> What makes all subjects discontent
> Against a prince's government,
> And princes take as great offence
> At subjects' disobedience,
> That neither th'other can abide,
> But too much reason on each side?

> Authority is a disease and cure,
> Which men can neither want nor well endure.[12]

Butler's criticism of secular Vicars of Bray, which anticipates Dryden's Achitophel, seems to extend to all politicians:

> So politic, as if one eye
> Upon the other were a spy; . . .
> H'ad seen three governments run down,
> And had a hand in every one . . .

> Our state-artificer foresaw
> Which way the world began to draw;
> For as old sinners have all points
> O'th compass in their bones and joints, . . .
> So guilty sinners in a state

Can by their crimes prognosticate
And in their consciences feel pain,
Some days before a shower of rain. (III. ii. 355–62, 403–14)

The traditional feudal concept of honour, whether social or military, is the object of sneers:

Honour is like a widow, won
With brisk attempt and putting on;
With entering manfully, and urging;
Not slow approaches, like a virgin. (I. i. 905–8)

But Hudibras gave him a twitch,
As quick as lightning, in the breach,
Just in the place where honour's lodged,
As wise philosophers have judged
Because a kick in that place more
Hurts honour than deep wounds before. (III. ii. 1065–70)

Timely running's no mean part
Of conduct, in the martial art.
By which some glorious feats achieve,
As citizens, by breaking, thrive . . .
That spares the expense of time and pains
And dangerous beating out of brains. (III. iii. 245–54)

We should therefore not think of Butler merely as a disillusioned backward-looking royalist. He was abreast of many modern ideas, and when he criticizes them he does so with first-hand knowledge. His attitude towards science, for instance, is curiously ambivalent throughout his writings. He is notorious for his mockery of the Royal Society, yet he was extremely accurately informed about its goings-on[13] He accepted the superiority of the Moderns to the Ancients ("Charleton excepted") and had a Baconian rational optimism. He approved of the experimental method.[14] Unlike many Fellows of the Royal Society, Butler was sceptical of apparitions, and contemptuous of Glanville's attempt to prove the existence of witchcraft.[15] He was prepared to believe that the stars might be other worlds, but was sarcastic about Wilkins's proposal "for virtuosos to make voyages to the moon".[16] In attacking astrologers' interpretations of men's characters, Butler insisted on the importance of pre-natal influences.[17] He shows in *Hudibras* his awareness of the significance of Harvey's demonstration of the circulation of the blood, and of Hooke's invention of the microscope—before Hooke had published on the subject.[18]

But Butler was as harsh as any interregnum radical against the medical profession. "The reason why great persons have the gout and other diseases in greater extremity than those of a meaner condition is because they are apter to take physic, and try the experiments of medicines upon themselves".[19] Chemistry—by which Butler meant alchemy—"is for the most part but an introduction to coining".[20] He was also hostile to those enemies of the radicals, abstract academic theorists who neglect practice.[21] Sidrophel was both experimental scientist and astrologer. He made a living as a "cunning man", a white witch who pretends to recover lost property and heal diseases. Yet Butler recognizes that he is learned in

> Mathematics,
> Optics, philosophy, and statics. (II. iii. 205–6)[22]

It was Ralpho who defended astrology because of its political usefulness to the Parliamentarians:

> Do not our great reformers use
> This Sidrophel to forebode news?
> To write of victories next year,
> And castles taken yet in th'air?

Had he not

> Made Mars and Saturn for the Cause,
> The moon for fundamental laws?
> The Ram and Bull and Goat declare
> Against the Book of Common Prayer? (II. iii. 171–84)

Butler's scientific approach extends to a rejection of the role of "accidents" in history which might with advantage be studied by those who think the civil war happened by accident. "Accident is but a term invented to relieve ignorance of causes, as physicians use to call the strange operations of plants and minerals occult qualities, not that they are without their causes, but that their causes are unknown. And indeed there is not anything in nature or event that has not a pedigree of causes, which though obscure to us cannot be so to God who is the First Cause of all things".[23]

One of the remarkable things about Butler is the consistent virulence of his anti-clericalism, comparable with that of Winstanley, Milton or Rochester. In *Hudibras* it is directed against the Laudian "etcetera oath" no less than against Presbyterians and Independents (I. ii. 649–50). "Clergymen have no wit and very little or no sense

until they come to encounter with some other party of the same
religion where their interests differ, and then they are implacable".
They always join the strongest side, and "share with those whom
they opposed before in dividing that which they endeavoured with
the utmost of their power to secure to themselves". "But in matters
. . . in which their wits are not engaged by their gains or losses, they
are always to be found very dull and insignificant".[24] The clergy
have discovered "nice and curious subtleties . . . to debauch and
corrupt the native simplicity of the Christian religion". It has "given
occasion to some to suspect that they who can make what use of it
they please, may have made it themselves".[25]

Butler almost echoes Winstanley when he writes "clergymen
expose the kingdom of heaven to sale, that with the money they may
purchase as much as they can of this world".[26] "Religion has always
been a traffic".[27] Experience of the changes of régime between 1640
and 1660 led Butler to denounce the Vicar of Bray, who is "very
zealous to show himself, upon all occasions, a true member of the
church for the time being. . . . For suffering is a very evil effect, and
not likely to proceed from a good cause".[28]

> What makes all doctrines plain and clear?
> About two hundred pounds a year.
> And that which was proved true before
> Prove false again? Two hundred more. (III. i. 279–80)

Butler observed that "when the cheats and impostures that are acted
under the cloak of religion have discovered the hypocrisy and
superstition of one age", the next is apt to run into an "extreme of
impiety and profaneness".[29] "Popery made the Christian religion a
fable, and reformation, by discovering the cheat, will in time bring it
to nothing".[30] If Butler had not had serious intentions of being a
good poet, he tells us, he might have

> Had nothing in the world to do or think
> Like a fat priest, but whore and eat and drink.[31]

The savagery is remarkable, again recalling the most radical
sectarians. "Priests in the church are the same things with guards in
the state"—to keep the rabble from falling foul upon either the
government or religion. The point had already been made by a
defender of the clergy: "if there were not a minister in every parish,
you would quickly find cause to increase the number of constables".[32]

Butler nevertheless was hostile to "fanatics"—"worse than the devil, for he never does any harm to mankind without a commission from God." Butler bracketed "revelations and revolutions".[33] "Nothing can prevail more to persuade a man to be an atheist as to see such unreasonable beasts pretend to religion". Yet he admitted, rather curiously, that "the modern fanatics . . . perhaps come nearest to the outward form of the primitive times"—almost echoing Milton.[34] Perhaps Butler intended this as a covert jibe at all creeds: "for religion, that was first planted among the rabble, can never so perfectly and naturally agree with anything else".[35] Butler was opposed to tolerating "seditious meetings in conventicles"; he believed that all religions "naturally incline to suppress and destroy all others".[36] But he accepted that "he that believes as the church believes is more violent, though he knows not what it is, than he that can give a reason for his faith", and to that extent favoured tolerance.[37]

Butler himself skirts very near some of the heresies of the "fanatics". He denied that the Scriptures were the Word of God, like Clement Writer, the Ranter Jacob Bauthumley and the Quaker Samuel Fisher. Butler used Hobbist arguments against miracles.[38] Faith is not above reason, but "below ignorance which it depends upon". Butler may have had doubts about the after life and the existence of hell.[39] He noted the paradox that papists and Laudians, who asserted free will, supported obedience to authority; whilst "Presbyterians and fanatics", who utterly deny free will, "assume all freedom . . . to oppose their governors at their own will and pleasure".[40]

With Milton, Butler thought popery was not a religion but the fifth column of a foreign prince.[41] He came to fear that English bishops were prepared to re-establish catholicism, as the only guarantee of their lands against "the general ill will and hatred they have contracted from the people, of all sorts, by their imprudent demeanour and unjust dealing since their restoration".[42] So far from converting fanatics to a better opinion of the church, "these are the only people they have confirmed in their former faith".[43] This again reminds us of the thinking of Henry Stubbe, who attacked the Laudian bishops and the Royal Society for intending to restore Catholicism.[44] More specifically it recalls Buckingham, Milton, Traherne, Marvell and others who in the seventies were thumping the protestant drum against popery and absolutism.[45]

It is often said that Butler's ideas derive in large part from Hobbes;

and there is evidence to support this.[46] But he is no uncritical disciple. "The Hobbists will undertake to prevent civil wars by proving that mankind was born to nothing else", to "reduce men to subjection and obedience by maintaining that Nature made them all equal", to "secure the rights of princes by asserting that whosoever can get their power from their hands has right enough to it; and persuade them and their subjects to observe imaginary contracts by affirming that they are invalid as soon as made".[47] Such witty comments show a pretty thorough appreciation of the strengths and weaknesses of Hobbes's position. But Butler also draws on what is often called "French court libertinism", though it might just as well be called "rational protestant heresy".[48] Butler himself goes out of his way to point out analogies between the doctrines of the libertines and the saints, and to show that "the modern false doctrine of the court, that men's nature and parts are rather impaired than improved by study and learning is . . . no more than what the Levellers and Quakers found out before them".[49]

Why did Butler publish relatively little when he left so much in manuscript? Clearly he intended to incorporate some of the contents of his notebooks in poems. But the characters exist in their own right, as do some of the philosophical reflections and criticisms. One reason may have been the very subversive nature of his ideas, which might well have got him into trouble if he had printed them. In this respect he died too soon: none of his prose was published before 1759.[50] This material helps us to understand the philosophy behind *Hudibras*, just as *Of Christian Doctrine* helps understanding of Milton's poems.

With Butler's pragmatic Hobbist approach to politics went cynicism about traditional methods of maintaining loyalty. Oaths, for instance: "as soon as a man has taken an oath against his conscience and done his endeavour to damn himself he is capable of any trust or employment in the government". This is "the most compendious way to exclude all those that have any conscience and to take in such as have none at all".[51] There was a lot of historical experience behind that remark, since each successive régime in the sixteen-forties and fifties had imposed an oath of some sort. But, said Butler, "oaths and obligations in the affairs of the world are like ribbons and knots in dressing, that seem to tie something but do not at all. For nothing but interest does really oblige".[52]

For Butler "there is no difference between a government that is managed by law and one that is maintained by force but that the one oppresses in a gentle and the other in a rugged way".[53] Butler is sarcastic at the expense of lawyers, like almost everybody (except members of the profession) who mentions them in the seventeenth century. He joins the mumbo-jumbo of lawyers and priests in terms reminiscent of Winstanley and the interregnum radicals.[54]

His political experiences had embittered him: royalists in general, and Butler in particular, had not gained what they expected from the restoration. "Rebels have been used in this kingdom like sinners in the kingdom of heaven, where there is more rejoicing over one sinner than forty just men that need no repentance".[55] "The royal party . . . had nothing left but merit . . . to pay for new employments". What was worse, the favoured ex-Parliamentarians "made their preferments pass for dispensations and out-goings of Providence, that had utterly exposed and disowned them before".[56] Like many on the opposite political extreme, Butler experienced a reversal of all his expectations.

Yet he was capable of a realistic assessment of the changes which the Revolution had brought about in England:

> For whatso'er we perpetrate,
> We do but row, w'are steered by Fate,
> Which in success oft disinherits
> For spurious causes, noblest merits. (I. i. 873–6; cf. p. 261)

"It is more than possible", Butler reflected, that another King may be forced to make the sort of concessions Charles I had to make in 1641, "especially when there is a precedent for it"; for, Butler added ominously, what had been fictitious charges against Charles I had become "matter of fact". The execution of Charles would be "a precedent to deal with all future princes that shall attempt to invade the rights of their subjects, or prove so weak as to have such pretences how false soever imposed on them. For to be guilty, or capable of being put upon for such, is all one to those who are not able to defend their own innocence".[57]

The interests of King and Parliament "are really the same", yet factions force the King into alliance with "his most implacable enemies". The Cavalier Parliament "has supplied the K— with money, as usurers do young heirs, to get a hold upon their estates".[58] "The power and interest of our House of Commons cannot but be greatly increased when elections are become so strangely dear and chargeable: for every new member is but a kind of Merchant

Adventurer, that would never lay down so great a stock if he did not expect a suitable return. And this swelling greatness can proceed from no other cause than an equal decrease of power and authority in the King and House of peers". Some of the latter "are no less greedy than the Commons to be sharing the remainder of his decaying interest".[59]

> The people have as much a neg'tive voice
> To hinder making war without their choice
> As kings of making law in Parliament,
> "No money" is as good as "No assent".[60]

> For money b'ing the common scale
> Of things by measure, weight and tale;
> In all th'affairs of church and state,
> 'Tis both the balance and the weight. (*Hudibras*, II. iii. 851–4)

So *via* a modified Harringtonianism Butler the former royalist is transformed into the sort of oppositionist who later formed the country party. A young republic, he observed with surprisingly sympathetic insight, like a young King, "must of necessity be under tutors, protectors and Keepers of Liberties" until they "are able to govern of themselves". "Though a foundation of liberty be laid, the fruition of it is for after ages. . . . For what protection can a nation have from a government that must itself be protected?" The reference to the English Commonwealth and the Army is clear; Harrington described post-revolutionary England as a commonwealth headed by a prince. But Butler was, on pragmatic grounds, against constitution-making.[61]

We can therefore understand why in the sixteen-seventies Butler was a supporter of the Duke of Buckingham, an ex-royalist who had been prepared to come to terms with the Protectorate, and who had no sympathy for high Anglican Toryism. Butler acted as secretary to the Duke in 1673 when the latter was Chancellor of Cambridge University.[62] Wood suggests that Butler helped Buckingham with *The Rehearsal*.[63] But Butler's reference to divines being "hen-pecked by their comfortable importances", though an allusion to *The Rehearsal*, could equally well derive from the hilarious use Marvell made of the phrase in *The Rehearsal Transpros'd*.[64] Butler appears to have had little respect for Charles II, and less for his brother: indeed he predicted that James's aspirations "would utterly deprive him of it [the crown], if he had it".[65] Butler was, on cultural grounds, anti-

French.[66] "The only writer with whom some exchange of ideas can be established", Professor de Quehen says, is the Whig Thomas Shadwell—who probably attended Butler's funeral.[67]

In the sixteen-fifties Abraham Cowley had advocated ideological disarmament for royalists.[68] Robert Boyle attacked traditional aristocratic concepts of honour, as Falstaff had done before him.[69] Butler followed suit. "Since the invention of guns came up, there can be no true hero in great fights, for all men's abilities are . . . levelled by gun-shot".[70] But ideas lag behind facts: Butler describes as "a degenerate noble" the man who thought he could live on inherited honour. "As those that are born to estates neglect industry and have no business but to spend, so he being born to honour believes he is no further concerned than to consume and waste it". He "trusts both to the management of his servants, by whom he is equally cheated in both".[71] This emphasis on improved estate-management is the authentic restoration note.

Here Butler comes at the end of a tradition. C.L. Barber's admirable *The Idea of Honour in the English Drama, 1591–1700*, traced the way in which concepts of honour changed. He suggested that from about 1615 there was a new emphasis, which cannot be explained by theatrical changes alone: it is a response to wider social transformations. Middle-class morality is being repudiated as the gap between court, country and City widens.[72] Falstaff mocks the concept of honour expressed by Hotspur. In *Richard II* Bolingbroke and the Duke of Norfolk indulge in a slanging match on behalf of honour. The main point seems to be that if you appeal to honour you do not have to prove anything: you simply fight it out. Coriolanus puts honour before patriotism: the honour to which Volumnia appeals is a euphemism for class interest, just as Shylock's sneers at honour merely represent his self-interest. In *King John* the Bastard has a critical function as against the honour-mongers. Hamlet mocks those who wish

> Greatly to find a quarrel in a straw
> Where honour's at the stake (IV. v).

And in *Troilus and Cressida* Hector demolishes Paris's argument that honour forbids the handing back of Helen to the Greeks, but then concludes that honour must override reason and prudence. So Troy is destroyed.[73]

With Beaumont and Fletcher the theatrical cult of honour, exalted and exclusive, established itself as the main substance of tragedy and comedy. Massinger takes it over from them. Middleton, on the other hand, as we might expect, is much more astringent:

> I'm forced to love thee now
> 'Cause thou provid'st so carefully for my honour,

Beatrice tells De Flores. He replies, with brutal realism,

> 'Slid, it concerns the safety of us both,
> Our pleasure and continuance. (*The Changeling*, V. i).

So Butler is taking sides against the court and Cavalier concept of an "honour" which is differentiated from "virtue". "Honour" derives from good birth: it is to be preserved, not won. In 1595, in "Ovid's Banquet of Sense", George Chapman had written:

> 'Tis for mere look-alike ladies, and for men
> To boast of birth that still be childeren
> Running to father straight to help their needs . . .
> Virtue makes honour, as the soul doth sense,
> And merit far exceeds inheritance.[74]

Butler laughs when

> Heralds stickle who got who
> So many hundred years ago (III. iii. 480–1)

"Virtue" is possible to those of lowly origin; "honour" might make demands which conflicted with Christianity, as in duelling or in sexual relations.

Butler's scepticism about traditional ideas of honour extends to the relation of the sexes. He showed up illusions about romantic love by contrasting it with the realities of property marriage which so often got mixed up with it.

> 'Tis true, no lover has that power
> T'enforce a desperate amour
> As he that has two strings t'his bow
> And burns for love and money too. (III. i. 1–4)

> Their fortunes! the perpetual aims
> Of all their ecstasies and flames! (III. i. 957–8)

Who would

> Be under vows to hang and die,
> Love's sacrifice, and all a lie? (II. i. 861–2)

"Virtue, as it is commonly understood in women, signifies nothing else but chastity, and honour only not being whores: as if that sex were capable of no other morality but a mere negative continence".[75]

Property marriage, Butler observed, deprived "great persons" of freedom of choice. Most women of the propertied class "are either forced by their parents or betrayed and sold by their friends" into unhappy marriages. Consequently "a good woman is infinitely more to be valued than a good man, because they pass through greater difficulties to become such".[76] Butler indulges in some conventional misogyny,[77] but insists that beautiful women—"the greatest rareties in the world in Paris"—abound in London.[78] Like almost all seventeenth-century commentators who discuss the subject at all Butler contradicts Lawrence Stone's idea that parents did not love their children. He thinks, on the contrary, that "nature has ordered it so, that parents have a great inclination to the love of their children, because they cannot subsist without it".[79]

Butler accepted the individualistic view that conquest of oneself is more important than dependency "upon the uncertain loves or fears of other men", upon the vain opinion of the world.[80] The cult of the golden mean extends to society. The very rich "are commonly insolent and proud"; the very poor are "mean and contemptible". "Those that are between both are commonly the most agreeable".[81] The doctrine was familiar in Puritan sermons, but perhaps rather unexpected in Butler.

Butler anticipated Mandeville in recognizing that conspicuous consumption by the traditional aristocracy performed a useful function in capitalist society. "Prodigality and luxury and vanity are great consumers . . . of all commodities of the growth of any nation, which (as men of politics affirm) is the only way to distribute and propagate trade among all people". "Destructive always to those that use them", such "extravagant follies . . . are very beneficial to all others that have to do with them"—not least to doctors and lawyers.[82] Hoarding is therefore anti-social.[83]

Butler was contemptuous of the lower classes,[84] of any form of political activity by them, and of egalitarian ideas. Sometimes he sounds like Coriolanus: "I do not remember in all history any one good thing that ever was done by the people, in any government, but millions of bad ones."[85] But the experience of the revolutionary decades had given Butler insights which Coriolanus lacked: "the natural frenzies of the rabble are best tempered by being kept in ignorance"—a lesson which the Church of Rome had learnt long ago.[86] And Butler knew that "the rabble" in the last resort paid for church, state and society.[87] For Butler, as for Cromwell and Harrington, "all bad men are levellers". Quakers are like Levellers in that their design was "to bring down all other men. . . . to an equality with themselves".[88]

We do not know much about the public to which *Hudibras* appealed. Both Pepys and the Puritan Henry Newcome disliked Part I on first reading—a "senseless poem", Newcome declared: "he would be wicked without wit". That did not stop him from reading Part II when it came out.[89] Pepys found Part I "so silly an abuse of the Presbyterian Knight" that he sold his copy at a loss; later attempts to read it were unsuccessful. But ultimately the fame of the poem was so great that he bought another copy of Parts I and II[90] Clarendon, who collected portraits of "the most illustrious of our nation", gave Butler's a special place of honour.[91]

Clarendon was a politician who tried to conserve the good old feudal virtues whilst adapting to the politics of a later age. This may be his link with Butler. Michael Wilding sees in *Hudibras* an appreciation of the traditional virtues of rural life—village sports, country food, the domestic simplicity of the small farmer's life rather than that of his landlord.[92] We owe to Butler our best description of that popular phenomenon, a Skimmington ride.[93] Butler's own views on prose style were firmly held. "Although the plainest and most significant style be undoubtedly the best, *yet it is only so where the excellency of the sense will bear it*".[94] He does not always follow the implications of this. Sometimes his prose reads like a late version of metaphysical poetry, aiming to get effects only by contradiction, by paradox for its own sake. In verse these are the vices for which Butler castigated Benlowes as "a small poet".[95] Southey saw John Taylor the Water-Poet as a predecessor in Hudibrastic rhymes. Dame Veronica Wedgwood suggested that Marchamont Nedham anticipated Butler's characteristic verse style.[96] Some of the ironical stanzas of Marvell's *Upon Appleton House* read like Hudibrastics.[97]

We know little of Butler's personality, but it has to be admitted that he may not have been the most agreeable of men. He often attacks those who were, or had been, his friends or patrons—Selden, for instance, or the Duke of Buckingham.[98] We have seen how he made jibes about Hobbes; he did the same for Harrington's Rota.[99] Does he ever, in his writings, praise anybody sincerely?

Butler wrote at a time when the idealists on both sides in the civil war had been ditched by the practical politicians: it was natural for him to look for material interests concealed under hypocritical phrases, though Hobbes and Harrington may have helped him. Property, Butler suggested, is theft. "Courts of justice, for the most part, commit greater crimes than they punish". "The solemn professions of religion, justice and liberty are but pretences to conceal ambition, rapine and useful cheat".[100] With all his contempt for "the rabble", he knew that the rich and the state lived on their backs.[101] One of his special aversions was also Milton's: "that cursed sin/Hypocrisy" (*Hudibras*, III. i. 1221–2; and pp. 223–4, 272 *passim*).

He was especially suspicious of ideology: its good intentions could do incalculable harm.

> As if religion were intended
> For nothing else but to be mended. (I. i. 203–4)

> Opinion governs all mankind, . . .
> And nothing's so perverse in nature
> As a profound opinionator. (*Poetical Works*, II, pp. 250–1)

> A teacher's doctrine, and his proof,
> Is all his province, and enough;
> But is no more concerned in use
> Than shoemakers to wear all shoes. (*ibid.*, p. 251)

Butler regarded himself as the spokesman of the man whom the shoe pinched. His enemies were religious fanaticism, romantic professions which concealed sordid reality, whether in love or war or politics; science that was all speculation and no practice. His "there is no ignorance so impertinent as that which proceeds from curiosity and over-understanding of anything" compares with Milton's rejection of learning in *Paradise Regained*—itself a familiar radical position.[102] Butler's pose is that of the plain blunt man:

> Was no dispute afoot between
> The caterwauling brethren?
> No subtle question raised among
> Those out-o'-their-wits and those i'th'wrong? (*Hudibras*. I. ii. 700–4)

Ideology was self-indulgence, and led merely to self-indulgent quarrels—

> As pedants out of school-boys breeches
> Do claw and curry their own itches. (II. ii. 465–6)

Like many later clever men whose ideals had turned sour, Butler proclaimed, a little prematurely, the end of ideology for everyone else too.

NOTES

1. I have drawn on a review of *Hudibras* (ed. John Wilders, Oxford U.P., 1967) in *Essays in Criticism*, XIX (1969). I cite *Hudibras* from this edition, but I have modernized the spelling.
2. Barbara Everett, "The Sense of Nothing", in *Spirit of Wit: Reconsiderations of Rochester* (ed. J. Treglown, Oxford, 1982), p. 37.
3. D. Farley-Hills, *The Benevolence of Laughter: Comic Poetry of the Commonwealth and Restoration*, p. 70.
4. Defoe quoted these lines in his *Serious Reflections during the Life and Surprising Adventures of Robinson Crusoe* (1720), p. 170.
5. Cf. Butler, *Genuine Remains*, in *Poetical Works* (1854), II, p. 250.
6. Cf. pp 101–2 above.
7. See pp. 289–90 above.
8. With the sun in Tethis's lap Michael Wilding compares Milton's sun supping in the ocean ("The Last of the Epics: the Rejection of the Heroic in *Paradise Lost* and *Hudibras*", in *Restoration Literature: Critical Approaches*, ed. H. Love, 1972, p. 110). Peter le Motteux cribbed Butler's phrase about a lobster boiled for his translation of Rabelais (*Pantagruel's Voyage*, 1694, Book V, Chapter 8). There is nothing corresponding to it in the original.
9. Cf. Butler's letter to Sir George Oxenden, *Hudibras*, p. 451; and Farley-Hills, *The Benevolence of Laughter*, pp. 36, 52, For epic and inspiration see pp. 324–5, 329–30 below.
10. Butler also received £200 secret service money (E.S. de Beer, "The Later Life of Samuel Butler", *Review of English Studies*, 4, 1928, p. 164).
11. Cf. "A Court Beggar, in *Characters and Passages from Note-Books* (ed. A.R. Waller, Cambridge U.P., 1908), pp. 38–9. The ingratitude of the restoration government recurs at pp. 3–4, 384, 390, 458.
12. *Miscellaneous Thoughts*, in *Poetical Works*, II, pp. 262, 259.
13. Butler, *Prose Observations* (ed. H. de Quehen, Oxford U.P., 1979), pp. 92–8, 134.
14. *Ibid.*, pp. 160, 185; Waller, *op. cit.*, pp. 320, 337–8, 479; cf. Farley-Hills *op. cit.*, pp. 60–2.
15. *Prose*, pp. 91, 137; *Hudibras*, p. 156.
16. *Prose*, pp. 87, 179.
17. *Ibid.*, p. 191.
18. *Hudibras*, pp. 181–2, 188; cf. 232; M. H. Nicolson, *Pepys's Diary and the New Science* (Virginia U.P., 1965), p. 129. Butler must have known Sprat well, since both were members of the group which accompanied Buckingham to Versailles in 1670 (*Hudibras*, p. xx).

19. *Prose*, p. 205.
20. Waller, *op. cit.*, p. 207.
21. Cf. *Poetical Works*, II, p. 251.
22. Cf. Butler's character of a Hermetic philosopher in Waller, *op. cit.*, pp. 97–108.
23. *Ibid.*, p. 300.
24. *Prose*, p. 200.
25. *Ibid.*, p. 204; cf. pp. 127, 168, 177, 293–8; Waller, *op. cit.*, pp. 74–5.
26. *Ibid.*, p. 322; cf. Winstanley, *The Law of Freedom and other Writings*, pp. 298–300.
27. *Prose*, p. 240.
28. Waller, *op. cit.*, p. 95; cf. p. 141.
29. *Prose*, p. 208; cf. pp. 212–13.
30. *Ibid.*, p. 196.
31. *Poetical Works*, II, p. 158.
32. Waller, *op. cit.*, p. 308; Robert South, quoted in *Three Restoration Divines: Barrow, South, Tillotson* (ed. Irène Simon, Bibliothèque de la Faculté de Philosophie et Lettres de l'Université de Liège, Fascicule CLXXXI, 1967–76), p. 60.
33. *Prose*, pp. 200, 246; cf. pp. 31, 282, and Waller, *op. cit.*, pp. 67–8: "A Ranter". See also *Hudibras*, II. ii. 235–8.
34. *Prose*, pp. 211–12, 166; but cf. p. 119 for irony at the expense of "the most pure and primitive times". For Milton see *M.E.R.*, p. 96.
35. *Prose*, p. 298; cf. pp. 275–6, 296–7. Butler's technique here recalls that used by Henry Stubbe to convey his criticisms of traditional Christianity. See Jacob, *Henry Stubbe, passim*. Cf. Butler's reference to Stubbe in *Poetical Works*, II, p. 116.
36. *Prose*, pp. 115, 160–1; cf. pp. 81, 122, 132, 196–9.
37. Waller, *op. cit.*, p. 168.
38. *Prose*, p. 124; cf. p. 85, and Waller, *op. cit.*, p. 355.
39. *Prose*, p. 253; cf. pp. 36, 42, 44, 67, 92, 236; and Waller, *op. cit.*, pp. 337–8. Contrast Farley-Hills, *op. cit.*, pp. 57–8.
40. *Prose*, p. 229. "The Stoical necessity and Presbyterian predestination are the same" (*ibid.*, p. 14).
41. *Prose*, pp. 275–6; cf. *Poetical Works*, II. pp. 264–5.
42. *Ibid.*, pp. 50–1. Cf. Pepys, p. 268 above.
43. *Prose*, p. 194.
44. Jacob, *op. cit.*, esp. Chapters 5 and 8, Cf. p. 102 above.
45. See pp. 168–9, 203, 228–30 above.
46. Cf. "A Modern Politician", in Waller, *op. cit.*, pp. 1–15, though this *attacks* a Hobbist politician. But see *Prose*, pp. 29, 68, 111, 115, 124.
47. *Prose*, p. 227.
48. Cf. Jacob, *op. cit.*, p. 48.
49. *Prose*, p. 17.
50. Cf. p. 233 above.
51. *Prose*, p. 6; cf. *Hudibras*, pp. 130–7, 303. See my *Society and Puritanism in 17th-century England* (Panther edn., 1969), Chapter 11.
52. *Prose*, p. 23.

53. Waller, *op. cit.*, p. 391.
54. *Ibid.*, pp. 74–5, 310; *Poetical Works*, II, pp. 259–61. Butler's own legal expertise adds point to these remarks.
55. *Prose*, p. 15.
56. *Ibid.*, p. 197; cf. Waller, *op. cit.*, pp. 38–9, 154, and p. 281 above.
57. *Prose*, p. 216. Butler was explaining how right Queen Elizabeth had been to oppose the execution of Mary Queen of Scots, because of the precedent it set.
58. *Prose*, pp. 282, 163; cf. p. 242, and Waller, *op. cit.*, pp. 454–5, comparing the King to a bankrupt merchant.
59. *Prose*, pp. 282–3.
60. *Poetical Works*, II, p. 258.
61. *Prose*, p. 113. Henry Stubbe, a Harrington-influenced radical, also thought the men of the Commonwealth were building for posterity (*Legends no Histories*, 1670, Sig. *2).
62. De Beer, "The Later Life of Samuel Butler", p. 163.
63. Wood, *Athenae Oxonienses* (1721), II, p. 804; cf. *Prose*, pp. xxvii–iii; *Hudibras*, p. xx; *Poetical Works*, II, p. 246 (against the court). But cf. the very hostile character of "A Duke of Bucks"—"one that has studied the whole body of vice"—in Waller, *op. cit.*, pp. 32–3. Some phrases here and in *Hudibras*, III. ii. may have given Dryden ideas for his famous character in *Absalom and Achitophel*.
64. *Prose*, p. 189; *The Rehearsal Transpros'd*, pp. 5–6.
65. *Prose*, pp. 154, 288; cf. p. 286.
66. *Hudibras*, I. iii. 923–8; *Poetical Works*, II, pp. 163–7.
67. *Prose*, p. xxix; de Beer, "The Later Life", p. 166. John Aubrey was at the funeral too. See pp. 303, 307 below for Rochester, Buckingham and Shadwell.
68. Cowley, Preface to *Poems* (1656). This passage was omitted in his *Works* (1668).
69. J.R. Jacob, *Robert Boyle and the English Revolution: A Study in Social and Intellectual Change* (New York, 1977), Chapter 2 and p. 101.
70. Waller, *op. cit.*, p. 468 Cf. *Poetical Works*, II, p. 234. Butler saw a connection between this military fact and the end of heroic poetry, of which *Hudibras* is a critique. Cf. p. 280 above.
71. Waller, *op. cit.*, pp. 34–5; cf. *Prose*, pp. 271–2.
72. Barber, *op. cit.* (Göteborg, 1957), pp. 20, 29–32, 99–100, 114, 116, 131–2, 136, 266–72.
73. A.L. Morton, *Shakespeare's Idea of History* (*Our History* pamphlet, 33, 1964, pp. 13–15).
74. Chapman, *Minor Poems and Translations*, p. 34.
75. Carew had earlier made the same point at the conclusion of his "A Rapture".
76. *Prose*, pp. 269–70; cf. *Hudibras*, pp. 148–9, 191, 206–9, 216–17, 312–21. Winstanley and Harrington agreed that it was easier for the poor to marry for love (*The Law of Freedom and other Writings*, p. 388; *The Political Works of James Harrington*, ed. J.G.A. Pocock, Cambridge U.P., 1977, pp. 239–40).

77. *Prose*, pp. 44, 196.
78. *Ibid.*, p. 252.
79. *Ibid.*, p. 95.
80. Waller, *op. cit.*, p. 7.
81. *Prose*, p. 14.
82. *Ibid.*, p. 73; cf. p. 325.
83. Waller, *op. cit.*, pp. 472–4.
84. "A Clown", "A Rabble", in Waller, *op. cit.*, pp. 89, 147. Cf. *Hudibras*, I. ii. 492–608; III. ii. 1611–14.
85. *Prose*, p. 103; cf. pp. 207, 266–7, 296–8.
86. *Prose*, p. 6; cf. Waller, *op. cit.*, pp. 295, 315; cf. pp. 282, 288, 291, 334–5, 464.
87. *Poetical Works*, II, pp. 241–2.
88. *Prose*, p. 74; cf. p. 226, and Waller, *op. cit.*, pp. 217, 286. For Cromwell see Abbott, *op. cit.*, III, pp. 435–6; for Harrington, see Pocock, *op. cit.*, p. 292.
89. *The Diary of the Rev. Henry Newcome, 3 Sept. 1661 to 29 Sept. 1663* (ed. T. Heywood, Chetham Soc. publications, 18, 1849), pp. 156, 191.
90. Pepys, *Diary*, 26 December 1662, 28 November and 10 December 1663.
91. Evelyn, letter to Pepys, 12 August 1689, in *Critical Essays of the Seventeenth Century*, II, *1650–1685* (ed. J.E. Spingarn, Oxford U.P., 1908), p. 320.
92. M. Wilding, *op. cit.*, pp. 116–17.
93. *Hudibras*, pp. 143 ff. Marvell appears to be the only competitor (*Last Instructions to a Painter*, ll. 373–89). In Kent in 1650 it was alleged that a Skimmington ride was used as a cover for a royalist rising (J. Nickolls, *Original Letters and Papers of State*, 1743, p. 66).
94. Waller, *op. cit.*, p. 414. Italics in the original.
95. *Ibid.*, pp. 47–57.
96. R. Southey, *The Lives and Works of the Uneducated Poets* (ed. J.S. Childers, 1975), p. 44; C.V. Wedgwood, *Seventeenth-Century English Literature* (Home University Library, Oxford U.P., 1950), p. 124. There is an unfriendly reference to Nedham in Waller, *op. cit.*, p. 241.
97. Many of Sir John Berkenhead's poems were attributed to Butler. For comparisons between the two poets see Thomas, *Berkenhead*, pp. 113–14, 146–9, 182.
98. See pp. 285, 288 above.
99. See pp. 285–6 above; for the Rota, *Hudibras*, II. iii. 1108.
100. *Prose*, p. 111; cf. p. 53; Waller, *op. cit.*, pp. 8, 389; cf. pp. 74–5, 292. We recall Winstanley and other interregnum radicals.
101. See p. 292 above.
102. *Prose*, p. 301; cf. *ibid.*, p. 10, p. 146 above, and *M.E.R.*, pp. 423–6.

14. *John Wilmot, Earl of Rochester (1647–80)*[1]

Rochester is one of the most exciting, and the most paradoxical, of English poets. Sexually ambivalent, a notorious member of the gang of young roués at the court of Charles II, he nevertheless managed to write a few poignant and haunting poems which suggest that his public notoriety concealed an exceptional sensibility reacting to the intellectual crisis of the later seventeenth century.

> All my past past life is mine no more;
>   The flying hours are gone,
> Like transitory dreams given o'er
> Whose images are kept in store
>   By memory alone.

> Whatever is to come is not:
>   How can it then be mine?
> The present moment's all my lot,
> And that, as fast as it is got,
>   Phyllis, is wholly thine.

The ideas in the poem derive from Hobbes;[2] it is not the sort of thing the average seducer wastes his time on.

Dying at the age of thirty-three, probably from the consequences of venereal disease and alcoholism, Rochester—extravagant to the last—was on his death-bed spectacularly converted to Christianity by Gilbert Burnet. He thus became a moral story for all rakes and a mystery for later critics.

In our generation Rochester's full stature as a poet has been demonstrated by the publication of an acceptable canon of his work.[3] Moreover, today's greater libertarianism has made it possible to print Rochester's bawdy poems unbowdlerized. So we can reconsider his small *oeuvre* as a whole. Jeremy Treglown's recent publication of a complete edition of Rochester's correspondence aroused expectations that a unified personality might be revealed behind the turbulent rake and the agonized poet, behind the courtier and friend of Charles II who wrote savage republican verse. But these hopes were disappointed.

Clearly the mind of Rochester the exhibitionist rake was grappling seriously with intellectual problems left over after the ferment of discussion during the sixteen-forties and fifties, and the sudden reversal of 1660. But there is as yet no agreement on what this mind was up to, how original it was and how consistent. Rochester translated select bits of Lucretius and Seneca which appealed to him. His senior contemporary Lucy Hutchinson translated all six books of the *De Rerum Natura*, which she then suppressed. John Evelyn's translation of the first book was published in 1656. It is curious to ask what it was in the great Epicurean poet that fascinated the very Puritan wife of a regicide, the prim and conventional Evelyn and the lecherous peer—or for that matter what it was that drew both Traherne and Rochester to Seneca. But anyone could have called Rochester's attention to the passages which he translated: indeed English versions of both Seneca and Lucretius were available.[4] What seems to me significant is that the lines which Rochester chose to translate, or to use as starting-points for poems of his own, related directly to controversies about the reality of heaven and hell, the immortality of the soul, which had raged in the sixteen-forties and continued to be topical. There is no reason to suppose that Rochester's heretical ideas—any more than Milton's—derived from classical sources alone. His theoretical libertinism might come from France, or it too might come from interregnum discussions initiated by the Ranters. His defence of divorce is most likely to derive from the controversies opened up by Milton in the sixteen-forties.[5]

Mr Treglown is healthily deflationary about Rochester's intellectual milieu. "No letter to Rochester from any of his friends survives in which any poem of his is referred to, except in relation to the scandalous content of lampoons attributed to him". "Rochester's own letters never allude to his writing". There is no literary criticism in the correspondence comparable to that in "An Allusion to Horace". "Some modern scholars have tended to over-estimate his first-hand knowledge of many philosophical works, and it is clear that his ideas were often picked up second-hand from contemporary sources".[6] There is a general indebtedness to Hobbes; and Rochester echoes *Paradise Lost en passant* in a way that assumes that his correspondent will recognize the allusion.[7] (It has been suggested that his poem *Sab. Lost* alludes to *Comus* as well as to Milton's epic).[8] What Mr Treglown does emphasize, illuminatingly, is Rochester's frequent Biblical phraseology, often used ironically, and often quoted *via* the Book of Common Prayer. Mr Treglown makes the interesting point that Rochester echoes the pre-1662 prayer book, ignoring alterations made in that year. This suggests not only that his religious education ceased in his teens, but also that in the sixteen-fifties the Book of Common Prayer was used at least by the family chaplain, although it was officially prohibited.[9]

Brought up by a pious mother, Rochester had been an undergraduate at Wadham, the most advanced Oxford college of his day. He was among other things settling accounts with the Puritanism of the sixteen-fifties in which he grew up, and indeed with Christianity. Professor Pinto suggested that Rochester was trying to escape from "a world which had been suddenly transformed by the scientists into a vast machine governed by mathematical laws, where God had became a remote first cause and man an insignificant 'reas'ning Engine'"; he was trying to escape from "the Cartesian-Newtonian world picture, a civilised city of good taste, common sense and reason".[10] This is a valuable insight, though in fact Rochester died before there was a "Newtonian world picture".

Mr Farley-Hills developed this line of thought by depicting Rochester as one of the first modern men, exploring a world without God, or at least without a God who takes any notice of humanity. Mr Farley-Hills contrasts Boileau and Dryden, clinging on to the ordered certainties and immutable values of the medieval world, and even—less plausibly to me—associates Marvell with them rather than with Rochester. Rochester accepts instability and change,[11] and was unique among poets in challenging the Christian assumptions of his society. Man is alone in an irrational world. Our fallible reason is all we have to impose a limited coherence on an incoherent universe, to come to terms with the insoluble absurdity. Gilbert Burnet records that Rochester felt no remorse for his past actions as offences against God, but only as injuries to himself and to mankind.[12]

For Rochester the individualism of passion and the order and decorum necessary to society are both desirable but they are absolutely incompatible.[13] These may or may not be, as Mr Farley-Hills suggests, "contradictions inherent in human nature".[14] But they were contradictions which obtruded themselves on particular individuals at this particular stage of historical development. Since Marlowe's and Shakespeare's tragic heroes the individualist virtue of honesty to one's own feelings had been challenging the public virtues necessary to the maintenance of social order. During the interregnum

Hobbes and radical sectaries had either removed God from the universe or at least severed the cords which linked him to human beings.

The aristocrats who regained their privileged position after 1660 had no significant role to play in the reconstructed social order. Flocking to the court, they ceased even to take their traditional part in local government; and at court their role was decorative rather than functional. Courtiers were freer than other men to indulge their passions; but this only emphasized their social irrelevance. They could sleep around, and beat up the watch.[15] Rochester's arbitrary and arrogant bad temper, his "public chiding of his servants",[16] his assumption that his rank combined with his great gifts entitled him to lay down the law to other poets, his sordidly tedious quarrels with Sir Carr Scrope, these unattractive aspects of his personality must all relate to his position as alienated aristocrat. It was this that left him feeling betrayed, not just the inadequacy of human reason. Dr Farley-Hills quotes Sir William Temple's shrewd remark that "the wits in vogue" were heirs to the sort of discourse "which was formerly left to those that were called fools and were used in great families only to make the company laugh".[17] The laughter might be purgative:

> Nature's as lame in making a true fop
> As a philosopher; the very top
> And dignity of folly we attain
> By studious search and labour of the brain,
> By observation, counsel, and deep thought:
> God never made a coxcomb worth a groat.
> We owe that name to industry and arts:
> An eminent fool must be a fool of parts.[18]

But the role of court fool was now peripheral to the concerns of society. In his pious phase Rochester himself sneered at those who delighted in "A fool's-coat". The tensions between Rochester's social position and his social irrelevance may account for some of the bad temper in his satire, and perhaps for his turn towards the Whigs at the end of his life. Graham Greene pointed out that other "profane wits" like Sedley, Buckhurst and Henry Savile were becoming political in the sixteen-seventies.[19]

But even this may oversimplify. For Dryden and official Anglicans by no means stood for traditional mediaeval values. The Church of

England was surreptitiously taking over many of the doctrines of discredited Puritanism (Sabbatarianism, the all-importance of preaching, "the protestant ethic"). The royalist Matthew Wren adopted the ethos of possessive individualism.[20] The scientists of the newly-founded Royal Society, determined to cover up their inter-regnum origins and clear themselves of imputations of an atheism which genuinely scared them, spent a great deal of time and energy arguing that science demonstrated the existence of God. Rochester clearly wished to *épater* the bourgeoisie. But in order to do so he not only played the reckless irresponsible aristocrat but also drew on the serious counter-ideas preached by political and religious radicals during the revolutionary decades, and by the hardly less disreputable Hobbes.

Mr Trotter has plausibly and valuably argued that one of Rochester's particular aims was to attack the moderate, middle-of-the-road attitudes of those who called themselves Latitudinarians. Men like Wilkins, Sprat, Stillingfleet, Boyle, Glanvill, Burnet were soon to dominate in the Church of England and many of them were already prominent in the Royal Society.[21] Latitudinarians were mostly "Cromwellian renegadoes", former Puritans who had con-formed without difficulty first to the Cromwellian and then to the restored episcopalian Church of England: "renegado-presbyterian turned Latitudinarian" was Henry Stubbe's phrase for Joseph Glanvill.[22] Even Marvell's butt, Samuel Parker (whom Mr Trotter classes as a Latitudinarian but I should have thought a high-flyer) had been an enthusiastic Cromwellian when that was the way to preferment. The word "Latitudinarian" indeed has magically ended controversies about whether the founders of the Royal Society were "Puritans" or "royalists". Call them "Latitudinarians" and then the question does not arise; any aspiring ex-Puritan was a Latitudinarian after 1660. The Latitudinarians—and the Royal Society—disap-proved above all of fanatical extremism, of enthusiasm, whether religious or literary. Moderation, common sense, tolerance, all the sober bourgeois virtues were theirs. Rochester, by temperament no less than by social position, found all this decidedly alien. Dorimant in Etherege's *The Man of Mode* was often taken to be a portrait of Rochester, as well as relating to Milton's Satan in *Paradise Lost*, a rebel hero.[23]

Consideration of Professor J.R. Jacob's *Henry Stubbe, radical Protestantism and the early Enlightenment* puts Mr Treglown's insight into an even wider context. Professor Jacob has brilliantly demonstrated continuity between the radical sectarianism of Stubbe in the sixteen-fifties and his Aristotelian attacks on the Royal Society in the seventies. The common factor, Professor Jacob suggests, is Stubbe's opposition to the Puritan/Latitudinarian establishment which dominated Oxford and Richard Cromwell's government in the sixteen-fifties and which preponderated in the Royal Society after the restoration. Dislike of the "latitude men" unites interregnum radicals, Stubbe and Marvell with Samuel Butler and Rochester.[24] Rochester's ire was roused by the dull moderation implicit in the Latitudinarian creed.

> Your reason hinders, mine helps to enjoy,
> Renewing appetites you would destroy.
> My reason is my friend, yours is a cheat;
> Hunger calls out, my reason bids me eat;
> Perversely, yours your appetite does mock:
> This asks for food, that answers, "What's o'clock?"[25]

It is a splendid brief assertion of enjoyable life against the clock-dominated civilization, of natural freedom against the discipline necessary to nascent industrial society, against the protestant ethic. Rochester started by aristocratic revolt against the contrived nullity of this stereotyped mediocrity. But what alternative standards could he produce except a sort of anarchical existentialism?

Rochester's explosions of rage, his sexual excesses, his drunkenness, could all be seen as protests against the common-sense moderation of the Latitudinarians. Conversely, Latitudinarians thought the swearing and profanity of the court wits not only wicked but—almost worse—unreasonable and unnecessary. The scoffer, Tillotson argued, "serves the devil for nought, and sins only for sin's sake"; he risks the fires of hell "for no other reward but the slender reputation of seeming to say that wittily, which no wise man would say". Scoffing was wanton, extravagant, gratuitous; an unprofitable waste of time and energy merely in order to provoke. Glanvill noted that "sects and jovial atheists" combined to lampoon the clergy, as Marvell did in *The Rehearsal Transpros'd*—again totally gratuitously, Glanvill thought. Rakes and enthusiasts had become the main source of contempt for the clergy; to Stillingfleet rakes were "zealots in wickedness".[26] (We recall Sir Francis Fane's description of Rochester as "an Enthusiast in Wit", which Pinto used as the title of his book on Rochester.) Sprat, Latitudinarian spokesman for the Royal Society, thought that prose should be purged of all enthusiasm.[27]

Professor Jacob helps us to push the point further. Concern for moderation, clarity, scepticism, courtesy in discourse, had social origins, as did the philosophy which underlay it. Professor Jacob has shown how Boyle's philosophical and scientific thinking was dominated by fear of the ideas of radical sectaries, which he believed tended towards atheism. Like many others in the sixteen-fifties, Boyle abandoned his early interest in Hobbes and Descartes because he thought that their philosophies too led to atheism; the corpuscular philosophy was designed to obviate this danger.[28] Those who write about Rochester are apt to attribute his materialist ideas to Hobbes: his contemporaries saw their connection with the ideas of Ranters and "mechanic" (i.e. lower-class) sectaries as well. Glanvill, in dedicating *Scepsis Scientifica* to the Royal Society in 1664 stressed the Society's role in "securing the foundations of religion against all attempts of mechanical atheism". "The folly and nonsense of mere mechanism", we are told in 1681, had passed to the very craftsmen and labourers, who were "able to demonstrate out of *Leviathan* . . . that all things come to pass by an eternal chain of natural causes".[29] Samuel Parker in the same year agreed that "plebeians and mechanics have philosophized themselves into principles of impiety, and read their lectures of atheism in the streets and highways".[30]

Rochester had no doubt read *Leviathan*; but Hobbes's ideas were in the air, particularly among court wits. It was difficult to avoid them. Towards the end of his life, when he was taking politics more seriously, Rochester came into direct contact with the interregnum radical tradition through Charles Blount, who was influenced by Henry Stubbe. Rochester sent Blount his translation of Seneca, and in reply received a letter concerning, among other things, the mortalist heresy.[31] Blount's letter was mainly cribbed, without acknowledgement, from Stubbe's *Account of the Rise and Progress of Mahometanism*, one of the great documents of the radical critique of orthodox religion.[32] In his ostensible translation of Seneca Rochester had written:

> After death nothing is, and nothing, death:
> The utmost limit of a gasp of breath.
> Let the ambitious zealot lay aside
> His hopes of heaven, whose faith is but his pride;
> Let slavish souls lay by their fear,

> Nor be concerned which way nor where
> After this life they shall be hurled.
> Dead, we become the lumber of the world,
> And to that mass of matter shall be swept
> Where things destroyed with things unborn are kept.
> Devouring time swallows us whole;
> Impartial death confounds body and soul.
> For hell and the foul fiend that rules
> God's everlasting fiery jails
> (Devised by rogues, dreaded by fools),
> With his grim grisly dog that keeps the door,
> Are senseless stories, idle tales,
> Dreams, whimseys, and no more.

That reads like not only mortalism but annihilationist mortalism.[33] No wonder Burnet was particularly anxious to emphasize that Rochester on his penitent death-bed had rejected mortalism. But in the conversations which Burnet records Rochester still attacked the sacred character of the Bible, and still thought that all came by nature—a specifically Ranter belief.[34]

Rochester translated lines from Lucretius which suggested that the gods took no notice of human life on earth.

> The gods, by right of nature, must possess
> An everlasting age of perfect peace;
> Far off removed from us and our affairs;
> Neither approached by dangers, or by cares;
> Rich in themselves, to whom we cannot add;
> Not pleased by good deeds, nor provoked by bad.[35]

("Not one god took care to save" fair Chloris when she fled from her dream-rapist).[36] This was a doctrine elaborated by the Ranter Laurence Clarkson and taken over by the Muggletonian sect which he joined.[37] Even in Burnet's account Rochester was not persuaded "that prayers were of much use", since God would not "be overcome with importunities. . . . He doubted much of rewards or punishments"—i.e. of the Christian doctrine of heaven and hell, another familiar Ranter heresy. In revising Fletcher's *Valentinian* Rochester added some lines asking how the gods could permit evil to exist. His answer there was Manichaean: evil was co-eternal with the gods.[38] Rochester, again like the Ranters, could believe the Biblical stories of the Creation and the Fall only if they were parables.[39]

Among other unorthodox views which Rochester continued to defend against Burnet was his fierce anti-clericalism, which recalls Milton, Winstanley and many other interregnum radicals, as well as

Samuel Butler. "Why must a man tell me that I cannot be saved unless I believe things against my reason, and then I must pay him for telling me them?" "The restraining a man from the use of women, except one in the way of marriage, and denying the remedy of divorce, he thought unreasonable impositions on the freedom of mankind"; that recalls Milton on divorce and polygamy, Clarkson on free love.[40]

Mr Treglown refers to the poet's violence, "apparent throughout his adult life, whether in his duelling, in the hectoring tone of a few of his letters both to his wife and to Elizabeth Barry, or in the domineering machismo of poems like *The Advice* or *Phyllis, be gentler, I advise*, and his sexual satires". "Machismo" is the appropriate word. Mr Treglown warns against "a modern tendency to generalize sentimentally about his relations with his wife", and indeed now that Rochester's letters to his wife and his mistress have been printed side by side, together with his wife's letters to him, it is difficult to retain illusions about the relationship.[41]

Nor can we be sentimental about his love affairs. The longest and strongest seems to have been that with Elizabeth Barry, which lasted for two or more years from 1675. But when she bore him a daughter, the fact had to be reported to Rochester by his friend Henry Savile, who added "I doubt she does not lie in in much state, for a friend and protrectess of hers in the Mall was much lamenting her poverty very lately, not without some gentle reflexions on your lordship's want either of generosity or of bowels toward a lady who had not refused you the full enjoyment of all her charms".[42] That is the seamy side of the philosophy of living only in the present, so beautifully expressed in *Love and Life*:

> Then talk not of inconstancy,
>   False hearts, and broken vows;
> If I, by miracle, can be
> This livelong minute true to thee,
> 'Tis all that heaven allows.[43]

Upon His Leaving His Mistress, written apparently after his affair with Mrs Barry had ended, put the point rather differently:

> 'Tis not that I am weary grown
> Of being yours, and yours alone;
> But with what face can I incline
> To damn you to be only mine?
> You, whom some kinder power did fashion,
> By merit and by inclination,
> The joy at least of one whole nation.[44]

Rochester's double standard is offensive to modern tastes. But lines added to Sir Robert Howard's *The Conquest of China* (c. 1675?), which have been attributed to Rochester, defend women's liberty against the constricting roles which society allotted to them:

> Treacherous man misguides her in her aim;
> Makes her believe that all her glories lie
> In dull obedience, truth and modesty,
> That to be beautiful is to be brave
> And calls her conqueror when she's most his slave, . . .
> With this poor hypocritical pretence
> That woman's merit is her innocence.[45]

And it should be added to Rochester's credit that, great though his debts were, he managed mostly to keep his wife's estate for her use, separate from his own, though it was legally his property.[46]

It may help to put Rochester's sexual attitudes in historical perspective if we recall that the main objection which Burnet raised against libertinism was that "men have a property in their wives and daughters, so that to defile the one or corrupt the other is an unjust and injurious thing"—not to the women concerned but to their male owners. Only the case of polygamy reminded Burnet that "women are equally concerned in the laws of marriage", presumably because polygamy did not harm any man.[47]

Perhaps not quite enough attention has been paid to Rochester's turn to politics in the last three years of his life when he was closely associated politically with the Duke of Buckingham (another court rake and wit) and voted consistently with the Whig leaders. This is interesting, since during these years he seems to have been thinking out his position more consistently than earlier. David Trotter suggested that "there was a political aspect to Rochester's wit, and that his greatest poem (*A Satyr against Reason and Mankind*) was generated . . . out of the tension between points of view in society".[48] This "political aspect to Rochester's wit" was not new. He participated in the Second Dutch War, acquitting himself well; but he ridiculed the Third War, and even expressed anti-war sentiments.[49] The Third Dutch War, fought in alliance with Louis XIV against the Dutch republic, was thought to endanger Parliamentary institutions in England: it was accompanied by toleration for papists as well as nonconformists, based on the royal prerogative and in defiance of Parliament. In 1669 Rochester had attacked Louis XIV; by 1674 he extended his attack:

> All monarchs I hate, and the thrones they sit on,
> From the Hector of France to the Cully of Britain.[50]

Graham Greene pointed out that Fletcher's *Valentinian*, which Rochester revised, may have attracted him because of its depiction of a lustful monarch and a corrupt court.[51] Swift's relationship to Rochester has often been noted; the Houyhnhnms may well derive from the horse at the conclusion of *A Satyr against Reason and Mankind*. But Defoe also was always intrigued by Rochester, though he could hardly admire his private life.[52] Defoe drew attention to the political significance of lampoons and satires, in "the days of King Charles II, when the licence tyranny reigned over the press". Such attacks "went far in ruining the parties they were pointed at, more than has ever been practised since the liberty of the press". Defoe mentioned Marvell, Denham, Rochester and Buckhurst among those "whose wit made the Court odious to the people, beyond what had been possible if the press had been open".[53] Under William III, Defoe thought, things were different: now "satire has no business with the crown".[54] It is a shrewd point, whose implications are worth pondering. Marvell as a commoner ran great risks from his satires; he feared assassination. But aristocrats like Rochester and Buckhurst were relatively immune: they could say things that commoners could not. Emile Forgues indeed suggested in 1857 that "perhaps there is more morality than we quite like to admit in the vengeful sallies hazarded by debauchees in their moments of revulsion", referring specifically to "the free satires of Rochester", which show "a vein of almost democratic independence".[55] It is possible to make too much of this (as in "democratic"); but the point should not be overlooked. Since we have mentioned Defoe, consider Rochester's picture of "my young master's worship", who was

> The heir and hopes of a great family;
> Which, with strong ale and beef the country rules,
> And ever since the Conquest have been fools".[56]

The author of *The True-Born Englishman* must have enjoyed those lines. Defoe quoted *A Satyr against Reason and Mankind* in his *Serious Reflections during the Life And Surprising Adventures of Robinson Crusoe*, to illustrate the fact that "man undoes man, to do himself no good".[57]

Dr Selden draws attention to Rochester's "anti-bourgeois, anti-plebeian stance", and distinguishes it from Samuel Butler's by Rochester's "sympathy with the unaffected vigour of the lowest orders".[58] We are reminded of Rochester's championing (with other Somerset gentlemen) of "commoners and cottagers" in Gloucestershire around 1670[59]—just about the time when Stubbe was taking radical politics to "the apron-men" and "the common sort" of Bristol and Somerset, denouncing the Royal Society as "a company of atheists, papists, dunces".[60]

It may be that the re-polarization of politics in the sixteen-seventies made Rochester think for the first time that there might be some point in political activity. I suspect that he turned to the deist Charles Blount as the repository of the radical critique of Christianity. In their correspondence during the last eighteen months of Rochester's life Blount reproduced many of the heresies publicized during the interregnum—God is in matter, the soul is mortal, religious changes derive from temporal interests. Such arguments would help Rochester to resist the religious orthodoxy which was being pressed on him. We find him echoing Blount in a letter to his friend Henry Savile.[61] The argument of Burnet's which Rochester found most convincing was that libertinism set a bad social example. He agreed to stop attacking Christianity, Burnet tells us, even before he was convinced of its truth—if he ever was.[62]

Rochester's famous death-bed conversion aroused some scepticism in the seventeenth century. As Mr Treglown puts it, "clearly his almost unendurable last illness drove him out of his mind for considerable periods of time, he was under intense pressure to repent and to be seen to do so, and any decision he reached was not only influenced by these circumstances but reported to the outside world in a determinedly cosmetic way".[63] The correspondence shows that his mother dominated the last weeks of his life: hers was the "stage-management" (Mr Treglown's word) of the "conversion" which she was determined to bring about. She admitted that William Fanshaw and other friends thought that Rochester was suffering from the madness which terminal syphilis brings with it; but she (alone) reported on what he thought and said in his lucid moments when they were absent. The great Marquis of Halifax wrote a significant letter to Burnet, exactly a month after the earl's death, when Burnet had clearly been commissioned to write up the conversion. "It is not possible for you to write on a subject that requireth more care. . . .

Let me beg of you to be exactly careful in it, and to file it over oftener than you have ever done anything that hath come from you".[64]

There is an appropriate irony in the fact that Rochester's death-bed repentance—if there was one—was received by the Latitudinarian Burnet, a man of moderate common sense *par excellence*. Burnet was an up-and-coming, not to say pushing, Scottish episcopalian, only four years older than Rochester. He was hardly likely to ignore such advice from a Marquis, reinforcing the insistent demands of the family. He wrote a brilliant account of the poet's last days, in which his own replies receive more than fives times as much space as that given to Rochester's statements of his beliefs.[65] Burnet firmly proclaimed the authenticity of the conversion. Rochester, Burnet tells us, welcomed him as "my best friend". It comes as rather a shock to work out that Burnet delayed for three weeks before responding to the call to the dying Earl's bedside, that he stayed for only four days and left two days before Rochester died—without saying farewell to him.[66] It is perhaps not unfair to suggest that Burnet got on better with his "best friend" after he was dead.

Grahame Greene quotes effectively from *Venice Preserv'd*, by Rochester's protégé Otway. The libertarian hero, Pierre, condemned to execution, refuses the ministrations of a priest. Pierre echoes Rochester when he denounces the priest:

> You want to lead
> My reason blindfold,

and make it

> Show strange tricks which you call signs of faith:
> So silly souls are gulled, and you get money.
> Away, no more . . . I would hereafter
> This fellow write no lies of my conversion,
> Because he has crept upon my troubled hours.[67]

More directly, Lee's *The Princess of Cleve* (1680 or later—published only in 1689) "debunking the Dorimant-style hero" concludes with "an icy judgment on Rochester's famous death-bed conversion":

> He well repents that will not sin, yet can;
> But death bed sorrow rarely shows the man.[68]

Since Rochester's full stature as a poet has been recognized critics have tried to find reasons for liking him—sentimentalizing his family life, sanitizing his follies, emphasizing his turn to Whig politics, seeing him as a modern man endowed with all our sensibilities and agonies. But the publication of his letters has made it harder to paint an attractive portrait. I must admit failure actually to like Rochester. So what I have written is in no sense an attempt to improve his image. One could be a Whig of 1678 without being a nice man; too much niceness indeed would have been a handicap. I have tried to draw attention to the nature of the society which produced a fringe of alienated aristocrats to whom Defoe looked back with respect because of the vigour and effectiveness of their anti-court satire. Defoe helps us to see them in social as well as personal terms, though of course each individual had his own reactions of pique, injured vanity, boredom, etc., etc. But just as restoration comedy gives us a pretty objective critique of the sexual mores of court and aristocracy, so Rochester's satires reveal a highly intelligent man seeing right through the shams of that glittering world to the hollow compromise underneath.

From its nature such satire could have no social roots, unlike that of Overton or Walwyn a generation earlier. I hope Rochester did not surrender to Burnet, but if he did it is understandable: his sceptical materialism was the negative-critical reaction of an individual dissatisfied with the flippant, frivolous milieu from which he could not escape. (Sedley too underwent "conversion" at about the same time). Hazlitt noted the negative power of Rochester's satire: "his contempt for everything that others respect almost amounts to sublimity".[69] *A Satyr against Reason and Mankind* shows that he could conceive of no alternative society—as Milton, Marvell, Stubbe and perhaps even Butler could.[70] Whether or not Rochester was "converted" at a time when he knew what he was doing, the unctuousness of his last two letters, to Burnet and to Thomas Pierce, another death-bed visitant, suggest that he was a badly frightened man. Faced by the combined assaults of death and Burnet, his Hobbist libertinism turned out to be pretty shallow.

This suggests that behind the court rake there was only the court rake. Mr Treglown writes sharply of "the clever, self-destructive group" of "court wits"; "even their negligence was calculated, their private life ostentatious". Drinking and copulation are major themes of Rochester's private correspondence as of his public image.[71] His advice to Nell Gwyn (conveyed through Henry Savile) on how to handle the King was "with hand, body, head, heart and all the faculties you have, contribute to his pleasure all you can and comply with his desires throughout". It was indeed sound advice: compare *A Satyre on Charles II*:

> His sceptre and his prick are of a length;
> And she may sway the one who plays with th'other.[72]

Riotous behaviour like smashing the King's sundial may perhaps be regarded as undergraduate fun. But such frolics could lead on occasion to murder, whether in a duel or in resisting the local minions of law and order. In either case there was no danger of a peer suffering any worse consequence than temporary exile from court. Things were different if you were a poet of lesser rank. Rochester may or may not have been responsible for the cudgelling of Dryden in 1679: "not proven" seems a fair verdict. But three years earlier Rochester had suggested to Henry Savile, no doubt playfully, that such punishment might be appropriate; and he was accused of having had John Crowne cudgelled for "greatly abusing him in a play".[73]

Yet the poetry remains. Intellectual lyricist, lyrical satirist, Rochester bridges the gap between the metaphysical and Augustan modes.[74] Critics argue about whether he was a better satirist than Marvell (who called Rochester "the best English satirist"); at his peak Rochester seems to me superior to either Marvell or Dryden.[75] *A Satyr against Reason and Mankind* is a great poem, with the flashes of paradoxical insight which give Rochester's poetry its peculiar strength.

> All men would be cowards if they durst. . .

> But thoughts are given for action's government;
> When action ceases, thought's impertinent.[76]

We must end with Rochester at his unforgettable best, his picture of "the misguided follower" of reason, who

> Stumbling from thought to thought, falls headlong down
> Into doubt's boundless sea, where, like to drown,
> Books bear him up awhile, and make him try
> To swim with bladders of philosophy;
> In hopes still to o'ertake th'escaping light,
> The vapour dances in his dazzling sight
> Till, spent, it leaves him to eternal night.
> Then old age and experience, hand in hand,
> Lead him to death, and make him understand,
> After a search so painful and so long,
> That all his life he has been in the wrong.[77]

It is no good feeling morally superior to a man who could write like that.

NOTES

1. Expanded from a review of *The Letters of John Wilmot, Earl of Rochester* (ed. J. Treglown, Oxford U.P., 1980), in *London Review of Books*, 20 November–4 December, 1980.
2. Treglown, *Letters*, pp. 12–13; ed. D.M. Veith, *The Complete Poems of John Wilmot, Earl of Rochester* (Yale U.P., 1968), p. 90.
3. *Complete Poems* (ed. Veith).
4. Seneca, *Troas*, translated by Jasper Heywood in 1559, and by Samuel Pordage in 1660. Traherne translated some lines from *Thyestes* (*Poems*, p. 163).
6. Treglown, *op. cit.*, pp. 24, 12–13.
7. *Ibid.*, p. 202.
8. *Complete Poems*, p. 34; ed. J. Treglown, *Spirit of Wit: Reconsiderations of Rochester*, pp. 78–9. A rude poem which Veith thinks is not Rochester's was attributed to Milton in 1708 (*ibid.*, p. 73).
9. Treglown, *Letters*, pp. 15, 244.
10. V. de Sola Pinto, Introduction to Rochester's *Poems* (1953), pp. xxxvii–ix; cf. *W.T.U.D.*, pp. 412–13.
11. Farley-Hills, *The Benevolence of Laughter*, pp. 132, 164, 166, 189.
12. *Ibid.*, pp. 183, 185, 189; Ed. Farley-Hills, *Rochester: The Critical Heritage* (1972), p. 56; cf. p. 53.
13. Farley-Hills, *The Benevolence of Laughter*, pp. 141, 145, 156, 174.
14. *Ibid.*, p. 139.
15. See pp. 328–9 below.
16. Robert Wolseley (1685), in Farley-Hills, *Rochester*, p. 139; cf. Burnet, *ibid.*, p. 85. Wolseley added that what "would have been ill-breeding and intolerable in any other man became not only civil and inoffensive but agreeable and entertaining in him". There is no record of what Rochester's servants thought.
17. Temple, "Of Poetry", quoted in Farley-Hills, *Rochester*, p. 151.
18. *Complete Poems*, p. 109. The point had been made by Etherege's Medley in *The Man of Mode* (1, i).
19. Farley-Hills, *Rochester*, pp. 82–3; Graham Greene, *Lord Rochester's Monkey* (1974), p. 105. For fools and folly cf. *W.T.U.D.*, Chapter 13.
20. For Wren see J.G.A. Pocock's Introduction to *The Political Works of James Harrington*, pp. 84–9; for possessive individualism see C.B. Macpherson, *The Political Theory of Possessive Individualism: Hobbes to Locke* (Oxford U.P., 1962).
21. Mr Trotter rightly argues for a restoration of "Stillingfleet's replies" in *A Satyr against Reason and Mankind*, rather than the amendment

adopted by Veith, "Sibbes's soliloquies". The other authors whom Rochester attacks are all post-restoration, so there is no point in going back to Sibbes (died 1635), who published no work with "soliloquies" in the title (in Treglown, *Spirit of Wit*, pp. 112–13).

22. Stubbe, *The Lord Bacons Relation of the Sweating Sickness Examined* (1671), Preface to the Reader, p. 9; Stubbe, *A Praeface against Ecebolius Glanvil; Fellow of the Royal Society and Chaplain to Mr. Rouse of Eaton, late member of the Rump Parliament*, p. 34, quoted in *The History of the Royal Society* by Thomas Sprat (ed. J.I. Cope and H.W. Jones, 1959), Notes, p. 72. I have not seen this tract myself.

23. M. Neill, *op. cit.*, p. 133 and *passim*. I return to this subject in my concluding chapter.

24. See *Complete Poems*, pp. 75–6 for Rochester and Marvell; for Butler p. 289 above.

25. *Complete Poems*, p. 98; cf. Farley-Hills, *The Benevolence of Laughter*, p. 169.

26. Trotter, in Treglown, *Spirit of Wit*, pp. 126–8, 115. Jeremy Collier took up the points later (pp. 331–2 below).

27. Sprat, *The History of the Royal Society*, pp. 111–13; cf. Trotter in Treglown, *Spirit of Wit*, pp. 120–2.

28. J.R. Jacob, *Robert Boyle and the English Revolution, passim*.

29. My *Change and Continuity in 17th century England* (1974), p. 259; Treglown, *Spirit of Wit*, p. 8. For Rochester and the Ranters, see Neill, *op. cit.*, p. 131.

30. S. Parker, *A Demonstration of the Divine Authority of the Law of Nature and of the Christian Religion* (1681), pp. iii–iv.

31. Charles Blount, *Miscellaneous Works* (1695), pp. 117–18.

32. J.R. Jacob, *Henry Stubbe*, pp. 140–1.

33. *Complete Poems*, pp. 150–1. For mortalism see *M.E.R.*, Chapter 25. It was much discussed in the sixteen-forties and fifties.

34. Farley-Hills, *Rochester*, pp. 53–72.

35. *Complete Poems*, p. 35.

36. *Ibid.*, p. 28.

37. See *The Experience of Defeat*, pp. 48–9, and a discussion in *P. and P.*, 104 (1984).

38. Quoted in Greene, *op. cit.*, p. 204.

39. Farley-Hills, *Rochester*, pp. 60–1, 65–6; cf. *W.T.U.D.*, pp. 170–83; *M.E.R.*, pp. 308–11.

40. Farley-Hills, *Rochester*, pp. 72–3; cf. *W.T.U.D.*, pp. 210–17 and Chapter 15. For Butler see pp. 283–4 above.

41. Treglown, *Letters*, pp. 17, 27, 169.

42. *Ibid.*, p. 174; cf. Greene, *op. cit.*, pp. 137–8.

43. *Complete Poems*, p. 90.

44. *Ibid.*, p. 81.

45. Pinto, *Enthusiast in Wit*, pp. 109–11; cf. *Complete Poems*, pp. lxii, lxviii. The Empress of China is defending women's right to military command.

46. Pinto, *op. cit.*, p. 144.

47. Farley-Hills, *Rochester*, pp. 75, 58. Burnet's attitude was not unusual; an

Essex man convicted of rape was ordered to make a public apology *to the parents* of the girl involved (J.A. Sharpe, *Crime in 17th-century England: A county study*, Cambridge U.P., 1983, p. 63).

48. Trotter, in Treglown, *Spirit of Wit*, p. 113.
49. *Complete Poems*, p. xxxviii.
50. *Ibid.*, pp. 20–1, 60–1. Sir Nicholas Cully, "knighted by Oliver", was a character in Etherege's *Love in a Tub* (1664). Rochester referred in *Tunbridge Wells* to "a mere Sir Nicholas Cully;/A bawling fop" (*Complete Poems*, p. 73).
51. Greene, *op. cit.*, p. 204; cf. Pinto, *Enthusiast in Wit*, pp. 159–60. See pp. 13–14 above. Rochester's *Valentinian* was acted in 1684, first printed in 1685.
52. "One man reads Milton, forty ——", Defoe wrote disapprovingly in *More Reformation* (1703). The missing name rhymes with "character" and must I think be Rochester. (G. Chalmers, *Life of De Foe*, Oxford, 1841, p. 94, quoting *More Reformation*. I cannot find these lines in the 1703 edition. But cf. p. 12 for critical reference to Rochester).
53. Defoe, *The Review*, 29 March 1711, in Farley-Hills, *Rochester*, p. 186.
54. Defoe, *More Reformation: A Satyr upon himself* (1703), p. 31.
55. Farley-Hills, *Rochester*, pp. 227–8, 232.
56. *Complete Poems*, p. 111.
57. *Op. cit.*, (1720), p. 122; cf. pp. 99–100; *Complete Poems*, p. 99. For *The True-Born Englishman* see pp. 124–5 above.
58. Raman Selden, "Rochester and Shadwell", in Treglown, *Spirit of Wit*, pp. 186–7; cf. *Complete Poems*, p. 48. Dr Selden's article is interesting on Rochester's relations with the very bourgeois, very Whig Shadwell. Cf. pp. 288–9 above for Butler and Shadwell, Butler and Buckingham.
59. Pinto, *Enthusiastic in Wit* (1962), p. 146. Rochester seems to have been an easy-going landlord in Somerset (R. Clifton, *The Last Popular Rebellion: The Western Rising of 1685*, 1984, p. 256. For the county in Charles II's reign see *ibid.*, chapters 1 and 2.
60. See *The Experience of Defeat*, pp. 274–5 quoting Jacob, *Henry Stubbe*, Chapter 5.
61. Treglown, *Letters*, pp. 208–41.
62. Farley-Hills, *Rochester*, p. 79.
63. Treglown, *Letters*, pp. 36–7.
64. *Ibid.*, pp. 34–7, 250–5.
65. Greene, *op. cit.*, p. 208.
66. Farley-Hills, *Rochester*, pp. 80–1, 85–6.
67. Greene, *op. cit.*, pp. 188–9, quoting Otway, *Venice Preserv'd*, Act V (1682).
68. Hume, *op. cit.*, pp. 356–7.
69. Farley-Hills, *Rochester*, p. 214.
70. See Butler's "Satire upon the Weakness and Misery of Man", a poor thing by comparison with Rochester, in *Poetical Works*, II, pp. 139–46.
71. Treglown, *Letters*, p. 1.
72. *Ibid.*, p. 189; *Complete Poems*, p. 60.
73. Treglown, *Letters*, pp. 119–20; Hume, *op. cit.*, pp. 366–7.

74. *Complete Poems*, pp. 2–3.
75. Aubrey, *Brief Lives*, II, p. 304; Emile Forgues, in Farley-Hills, *Rochester*, p. 233; Pinto, "Rochester and Dryden", *Renaissance and Modern Studies*, V (1961), pp. 29–48; Farley-Hills, *Benevolence of Laughter*, *passim*.
76. This is another radical commonplace; cf. Winstanley, *The Law of Freedom and other Writings*, pp. 127–8, 364; Sabine, *op. cit.*, p. 193.
77. *Complete Poems*, pp. 95–100.

VI *Some conclusions*

Some Conclusions

In Chapter 3 I suggested that the mid-century English Revolution had a decisive effect on the evolution of popular prose in England. Perhaps other chapters have helped us to extend this generalization. But first let me briefly summarize what I see as the most decisive social changes resulting from the Revolution.[1]

The great divide of the two generations before 1640 was confirmed and solidified. In these decades a class of permanent poor emerged, as a result of population growth, inflation, loss of land by the poorer peasantry. The struggle of Levellers and others during the Revolution to win security of tenure for copyholders and to check enclosure (or regulate it in the interests of the poor) failed. In the sixteen-fifties the Levellers' former allies from the middling sort came to support Oliver Cromwell the defender of property. Parish élites drawn from richer villagers were confirmed by the Revolution in their positions of control in alliance with the gentry from whom J.Ps. were drawn. Laud and the Major-Generals both failed to impose policies on local government; after 1660 the central government lacked the means of coercion.

The gentry won absolute ownership in their lands by the abolition of feudal tenures. Relieved from the arbitrary death duties incident to wardship, they had now every incentive to invest capital in agricultural production. Land was transformed into a commodity like any other in capitalist society. This has been called "the decisive change in English history which made it different from that of the continent. From it every other difference in English society stemmed"; "a new chapter in the [rural] world".[2] It led to agricultural improvements which increased output and reduced prices. Before 1640 England was a corn-importing country; by the end of the century she exported corn. The abolition of monopolies and of Privy Council control enabled British industry to take advantage of the slowing down of population expansion and inflation.[3] So, paradoxically, the triumph of the gentry over copyholders led not only to increased national prosperity but also to rising real wages. Expanding employment brought vagabondage under control.

Prosperity was aided by a revolution in foreign policy. The Navigation Act of 1651 created a closed imperial market for British traders, excluding the Dutch who had previously looked like monopolizing trade with England's overseas possessions. Three Dutch wars deposed the Netherlands from their position as Europe's premier trading nation. The great navy created for this purpose in the sixteen-fifties also made possible, for the first time, a vigorous policy of colonial expansion, starting with Cromwell's annexation of Jamaica in 1655 and the subordination of English colonies in the West Indies and North America to metropolitan economic policy. England's monopoly of trade with an empire expanding in size and population led to rapid increases in the mercantile marine, in the slave trade, in the re-export trade in colonial goods and in exports of consumer goods to the colonies. Once started, the upward spiral was continuous. The reorganization of taxation in the sixteen-forties put far greater financial resources at the disposal of the state, which assumed responsibilities hitherto left to private enterprise. Parliamentary control of taxation and foreign policy after 1660 ensured that these policies survived the restoration. After 1688 most remaining obstacles were removed.

Landowners increasingly involved in agricultural production for the market were also drawn into closer association with commerce. Before 1640 some gentlemen had begun to invest in trading companies, especially those who had been to London as M.Ps.[4] By the end of the century political stability had made possible the foundation of the Bank of England, to which gentry subscribed no less enthusiastically than merchants. As Harrington had foreseen, competitive capitalism with no upper limit on property holdings led inevitably to the growth of oligarchy. The aristocracy, restored to its privileges in 1660, was able to consolidate its position by City marriages. The distinction between landed and monied interests, on which Swift harped so insistently, was becoming more apparent than real.[5] All these changes made it possible for England to become the country of the first industrial revolution.

Before and after the Revolution England was a highly mobile society—mobile downwards (Quarles, Benlowes) as well as upwards (Traherne). The events of the mid-century came as a profound political shock. *"Le supplice public d'un roi"*, said Diderot, *"change l'esprit d'une nation pour jamais"*.[6] But regicide was only the most obvious symbol of the changes of the forties and fifties. The powers of the natural rulers were restored in 1660, and even enhanced by the abolition of central controls (Star Chamber, High Commission); but the minds of men were never quite the same again.

Before 1640 men had been conscious of great economic possibilities but also of economic frustration.[7] We cannot tell how much millenarianism and the belief that England was a chosen nation contributed to making revolution possible.[8] But as the Revolution translated millenarianism into a cosmic optimism it contributed to a sense of England's historic destiny which was soon expressed in more secular terms. Harrington, who gave a socio-economic explanation of the Revolution, advocated a policy of imperialist expansion. We have seen how his ideas influenced Marvell, Butler and Dryden; soon they became Whig orthodoxy.[9] Defoe was a Harringtonian: in 1715 he associated the commercial foreign policy with defence of the protestant interest.[10] John Bull with his cudgel, the independent yeoman who has become an international bully, symbolizes the way in which the middling sort had been subsumed into the imperialist economy.

Some natural rulers and emerging parish élites had been sympathetic to Puritanism before 1640 because its emphasis on hard work, discipline, asceticism, fitted in with their aspirations to control the poor.[11] But during the Revolution the main threat to their social position had come from enthusiastic religion, which had offered means of self-expression to classes hitherto excluded from power—and to women. The lower and middling sort organized in congregations and ultimately in national sects. This perhaps helps to explain the acquiescence of parish élites in the restoration.

I have noted from time to time a passionate anti-clericalism about which Butler and Rochester felt hardly less strongly than Wither, Milton, Marvell and revolutionary radicals like Walwyn, Winstanley, Ranters and Quakers. The clergy were crucial to the ideological problems of our age. The reformation and expanding literacy had put the Bible before lay readers. So long as there was a monopoly state church, the clergy remained the authorized interpreters of the sacred text. But with the breakdown of that church in England after 1640 free trade in ideas replaced monopoly: any attempt to restore a group of professional expert interpreters roused the most intense resentment.[12] The blind hatred of Jack Cade and his like to learning was transformed into bitter hostility towards the universities which turned out accredited interpreters of the Scriptures. This hostility was shared by Milton and William Dell, Master of Gonville and Caius College, Cambridge, with mechanic preachers and their congregations. One of the major achievements of 1660 was the reimposition of a single state church and the preservation of the universities. It reflected a consensus among the propertied class.

But it was no longer a monolithic state church: the ideas of the interregnum critics could not be wished away, as Butler and Rochester show, and as Collier was painfully aware. When Lady Brute in Vanbrugh's *The Provoked Wife* was reminded of the Biblical adjuration to return good for evil she replied "that may be a mistake in the translation".[13] Mary Astell was a Tory and high Anglican, but in defending the equal rights of women she too used interregnum techniques, questioning the divine right of self-appointed interpreters of the Bible. They were all men, she pointed out, so naturally they proclaimed the superiority of male over female, on the grounds that God created Adam before Eve. Had they not noticed, she asked, that God created all other animals before man? What conclusion should they logically draw from that?[14] As Butler did not fail to notice, the religious controversies of the Revolution, as of the sixteenth-century reformation, helped to spread lower-class scepticism about religion as such.[15] But ideas of that sort could no longer be expressed in print, for reasons which Rochester came to appreciate.

England after 1660 was a more law-abiding country than it had been before 1640. In part this was due to the prosperity which dates from the sixteen-fifties. It was also due to the defeat of the radicals and to acceptance by the sects that Christ's kingdom was not of this world. They were excluded from politics again. But still more it was due to the liberation of gentry and parish élites to control their localities as they wished, and through Parliament to control the central government. The country could be run peaceably only when the natural rulers fully co-operated with government; this co-operation was re-established after 1660, though now governments knew that in the last resort they could not rule without the consent of the gentry.

In the decades before 1640 there had been (in Essex at least) "a high level of witchcraft accusations between villagers, a staggeringly high rate of denunciations of neighbours for sexual deviance, and a high rate of suits for slander of all kinds by neighbours". The number of executions increased. After the interregnum this changed: the rate of homicide begins to fall. There was a simultaneous decline in offences against property, and in executions for all kinds of offences.[16] From the mid-century witches ceased to be sentenced to death. John Aubrey, who saw the Revolution as a turning-point in all sorts of ways, dated from it a decline of belief in spirits as well as more affectionate treatment of upper-class children by their parents.[17] In 1671 a statute was passed against nose-slitting or other mutilations of the person—in consequence of Sir John Coventry having his nose slit for criticizing Charles II's fondness for actresses.[18] What is significant is that such aristocratic thuggery had not been treated as a crime earlier. With the relaxation of political tensions after 1688, spoken words ceased to be treasonable, and treason trials were conducted with some appearance of fairness to the defendant. Benefit of clergy was extended to female defendants in criminal trials in 1692.[19] This new climate must have had its effect on literature.

Post-revolutionary society was more effectively self-controlled than it had ever been controlled from on top before 1640. Parish élites exercised "a far more subtle control of the labouring population than could possibly be achieved by court prosecution".[20] Peter Clark has shown how that old centre of seditious talk, the ale-house, which had defied the attempts of governments and monopolists to control it, was brought to heel in the later seventeenth century by the increasingly monopolistic brewers. They wanted to remain on the right side of the government from whom they derived their privileges, and used their economic strangle-hold over ale-house keepers effectively.[21] Similarly self-censorship rendered government licensing and the Stationers' monopoly superfluous. Private enterprise, now that it operated under a sympathetic government, could police society more efficiently than Star Chamber or High Commission.

From the revolutionary decades, it has been suggested, there was a "crisis of language", illustrated by the prose experiments of Coppe and Fox and by the glossolalia, the speaking with tongues, of some sectaries and of Lady Eleanor Davies.[22] The resolution of the crisis was accompanied by the reconstitution of an intellectual if not a social élite in a formally equal society. The classicism in which Berkenhead had found consolation in the sixteen-fifties once more excluded those whose education had been unsatisfactory. The Royal

Society emphasized the "common sense" not of all men but of members of the limited ruling group.[23] The exclusion of the vulgar was conventional, artificial, no longer legal; it was the more important to stress class distinctions—e.g. by excluding dissenters from the universities as well as from central and local government. The old society had been unashamedly unequal, hierarchical: inequality did not trouble men's consciences because equality did not seem a possible, still less a desirable, ideal. Levellers and *Leviathan* had changed that: the Coriolanus approach was now too simple. The vast mass of potentially equal political atoms had to be controlled— and language did this better than more violent measures. To rise above one's station could be heroic in Elizabethan drama; it was funny in restoration comedy. Sprat's initial emphasis on the language of artisans was not the last word. By 1672–3 Dryden was calling for improvements, for a more conversational style, the norm for good conversation being naturally the court. The ideal shifted from a "plain" to a "correct" style, from private to public prose.[24] It was not as alien from popular speech as Latin had been, but it had the same exclusive effect.

But from 1688 the court ceased to be the sole cultural centre. With the revival of popular journalism after the expiry of the Licensing Act in 1695 the chasm between upper-class and popular prose narrowed. Bunyan is clearly outside the establishment: Defoe hovers on its brink; by Richardson's time the gap is minimal. Addison made the necessary adjustments.

The novel is to bourgeois society what the epic had been to feudal society. The epic had its heyday in the baronial hall, where the military leader celebrated with his dependent warriors. Despite the efforts of Ariosto, Tasso and Spenser to update, the epic's values remained military: courage, honour, chivalry. We noted above Butler's rejection of epic.[25] The peculiar example of Spenser apart, there had been no successful modern English epic. The fact that Davenant could not finish *Gondibert*, and that Cowley finished neither *Davideis* nor *The Civil War*, suggests that they both felt something was amiss. (Spenser too failed to complete *The Faerie Queene*). Henceforward no significant poet writes epic. Dryden and Pope turn to translation; others follow Butler's example and produce burlesque. There was a vogue for travesty in the later seventeenth century.[26] Epic is left to the likes of Edward Howard[27] and Sir Richard Blackmore—and in the eighteenth century to Defoe's biographer, George Chalmers. The one apparent exception, *Paradise Lost*, is in its very different way also an anti-epic; Milton is as much opposed as Butler to the traditional epic virtues, to

> Wars, hitherto the only argument
> Heroic deemed.

He was

> not sedulous to dissect
> With long and tedious havoc, fabled knights
> In battles feigned (IX. 27–31).

Milton's treatment in the war in heaven of the angelic response to Satan's invention of gunpowder verges on burlesque.[28] It is an intriguing thought that Butler was writing *Hudibras* from about 1656 till shortly after the restoration, precisely the years in which Milton was writing *Paradise Lost*.[29] The "brief epic" of *Paradise Regained* has been compared to a psychological novel: it looks forward to the new genre as *Robinson Crusoe* and *Tom Jones* look back to epic. The novel deals at epic length with ordinary people, not just with kings and knights; with love, marriage and property, not with honour. *Pamela* and *Tom Jones* are both in their very different ways epics of social mobility. The villagers of Slough who rang the church bells when Pamela attained to matrimony are symbolic of the new audience for the new values.[30]

There were other approaches to the novel. Keeping diaries and writing spiritual autobiographies contributed. Baxter, Bunyan and Defoe all specialized in what we may call shop-keeper casuistry—grappling with the problems of the honest man brought up to believe in the just price who found himself in the world of competitive self-interest. *Mr. Badman* and *Religious Courtship* show this genre on the way to transformation into the novel.

There is a theme here too large to be pursued now. Pepys regarded singing and playing musical instruments as part of normal social intercourse. But the virtuoso concert performer and opera were diminishing the role of the individual performer, just as novel-reading in private accompanied the decline of the eighteenth-century theatre.[31] Davenant had intended *Gondibert* to be sung: the decline of epic relates to the decline of music-making, of song and dance. Ultimately this is part of the rejection of popular rural culture. James I and Charles I had defended rural sports against Puritans;

nonconformists began to make hymn-singing part of their worship just as their betters were turning away from madrigals.

The social facts we have been considering may help us to answer Saintsbury's question about the quatrain.[32] Used to such brilliant effect from Spenser to Rochester, how was it that it fell from favour in polite literary circles? One possible answer might be that the quatrain was the metre of popular verse, whether ballads or Sternhold and Hopkins's metrical psalms. "The golden age of the ballad", wrote Douglas Bush, "may be said to have ended, like that of the drama, with the beginning of the civil war".[33] As the cultivated wish to distinguish themselves from the taste of the vulgar, the quatrain in which their hymns and songs were sung may have been a victim. Rochester was the last of the metaphysical poets as well as an early Augustan. Carols too, we are told, were remembered only by the lower classes after 1660, who kept them alive until the nineteenth-century revival under middle-class auspices.[34] Emblems also lost the fascination they had held so long as Hermeticism was a respectable intellectual system. With the dominance of the new science they ceased to be pored over by sophisticated intellectuals; they became unsophisticated illustrations for children's books like Bunyan's *A Book for Boys and Girls.*[35]

Historians of the drama are working out a satisfactory account of its relation to the political and social changes of the seventeenth century.[36] The "Shakespearean moment" was short-lived. As we saw, the great Elizabethan and Jacobean tragedies, and the best City comedies, date from the years of balanced tension, when men were beginning to be conscious of its precariousness, of impending social conflict. It would have been impossible to write *Macbeth* after Charles I's execution in 1649, to combine mystical reverence for kingship with a sympathetic presentation of the murderous usurper.[37] Real tragedy had to be replaced by heroic drama in which kings concern themselves with imaginary points of honour in love and war because real political issues have become too hot to touch. Many leading practitioners of heroic drama were ex-Cromwellians like Dryden. Broghill, a former royalist, had been one of Cromwell's right-hand men before helping to bring about the restoration in Ireland. He no doubt had "honour" problems of his own.

Tragedy becomes empty and self-caricaturing as comedy becomes more daring and witty. Similarly Butler could use Benlowes's conceits comically. "The frivolity and preposterousness of the political ideas and situations represented in the drama", Susan Staves remarks, reflect "the extravagance and preposterousness of restoration political experience itself".[38] Restoration comedy is more directly related to "a competitive and bargaining social order in which title and property were both determined and seen as determined in ways and by values different from those of a feudal and post-feudal world".[39] "The excellence of the major social satires of this period", Laura Brown agrees, "resides . . . in their daring formal and ideological representation of the fundamental moral and social contradictions of their time and place".[40] Restoration comedy contrasts the standards of behaviour of the two social groups that are fusing into a single ruling class—on the one hand the new rich, hastily shedding their Puritanism and learning court manners and language, on the other the aristocracy, learning the importance of money, adjusting themselves to processes which they despise but which are necessary to obtaining and keeping money.

"Here you see a bishop bowing low to a gaudy atheist; a judge to a door-keeper; a great lord to a fishmonger, or scrivener with a jack-chain about his neck; . . . and so tread round in a preposterous huddle of ceremony to each other, whilst they can hardly hold their solemn false countenances". So Manly, the hero of Wycherley's *The Plain Dealer*. "Well, they understand the world", replied Freeman, who was "a complier with the age". (I. i).[41]

The machismo of Etherege's Dorimant succeeds where the bombast of the analogous tragic heroes fails because the attack on property marriage and bourgeois hypocrisy was a real issue.[42] Restoration satirists like Rochester draw on the ideas of interregnum radicals to attack their mutual enemies, Puritans and Latitudinarians.[43] Only towards the end of the century does a reaction set in, as the court loses interest in the theatre and audiences become increasingly bourgeois. Dorimant had acted according to "nature" rather than in accordance with social convention. Now however morality is no longer seen as conventional but as "natural"; the accepted concepts of nature and natural law have changed since before the civil war.[44] Both in tragedy and in comedy inner moral worth replaces conformity to external standards of honour or social correctness.[45]

The subject of eighteenth century tragedy and comedy shifts from kings and dukes to ordinary people, just as the bourgois novel replaces the aristocratic epic. Collier was the belated spokesman for the new respectability. His attack on the stage stresses the *social* dangers of libertine flippancy, just as Burnet had done to Rochester.[46] "To break through the laws of a kingdom is bad enough; but to make ballads upon the statute-book and a jest of authority is much worse". "If eternity were out of the case, general advantage and public reason and secular policy would oblige us to be just to the priesthood". "What necessity is there to kick the coronets about the stage, and to make a man a lord only in order to make him a coxcomb? I hope the poets don't intend to revive the old project of levelling, and vote down the house of peers". "To breed all people alike, and make no distinction between a seat and a cottage, is not . . . very ceremonious to the country gentlemen."[47]

So we move on to sentimental comedy. As the alienated aristocrats get drawn into the expanding armed forces and professions, or retire to the country to live off their expanding rent rolls, there are no more Dorimants or Horners, just as after 1660 there had been no more Ranters.[48]

In the sixteen-thirties coterie and popular theatres between them had seats for up to 13,000 persons. After 1660 there were only two theatres, with a total seating capacity of 1200; they rarely seem to have been full. The audience from the middling sort had dwindled before 1640, and it was long after the restoration before it began to predominate. This shrinkage in the audience is perhaps the most important fact relating to drama in the later seventeenth century. Audience numbers did not increase significantly until the eighteenth century.[49] By then the "two nations" had separated: a section of the middling sort had disowned their "fanatical" brethren and had adopted some aristocratic postures, including literary attitudes. Pepys illustrates the process.[50]

Before 1640 the aristocracy had been of great social significance, and of considerable importance to the business world, if only as mediators working the court to procure monopolies for merchants. The restored aristocracy of the post-1660 generation found itself playing a largely decorative role. They were even more remote from productive economic processes than their pre-revolutionary predecessors. Hence their intensified contempt for trade and industry, which had rendered them irrelevant. The more intelligent among them—like Rochester—had little respect for the social order as such.[51] What seems to us the empty extravagance of "heroic" drama may have been a form of protest against a very unheroic age. But there was a hollowness in restoration comedy too. The dramatists contrast the humbug of property marriage with an irresponsible Ranter-like sexual "freedom". Yet City marriages were one means by which aristocrats could benefit from trade and industry without actually soiling their hands.[52] Meanwhile the society reeks with shams. Court culture is no longer really superior; its values are now those of the City. There is no real class conflict, only snobbery.

In poetry the chronology is significant. The double heart of the metaphysicals appears around the turn of the century. The lyric of conflict reached its peak during the interregnum, when Vaughan, Crashawe and Marvell wrote their best poetry.[53] After the Revolution metaphysical lyric declines. Society became more prosaic after the defeat of the two extremist wings—high-flying royalists and enthusiastic sectaries. The rhymed couplet conveys balance, order, stability and moderation—all the post-revolutionary virtues. It was more appropriate to poetry of the head than of the heart, to satire than lyric, to burlesque than epic.[54] Milton failed to recover "ancient liberty . . . from the troublesome and modern bondage of rhyming".[55]

There was a simultaneous decline of confidence in inspiration. "Inspiration, a dangerous word", wrote Sir William Davenant, thinking of literature. His correspondent, Thomas Hobbes, thought inspiration equally dangerous in religion.[56] Both types of inspiration were unpopular in polite restoration society, and in the Royal Society; and they were often lumped together, mainly in order to disparage those who relied on poetic inspiration. Dryden called Settle a "kind of fanatic in poetry", who "writes by inspiration", from the inner light. Oldham denounced "fanatics and enthusiasts in poetry"; Rochester was called an "enthusiast in wit."[57]

For sectaries of the revolutionary decades, reliance on the spirit within symbolized a rejection of existing society and its culture, especially its universities. Winstanley insisted that he got his ideas from no one else; like Bunyan, he minimized the extent of his own reading. For such people knowledge of "the rules" signified mastery of a classical education, and therefore a certain social eminence. Shakespeare's Jack Cade had made the point.[58] Whereas for the defeated royalists, as Dr P.W. Thomas has shown, classicism became a shield under which to recover from defeat. Accepted certainties had been dissolved in the society around them, but elsewhere and in the best times decorum, the rules, prevailed and tamed the horrors of uncontrollable democracy.[59]

No doubt for similar reasons, the liberal royalist intellectuals of

Falkland's Great Tew circle had been wary of enthusiasm.[60] This tradition, with many others, was picked up by the Latitudinarians of the Royal Society, whose alarm had been intensified by the experience of the revolutionary decades.[61] Wither characteristically held himself to be inspired,[62] and the Muse continued to visit Milton nightly. But Samuel Butler had no use for inspiration.[63] Inspiration (and ballad metres) returned with the Romantic movement after the Industrial Revolution in England and the French Revolution had given fresh confidence and hope to those whom we may begin to call the middle class.

Professor Eisenstein suggests that there is a natural affinity between belief in inspiration, revelation, and the popular culture of folk singers and tellers of tales. Bards were moved by the spirit. So the attack on inspiration was directed not only against religious radicalism; it was also directed against part of the traditional culture of the villages. Art was no longer something that flowed from the people, spontaneously; it depended on skills, decorum, rules which had to be learnt.[64] Getting rid of inspiration was part of a conscious reconstruction of language and literature. Belief in inspiration consorted ill with the myth that culture percolated down from the ruling class to the populace.

Satire, silenced in 1599, revived in the freedom and conflict of the civil war, and became a major genre in the party political struggles of Charles II's reign, as we have seen in considering Berkenhead, Marvell, Butler and Rochester.[65] " 'Tis the persecuting spirit has raised the bantering one", the third Earl of Shaftsbury observed after the event.[66]

The restoration of 1660 was not a total defeat even for the radicals. Ideas survived better than institutions. Although the interregnum legislation on law reform was repealed in 1660, its underlying ideas, Dr Staves assures us, were not forgotten.[67] Libertines borrowed from Ranters; Latitudinarians carried much of Puritanism into the restored Church of England,[68] just as Professor Gura has shown that the New England Way absorbed much from the radicals it suppressed.[69] "The middling sort of men", wrote the old revolutionary Adolphus Warren in 1680, "will not be brought to rest with an implicit faith in their authorized teachers; that will not do in England. The people apprehend well enough, for they feel soonest" and must therefore be convinced by reason.[70] The Marquis of Halifax had attributed this consequence to "the liberty of the late times".[71]

Dr Spufford observed that chapbooks of late seventeenth and early eighteen century England differed from those of France in that they no longer focused mainly on the aristocracy: there were abundance of humble heroes and heroines who could hope to thrive by self-help. "It seems that English society was less subservient, more aware of the possibilities of upward social movement, and more liable to ridicule its 'betters' than the French".[72] In 1724 Defoe noted that England was superior to France in security of property and religion but inferior in the subordination of servants. The lower orders in England abused the idea of liberty by claiming it for themselves. (The Ireton of the Putney Debates would have agreed). Defoe attributed the difference between England and France to England's Revolution of the sixteen-forties.[73] The material collected in this book may help to substantiate his judgment.

NOTES

1. I have discussed these matters at greater length in *Some Intellectual Consequences of the English Revolution* (1980), Chapter 6.
2. H.J. Perkin, "The Social Causes of the British Industrial Revolution", *Transactions of the Royal Historical Soc.*, 5th Series, 18 (1968), p. 135 and *passim*; E. Le Roy Ladurie, quoted in my *Some Intellectual Consequences of the English Revolution*, p. 35.
3. For the upturn from the sixteen-fifties see Joan Thirsk, "Plough and Pen: Agricultural Writers in the 17th century", in *Social Relations and Ideas: Essays in Honour of R.H. Hilton* (ed. T.H. Aston, P.R. Cross, C. Dyer and J. Thirsk, Cambridge U.P., 1983), pp. 315–17. In the first half of the eighteenth century corn export was "the fastest-growing component of all English domestic exports". Thirsk, *Economic Policy and Projects: The Development of a Consumer Society in Early Modern England* (Oxford U.P., 1978), p. 161.
4. T.K. Rabb, *Enterprise and Empire: Merchant and Gentry Investment in the Expansion of England, 1575–1630* (Harvard U.P., 1967), p. 93.
5. Geoffrey Holmes, *Augustan England: Professions, State and Society, 1680–1730* (1982), pp. 15–17.
6. Quoted by József Szigita, *Denis Diderot: une grande figure du materialisme militant du 18e. siècle* (Budapest, 1962), p. 82.
7. See pp. 148–9 above.
8. See pp. 20–1 above.
9. See pp. 172, 288, 292–3 above. Cf. M. McKeon, *op. cit.*, *passim*; G.M. Maclean, "Poetry as History: The Argumentative Design of Dryden's *Astraea Redux*" (*Restoration* 4, 1980).

10. See pp. 112–13 above.
11. W. Hunt, *The Puritan Moment, passim.*
12. See p. 85 above, Walwyn.
13. Act I, scene i.
14. Mary Astell, *Reflections upon Marriage* (3rd ed., 1706), Preface. I am indebted to Bridget Hill for this reference.
15. See pp. 283–5 above; cf. Dollimore, *op. cit.*, pp. 13–14, 105–6.
16. L. Stone, "Interpersonal violence in English society, 1500–1980", *P. and P.*, 101 (1983), pp. 28–32; J.A. Sharpe, *Crime in 17th-Century England: A county study* (Cambridge U.P., 1983), esp. pp. 97–102, 112, 133–5, 144, 149, 188. Again the evidence comes from Essex only, but there is no reason to expect this county to be exceptional.
17. Aubrey, *Brief Lives*, II, p. 318; *Remaines of Gentilisme and Judaisme* (ed. J. Britten, 1881), pp. 26, 67–8, and *passim.*
18. Susan Staves, *Players' Scepters: Fictions of Authority in the Restoration* (Nebraska U.P., 1979), p. 186. She illustrates the point with much illuminating detail.
19. Just as the sixteenth-century inflation had extended the franchise by devaluing the 40s. freehold, so the spread of literacy in the sixteenth century had greatly increased the numbers of those who could escape hanging for a first offence by claiming benefit of clergy.
20. K. Wrightson, quoted by Sharpe, *op. cit.*, p. 179.
21. P. Clark, *The English Ale-House: A Social History, 1200–1800* (1983), pp. 178–84.
22. Hugh Ormsby-Lennon, "Speaking in many Tongues: Millenarian Linguistics, Glossolalia and Shamanism during the Puritan Revolution", in *Studies in the Social History of Language* (ed. P. Burke, Cambridge U.P., forthcoming). I am grateful to Mr Ormsby-Lennon for letting me read this in advance of publication, as well as several other unpublished papers.
23. Raymond Williams, *Culture*, p. 160. Cf. *The Experience of Defeat*, p. 297.
24. Dryden, *Of Dramatic Poesy and other critical essays* (Everyman edn.), I, p. 181; cf. Eagleton, *Literary Theory: An Introduction* (Oxford, 1983), p. 203.
25. See p. 280 above.
26. Sutherland, *op. cit.*, p. 161; cf. p. 102 above. Davenant thought "the most effectual schools of morality are courts and camps" (*Gondibert*, ed. D.F. Gladish, Oxford U.P., 1971, pp. 12–13).
27. See Butler, *Genuine Remains, Poetical Works*, II, pp. 167–72.
28. See p. 289 above for Butler on the effects of gunpowder in exploding chivalry. Samuel Pordage, who also published a post-restoration epic on the Fall of Man, also insisted that he sang "No hero's doughty gests in wars/ . . . Nor the dread fury of the wars" (S. Pordage, *Mundorum Explicatio: Or, the Explanation of an Hieroglyphical Figure*, 1661, Sig. b 8).
29. Farley-Hills, *The Benevolence of Laughter*, p. 46; cf. M. Wilding, *op. cit.*, *passim.*

30. J.D. Chambers, *Population, Economy and Society in Pre-Industrial England* (Oxford U.P., 1972), pp. 52–3. I owe this reference to Bridget Hill.
31. L. Brown, *op. cit.*, p. 208.
32. See p. 4 above.
33. Bush, *English Literature in the Earlier Seventeenth Century*, p. 48.
34. Gillian Widdicombe, "Tidings of Comfort and Joy", *The Observer*, 18 December, 1983.
35. Rosemary Freeman, *English Emblem Books* (1948), *passim*. Cf. p. 196 above.
36. I am thinking especially of Hume, *Development of English Drama*, Susan Staves, *Players' Scepters* and Laura Brown, *English Dramatic Form, 1660–1760*. They are usefully discussed by J. Thompson, "Histories of restoration drama", *The Eighteenth Century: Theory and Interpretation*, 24 (1983), pp. 163–72. The whole issue of this valuable periodical is relevant. See also chapter 1 above, especially notes 32 and 141.
37. P. Cruttwell, *The Shakespearean Moment* (1954), esp. pp. 197–8; Dollimore, *op. cit.*, pp. 8, 91. For the importance of the Revolution for drama see R. Markley, "History, Ideology and the Structure of Restoration Drama", in *The Eighteenth Century: Theory and Interpretation*, 24, esp. p. 100; M. Neill, "Heroic Heads and Humble Tails: Sex, Politics and the Restoration Comic Rake", *ibid.*, esp. p. 116.
38. Staves, *op. cit.*, pp. 47–8. She cites many examples. For Butler see p. 203 above.
39. R. Williams, *Culture*, pp. 160–3.
40. Brown, *op. cit.*, p. 63.
41. *Ibid.*, Chapter 2 and *passim*; A.N. Kaul, *The Action of English Comedy* (Yale U.P., 1970), p. 104; John Barnard, "Drama from the Restoration till 1710", *English Drama to 1710* (ed. C. Ricks, 1971), pp. 379–81.
42. See pp. 280, 291 above; cf. Neill, *op. cit.*, p. 133.
43. Brown, *op. cit.*, pp. 41–8; cf. pp. 302–3 above.
44. Staves, *op. cit.*, pp. 300–3, 313–14. Cf. my *Change and Continuity in 17th-century England* (1974), Chapter 4.
45. Brown, *op. cit.*, p. 102.
46. See p. 309 above.
47. J. Collier, *A Short View of the Immorality and Profaneness of the English Stage* (4th. edn., 1699), pp. 95–6, 129, 175, 221.
48. See pp. 301, 311 above.
49. *The Restoration of the Stuarts, Blessing or Disaster? A Report of a Folger Library Conference* (Washington, 1960), pp. 86–8: comments by G.E. Bentley and W.D. MacMillan. Cf. R. Williams, *Culture*, pp. 156–8.
50. See pp. 260–1 above.
51. See pp. 300–4 above.
52. See p. 252 above.
53. See pp. 22–4 above.
54. Eagleton, *Literary Theory*, p. 17.
55. "The Verse", prefixed to the second edition of *Paradise Lost*. See pp. 180–1 above.

56. Davenant, *Gondibert*, pp. 22, 49; cf. Hobbes, *Leviathan*, Chapter 2.
57. Quoted by Sutherland, *op. cit.*, pp. 65, 166. Cf. Dryden's dismissal of Robert Wild, author of *Iter Boreale* (1660), as "a Leveller in poetry" and "the Wither of the City" (*D.N.B.*), presumably because of his vulgar popularity. Pepys liked Wild's poem (*Diary*, 23.8.63, 21.12.67). For Rochester, some of whose poems were attributed to Wild, see pp. 303–4 above.
58. See p. 15 above.
59. See pp. 100–1 above.
60. Cf. Ruth Wallerstein, *Studies in Seventeenth-Century Poetic* (Wisconsin U.P., 1965), pp. 116–17.
61. See pp. 302–3 above.
62. Wither, *Echoes from the Sixth Trumpet* (1666), in *Miscellaneous Works*, VI; cf. pp. 133–41 above.
63. See p. 285 above.
64. Eisenstein, *op. cit.*, I, p. 322.
65. See pp. 4, 34–5, 98–9, 158, chapters 13 and 14 above.
66. Quoted by Ruth Nevo, *The Dial of Virtue*, p. 210.
67. Staves, *op. cit.*, pp. 15, 97–100, 184.
68. See my *Society and Puritanism* (Panther edn.), pp. 490–5.
69. P. Gura, *A Glimpse of Sion's Glory: Puritan Radicalism in New England, 1620–1660* (Wesleyan U.P., 1984), pp. 13–15, 212–14 and *passim*.
70. [A. Warren], *An Apology for the Discourse of Humane Reason written by Ma[rtin] Clifford Esq.* (1680), p. 8. This tract was dedicated to Shaftesbury. The sentiment echoes Harrington, whom Warren admired (*The Political Works of James Harrington*, p. 764); it anticipates Rousseau.
71. H.C. Foxcroft, *The Life and Letters of Sir George Savile, First Marquess of Halifax* (1898), II, p. 308.
72. M. Spufford, *Small Books and Pleasant Histories: Popular Fiction and its Readership in Seventeenth-Century England* (1981), pp. 71, 147. Dr Capp made a similar observation about almanacs (*Astrology and the Popular Press*, pp. 271–4).
73. Defoe, *The Great Law of Subordination considered; Or the Insolence and Insufferable Behaviour of Servants in England duly enquired into* (1724), pp. 16–20, 52–62.

Index